THE INTER-AMERICAN HISTORICAL SERIES

Edited by JAMES A. ROBERTSON

A HISTORY OF BRAZIL

A HISTORY OF
BRAZIL

By JOÃO PANDIÁ CALOGERAS

Translated and Edited by

PERCY ALVIN MARTIN

Professor of History, Stanford University
Socio Honorario do Instituto Historico e Geographico
Brasileiro

NEW YORK
RUSSELL & RUSSELL · INC
1963

PREFACE BY THE GENERAL EDITOR

For a brief sketch relative to the genesis of the Inter-American Historical Series and its final realization, see the preface of the General Editor of the series in Professor William Spence Robertson's translation of Dr. Ricardo Levene's *Lecciones de Historia Argentina,* which was published by the University of North Carolina Press in 1937, as the first volume of the series.

Of that series, the present volume, translated and adapted by Professor Percy Alvin Martin, from João Pandiá Cologeras' *A Formação historica do Brasil,* is the third. Obviously, no scholar of the United States of North America, more fitted by his predilections, his special studies, his classroom experience, and his reputation, could be chosen by the Inter-American Historical Group to essay the task of presenting in English dress a work on the history of Brazil as seen through Brazilian eyes. Just as obviously, no volume written by a Brazilian scholar and used currently in Brazilian educational institutions as a text could have better claims for translation into English than that of Pandiá Calogeras.

Dr. Pandiá Calogeras, whose lamentable death occurred but recently, not only wrote excellent history, but was himself one of the makers of latter-day Brazilian history. His vision was broad, so broad, indeed, that he did not hesitate to criticise when he thought criticism was needed. The fact that his book finds considerable and continuous use in Brazil itself is his best vindication. He wrote logically and earnestly, and it is evident throughout the pages of his book that he took the history of Brazil seriously and in consequence put his best efforts into the writing of his admirable exposition of the Brazilian drama as it unfolded itself.

Dr. Martin has been no less happy than his author in his translation and adaptation of *A Formação historica do Brasil.* In the course of his translation, he found it necessary often, because of the involved language, to adapt freely, rather than to translate directly, certain passages; but in so doing, he has lost nothing of the flavor of the original. The result is a readable volume which will give to those who can not read the original Portuguese an excellent idea of the forces that have made Brazilian history and of the evolution of the people of Brazil into a nation.

Dr. Martin's excellent introduction, his illuminating footnotes, and his discriminating bibliography with its brief, critical comments will aid in the understanding and the appreciation of the largest country of South America and the only one stemming from Portugal. The concluding chapter, covering the last decade of Brazilian history, is also from his pen.

It is the hope of those connected with the Inter-American Historical Series that this volume, as well as the two which have preceded it and those which will follow it, will draw closer the intellectual and cultural bonds between Anglo and Hispanic America.

JAMES A. ROBERTSON

February, 1939

INTRODUCTION BY THE TRANSLATOR AND EDITOR

ALTHOUGH the study and investigation of history have long been assiduously cultivated in the leading countries of Hispanic America, the number of really adequate, one-volume surveys, embracing the entire history of any particular republic, is exceedingly small. There are several reasons for this unfortunate situation. A really valid synthesis of a nation's entire history may be written in one or two ways. The author may conceivably work up his subject *de novo* relying entirely on original material. Few writers, however, are disposed to essay such an arduous task. The more likely procedure is to attempt to erect the historical structure on monographs, articles, and other data, which in turn embody the results of investigations of the sources. Yet for reasons presently to be noted, conditions in Hispanic America are rarely propitious for the successful use of this latter method when it is a question of covering the entire span of a nation's history. Why should such be the case?

The conscientious investigator of Hispanic America, intent on doing really worthwhile spade work, naturally turns to periods for which the sources are at least reasonably complete, authoritative, and available. In most instances only the colonial epoch, the era of independence, and perhaps the first half of the nationalistic period meet these requirements. As the student reaches more recent times his material becomes more and more refractory. Documents are widely scattered and in many cases have not yet found their way into public libraries and archives. Diplomatic correspondence, being "confidential" and hence sacrosanct, is usually not accessible. Really significant memoirs are few and far between. The dearth of adequate monographic material on the last half century is, under these circumstances, quite understandable.

The would-be investigator of contemporary or nearly contemporary history is at the same time confronted with another obstacle which he seldom surmounts successfully. This we may call the personal equation. As we approach more closely the modern period the evaluation of the human factor in the march of events becomes more baffling. The rôle of statesmen and other persons in public life is almost invariably interpreted from the standpoint of the particular ideology of the writer. Prejudices engendered by political passion evaporate slowly. As a natural consequence of all of this, the cautious, professional historian who hopes that his work will possess a certain stamp of finality seldom concerns himself with the history of the last fifty years.

This situation is particularly true as regards Brazil. Several illustrations at once come to mind. The greatest of all Brazilian historians is probably Varnhagen. Though he lived and wrote during some of the most stirring years of the empire, the works for which he is best known deal almost exclusively with the colonial period. The foremost representatives of the newer school, Oliveira Lima and Capistrano de Abreu, though they produced works of enduring value, wrote next to nothing on the republican era. The late João Ribeiro, whose excellent one-volume *Historia do Brasil* went through many editions and is still the standard text for Brazilian secondary schools, did not go beyond the fall of the empire in 1889. For this emphasis on the pre-republican era, the Brazilian Historical and Geographical Institute (*Instituto Historico e Geographico Brasileiro*) has, perhaps, been partly responsible. This venerable body, established in 1838, has for almost a century been publishing through its *Revista* and special volumes a vast amount of material dealing with the history and geography of Brazil. But with rare exceptions it has excluded from the field of its endeavors the history and institutions of the last forty or fifty years.

The preceding remarks are in no wise intended to be strictures on the great historians of Brazil. No one with even a cursory knowledge of South American historiography would wish to criticise either the extent or importance of their output. Yet it is an indubitable fact that some of the most useful works in their domain have been written by men who could not be described as historians in the narrower sense of the term. Few would deny, for instance, that the most penetrating work on the empire is the three-volume work on the life and times of his father by Joaquim Nabuco,[1] and yet Nabuco is chiefly remembered as a statesman, diplomat, and abolitionist. And if we are in quest of an authoritative, one-volume survey of the whole sweep of Brazilian history from the epoch of discovery to the present time we must turn to a man for whom history was at best an avocation, Dr. João Pandiá Calogeras.

Anything like an adequate biographical sketch of this remark-

---

[1] *Um estadista do imperio, Nabuco de Araujo* (3 vols., Rio de Janeiro, 1897).

able man would expand this introduction to unconscionable length. Yet the *Formação historica do Brasil* bears such a marked imprint of the public and even private life of Calogeras that at least a summary account of his career is in order. It is hoped, too, that a useful purpose will be served in bringing to the attention of English readers the life and achievements of one of the really notable figures in Brazilian public life. As statesman, financier, administrator, economist, and historian, Calogeras played a conspicuous and exceedingly useful rôle in the public life of his country during the last half century.

A passing notice may be accorded Calogeras' antecedents. As his name would indicate, he was of Greek extraction. His family was a very old and honorable one. It possibly goes back to the fifth century when we hear of a certain St. Calogeras in the hagiology of Byzantium. The record becomes clearer by the twelfth century when the historian Anna Comena mentions the arrival of the Calogeras family at Constantinople and its alliance with the imperial dynasty. From that time its members are involved in almost all of the vicissitudes of the last centuries of the Byzantine Empire. After the fall of Constantinople we meet them in Venice and other Italian cities as admirals, bishops, knights of St. Mark; yet they never entirely abandoned their Greek affiliations, and for the most part remained members of the orthodox Greek Church.

The grandfather of our Calogeras was born on the island of Corfu in 1810. He was a man of wide interests and vast culture. Much of his early life he spent in France. He was an intimate friend of Baron Lafitte, the financier and minister of Louis Philippe. In 1841, he was sent to Brazil to take charge of one of Lafitte's financial ventures. He became a naturalized Brazilian in 1854. So great was his interest in his adopted country that he wrote a number of historical texts which were long used in the imperial secondary schools. His son, Michel Calogeras, though lacking the erudition of his father, was an enterprising engineer and business man who especially interested himself in the extension of the Brazilian railway system.

The object of our study, João Pandiá Calogeras, was born in Rio de Janeiro, June 19, 1870. His early education was in charge of his grandfather and father and a number of excellent private tutors, especially Germans residing in Petropolis. So well were the foundations laid that on his entry into the Collegio Pedro II he passed in a single year the three courses ordinarily necessary for matriculation in the celebrated School of Mines of Ouro Preto. One of his examiners was the eminent historian Capistrano de Abreu. Here began a friendship which terminated only at Capistrano's death and which exercised a tremendous influence on Calogeras' intellectual development.

At the age of twenty he graduated from the School of Mines and for the next seven years devoted himself to the profession of mining engineer. He soon gained a reputation as an able geologist and mineralogist. Articles and monographs came from his pen in increasing volume. In 1904-1905 he published his first comprehensive treatise, a three-volume work entitled *As minas do Brasil e sua legislação*. The book at once made him famous. It contains in effect a comprehensive history of mining in Brazil, and is of the utmost interest to students of colonial history. Here is to be found for instance one of the best accounts of *bandeiras* and *entradas*[2] in existence.[3] It is not surprising therefore that it at once opened the doors of the *Instituto Historico e Geographico Brasileiro*, admission to which is one of the highest honors to which a Brazilian historian may aspire.

It was inevitable that a man of Calogeras' broad culture and technical accomplishments should gravitate to politics. In 1897, he was elected federal deputy from Minas Geraes and, save for the years 1899-1903, he held this office until 1914. He was soon acclaimed as one of the outstanding figures in the Chamber of Deputies. On such varied subjects as the army and navy, boundaries, mineral resources, and railroads, he spoke with authority. His addresses, which were quite devoid of oratorical embellishments, were carefully prepared and always commanded attention.

Calogeras took little interest in partisan politics and had a profound distrust of party leaders. He was never amenable to party discipline and at no time courted popularity. Though he was a deputy from the great state of Minas Geraes, he assumed at all times that he had a mandate from all of Brazil. To one of his opponents who taxed him with being the advocate of local in-

---

[2] Expeditions into the interior of Brazil in search of Indian slaves and precious metals. They resulted in exploration and eventual settlement of large sections of Brazil and helped push the frontier far to the west of the line of demarcation between Spanish and Portuguese America.

[3] Calogeras' nephew, the geologist Djalma Guimarães, is preparing a second edition for the press.

terests Calogeras scornfully replied: "For me there is no parcel
of Brazil apart from Brazil itself; I do not understand regional
conflicts." The deputy Martim Francisco de Andrada, one of the
most cultivated men in Brazilian public life, was wont to declare
that he "never missed a single one of his addresses, as it was an
education in itself to listen to Calogeras, 'a specialist in encyclo-
paedias'." In his still unpublished memoirs this scion of the great
José Bonifacio speaks of Calogeras as having in him the stuff of
"a minister of any department in any country in the world." While
this statement is perhaps an example of Lusitanian exuberance it
certainly contains a kernel of truth. Calogeras did, in fact, treat
with equal competency such disparate subjects as mining legislation, foreign affairs, coffee valorization, the conversion bureau
(*caixa de conversão*), tax reforms, public instruction, transportation, budgetary laws, and banking reforms. Especially noteworthy
was his magisterial address of January 23, 1904, on the Acre
question—a controversy which threatened at one time to involve
Brazil in a war with Bolivia. In the space of five hours Calogeras
explored every aspect of the subject, admittedly one of the most
thorny and difficult in the entire history of Brazilian diplomacy.

With his passionate interest in all that concerned Brazil's international status it was inevitable that he should become an admirer
and collaborator of the Baron of Rio Branco, the great Brazilian
minister of foreign relations. The Baron, in turn, fully appreciated
the abilities of Calogeras. He appointed him a member of the Brazilian delegation of the Third and Fourth Pan-American conferences held in Rio de Janeiro and Buenos Aires in 1906 and 1910
respectively. Owing to the captious refusal of the Chamber of
Deputies to grant Calogeras a leave of absence, he was unable to
attend the latter of these two gatherings in person. He did however submit to the Conference one of his best works, *La Politique
monétaire du Brésil.*[4] Aware that books written in Portuguese
secure little hearing beyond the confines of Brazil and Portugal,
Calogeras wrote it in French. The work is both a financial history
of Brazil and a monograph on Brazilian currency. As was to be
expected Calogeras' financial views were at all times orthodox.
Especially did he deprecate the excessive issue of paper money
and the co-existence of two kinds of currency—the so-called gold
and paper milreis. Copies of this book, which were presented to all

[4] Rio de Janeiro, 1910.

members of the Conference, elicited praise in all quarters. In successive numbers the great Argentine daily, *La Nación*, published the work *in extenso*. It evoked the enthusiastic commendations of such eminent French financiers as Emile Lavasseur, Charles Gide, and Raphael Georges Lévy. In fact this monograph is still regarded as so important that the Calogeras Foundation (*Fundação Calogeras*) is about to bring out a new and up-to-date edition under the direction of the Foundation's president, the distinguished engineer, Dr. Roberto Simonsen of São Paulo.

It is the history of republics the world over that the so-called practical politicians set little store by public men who place devotion to national issues and problems above partisan interests. Calogeras is a case in point. In 1914, there took place in Minas Geraes a radical shift in state politics the details of which are no concern here. It would appear that the party chiefs, intent on feathering their own nests, had no real appreciation of their eminent representative and Calogeras failed to be reëlected to the federal congress. He never again set foot in the Chamber of Deputies.

Fortunately, his merits as a statesman and administrator were well understood in higher quarters. Wenceslau Braz, former governor of Minas Geraes, was inaugurated chief magistrate of the nation on November 15, 1914. One of his first acts was to invite Calogeras to assume the portfolio of agriculture. The new minister was well equipped for his new duties. Thanks to his frequent addresses in congress, his ideas on the needs of Brazilian agriculture were well known. He had shown himself to be an enemy of rash experiments and capricious improvisations. Especially noteworthy was an attack in 1912 on an extravagant and ill-conceived attempt made by President Hermes da Fonseca to "valorize" rubber, and thus revive an industry which was in its last gasp as a result of faulty methods of production and the competition of plantation-grown rubber in the Far East. Calogeras' criticism of the *defesa da boracha*[5] was fully vindicated by the disastrous failure of the project.

Unhappily, Calogeras held office too short a time to achieve any definite results. The reforms which he put into effect were largely neutralized by his successors. Yet all qualified critics agree that in theory these reforms were sound. His chief preoccupation

---

[5] "Defense of rubber."

was the increase of agricultural production. This, in his judgment, could be accomplished only through the abandonment by the planters or *fazendeiros* of routine methods which had been in existence for generations. For this purpose, Calogeras did not feel that agricultural schools offered the most effective instruments. Colleges of this type, of which a number had recently been established, were indeed desirable, and in time their influence could be beneficial and far-reaching. But from their very nature they could mean very little to the existing agriculturists. It was Calogeras' idea to offer direct instruction to the *fazendeiros* by means of itinerant, practical agronomists, men whose hands were calloused by the use of farm machinery, and who were skilled in the technique of stock-raising. In addition there were to be established demonstration farms in certain strategic localities to which the agriculturalists could have ready access.

As events fell out, Calogeras was denied the opportunity of carrying out with anything like effectiveness these and other reforms. At the expiration of a few months, President Wenceslau Braz summoned him to a post in which, owing to the tragic situation in Brazil, the gifted minister could render greater services to his country. To Calogeras was entrusted the responsibility of guiding the financial destiny of Brazil through the most trying years of the Great War.

The new minister of finance was faced with a task of extraordinary difficulty. To almost all of the neutral countries the outbreak of the conflagration had brought a serious dislocation in their finances but the situation was greatly aggravated in the case of Brazil by a severe internal crisis. The country was in truth in a desperate plight. The great Ruy Barbosa compared Brazil to a house that had been gutted by thieves.[6] The statement is hardly overdrawn. It is now agreed that the administration of Hermes da Fonseca, which came to an end in 1914, was the most disastrous in the history of the republic. Corruption went hand in hand with the most wanton extravagance. When Calogeras took over the portfolio of finance early in 1915, he found the national income insufficient to meet the most urgent needs. The proceeds from the custom house—the greatest single source of income of the federal government—was reduced by a third. Commerce was paralyzed by the outbreak of the European War and by the dearth of available

---

[6] "O Brasil é espolio de uma casa roubada."

tonnage. Worst of all, the new minister had to make provisions for meeting the funding loan contracted during the latter part of the Hermes administration.

This is not the place to rehearse the measures adopted by Calogeras to meet the financial crisis and to husband the nation's resources. He himself tells us that "only those who had to grapple with these terrible problems can appreciate the magnitude of the task which made a veritable agony of each day's labor." [7] It is sufficient to point out that his efforts were conspicuously successful. All authorities concede that he was one of the ablest ministers of finance in the entire history of Brazil. On his resignation in September, 1917, Messrs. Rothschild, the British financial agents for Brazil, cabled Calogeras:

"Under your able guidance, Brazilian finances have never been so flourishing, and it is with a very great feeling of satisfaction that we both can say that we have been able to combat the difficulties which have presented themselves these last few years. Once more we thank you."

On the conclusion of the World War, Brazil, as one of the Allies, was entitled to a place at the Paris Peace Conference. The minister of foreign affairs, Domicio do Gamma[8] was an intimate friend of Calogeras. It was both natural and fitting that one whose grasp of international affairs had been so often demonstrated should be invited to be a member of the Brazilian delegation, even before the chief, Epitacio Pessôa, was appointed. Calogeras accepted the invitation, sailed immediately for France, and took an active part in the preliminary sessions of the Conference. The eminent Brazilian jurisconsult, Rodrigo Octavio, who was attached to the delegation as legal counsellor, has left a graphic recital of the activities of Calogeras at this time. A paragraph from his account is perhaps worth quoting.

"When I arrived at Paris, Dr. Alberto de Oliveira, the delegate of Portugal, at once came to see me and acquainted me with the surprise caused by Calogeras' first appearance in the Assembly. Everyone was eager to learn something about this unknown Brazilian delegate with the Greek name. . . . I soon heard from a variety of sources that the speeches of Calogeras were producing

---

[7] See below, p. 319.
[8] Later Brazilian Ambassador to the United States.

a profound impression, not only by the correctness of his language and diction, but also by the good sense of his proposals."

In the pages of his *Diario da Conferencia da Paz*, published in 1934 shortly after his death, it is possible to follow the activity of Calogeras during the memorable period from December 13, 1918, to March 6, 1919. The accounts which he gives of his interviews with Clemenceau, Briand, Wilson, Ribot, and Millerand are intensely interesting and evince keen psychological insight. One writer characterizes the pictures of these men as veritable historical miniatures. As a useful and hardworking committeeman his services were in constant demand. He became the leader and spokesman of the assembly when he denounced the efforts of Clemenceau to exclude the delegates of the smaller countries from the more important commissions. It was owing in considerable part to his efforts that Brazil was represented on the League of Nations Committee. In his championship of the rights of the lesser powers he so profoundly impressed King Albert that the latter personally invited Calogeras to visit Belgium, an honor extended to no other delegate at this time.

The chief of the Brazilian delegation to the Peace Conference was, it will be recalled, Epitacio Pessôa. While serving in Paris in this capacity, Pessôa was elected president of Brazil for the quadrennium 1918-1922. One of the first acts of the new executive was to appoint his friend and fellow-worker Calogeras to the post of minister of war, an office which he held from September 19, 1919, to November 15, 1922. In making this appointment the president broke sharply with existing traditions. Though civilians had frequently held the portfolio of war under the empire, Calogeras was the first to be so designated under the republic. He may be said to be one of that small group of gifted civilians, like Stanton and Baker in the United States, Sainte Beuve in France, and Araña in Spain who had a better appreciation of the real military needs of their country than the generals themselves.

Calogeras was no novice in these matters. During his long service in the Chamber he had frequent occasion to subject the war budget to a searching analysis and his various written reports show that he was fully alive to the necessities of the army. From his seat in parliament he had vigorously supported the idea of contracting for a French military mission and when General Gamalin and his staff arrived in 1919 he coöperated with them in every possible way in their formidable task of raising the morale and of augmenting the efficiency of every branch of the military service.

In his efforts to supply the army with the necessary *matériel* Calogeras was indefatigable. The arsenals and factories were the objects of the minister's particular care. For the first time the army was adequately housed in barracks. These the minister visited almost daily. He really lived with the troops. He ate at the soldiers' mess, was present at their drills, and scrutinized the functioning of the military machine in all its details. And it is indeed a splendid tribute to the character of Calogeras that when he resigned from his post he could look upon almost every officer as a personal friend.

The writer Baptista Pereira, in his introduction to a collection of Calogeras' essays called *Res Nostra*, relates that the workmen who were installing machines in the arsenals or shops were frequently joined by an unknown foreman who took an active and intelligent part in their tasks. But not for long could the rough blue blouse disguise this strange operative of almost uncanny skill. "It is the minister himself" was the word whispered from group to group, and such indeed was the case.

It is no exaggeration to say that Calogeras was the ablest minister of war who has yet held office under the republic. The French mission, for whose success he was largely responsible, really marked a turning point in Brazilian history. So true is this that the brilliant journalist Assis Chateaubriand once declared that there have been two armies in Brazil: the one before and the one subsequent to the French mission.

Yet when all has been said and done the greatest service rendered by Calogeras as minister of war was to attack—with some success —the unholy alliance between the army and politics. The part which the army had played and still plays in overturning governments, seating and unseating ministers, and dictating the march of public events is in the main a sorry and sordid one, the details of which are given in the present text. Calogeras had taken these lessons to heart. He was determined that henceforth the army should confine itself to its legitimate rôle of protecting the state from foreign aggressions and domestic uprisings. While he could not entirely eradicate an ill which harks back to the early days of the empire he did succeed in infusing a new spirit into the younger officers who from now on resolved at all costs to remain true to the code of their profession and to the principles of military discipline. Though subsequent events were to show that Calogeras strove for ideals incapable of complete fulfilment, it can at least be said that since his day the army has been a much less fertile field for the intrigues and machinations of unscrupulous politicians.

When Calogeras laid down the portfolio of war in 1922, his career as a public man virtually came to a close. In many respects it was a great pity. Through observation and arduous study he had gained a remarkable insight into the basic problems of Brazil and he was eager and willing to apply his great talents and abilities to their solution. His amazing versatility has been abundantly illustrated. It could be said of Calogeras as it was said of Nabuco: He could occupy all ministries with equal competency.

This is not the time or occasion to attempt an analysis of the causes which deprived Brazil of the services of one of its greatest public officials. The reasons apparently lie in the nature of Brazilian political life and the character and temperament of Calogeras himself. The truth of the matter is that Calogeras never adapted himself fully to the political climate of Brazil. He was by nature forthright and fundamentally honest. He had none of the stuff of the *arriviste* and cherished no vulgar ambitions. He was no great success as a compromiser. As has already been intimated, intrigues, maneuvers, wirepulling, and all the devices dear to the heart of the politician were repugnant to him. Such considerations may explain in part why Calogeras withdrew to private life at the very height of his public career.

For the next decade, then, he remained aloof from political life. This "tragedy of isolation," as one writer puts it, was not without its advantages and compensations. Inactivity was entirely foreign to Calogeras' nature and his restless and enquiring mind quickly turned to new fields. He had long been interested in the history of Brazil, and this predilection was naturally encouraged by his friend, the eminent historian, Capistrano de Abreu.

For a number of years Calogeras had been toying with the idea of a comprehensive survey of the foreign policy of Brazil. The project took definite form when, in 1924, the *Instituto Historico e Geographico Brasileiro* invited him to collaborate in the homage which the Institute planned to render to the memory of its former protector, Dom Pedro II, on the centenary of his birth. The period for treatment assigned to Calogeras was the years 1850-1864,

which included the suppression of the slave traffic, the foreign
policy of the empire, and the problem of the equilibrium of La
Plata. But he quickly discovered that these topics could not be
adequately handled without a careful analysis of the preceding
periods. The result was the publication of the first volume of what
eventually became the only comprehensive and detailed survey we
possess of Brazil's foreign policy. *A Politica Exterior do Imperio*
was designed to embrace the full sweep of Brazil's contacts with
its neighbors from the Treaty of Tordesillas in 1494 to the fall of
Rosas in 1852. The first volume, *As Origins*, appeared in 1927. It
brought the story up through the reign of Dom João and the eve
of Independence. The second volume, *O Primeiro Reinado*, exclusively devoted to the period of Dom Pedro I, was issued in 1928.
The third, published in 1933, the year before Calogeras' death, is
entitled *Da Regencia á Queda de Rozas*. Since the reputation of
Calogeras as a historian will rest chiefly on this work, we may
pause for a moment to consider its excellencies and shortcomings.

The merits of the book are obvious. Realizing that his study,
if it was to have any stamp of authority, must be based on the
wide use of source material, Calogeras worked carefully through
the extensive documentary material in both the National Archives
(*Archivo Nacional*) and the Foreign Office (*Palacio Itamaraty*).[9]
He also placed under requisition most of the important monographs and secondary works dealing with the periods covered. He
enjoyed other advantages too. Thanks to his intimate association
with the Baron of Rio Branco and his own official activities he had
acquired a first-hand acquaintance with the foreign relations of
Brazil of his own day, and he was thus in a better position to interpret the spirit and tendencies of the whole span of Brazilian
diplomatic history.

Yet this work, for the completion of which Calogeras courageously sacrificed his health and probably shortened his life,[10] is subject to a number of qualifications. In perusing some of the chapters
one cannot escape the conviction that the narrative is at times

---

[9] In the latter repository he was fortunate enough to find the cipher used in
the diplomatic correspondence relative to the recognition of the empire. A later
investigator, Sr. Mozart Monteiro, discovered that Calogeras had left written
in his own hand copies of the deciphered documents along with the originals,
for the guidance and convenience of future students of the archives.

[10] The last chapters of the concluding volume were written while Calogeras
was confined to his bed. It was literally a race against time.

rather thin and that source material has not always been exhausted. Especially is this true of the section dealing with the recognition of the Brazilian empire by the United States. It would be surprising indeed if the book did not have its purple patches. The composition of a work of fifteen hundred closely written pages, embracing three and a half centuries of Brazilian history, would have been regarded by many professional historians as the task of a lifetime. Yet Calogeras could devote only seven or eight years to the project, and even this period witnessed the publication of a number of other books, notably the *Formação Historica do Brasil.*

But the chief complaint of the serious reader is the almost complete absence of critical apparatus. Footnotes and references to authorities are exceedingly rare. Such as exist are calculated to whet rather than to satisfy the appetite of the reader. A single example will make this clear. Perhaps the most important section in the entire work is that dealing with the recognition of the independence of Brazil by Portugal and England.[11] In a note at the beginning of this chapter Calogeras tells us:

"In the preparation of this chapter, in addition to the general works on the subject (not specified) we utilized the *Archivo Diplomatico da Independencia,* the correspondence of Palmella, the works of Stapleton and Temperley on Canning, and Rocha Martim's *Independencia do Brasil.* For the English side of the negotiation, we above all used the official correspondence of Canning with Stuart, as transcribed by Alberto Rangel at the instance of the Minister of Foreign Relations."

This is surely a formidable array of material. But in the section embracing over a hundred pages the author does not give us a single specific reference and in most cases we are left quite in the dark as to which of his sources or authorities he has drawn upon. Furthermore, it should be noted that the book is quite innocent of any general bibliographies, and the index is limited to proper names.

In justice to Calogeras one should not attach too much weight to these criticisms. In some respects they are captious. The author was writing for a Brazilian audience interested primarily in a detailed and authoritative account of the period. As for the value of the sources and authorities, the reader is quite willing to take

[11] Vol. II, Chap. IX, "Reconhecimento por Portugal e Inglaterra."

Calogeras' word for it and accept his interpretation. He is not interested in the mechanics of scholarship. Footnotes, references to manuscripts buried in archives, critical bibliographies, and such scholarly machinery merely clutter up the text and distract one's attention. Why not then omit these unnecessary refinements?

If we assume that such is the attitude of the overwhelming majority of Cologeras' readers we can well understand why the author made little or no effort to present his work in monographic form. And while this method of presentation does not commend itself to the more critical wing of the scholarly fraternity, few will be disposed to deny that *A Politica Exterior do Imperio* will remain a monument to Calogeras' patient research and fine erudition.

The Formação Historica do Brasil, of which a translation is now offered to the English reading world, was written *con amore*. Calogeras had a real admiration for the United States and a genuine affection for many of its citizens. He had an excellent command of spoken English and for many years he cherished the ambition to give a series of lectures on Brazilian history at our institutions of higher learning, particularly Stanford University, whose former president, Dr. John Casper Branner, was an intimate friend.

For a variety of reasons these hopes were never realized. Yet this generous and fruitful idea did not entirely perish. In 1930 was held in Rio de Janeiro a summer school for foreigners, particularly North Americans. Though this initiative was unhappily abandoned after a single year, it had to its credit one achievement —the publication of Calogeras' excellent survey of all of Brazilian history, based on informal lectures delivered at the time.

Brazilian writers are one in acclaiming the merits of this work. The opinion of the critic Baptista Pereira is perhaps worth quoting.

"No other work embraces with equal thoroughness all of the elements which have entered into our formation as a people, or treats with such insight and method the different phases of our evolution. It is a work quite indispensable, especially to teachers and students of Brazilian history, to whom its didactic qualities will make a special appeal. It would be the counsel of wisdom to require its adoption in our institutions of learning."

As intimated elsewhere in this introduction, perhaps the chief merit of the work—aside of course from the scholarship and competency of the author—is its comprehensiveness. It carries the

story from the discovery of Brazil in 1498 (as Calogeras would
have it) up to 1926, and as such occupies a unique place in Brazilian
historiography. The book is in no sense an arid chronicle. While
the chief events are chronicled in their proper sequence, considerable space is devoted to institutions. Even literature comes in
for a brief treatment. Though the book is designed to be objective
it is never colorless. Calogeras was an original and vigorous
thinker and it is not surprising that many phases of Brazilian history are considered from a new angle. Some critics might accuse
him of a certain clerical bias owing to the fact that in the last
years of his life he had become a fervent Catholic. Yet, in his account of the religious struggle of the latter years of the empire, he
tries to be fair to the civil authorities though it is evident that his
sympathies are with the Church. In his treatment of personalities
he has striven to mete out justice with an even hand. Especially
commendable is the restraint he has shown in his appraisal of the
leading men of the republic among whom he had many friends and
some enemies. Perhaps the most serious lapse in this portion of his
work is his failure to give the reader any real understanding of the
character and achievements of Ruy Barbosa, one of the most remarkable figures in the entire history of Brazil.

The translation of the *Formação historica do Brasil* has been
attended with a number of very real difficulties. Statesman, historian, financier, geologist, Calogeras undoubtedly was, but even
his warmest admirers would concede that as a writer he lacked the
golden touch of style. If he scorned those literary embellishments
which only too often take the place of thought, he at times failed
to appreciate the prime importance of clarity of presentation. His
style also reveals a certain lack of consistency. Only too often his
pages contain long passages in which his ideas are involved and occasionally obscure. A little later on we may find models of com-
pression, where the sentences are terse and almost lapidary in
style. It will be readily apprehended that under these circumstances
anything like a literal translation of Calogeras' works would make
almost impossible reading.

There are still further difficulties inherent perhaps in the nature
and genius of the Portuguese tongue. The noble language of
Camões, with all its beauties and possibilities, could hardly be
characterized as an instrument of precision, as is, for instance,
the French, and to a lesser extent the Spanish. To convey the

thought of a Portuguese or Brazilian writer with reasonable accuracy in anything like idiomatic English, it is frequently necessary to recast and rearrange an entire paragraph. At least such is the case with the works of Calogeras. It is the reasoned conviction of the writer of this introduction that of all the Romance languages, the Portuguese makes the most exacting demands upon the translator.

Limitations of space preclude anything but the briefest mention of Calogeras' remaining works. In 1930, a group of his friends collected some thirty-five of his lectures and briefer monographs, and published them under the title of *Res Nostra*. Though some of the items are fugitive and ephemeral in value, a score or more deserve a place in Brazilian historiography. Their scope is indicated by such titles as "Capistrano de Abreu," "Diario de Navagação de Pedro Lopes de Souza (1530-1532)," "A Orden de São Bento e a Civilisação," "Rio Branco e a Politica Exterior," "O Brasil e a Sociedade das Nações." In 1932 appeared a biographical study, *O Marquez de Barbacena*, one of the outstanding figures in the days of Independence. The year following appeared a formidable treatise called *Problemas de Administração*. The history of this work is worth noting. Back in 1917, Rodrigues Alves had been elected to the presidency a second time, although as events fell out he did not live to take office. He had been out of politics for several years and, in order to gain the necessary orientation for his new duties, he asked Calogeras to draw up a confidential report on the outgoing administration, that of Wenceslau Braz. Calogeras could write with authority since he held the portfolio of finance, as we have seen, from 1915 to 1917. The result is a minute and devastating appraisal of the inner workings of the Brazilian administration during four crucial years (1914-1918); nothing is concealed, nothing glossed over. Wenceslau Braz now appears in his true light, a well-intentioned but weak executive who allowed the gravest kinds of abuses to invade almost every branch of the administration. A decade and a half later, when passions had subsided and new men had come to the fore, Calogeras was persuaded to publish his report under the title *Problemas de Administração*. Though no one would claim it is easy reading, its importance as an analysis of the Brazilian body politic is beyond question.

Did this Introduction make any pretension to completeness it would be necessary to mention other works of Calogeras. In addition to innumerable articles in the press, many of which have never been collected, a complete bibliography would have to include well over a hundred different items. There still remains a vast amount of manuscript material, chiefly letters to his many friends. On his death in 1934 a number of these friends established the *Fundação Pandiá Calogeras,* of which the president is the eminent Paulista engineer, Dr. Roberto Simonsen. To this Foundation was committed not only all the rights to Calogeras' publications but also his archives. It already has to its credit two admirable studies on Calogeras, both of which were placed under requisition by the writer of this Introduction. The works are *Calogeras na opinião de seus contemporaneos* (São Paulo, 1934), consisting of a series of appreciations and estimates of his life by a large number of writers; and *Calogeras* by Dr. Antonio Gontijo de Carvalho (São Paulo, 1935). It is altogether likely that the next task of the Foundation will be the publication of Calogeras' correspondence. Certainly anything which may contribute to a better knowledge of one of the most useful, patriotic, and competent figures in the last quarter century of Brazilian history is worthy of every encouragement.

PERCY ALVIN MARTIN

March, 1939

CONTENTS

CHAPTER I

DISCOVERY AND EXPLORATION

The Problem of the Discovery.—According to the generally accepted opinion Brazil was discovered on April 22, 1500, by a Portuguese fleet commanded by Pedro Alvares Cabral while en route to India. For centuries this view was accepted without question. But during the past few years the priority of Cabral's discovery has been sharply challenged. As a result of researches in the archives of Lisbon and other repositories of fifteenth and sixteenth century material the evidence is all but conclusive that prior to the landfall of Cabral other Portuguese navigators visited Brazil and adjacent portions of South America.

If we consider for a moment the situation in Portugal on the eve of the great period of discovery and exploration, the reasons for this long silence on the voyages of Cabral's predecessors will become clear. Occupying a narrow band along the Atlantic littoral of the Iberian Peninsula the Lusitanian kingdom contained at this time barely a million and a half inhabitants. Both in population and resources it was far outstripped by Castile, a nation shortly destined to be its chief competitor in the adventurous quest of new lands and continents. England, to a less degree, and France, on a larger scale, were soon to engage in this same rivalry. As the weakest of the maritime powers, Portugal was forced to follow one consistent policy in the defense of its rights: to conceal as best possible its activities from its rivals. Fortunately, Portugal had at its command the most competent pilots and the most skillful sailors of the period. Not only did these men make possible the great achievements of Portugal during the fifteenth and sixteenth centuries but they likewise rendered inestimable services to Spain. One needs only to recall the names of such intrepid navigators as João de Solis and Fernão de Magalhães,[1] engaged in Seville by the Spanish House of Trade or *Casa de Contratación*. Columbus, though a Genoese by birth, as a pilot and navigator largely followed Portuguese methods.

Official Secrecy.—Fully aware that they had no means of resisting attacks from their powerful rivals, the rulers of the house of

---

[1] Better known by the English form of his name: Magellan.—P.A.M.

Aviz[2] adopted in their transatlantic enterprises one consistent policy of defense: absolute secrecy. It was forbidden to publish maps, portolanos,[3] or accounts of voyages. If it were absolutely necessary to commit anything to writing, it was done in such a manner that no information of value could become public property. This invariable rule had been imposed from the dawn of the fifteenth century when the infante, Dom Henrique,[4] assumed the noble initiative of directing the maritime expansion of Portugal along the coast of Africa. His castle and observatory of Sagres became a school where great explorers were to gain their naval apprenticeship. It was also a center of instruction in nautical and geographical sciences, a promontory where burned the torch of energy and light which illumined the entire Atlantic.

Dom João II was his intellectual and political heir and in the conduct of his government he followed the lines traced by his great predecessor. From 1415 to 1495, during eighty years, there was no change in aims or methods. Dom Manoel I, who immediately succeeded Dom João, followed the same traditions up to his death in 1521. Thus did the policy of official secrecy become a political axiom of Portugal, consistently pursued for more than a century. Contemporary scientific progress permits us to investigate these problems, utilizing a certain number of documents which unfortunately are not sufficiently numerous or authoritative completely to establish our conclusions. But they abundantly prove the severity of the king's orders and the strict and even harsh manner in which they were carried out.

In certain respects, the Portuguese did but revive the ancient methods employed by the Phoenicians. These historic lords of the sea, in one of their maritime exploits, acquired secret knowledge of the tin mines of Cornwall, whose products they carried to Tyre. In order to maintain this monopoly they sank without mercy all foreign ships with their crews found beyond the columns of Hercules, the present Strait of Gibraltar. The Portuguese followed the same procedure as regards ships found within the limits assigned to the Portuguese possessions by a series of papal bulls. It proved an effective means of assuring to Portugal the islands in the At-

---

[2] A Portuguese dynasty which ruled from 1385 to 1580.—P.A.M.

[3] A medieval chart or map on which coast outlines and ports or harbors are indicated.—P.A.M.

[4] Better known as Prince Henry the Navigator (1394-1460).—P.A.M.

lantic and the maritime route to India. Frightful rules, these, which, implacably carried out, enabled the Portuguese to cast a veil of secrecy over their maritime discoveries.

We have here the explanation of the refusal of Dom João II to accede to the demands of Columbus. The immortal Genoese proposed a direct passage from Lisbon to Asia across the Atlantic. But the Portuguese rulers, together with their statesmen and their navigators, possessed a more exact knowledge of geographical conditions than did Columbus and were not ignorant of the fact that half way between Europe and India lay another continental land mass.[5]

The Portuguese Attitude at Tordesillas.—For this reason, when Columbus on his return from his first voyage proclaimed his supposed discovery of islands lying off the coast of China, the Portuguese, headed by their king, retorted that the lands which he had found were located within the domains of the house of Aviz, such as the pope had defined them. Labrador, for instance, had probably been reached as early as 1472 or 1474 by the Portuguese pilot João Vaz Corte-Real.[6] Another Portuguese, Estevão Fróes, in a letter to Dom João II refers to a voyage which he undertook to South America in 1498, perhaps earlier.[7] The protracted debates at Tordesillas[8] in regard to the location of the line of demarcation between the possessions of the Portuguese and Spanish crowns assumed a capital importance for the dynasty of Aviz as these de-

---

[5] This statement of Dr. Calogeras, though supported by a number of Portuguese writers, by no means represents the consensus of the historians who have written on this period.—P.A.M.

[6] This tradition goes back to the work of Gasper Frutuoso, a chronicler of the Madeira and Azores islands and appears in his *Saudades da Terra,* composed between 1580 and 1591, or over a hundred years later. In general, his work enjoyed little credit among Portuguese historians. The subject is investigated at length by the distinguished scholar Fidelino de Figueiredo in his *Estudos de Historia Americana* (São Paulo, 1930), pp. 52-60.—P.A.M.

[7] This Fróes was a semi-mythical figure who after visiting Brazil reached the West Indies where he was captured and incarcerated by the Spaniards. From his prison he wrote a long rambling letter in execrable Portuguese to Dom João II begging him to secure his release. Nothing more is known of him. The letter is published in facsimile in I, xxv ff., of the monumental *Historia da Colonização portugueza do Brasil* (3 vols., Porto, 1921).—P.A.M.

[8] The Treaty of Tordesillas, signed June 7, 1494, carried the papal line of demarcation, drawn up the previous year by Alexander VI, to 370 leagues to the west of the Cape Verde Islands. *Cf.* John Fiske, *Discovery of America* (2 vols., Boston, 1898), I, 96-99.—P.A.M.

bates were closely linked up with the mystery of the Portuguese discoveries.

Finally, Duarte Pacheco Pereira, in his celebrated work *Esmeraldo de situ orbis* makes the astounding assertion that he was in Brazil in 1498 by order of Dom Manoel.[9] In this event—and everything conspires to confirm the truth of this assertion—Duarte Pacheco should be considered the real discoverer of Brazil, while to Pedro Alvares Cabral merely falls the official title of "finder" (*inventor*).[10] By a curious irony of history, this same Duarte Pacheco accompanied Cabral when the latter on his way to India sailed so far to the West as to reach the shores of Brazil on April 22, 1500. To both heroes were reserved great exploits and a glorious destiny in India.

How are we to account for this strange silence in reference to the achievements of Duarte Pacheco? Why should the fame of one great Portuguese be so completely eclipsed by that of the other? This is one of the mysterious aspects of the problem. It is probably related to the policy of secrecy in national affairs followed by the authorities in Lisbon. To attempt further to explain the problem here would transgress the scope of the present study.

The situation of the Portuguese kingdom at the beginning of the sixteenth century was politically and socially one of extreme delicacy. After the triumphal voyage of Vasco da Gama in 1497-1499, there had sprung into existence a vigorous traffic with the East Indies, at first largely peaceful in character, but presently beset with military difficulties. The chief articles of trade were spices, bartered for such European wares as textiles, copper, and hardware. The quotations on pepper and cloves had fallen to one-fourth

---

[9] In attributing to Duarte Pacheco the priority in the discovery of Brazil, Dr. Calogeras has rallied to the thesis elaborated by Professor Luciano Pereira da Silva in chap. V of vol. I, *Historia da Colonização Portugueza do Brasil.* It is to be noted that Duarte Pacheco does not specifically state that he visited Brazil. His words are: "In the third year of your reign (*i.e.* 1498) in which Your Highness ordered us to discover the western part (*a parte occidental*) passing beyond the great expanse of the ocean sea." Pereira da Silva deduces that such a command could only apply to those regions beyond the Atlantic falling within the Portuguese zone as defined by the Treaty of Tordesillas, *i.e.,* Brazil.—P.A.M. [Arguments for the discovery of Brazil by the Portuguese, before 1492, are stated by Charles E. Nowell, in *The Hispanic American Historical Review,* XVI (August 1936), 311-38.—J.A.R.]

[10] The conventional view in regard to the discovery of Brazil by Cabral may be found in Fiske, *op. cit.* II, 96-99.—P.A.M.

of their former level as a consequence of the extensive cargoes brought to Lisbon and from there forwarded to Antwerp. But as late as 1510, trade in such articles continued to be profitable. From this time on, however, difficulties increased, and the commercial perspective appeared much less favorable. Though Portugal continued to be dazzled by the mirage of India, its new commitments in the East proved a heavy draft on the nation's energies and resources. By the first years of the third decade of the sixteenth century these enterprises became ruinous. The country fell back upon loans, both internal and foreign, which resulted in the failure of both borrowers and lenders.

The discovery of Brazil also inflicted new and increasing burdens on the royal treasury. The new colony turned out to be poor. No precious metals were discovered. Instead of diamonds, rubies, and pearls were found parrots, monkeys, and brazilwood. A few slaves were captured but these were of poor quality and were too accustomed to their independence to long survive their loss of liberty. In short, a wretched business!

Why the Conquest was Maintained.—Yet in the final resort it was not possible to abandon Brazil. Thanks to its position on the ocean route to India via the Cape of Good Hope the new colony might serve as a protection to Portuguese trade and furnish supplies and fresh water to the ships plying between Lisbon and the East. Moreover, on the Pacific coast of the continent had just been revealed the fabulous riches of Peru—a sequel to the treasures drawn from Mexico through the pillage of the Aztec empire. According to superstitions current at this period, the East was superior to the West; Brazil, therefore, should harbor in its soil even greater hidden wealth than the domains of the Incas. Unfortunately, the Treaty of Tordesillas, in dividing America, failed to meet all of the aspirations of Portugal.[11] Intent on the future, Portugal naturally hoped to perfect some arrangement that would improve its frontier. A first step toward such a consummation would be to establish itself firmly on the eastern littoral.

Happily, at this time, the relations between Lisbon and Madrid were thoroughly cordial. Family bonds and common interests united

---

[11] According to F. A. de Varnhagen (*Historia do Brasil*) the line of demarcation entered Brazil in the north in the vicinity of Pará and emerged in the south a little to the west of Laguna in the present state of Santa Catharina. —P.A.M.

the Spanish and Portuguese courts despite the fact that in America their policies were in conflict. Moreover, Francis I of France was an adversary of both Iberian powers. He challenged their pretensions to a common ownership of the non-European world and declared that he had never seen the clause of the testament by which Father Adam had bestowed such an empire exclusively on Dom Manoel and Charles V. Nor was the French menace confined to mere words. Brazilwood remained a valuable commodity, even if it could not compete in importance with the products of India. French corsairs were wont to cruise between the Azores, the Cape Verde Islands, and Portugal, cutting athwart the route which the ships followed on their return from South America to Lisbon, and seizing the ships together with their crews and cargoes. The losses to the Peninsula from such captures were very heavy and were the occasion of long and difficult diplomatic controversies in Paris. But efforts on the part of the Portuguese crown to secure redress were futile. To be sure, Francis undertook to grant no more letters of marque, and officially he carried out his promise; surreptitiously, however, concessions continued to be granted, and ships were captured as before. So critical did the situation become that by 1530 one might well hesitate to predict whether Brazil would remain under Portuguese control or fall as booty to the French.

To be sure these piratical expeditions from Normandy and Brittany did not always go unpunished. In 1516, Dom João III, driven to desperation, despatched a number of caravels under Admiral Christovão Jacques with stringent orders to sink all hostile ships plying in Brazilian waters. Thanks to the energy of the commander many vessels were disposed of and in a short time the activity of these interlopers greatly diminished. But it soon became evident that the only effective means of coping with this French menace was to establish permanent nuclei of population along the Atlantic coast.

The Mission of Martim Affonso de Souza.—This all-important task of placing the colony on an enduring basis was entrusted to Admiral Martim de Souza in 1530. With the achievements of this accomplished nobleman, doughty soldier, and able statesman the real history of Brazil may be said to begin. His ships followed the Brazilian littoral from North to South. The contour of the coast was carefully studied. The map of Viegas, completed in 1534, was one of the results of these geographical studies: even today it deserves attention and respect as the first attempt to fix an approximately true outline of the coast. To indicate the Portuguese ownership stone pillars (*padrões*) were set up at various points. In the North the first of these was located slightly to the west of the Tordesillas line. In the South, on the other hand, the pillars were placed far beyond it; in fact the boundary line was pushed so far to the West as to lie half way between the sites of the present Buenos Aires and Santa Fé. We have here the first active move leading to the reopening of the whole frontier question between Spanish and Portuguese America.

Meanwhile, Martim Affonso waged an implacable warfare against the French corsairs. Such captured ships as he did not sink were manned by his own seamen and brought to Portugal. Near Pernambuco he destroyed a French factory or commercial settlement and constructed another garrisoned with Portuguese troops. In the South, near the present port of Santos, he founded in 1521 a settlement called São Vicente, and then, beyond the neighboring *Serras*, on the interior plateau which drained into the Platine basin, he established another village, Piratininga, which in the fulness of time was to become the great city of São Paulo.

With these setlements as bases it was hoped that the Portuguese were at length in a position to confront the dangers growing out of the presence in Brazil of powerful rivals and neighbors. Pernambuco, the center of the zone producing brazilwood, might serve as an advance post in the war against foreign interlopers and corsairs, chiefly the French. To São Vicente-Piratininga would be entrusted the task of grappling with the problems created by the proximity of the Spanish-American frontier. This latter community might also serve as a point of departure for a movement, destined to extend over two centuries, to the South and West. This advance was not only to be launched against the Spanish province of Paraguay but also was to include in its scope distant Potosí and the fabulous wealth of Peru. So true was this that one of the first orders emanating from Martim Affonso was for the organization of an expedition "against the Inca," *i.e.*, against Peru.

Utilization of the Colony. Establishment of the Captaincies.— The settlements founded by Martim Affonso, though fated in later years to play a great rôle in Brazilian history, offered an insufficient protection against the encroachment of Portugal's enemies. As the sixteenth century wore on, it became increasingly clear that more effective means must be found to develop the resources of the colony and to provide adequately for its defense. Owing to its poverty and its commitments in India, the mother country was in no position to divert its resources to the support of its American possessions. At this critical juncture, the Portuguese crown fell back on methods that had proven successful in the Azores and Madeira. Here vast estates or fiefs had been granted to vassals of the crown known as donataries (*donatarios*) who had assumed responsibility for the settlement and exploitation of their grants and had agreed to pay the crown a portion of the taxes and revenues collected. In return, they had been invested with almost sovereign powers. An analogous method was now applied to Brazil. From Laguna in the South to Pará in the North, the coastline was divided into sections measuring fifty Portuguese leagues. In theory, each section, known as a captaincy, was assigned to a grantee or *donatario*. But in the case of Martim Affonso it was felt that his extraordinary services entitled him to a double portion, or one hundred leagues, while his brother Pero Lopes de Souza, who had shown himself a skillful sailor under the admiral's orders, obtained eighty leagues. Since Brazil was still in large part unexplored, no natural boundaries such as river courses or mountain ranges could be utilized as limits of the captaincies. As a consequence, the crown fell back on geographical divisions based on meridians and parallels.

This arrangement was not without its disadvantages. When the coast ran in a general way from north to south the maritime boundary of the captaincy corresponded more or less to the width of the fief in the interior of the country. But where the direction shifted from north to south to northeast to southwest the width of the fief was materially reduced. The western boundary of the captaincies was theoretically the meridian or line of demarcation established by the Treaty of Tordesillas. Owing, again, however, to the configuration of the coast, some of the fiefs extended much farther to the west than others. Thus there were great discrepancies in the size of the various captaincies. Yet these differences in area constituted after all one of the minor shortcomings of the system. In the final resort, all depended on the abilities of the *donatario*, his resources, his organizing capacity, and his skill as a commander. In these respects the majority of the captaincies failed lamentably. At the end of two decades, by 1554, only three could be described as successful: Pernambuco, São Vicente, and São Amaro. The method, nonetheless, was not essentially bad. Other colonizing nations, England for example, followed somewhat similar procedures in the case of their American possessions.

Breakdown of the Donatary System.—By the middle of the sixteenth century the failure of the captaincies had become clear to the authorities at Lisbon. Letters reached the king from his subjects in Brazil imploring help against the Indians and the French. "Send us aid," was the tenor of the majority of the complaints, "or the whole enterprise will perish." At Paris, where the tension between the French and Portuguese courts reached its height, the Portuguese ambassador was wont to conclude his letters in the same strain.

It was generally agreed that the powers of the *donatarios* were excessive. There was no real bond uniting the various captaincies. The efforts of the *donatarios*, instead of being bent toward the realization of common aims, were dissipated in all directions. Their authority, nominally unlimited, varied in practice from one fief to another. Duarte Coelho in Pernambuco, for example, had the reputation of being severe, obedient to the law, and a strict commander. Criminals gave his captaincy a wide berth. The difficulties of the *donatarios* were increased by the many turbulent and refractory elements among the colonists. This is not surprising when we recall that Brazil like Australia in the last century was looked upon for a time as a penal colony and was the recipient of many undesirables from Portugal. Along with the riffraff, however, were to be found many colonists of excellent origin, including even younger sons of the nobility.

By the middle of the sixteenth century it was clear that the captaincies had not served the purpose for which they were created. With a few exceptions the *donatarios* turned out to be unequal to their tasks. A complete change in the existing system was thoroughly necessary if Portugal were not to forfeit its American possessions. To cope with the growing anarchy it was imperative to establish a common code, both administrative and penal. As a supplement to the rule of the king in Lisbon, distant, theoretical, and slow in execution, it was essential to create in Brazil a superior authority sufficiently powerful to put its decisions instantly into effect. The decisive step was taken in 1549 when the king issued a royal decree, limiting the power of the *donatarios* and creating a governor general for the whole of Brazil. The first incumbent of this high office was Thomé de Souza, a Portuguese noble who had won his laurels in India and Africa. São Salvador or Bahia was selected as capital of the colony.

Religious Organization.—Moral conditions in Brazil were at this time deplorable. Religious sanctions, loose at best, had all but disappeared. Priests were few and such as there were led scandalous lives. Moreover, the immense extent of the captaincies and the widely scattered population would have made it almost impossible for the clergy to exercise any kind of spiritual control. All of these factors contributed to a moral collapse much worse than the spiritual life of the primitive Indians. In ecclesiastical matters, nothing could be settled *in loco* since everything depended on the decisions made by the Bishop of Funchal (Madeira) and the Metropolitan in Lisbon: the first the seat of the diocese, and the second the metropolitan church of the colonial territory. The creation of a diocese in Brazil was imperative. The unconverted masses of the Indians must be gathered within the folds of the Catholic Church and a special militia must be trained to preach and teach the gospel. To solve these problems, all of them vital, demanded considerable time. The creation of a diocese depended on Rome and it was not until 1551 that the first steps were taken. As regards the missionaries, they were sent over under Father Nobrega in the same squadron which carried the first governor general to the colony. They were recruited from the newly created order of the Jesuits, the product of the genius of Ignatius Loyola.

Collaboration of the Civil Power with the Church.—It was indeed a blessing for Brazil that the superior of the missions and the governor general were men of exceptional ability. They would in fact have been marked out for distinction in any country at any epoch. Thomé de Souza and Father Manoel de Nobrega were the real founders of Brazil, although their tasks had been facilitated by the pioneer labors of Martim Affonso de Souza. To these two excellent friends, working hand in hand, the new colony owed its impetus and its progress. To both Brazil was beholden for the beginnings of an era of peace, respect for authority, justice, and the organization of economic and social life.

The first governor occupied his post for nearly four years. His successor, Duarte da Costa, though worthy of no special mention, proved a happy choice. But the third of these high functionaries, Men de Sá, showed himself to be the true and worthy successor of Thomé de Souza, and like him, the friend of Nobrega and of the Jesuits. His term of office covered eighteen years, extending to 1572. His collaboration with Nobrega, who died in 1570, was at all times close. One may, therefore, assert that for more than two decades, Brazil was ably administered by men of marked capacity, all inspired by the same ideal.

The Spanish Dominion.—The latter years of the sixteenth century witnessed a great change in Portugal. In 1580 Dom Enrique, the cardinal-king and the last representative of the national dynasty of Aviz, died. Philip II of Spain, who through his mother had claims to the Portuguese throne, determined to make good his rights. He invaded the little kingdom and partly by force, partly by bribery, he contrived to be elected as legitimate ruler. As sovereign of both Spain and Portugal, Philip now became lord of the entire South American continent. He was already master of the Spanish colonies and now through inheritance and choice of the Portuguese Cortes he became ruler of Brazil.

This new situation had important consequences, especially as regards the Line of Demarcation. At the beginning, at least nominally, the line had been definitely fixed by the Treaty of Tordesillas. But under the new dispensation a certain amount of confusion was inevitable, and the Portuguese colonists quickly strove to derive the maximum benefit from this changed status by pushing their discoveries and explorations farther and farther to the west. In certain cases the government of Madrid even officially granted large territorial extensions to the Portuguese without reference to the geographical situation growing out of the treaty of 1494. These advantages were not lost when in 1640 Portugal regained its independence and a new national king, Dom João IV, the first of the Braganza line, mounted the throne. Thus the period of sixty years of Spanish rule turned out to be of capital importance to Brazil, not merely through the enlargement of its territory but also because it contributed to the growth of a certain sentiment of nationality.

The Local Element.—From its first days of the captaincies, and even earlier, racial crossing between the Portuguese and the Indians had become a common practice. At first such unions were regarded as illegitimate but with the passing of time they became perfectly legal and enjoyed the blessing of the Church; especially was this true after the conversion en masse of the Indian tribes. The members of the mixed race which resulted from these unions boasted of their paternity. This was all the more true from the fact that, contradictory to what happened in the case of the African Negroes, marriages between the whites and the Indians were not only encouraged, but also enjoyed the sanction of the Portuguese law. The products of these Indo-European crossings, known as mamelucos, played an important rôle in the conquest of the country. They possessed the astuteness of the Indian, together with the knowledge of the ways, mentality, and customs of their savage forebears, and to these advantages they added the immense superiority derived from the firearms and support of the Portuguese. Through the intervention of the mamelucos, entire tribes were brought from the forests of the interior to the settlements on the littoral where they were forced to labor in the sugar plantations or in the rude sugar factories constructed by the Portuguese.

Little by little were revealed the outlines of the various racial groups into which colonial society was eventually divided. First came the Portuguese from Europe, the so-called *reinóes*;[12] second, the Portuguese born in Brazil corresponding to the *criollos* or creoles in Spanish America; then, the mamelucos whose sympathies were with the whites rather than with the Indians; and finally, the peaceful and friendly Indians. Not always, to be sure, could the Indians be so characterized. Between the Portuguese and their Indian allies peace was by no means permanent; frequently it was in the nature of a truce which might, without warning, be broken at any moment. Yet taken by and large the friendly relations between the two races could be counted upon even in times of stress.

Such was the case, for instance, in the conflict with the French invaders, the smugglers of brazilwood. We have here the first instance of that solidarity of feeling which was to gain steadily

[12] *I. e.*, the inhabitants of the Kingdom (*Reino*) of Portugal.—P.A.M.

in strength with the passing of the years. We may even describe these struggles as our first national war, in spite of the relative exaggeration of the term. A feeling of unity based on hostility against a third party may hardly be said to constitute a national ideal. Nevertheless, the war over brazilwood which lasted almost a century (1520-1615) lent unity and cohesion to the scattered and heterogenous Portuguese elements whose collaboration under other circumstances would have been exceedingly difficult. The opposing group, consisting of the French and hostile Indians, did not possess the same power of prolonged resistance. The French came and went and their action was therefore episodic. The Portuguese settlements were permanent and their action was constant. But the real test of the solidarity of sentiment which united the Portuguese, the Indians, and the mamelucos was to come in the second quarter of the seventeenth century when the Honorable Dutch West India Company laid its plans for the conquest of Brazil.

The Struggle With the Dutch.—Portugal, since 1580 a part of Spain, found itself involved in a war with Holland. Both in the East and the West Indies the Portuguese colonies were attacked, captured, and lost. The first Dutch assault on Brazil, in 1624, resulted in the capture of Bahia; but the conquerors were expelled the following year. Two years later the same city was again attacked but the Dutch were repulsed after they had pillaged the city and harbor. In 1630, a large fleet dropped anchor in the harbor of Pernambuco and captured the two chief cities of the captaincy, Olinda and Recife. For the next two years the conquest made no further progress. But in 1632 the whole situation was changed through the adhesion to the Dutch of a clever and enterprising mameluco named Domingos Fernandes Calabar. Thanks to the counsel and aid of this renegade the Dutch were able to extend their rule until it embraced the better part of the coast of what are now the states of Sergipe, Alagoas, Pernambuco, Parahyba, Rio Grande do Norte, Ceará, Piauhy, and Maranhão. They even succeeded in crossing the Atlantic and seizing Loanda in Africa.

Involved as it was in numerous conflicts in Europe, Spain had few reserve troops available for use against the Dutch in Brazil. An effort was made in 1636 to send reënforcements but this proved a failure since the Spanish warships were inferior to the Dutch in fighting qualities. Thus the defense of Brazil was left almost entirely to the colonists themselves and to such irregular troops as they could put into the field.

The Restoration.—Meanwhile, the Portuguese restoration had occurred in 1640. All of the energies of the recently liberated kingdom were necessarily employed in the war against Castile and the colonists, as we have just seen, were left to their own ways and devices. They rose to the occasion, however, and with amazing energy set about unaided to expel the Dutch invaders. Their efforts were almost everywhere successful. A naval expedition put out from Rio, laid siege to Loanda and attacked the Dutch garrison of the local forts, obliging them to return to the Netherlands. In Brazil, the Dutch were gradually driven from the interior to the coast. They held out for a time in Recife and Olinda but in 1654 they were forced to capitulate and return to Holland.

The repulse of the invaders through the unassisted efforts of the colonists constituted a serious warning to Portugal. There was, to be sure, no thought of secession. On the other hand, the mother country was forced to recognize that credit for the victory belonged entirely to the colonists. The very terms of the peace itself, which followed hard on the unconditional surrender of Recife, were in accordance with the views and desires of the colonists rather than with the orders emanating from Lisbon. The colonists were filled with pride. They were the victors; they had shown themselves to be the equals, if not the superiors, of the Portuguese of Europe. From this time on, Brazil began to weigh more and more heavily in the balance of Portuguese politics and policies. And in America was born a national sentiment, which was steadily to grow in strength and consciousness.

The Viceroyalty. The Mines.—Even before the conclusion of the Dutch invasion, it was recognized by the metropolis that a mere governor general was not invested with sufficient authority to preside over the destinies of Brazil. In 1640, the year which ended the Spanish domination of Portugal, a viceroy with his headquarters in Bahia took the place of the governor general. Not until a century later, however, was the colony officially designated a viceroyalty. Growth in wealth kept pace with increasing political importance. Revenues mounted slowly but surely. Little by little, the colony began to pay its way and ceased to be a burden to the royal treasury. The income was derived from taxes, concessions, contracts, and royal monopolies. One source of wealth, however, was lacking, the very one on which the government most anxiously pinned its hopes: precious metals.

Small quantities of gold had already been found in the captaincies in the south and to stimulate zeal for further discoveries the Portuguese king, Dom Pedro II, deluged his Brazilian vassals with exhortations and promises of rewards. Especially were the notables of São Paulo, among whom were found the most intrepid explorers, urged to redouble their efforts. Such incentives were hardly necessary for the search was prosecuted with unflagging energy. The Brazilian El Dorado was at length discovered. In the period of thirty years from 1694 to 1724 the richest gold deposits of Minas Geraes, Matto Grosso and Goyaz were revealed. The result was little short of an economic revolution in both Portugal and Brazil.

Never had the metropolis dreamed of receiving such wealth from its colony. From the king down to the lowest officials the Portuguese authorities were consumed with one desire—to stimulate in every possible way the production of gold, thus augmenting the amount of the precious metal sent to the mother country. Hitherto, the exports of Brazil had consisted of agricultural and pastoral products; now the output of the mines took precedence over all else. Bahia, the formal center of the economic life of the colony, yielded the palm to Rio de Janeiro, the natural outlet for the wealth of Minas Geraes and the other mining centers. The fame of these riches was noised abroad and drew upon the harbor of Guanabara or Rio de Janeiro the greed of pirates and corsairs eager to conquer the city and force it to disgorge a heavy ransom.

Extension of the Demarcation Line.—Meanwhile, a vast shifting of the population was taking place. Explorers, miners, and slave hunters, swarmed toward the west, beyond the line of Tordesillas, encountering little or no opposition on the part of Castile and its American colonists. The newcomers quickly formed settlements about the gold washings, which for a time were worked with great profit. With this wholesale migration resulting from the discovery of gold, all possibility of observing the Line of Demarcation of 1494 was necessarily abandoned. An understanding was at length reached between the two Iberian courts whereby for the old frontier arrangement was substituted a new rule: the abandon-

ment of the old treaties which delimited territories by astronomical lines and the establishment of the legality of ownership on
the basis of effective and continuous possession. No such adjustment was necessary in the north since Spain took little interest in
the Amazon basin. For this reason, this vast area fell almost undisputed under Portuguese rule by the fourth decade of the seventeenth century.

In the south, however, the difficulties were numerous and vexatious. Effective and continuous possession was a conveniently
elastic term. Protracted controversies resulted from the progressive invasions of the Portuguese colonists. Their goal was the
line of the Paraguay River. In the course of their expeditions the
Portuguese authorities aided by local elements from São Paulo
had founded the colony of Sacramento as early as 1680, on the
left bank of the Río de la Plata. Forty years later, in 1719, gold
hunters had pitched their tents and established a settlement on
the margin of the Paraguay River in distant Matto Grosso.

This last thrust of the Portuguese westward movement constituted a terrible menace to the Spanish colonization of America.
In the first place, it revealed the tendency of the Braganza dynasty
to regard the Paraguay River, from its upper reaches to its outlet
into La Plata estuary, as the line dividing the Spanish from the
Portuguese possessions. Should the government of Lisbon make
good its claim, the fertile territory of Paraguay, one of the oldest Castilian foundations in southern South America, was doomed
to disappear. In the second place, once such a frontier was in the
power of the Portuguese, the road to Potosí would be open to the
subjects of the crown of Braganza, and the rich mines of Peru,
the chief source of the revenues of his Catholic Majesty, would be
imperiled.

The Spanish Crown naturally utilized every means in its power
to exorcise such a peril. Success could only be obtained at the cost
of a bitter struggle. The dispute, at times carried on by diplomatic,
at times by more lethal, weapons, lasted a century and a half.
The treaty of 1828, which gave birth to the Republic of Uruguay,
solved the problem as far as attempts to reach the Río de la Plata
were concerned. As regards the upper reaches of the Paraguay,
after 1720 the Portuguese virtually abandoned all attempts to
secure its right bank, thus allaying any fears which the Spaniards

harbored in regard to the safety of the mining regions of Potosí.

By the middle of the eighteenth century it was clear that the vital interests of Brazil required the shifting of the center of gravity of public life farther to the south. The reasons have already been discussed. The primary concerns of the government had to do with the economic development of southern and central Brazil, especially in the gold-bearing captaincies of Minas Geraes, Matto Grosso, and Goyaz, and with the complicated relations with Spain growing out of boundary controversies in La Plata basin. We have here the background for the act of 1763, which raised Brazil to the status of a viceroyalty and transferred the capital from Bahia to Rio de Janeiro. Such was the situation when in 1808 the prince regent, Dom João, later to become King Dom João VI, transferred to America the seat and capital of the Portuguese monarchy.

CHAPTER II

THE ECONOMIC ORGANIZATION OF THE COLONY

BEFORE we proceed further in our narrative of Brazilian history let us pause to consider the economic importance of this colony, a veritable giant in comparison with a mother country such as Portugal, small in area and limited in resources.

The Setting.—During colonial days the greater part of the immense area of Brazil was clothed with dense forests; even in our day it is calculated that 50 per cent of the surface is wooded. To estimate the forested area in times past it is necessary to deduct those sections now devoted to agricultural uses. The most reliable statistics would indicate that at least 60 per cent of Brazil was wooded during the sixteenth and seventeenth centuries.

Brazil is dowered with a rich and fertile soil, having a thick covering of humus. It is capable of yielding bountiful crops, appropriate to the region in which they are grown. We do not, however, find wheat, oats, or barley, for these were as they still are, exotic productions. On the other hand, the soil offers lavish returns in such food stuffs as corn, manioc, sweet potatoes, and plantains.

Seas, lakes, and rivers teem with fish of every kind. Hives, swarming with bees, abound. Game, not in excess, but in reasonable quantities, is to be found in the valleys, the grasslands (*chapadas*), and the forests. And finally, Brazil is blessed with a climate without extremes, tolerable even under the equator, thanks to periodical breezes and regular rains; while even in the temperate sections of Brazil the winters are rarely if ever cold.

The Population.—The Portuguese discoverers found a population scanty and widely distributed, rarely sedentary but prone to roam over the plains and through the forests. Physically, the Indians were strong and inured to hardship. They were cunning in woodcraft; cruel, dissimulating, and devoid of any feeling of individual responsibility. They were wont to visit upon the whole tribe or group of their enemies vengeance for the fault or crime of one of its members. They obeyed their chiefs (*caciques* or *morubixabas*) as well as their soothsayers and sorcerers (*pagés*). Incapable of persistent efforts or uniform labor, they had but rudimentary instruments for their household and agricultural needs. They were unfamiliar with metals and used axes of polished stone, wooden clubs, bows made of seasoned wood, arrows tipped with pointed bones or sharp stones, and bone fishing hooks.

The Indians generally lived in tribes consisting of a few hundred individuals. As they depended for their food on the largesses of nature they changed their habitat as soon as they had exhausted the possibilities of honey, game, and fish in the regions they had been occupying. Their industries were primitive; only exceptionally did they produce any object of artistic merit such as woven hammocks, nets, baskets, decorated pottery, or feather work. They were constantly on the warpath. Motives for hostilities were insignificant or entirely lacking: hunting grounds invaded or contested, theft of women, oracles of their sorcerers, threats of vengeance. Some tribes mummified their dead. Others, dwelling in the regions adjacent to the present republics of Peru and Colombia, extracted the bones from the heads which were then dried and mummified. Cannibalism was generally a ritual practice.

The Invaders.—The Portuguese invader was a rude human type. Pillage and bloodshed were normal attributes of such times; religion and superstition, hatred and persecution of the unbelievers were common traits. In the early years of the colony, the Portuguese were too few in number to cope with entire tribes and thus they were forced to remain on the defensive. When they were commanded by energetic and strict chieftains, who held them under rigid subjection and discipline, friction with the Indians was reduced to a minimum. But such a situation was at best only transitory. Racial crossing began early and broke down all barriers. The Portuguese repaired to the Indian villages; Indians found their way to the coast settlements, and quarrels of every kind began.

These local altercations frequently led to miniature wars between the two races. Thanks to the efforts of the Catholic missionaries, who were in almost constant contact with the natives, peace was in most cases soon reëstablished. But from time to time the offenses committed by the whites became so numerous and grave that the explosion of wrath on the part of the victims proved fatal to the colonists. In this manner, not a few of the factories established by the Portuguese were entirely wiped out. The coast from Espirito

Santo to Bahia was practically abandoned and even today reveals large gaps in its population as a consequence of these attacks.

In time, as the number and strength of the colonists increased, this spirit of turbulence began to subside. But the hunters of human flesh, recking little of time or distance, kept hot on the trail of the Indians until, in many cases, they reached or passed beyond the line of Tordesillas. Intermarriage with the Indian women took on greater proportions. The mamelucos became an increasingly important factor of the population. At the same time, the Jesuits penetrated far into the *sertão*[1] or hinterland in their self-appointed task of protecting and converting the natives. They baptized both children and adults. Frequently they lured to the coast entire communities who either were absorbed by the population or perished from the destructive contact with the so-called civilization of the whites.

But the Jesuits were not the only ones who plunged into the interior in quest of the Indians. Under the pretext of carrying on warfare against idolatry, the colonists assembled in large bands and conducted veritable raids into the *sertão*. They attacked the Indian settlements, captured their inhabitants, and returned to the coast with their quarry. While such expeditions, known as *picadas* or *bandeiras,* eventually resulted in the exploration and, to some extent, the settlement of vast areas in the interior of Brazil and offer an interesting analogy to the westward movement of the United States, for the Indians at least they proved a frightful scourge. The terror which these raids inspired caused the natives to flee farther and farther from the coast.

The Problem of Labor.—The real reason for these incursions was the crying need of labor. Prior to the discovery of gold, Brazil was necessarily an agricultural colony. The Portuguese, few in numbers, did not possess the labor requisite for the cultivation of their fazendas or plantations, or for the extraction of brazilwood. The only solution of this dilemma was the seizure, by all the means available, of the requisite number of Indian laborers from the apparently inexhaustible native population. From such an economic necessity did slavery arise.

From the very first, the Jesuits protested against such a policy

---

[1] A name given to the "back-country" of Brazil, particularly of the states of Bahia, Pernambuco, and Ceará.—P.A.M.

and for more than a century carried on an unremitting warfare against it. The missionaries tried to safeguard the natives; the colonists mercilessly pillaged Indian settlements under the pressure of economic needs. The Company of Jesus suffered much from this generous protection of its catechumens. But it never abandoned its noble defense of the natives and this brought immortal glory to the sons of St. Ignatius Loyola.

From a purely business point of view the Indians turned out to be poor risks. They were primitive creatures, children of the forest and the field; they could not adapt themselves to a life with four walls, nor could they become inured to the hard and continuous labor on the plantations or in the sugar mills. Once enslaved they died in droves; many committed suicide; the majority escaped to the woods. The remainder, beguiled or recaptured through the the wiles of the colonists, lost all hope and remained in captivity. Here their span of life was short; they fell defenseless victims to measles, smallpox, rum, or the fetid air of their confined quarters. Then new *bandeiras* plunged into the *sertão* and reappeared with new flocks of human cattle, though each time they were more difficult to secure since the source of supply progressively moved farther and farther into the interior.

In Central America and the Caribbean area similar situations developed, only in this instance the task of protecting the Indians was assumed not by the Jesuits but by the saintly Las Casas who raised his voice in indignant protest against the atrocities of the Spaniards. But both in Spanish and Portuguese America it was at length obvious that some substitute for Indian labor must be found. In the case of Brazil, both the colonists and the Portuguese government finally agreed on the desirability of importing Negroes from Africa to replace the refractory and indolent natives.

Negro Slavery.—There is great uncertainty as to the date when the first Africans reached Portuguese America. It is supposed that they arrived in Bahia as early as 1538. Once the movement was under way the influx of servile labor did not cease until the abolition of the slave trade in 1850. This traffic offered no novelty to Europeans; especially was this true of the Portuguese. Since the middle of the fifteenth century Lisbon had served as an importing market for Negro slaves who were sold to meet local needs or for export abroad. At first in Europe and later in both Americas

Portugal's African colonies were recognized as the most important source of supply; no effort was made to disguise this fact. As the human factor in the labor situation in Brazil, the Negro proved infinitely superior to the Indian. Culturally, the African was on a much higher level than the aboriginal American. While the latter was still in the neolithic period and had barely reached the stage of fetishism, the imported Negro knew how to work metals, especially iron, had an architecture of his own, and possessed a mass of revered traditions. Although a majority of the Negroes were pagans, many adhered to monotheism. They were accustomed to sedentary life, quickly learned to use tools, and proved to be good and skillful workmen.

The Indian, as we have seen, could not suffer confinement, while the Negro prospered under the living conditions of the whites. With his greater strength and powers of resistance, he far surpassed the aborigines in efficiency. Exposed to the same hardships which decimated the Indians, the Negroes grew and multiplied. Their birth rate was the highest of the three races in Brazil.

On the other hand, as a result of unfavorable conditions, or owing to other biological factors, the mortality of the Negro was greater than that of the white and even exceeded his own birth rate. As a consequence, his average life span was not greater than twenty-five years. But through fresh importations of these human cattle the slave population remained steadily in the ascendant.

It is no exaggeration to say that, under the direction of the whites, the Negroes furnished all of the material labor essential to the economic growth of Brazil. This was the more true as climatic and geographical conditions imposed upon the colonists a single line of activity, that which the Germans characterize as "natural economy," i.e., the direct and immediate utilization of natural resources. In the early days of the colony the settlers, closely confined to the littoral through their ignorance and fear of the sertão, were obliged to live as in a besieged camp. Within the confines of high wooden palisades and deep trenches they were forced to maintain their supply of fish, raise a few vegetables, and guard their poultry, swine and cattle brought in from Madeira or Cape Verde. These settlements served various purposes; means of defense against attacks from the natives; trading posts with the Indians, when these were disposed to be friendly; centers of cultivation of such crops as the limited area made possible.

Pacification. Economic Organization in the North.—A few years passed and the danger of Indian attacks became less pressing. Only then could the fazendas, as the farms of the colonists were called, expand into true plantations. At this same period, sugar cane was imported from Madeira and crude sugar mills, as well as evaporating pans, were constructed for the extraction of the cane juice and the manufacture of coarse sugar. These plants were called *engenhos* (literally "engines"), a term which was frequently synonymous with fazenda. The sugar plantations with their mills soon came to constitute the basic economic wealth of the country. They were autonomous, self-sustaining units: only a few articles contributing to the comforts of life were imported from Portugal, chiefly wine and olive oil. Cotton was cultivated and rude cloth was woven. Cattle, poultry, and swine grew and multiplied. The cattle furnished not only meat but hides and leather. The sugar mills supplied rum. In a short time there was a large surplus of such products and the colonists began to export them to the mother country in the Portuguese ships which came to America, the only vessels authorized to frequent Brazilian ports.

Such an economic organization required a large expenditure of labor. Woodcutters to clear away the forest for the plantations; agriculturists to prepare the ground for the sowing and reaping of the harvest and the transplanting of the sugar cane, corn, and other cultures; special workmen to set up or repair the sugar mills, water wheels, canals, and irrigating ditches; oarsmen and boatswains to man the barges which carried the products of the plantations down the river to the ocean; firemen to stoke the furnaces of the sugar mills; carpenters, joiners, smiths, masons, and tilemakers; domestic servants of all descriptions; fishermen and hunters to keep the larder stocked with fish and game; guards for protection of both family and property; such in brief were the most important types of work performed by servile labor. The Indians could endure only a few of these tasks; for most of them they proved inept, and either took refuge in flight or died in the harness. On rare occasion they proved successful in the care of livestock. As for the Negroes, it was difficult for them to escape from captivity, partly because the Indians would afford them no welcome. Thus from year to year the traffic in Negro slaves steadily grew.

Livestock had found conditions favorable for its development throughout the whole region about Bahia and Pernambuco. Along the ancient Indian trails, which struck out into the interior from the basin of the São Francisco River, primitive ranches were established, and the population, still pastoral in large part, gradually spread out in all directions. By the end of the sixteenth century the *sertão* had already lost in the minds of the settlers much of the terror which it had formerly inspired. The Indian tribes most feared had been pushed back from the coast. By the close of the following century cattle ranches had so multiplied in the river valleys of this portion of Brazil that the São Francisco was ordinarily spoken of as the *Rio dos Curraes* (River of Ranches).

This was one of the most important aspects of the colonization movement. The topography of Central Brazil shows that the watersheds dividing one river basin from another are of such moderate height as to offer no obstacle to the migration of cattle from the coastal region far into the interior. Setting out from Bahia pioneers began to establish their cattle ranches in the direction of the São Francisco; in time they crossed this stream and ascending its affluents penetrated far into the zone of the north or northwest.

Economic Organization in the South. The Mines.—Quite different was the situation in the south. Sugar cane had been imported into these regions, notably in São Vicente and São Paulo, but conditions proved to be less favorable than in the north. Cattle raising also was of less importance than in the districts about Bahia. The plantations were organized on a somewhat different basis. While Recife and Bahia produced an important surplus for exportation to Portugal, Santos, the harbor for the captaincies of São Amaro and São Vicente, sent comparatively little to the mother country. In their economic life these southern captaincies tended to become self-sufficing units. They produced everything necessary for their support, even to wine, grapes, and wheat; the latter was used for cakes, biscuits, and tarts rather than for bread. Naturally, life in southern Brazil was conditioned by the climate, which thanks to the lower latitude and the elevation of the interior plateau was much cooler than in the north.

One of the outstanding traits of the opulent classes in these remote days was the parade of their wealth and this was measured by the number of slaves each owner possessed. Much more than in the north—where the Negroes predominated—São Paulo evinced a preference for the Indian. Many reasons lay behind this choice. Mamelucos were numerous and this element of the population was turbulent and bellicose. The pursuit of slaves, combined with the political animosity between the two Iberian peoples, served as motive for the *bandeiras* or *entradas* which exerting a slow, constant, and irresistible pressure on the Spanish occupation forced it back to the Paraguay River. The Jesuit "reductions," those Indian colonies or missions dominated and governed by the sons of St. Ignatius, were little by little destroyed or obliged to move to other localities, principally between the Paraguay and the Paraná rivers and along the southern reaches of Uruguay. A sombre history, this, stained with bloodshed and cruelty, but one which contributed nonetheless to the expansion of Brazilian territory.

The quest for Indian slaves was not the only motive which lured the Paulistas, as the inhabitants of the captaincy were called, into the interior of southern Brazil. The hope of discovering gold deposits, rivalling in wealth those of Spanish America, was ever present in the minds of the *bandeirantes*[2] and the dwellers in the *sertão*. As a matter of fact small quantities of gold had early been found on both slopes of the great watershed which culminated in the Serra do Mar or Coast Range. This beautiful chain of mountains, whose average height was some twelve hundred meters, was on the east separated from the Atlantic by a narrow coastal strip from twenty to one hundred and fifty kilometers in width extending from Santos south to Santa Catharina. The vast area west of the Coast Range was drained by the tributaries of the Río de La Plata, of which the Paraná was the most important. In their explorations, the Paulistas eagerly scrutinized the sands and gravels of almost every stream they crossed. Seldom were their efforts rewarded. Possessing but a rudimentary knowledge of mining, they confined their attention to placers and neglected the solid lodes. Nearly a hundred years were to elapse before the great gold deposits of Minas Geraes revealed to the world the mineral wealth of Brazil.

Racial Crossing. The Slave Trade.—At the end of the sixteenth century, Brazil was inhabited by a motley Portuguese-speaking population not exceeding one hundred thousand in number. By and large, it was composed of six principal nuclei: Bahia, Pernambuco,

[2] Name given to those who made up the *bandeira.*—P.A.M.

Maranhão, Rio de Janeiro, and Santos-São Paulo. From our calcu-
lations have naturally been excluded the Indians outside the pale
of Portuguese settlements. Society was rather rigidly stratified
according to an artificial caste system. Of the total population,
the pure whites constituted a minority. At the top of the social
ladder were those born in Portugal, the so-called *reinóes*, from
whose ranks most of the official elements were recruited. Then came
colonials who were unlucky enough to be born in Brazil. Their
condition was somewhat similar to that of the *criollos* or creoles
of Spanish America. Naturally, they were looked down upon by
the *reinóes*, but on the whole they acquiesced in their inferior social
status. On the next rung of the social ladder we find the mestizos,
the cross between the whites and the Indians. The mestizos refused
to be placed on the same level as the mulattoes; they stressed the
fact that their paternal ascendants were white and fell back on
the encouragement, which officially, at least, the Portuguese government had extended to marriages between the Europeans and
natives. After the mulattoes came such nondescript racial crossings
as mulatto-Indian and Indian-Negro.[3] Finally near the foot of
the ladder came the Indian slaves, and lowest of all the pure-blooded
Negroes. Reliable statistics on the total population at this
period are not available. Nonetheless, a few suggestions may be
hazarded. Indian tribes beyond the radius of Portuguese action
numbered more than 800,000 members. The oldest chroniclers,
writing about 1583, estimated the population of Brazil as 57,000
souls: 25,000 whites; 18,000 civilized Indians; and 14,000 Negro
slaves. A majority of these last were concentrated in Pernambuco,
and the remainder in Bahia, with scarcely a hundred in Rio de
Janeiro. The chief point of debarkation of the Africans was, however, Bahia. This distribution of the Negroes was, of course, intimately connected with the conditions prevailing in agriculture.
In the north, where sugar cultivation was carried on so extensively
as to supply a surplus for export to Portugal, the Negro population was numerous. In São Vicente, Santos, and São Paulo, on the
other hand, where agricultural products barely sufficed for the
needs of the colonists, Indian slaves were more numerous than the
Negroes.

As a rule the Negroes were not ill-treated. Historians of slavery

[3] Known as *zambos* in Spanish America.

relate that in the West Indies captives were accustomed to beg for the adoption of the regulations in force in Brazil. These consisted of the royal orders and decrees (*alvarás*) of 1688, 1689, 1693, and 1704 according to which the owners of the Negroes were obliged to leave Saturday free for their slaves when they might labor on their own account. The comforts of religion were to be extended to them when they were ill or in peril of death. The masters were likewise obliged to support the aged and helpless.

It can hardly be questioned that the plight of the Negroes in their new habitat was no worse than their wretched existence in the land from whence they came. What was really horrible and beggars any description was the passage across the Atlantic in the holds of the small slave ships. In these constricted quarters the Negroes were deprived of all fresh air or space in which to move. Their food was scanty and filthy; their drinking water polluted. Not infrequently 30 or 40 per cent of the slaves died during the passage; in fact, such a proportion was not considered abnormal. An average mortality of 20 per cent was acceptable and even favorable. *Tumbeiros*, a term meaning floating coffins, was the name given to slave ships in Angola.

The slave trade reached its apogee in the eighteenth century after the discovery of the gold and diamond mines in the interior and the expansion of cultivated areas in the south. Tentative estimates, based on such data as may be gleaned from official documents, point to figures which oscillate around fifty thousand per annum. For the seventeenth century the number was perhaps ten thousand less. But unfortunately, no reliable statistics are available. If some points may be cleared up regarding the number of Negroes imported legally there is practically nothing on the number smuggled in, and these latter may well be double the former. According to a report presented to Philip II of Spain, 52,053 Negroes were exported directly from Angola to Brazil from 1575 to 1591, that is 3,100 per annum. But Angola was merely one of the African captaincies; how many did the others send? From Pernambuco we have statistics covering a decade of the Dutch occupation. From 1636 to 1645 a total of 23,163 slaves were imported, or 2,300 per year. These are practically all the figures we have for the sixteenth and seventeenth centuries. Documents dealing with the traffic during this period have disappeared. In Brazil they are not to be found. Perhaps some still slumber in the archives of Portugal, or in those of the former colonies along the African coast; up to the present, however, they have not yielded up their secrets to the investigators of our colonial history.

The Consequences.—In order to have an approximate idea of the extent of this influx of Negro blood, there apparently exists but one means of making an estimate and that is an indirect one. As our point of departure we may accept the first census of the slave population. Then through the utilization of available figures on birth, death, and average life span we may determine the annual quota capable of giving in x year the slave population as revealed by statistics at the beginning of the nineteenth century. Following this procedure, we find the average annual importation to be around 55,000 slaves. It is obvious the number would be smaller at the outset but would progressively increase as time went on.

The Negroes constitued the lowest social stratum of the population of the colony. Even human qualities were sometimes denied them. It was necessary for the Holy See to declare them men in order that they might be regarded as such. Yet, in spite of everything, racial crossing between the Negroes and the Portuguese began very early. The Mediterranean peoples do not evince toward the colored races the kind of repugnance characteristic of Nordic psychology. This attitude of Latin peoples persists still. The abundant progeny of the African began little by little to lose the purity of its racial blood; soon there appeared in ever growing volume various strata of mulattoes, such as the quadroons, and other racial mixtures. This thinning of the pigmentation has not ceased even today, for the same factors that operated in colonial days are still active; only to the Portuguese have been added Spaniards and Italians. We have in other words a progressive and noticeable whitening of the skin of the local population in large sections of Brazil.

Hence, we must pause to note a peculiar phenomenon. Unions with Indians of both sexes evoked no criticism except when they were illegal or contrary to religious sanctions. On the contrary, the crossing with the African was looked upon as degrading. While the mestizos encountered no obstacles in their path, provided they were free, the mulattoes were despised and were not regarded in the same class as their superiors even when they were free. Among the privileges denied to persons of color was the priesthood; for this reason families with even the most respectable antecedents made every effort to have among their members priests or friars; this was a proof of purity of blood, of reputed ancestry, of a stainless escutcheon. It may readily be understood that in many instances an additional infusion of white blood was considered indispensable if the families in question were to aspire to higher social levels. Under such conditions there was gradually taking place a fusion of the races. This process encountered no insuperable obstacles save in the case of the most illustrious families and even here the opposition was not always successful.

The early Portuguese colonists were frank and sturdy, simple, and sincere in speech. Rarely were they gay or expansive and it was only with an effort that they revealed intimate feelings of pleasure. The Indian, like the white, was grave. But the Negro element in general revealed a perpetual good humor, a childish and expansive joy, a delight in the slightest incidents of life. Nothing gave him greater happiness than to dance, to sing, to clothe himself elaborately and in gaudy colors. Filled with the joy of youth a ray of sunshine illumined his childish soul. Sensitive, worthy of confidence, devoted to those who treated him well, capable of being led in any direction by affection and kind words, the Negro helped to temper the primitive harshness of the Portuguese colonists. Such uprisings as occurred in Brazil were never comparable to the revolts of the slaves in the West Indies. In spite of abuses in the treatment of slaves by their masters, the relations between the two elements were generally characterized by kindness and consideration, and for this reason the lot of the Negroes in Brazil was envied by their brothers condemned to slavery in other countries. It may be noted in passing that some of the Negro characteristics which we have just discussed reappear in the psychology of the mulattoes.

But there were shades as well as lights to the picture. The morality of the masculine part of the white population left much to be desired. On the distaff side there was a comprehensible but unfortunate spirit of revenge and cruelty toward the Negro women owing largely to the incontinence and moral laxity of their masters.

It is difficult and hazardous to attempt to pass judgment on the Negro problem in Brazil. But after duly weighing the good and evil features of the system, it is only fair to recognize that from the material and economic point of view the Negro constituted the chief factor in the building up of Brazil. If morally he may be taxed with shortcomings these are being met and overcome by education and a general raising in the level of intelligence. Finally, the black stain is destined to disappear in a relatively short space of time because of the influx of white immigration in which the heritage of Ham is dissolving. Roosevelt rightly pointed out that the future has reserved for us a great boon: the happy solution of a problem fraught with tremendous, even mortal dangers—the problems of a possible conflict between the two races.

Antonil.—We have a piece of evidence of striking value on the reciprocal influence of these factors at the beginning of the eighteenth century. One of the important representatives of the Jesuits in the province of Brazil at this epoch was an Italian from Lucca, João Antonil, who published in 1711 an admirable book whose extraordinary importance may be judged from the fact that the Portuguese government confiscated the entire edition. Only a very few numbers escaped the pyre, some six all told. These survivors are now jewels beyond price in the collections of bibliophiles.

The work was suppressed because its author was guilty of the crime of offering too complete and exact information regarding the value of the land and its possibilities, thus giving other countries richer and stronger than Portugal the desire to conquer it. But there was still a more powerful reason for this *auto da fé;* the work revealed to the Brazilians the greatness and potentiality of their country, and might fire them with aspirations, especially after their success in expelling the French and the Dutch. Its very title was suggestive: *Cultura e Opulencia do Brasil, por sus Drogas e Minas* (*Culture and Wealth of Brazil as revealed in its Drugs and Mines*). By "drugs" is to be understood agriculture and its products.

When the book was published, the recently discovered gold mines were supplying a number of amazing statistics of which we shall speak presently. But the work is valuable also for the basic industries of the country: tobacco, hides, leather, sugar, livestock, and other items. Such types of activity varied little from year to year and we may accept the data here published as valid for the end of the seventeenth century, although they refer to the year 1711.

Thus we learn that Bahia had 146 sugar mills producing a surplus for exportation amounting to 14,500 cases of sugar weighing 35 arrobas[4] each. Pernambuco produced less: 246 mills did not export more than 10,300 cases. Rio, with 136 mills, exported 10,220 cases. This sugar weighed approximately 1,300,000 kilograms and was worth in this period 2,535:142 $800. in Portuguese money. Today its value would be some fifteen times this amount.[5] Maranhão set up some fifty sugar mills but subsequently abandoned them in favor of such products as nuts, cloves, and cacao.

Smoking, at first, was considered an unholy practice connected with the idolatrous rites of the Indians. Soon, however, the ecclesiastical ban was lifted and the use of tobacco was permitted. Its cultivation became one of the great industries of Brazil and remains so up to the present time. At the end of the seventeenth century, Bahia exported some 25,000 *rolos*, as the rolls of twisted tobacco were called, and Pernambuco and Alagoas, 2,500.

Cattle raising had by the end of the seventeenth century taken on large proportions. Capistrano de Abreu[6] went so far as to characterize the colonial epoch as the age of leather. In fact, the uses to which leather was put was almost legion. This was true not only in Brazil but throughout the continent as well. A Uruguayan scholar[7] has graphically described the multiple uses to which leather was put during the same period in the basin of the Río de la Plata. Curiously enough the statistics on tobacco exports shed light on the leather industry. Tobacco was exported in rolled bundles, sewn in rawhide coverings. Thus Bahia utilized 50,000 halves of leather; Pernambuco, 40,000; and Rio, 20,000. This last estimate included the leather which came from the Portuguese settlement of Sacramento on the La Plata estuary. These halves of leather would account for some 55,000 to 60,000 head of cattle. When one recalls, however, that implements, tools, furniture, gar-

---

[4] An "arroba" in Portugal and Brazil at this time was the equivalent of 32.38 lbs.—P.A.M.

[5] Possibly twenty million dollars.—P.A.M.

[6] Capistrano de Abreu (1853-1927), one of the outstanding figures in modern Brazilian historiography. He is best known for his *Capitulos da Historia Colonial* (Rio de Janeiro, 1928), and his critical edition of Varnhagen's classical *Historia do Brasil* (São Paulo, 1927).—P.A.M.

[7] The reference is to Alberto zum Felde, *Proceso Histórico del Uruguay* (Montevideo, 1919).—P.A.M.

ments, footgear, and a multitude of other objects were likewise
made of leather, it is not unreasonable to assume that the annual
demand was little short of a hundred thousand head.

Antonil furnishes some approximate figures on cattle breeding.
The great center of the industry was to be found along the lower
and middle reaches of the São Francisco River. In the region adjacent to the northern bank were more than 800,000 head, belonging to the inhabitants of the captaincy of Pernambuco. Farther to the north, over low-lying divides, large numbers of cattle
roamed over the pastures of Piauhy and Maranhão. The immense,
little known prairies extending along the right or southern bank
of the São Francisco, lying in Bahia, gradually were taken up by
cattle raisers whose ranches eventually numbered more than five
hundred. As the demand for new land increased, these ranches extended farther and farther southwest toward Minas Geraes and
the Rio das Velhas, a stream famous in the history of the gold
rush. Eventually half a million head of cattle were to be found
along the right bank of the São Francisco. As will be noted later,
the existence of these ranches along the upper reaches of the
São Francisco turned out to be one of the most fortunate developments in the whole history of Brazilian agriculture. In the latter
seventeenth and early eighteenth centuries, Minas Geraes was invaded by vast hordes of prospectors and adventurers intent on ex-
ploiting the newly discovered gold deposits. Much of this region
was virgin territory, entirely lacking in means of subsistence. Had
not the ranches along the São Francisco been able to furnish food
supplies, chiefly meat, many of the prospectors and miners would
have died of starvation.

Absence of a Circulating Medium.—It is a curious phenomenon,
deserving of a more detailed scrutiny than is possible at this point,
that the whole economic development of Brazil was being carried
on at this period without the use of money. Or, to be more accurate,
money appears only as a common measure of value, for little or
no currency was in circulation. In the hinterland, as a rule, the
colonists relied for their commercial transactions on a system of
barter. When debts could not be exactly balanced what was left
over was paid for in slaves, cattle, cotton thread, sugar, or textiles. Imported goods were paid for by export commodities; the
credit balance of the colonists furnished perhaps the only instance

of payments in coin. But this currency did not circulate except on a small scale in the coast cities. The coins were either hidden to escape theft by robbers and pirates or melted up and converted into crude adornments for the women.

Taxes, rents, and the proceeds of monopolies were paid in kind. Generally speaking, the administration farmed out at auction the privilege of collecting these revenues. The collectors were obliged to settle with the authorities in currency, but they gathered in the taxes *in natura:* calves or oxen, cloth or dyewood, sugar or rum. These commodities were sold in the coast towns or exported and the collectors made their profits from these transactions. Gambling, as is generally the case in such primitive societies, was a veritable scourge. Losses were always settled for in the same manner: land, slaves, jewels, commodities, and, very rarely, money. This situation prevailed for well over a hundred years and only began to change in the late seventies of the seventeenth century.

Tendencies Working Towards Political Emancipation.—The type of social life just described, with its peculiarities and drawbacks, was bound in time to affect Brazil's relationship with Portugal. It has already been suggested that it tended to develop in the colonists a feeling of confidence and self-reliance. In their struggles and triumphs they had received little or no aid from the mother country. They harbored no ill feeling toward the metropolis but had come to rely entirely upon their own means and initiative. *El Rey* (the king) was for the Portuguese in America a sort of demigod, respected, revered and even loved as some remote superhuman being. From the king came bounties and gifts, honors and preferments. But from the government itself few, if any, benefits were to be expected. Little by little, there began to emerge an obscure sense of equality between the Portuguese dwelling on opposite sides of the Atlantic. A feeling akin to resentment at the neglect of which they were the victims also appeared among the colonists. Thus was prepared the ground on which the seeds of liberty and independence were planted, although they were not destined to bud until a century later.

Mines and Mining.—In the closing years of the seventeenth century, Portugal was aroused to a frenzy of excitement by the news that gold and emeralds in fabulous quantities had been discovered in the hinterland of the captaincy of São Vicente. So rich were these deposits and so widely spread that eventually this region took the name of Minas Geraes, meaning "General Mines." This discovery represented the victorious culmination of a long, arduous, and heartbreaking search, extending well over a century and a half. Obstacles of every description had to be surmounted. Not the least of these had been a curious, and in a way grotesque, misunderstanding between the Portuguese and the Indians. These latter, as we have already seen, lived in the neolithic age. They were unfamiliar with metals and such instruments as they possessed were made of polished stones, wood, or bone. Hence, when the early invaders enquired about mines, silver or gold, the ignorant natives, in perfect good faith, understood stones, white or yellow. The eager questioners were informed that there were indeed immense deposits of stones white as the moon or yellow as the sun to be found in such and such places many days' march from the coast.

Convinced that they were on the track of precious metals, the Portuguese set out from São Salvador, the present Bahia, and from other points on the adjoining littoral, and with their Indian guides plunged into the interior. It proved a bootless quest. An examination of the sands and gravels pointed out by the Indians revealed no traces of precious metals. The mutual recriminations which followed still further embittered the relations between the two races. As a consequence of these failures, enthusiasm waned and for a long period interest in these expeditions, at least in the Bahia region, practically ceased.

As regards precious stones, the deception was not quite so complete. The first settlers observed that the Indians were wont to insert in their lips, noses, or cheeks bits of polished wood or stone or fragments of crystal. These ornaments were known as *tembetás*. Some of them, a brilliant and bright green in color, resembled crude emeralds. The settlers spoke of them as "unripe" emeralds, convinced that gems like fruit were a natural growth of the soil. Rumors soon gained currency that the Brazilian hinterland abounded in emerald mines. Many expeditions or *entradas* were organized in search of these precious stones and all but one failed. This expedition was commanded by Fernão Dias Paes Leme, one of the greatest of Brazilian explorers. After years of wandering and incredible hardship, he discovered in 1681 what he supposed were emeralds in one of the most remote sections of the present

Minas Geraes. In reality, they were tourmalines, beryls, and aquamarines; real emeralds, scientifically speaking, were only found a few years ago. Fernão Dias never learned the true character of his find. Worn out with hardships and toil he died at an advanced age[8] on the banks of the Rio das Velhas in Minas Geraes.

In addition to gold and precious stones, silver was eagerly sought for by the settlers in early colonial days. As a matter of fact, this metal in the form of silver ore has been found in Brazil only as an accessory element in the lead sulphite, galena. But the Portuguese colonists had no means of knowing this fact; they were entirely ignorant of the methods employed in the extraction of silver since deposits of this metal do not exist in Portugal and naturally they had never visited the great silver mines at Potosí in Upper Peru. Innocent of any knowledge of geology or mineralogy, they mistook any white or grey mineral which glittered for silver. Despite repeated failures, the quest for silver continued up until the end of the eighteenth century. This persistence is probably to be explained by the fame of the almost fantastic wealth of the silver deposits of Spanish America, especially those of Potosí and Mexico. The energy expended on this search for elusive silver mines was not wholly lost. Immense areas in the interior of Brazil were traversed and partially explored with results, political and geographical, of considerable importance. Nor should we fail to mention another by-product of this fruitless search. One of the most convinced believers in the existence of silver mines was a rich landowner of Bahia, Gabriel Soares de Souza. In order to secure a special royal concession from King Philip II of Spain, he wrote in 1587 a *Tratado descriptivo do Brasil* (*Descriptive Treatise of Brazil*). This work not only is an invaluable general history and description of the country but also is one of the noteworthy productions of Portuguese literature of the sixteenth century.

As was indicated at the beginning of this chapter, it was not until the end of the seventeenth century that Brazil's wealth in gold and precious stones was revealed to all the world. It is perhaps no exaggeration to say that one of the great incentives to renewed efforts, this time crowned with success, was a personal letter written in 1674 by Dom Pedro II to the great magnates of

---

[8] If we are to believe Southey he was eighty years of age when he embarked on his expedition in 1672. *History of Brazil*, III, 46 (London, 1822).—P.A.M.

São Paulo exhorting them to persevere in their search for gold and emeralds since a solution of this problem was essential to the public weal of Portugal. In those days a letter from *El Rey* to his subjects was so rare that its fortunate possessor bequeathed it to his heirs as a treasure beyond price. And among the recipients of this royal missive were some of the most daring and enterprising of the *bandeirantes* and *sertanistas* (explorers) to be found in all Brazil.

We have already seen that one of the greatest of these explorers was Fernão Dias Paes Leme, the searcher after emeralds. But the real reward for so many decades of toil and hardship finally came in 1698-1699 when important gold placers were found in the basin of the Rio das Velhas, one of the great tributaries of the São Francisco. From now on, month after month and year after year new deposits of amazing wealth continued to be discovered in the great inland region soon to be known as the captaincy of Minas Geraes. Naturally these finds served as a stimulus for new expeditions and in 1719 the existence of gold-bearing gravels was reported in Matto Grosso, in the remote western portion of Brazil. Six years later, in 1725, came the turn of Goyaz. At about the same time, or possibly a little earlier, gold was found in Bahia. And of the treasures which lavish nature had bestowed upon Brazil, the last to be discovered was diamonds. This happy event occurred in 1729 in a section of Minas Geraes largely devoid of gold deposits.

These new and unexpected sources of wealth naturally brought about an economic revolution both in the colony and the motherland. Unfortunately, Portugal was not in a position to derive the maximum advantage from this sudden increase of the national income. The Braganza dynasty had fallen upon evil days. The government was both inefficient and corrupt. The king, Dom João V, was chiefly intent upon amusing himself and dazzling his courtiers by his extravagance. As a consequence, the millions which poured into the royal coffers from Minas Geraes were for the most part squandered or dissipated. The chief results of this golden stream were the erection of a number of buildings of more than dubious taste,[9] the creation by the Holy See of the patriarchate of Lisbon, and fortunes lavished on favorites of both sexes. Intellectually,

---

[9] The most striking example was the enormous, barrack-like monastery of Mafra erected a short distance to the north of Lisbon.—P.A.M.

as well as politically, the reign was disastrous. Nothing sensible or constructive was to be hoped for from the monarch. The king's advisers were on his own level. And yet—such is one of the glaring ironies of the history of the period—Dom João V had available at this time the services of two of the ablest diplomats Portugal has produced, Luis de Cunha and Alexandre de Gusmão. But of what profit was such talent if the sovereign refused to read state papers or keep himself informed of the most pressing internal or foreign policies?

His successor, Dom José I, was an abler monarch. He belonged to that group of eighteenth-century rulers known as enlightened despots—sovereigns of the type of Charles III of Spain, Frederick II of Prussia, and Joseph II of Austria. He was served by able counsellors. Of these by all odds the most important was the world-famed Sebastião José de Carvalho e Mello, Marquis of Pombal. This aggressive and energetic prime minister was endowed with an iron will. But to this quality was united a monumental egotism and a pretension to a wide range of knowledge which he was far from possessing. Distrust, with him, had become a mental disease. Naturally of a vindictive character, his revenge would take the form of exquisite cruelty. Yet he knew how to govern and as long as he guided the ship of state the Portuguese administration ceased to be the utter nullity it had been during the preceding reign.

The Opening Up of Minas Geraes. Diamond Mining.—Meanwhile, as we have already seen, tremendous changes were taking place in the colony. The first result of the discovery of gold was an enormous rush into Minas Geraes, a shift in population which anticipated in some respects the days of Forty-nine in California. The stampede was at its height from 1699 to 1711, though it continued for some time later on a lesser scale. Fully to grasp the significance of this phenomenon, it must be recalled that the region was all but unknown and that no facilities existed to take care of the great invasion of miners who poured in by the thousands not only from Brazil but from the motherland as well. Famine, unspeakable suffering, and epidemics dogged the steps of the gold-seekers and decimated their ranks.

Antonil, in his invaluable treatise, notes that commodity prices rose from twenty-five to fifty times their normal figure. A full decade elapsed before conditions became anything like stabilized. The improvement was brought about through the opening of rude mule-tracks and so-called roads up into Minas Geraes from Rio de Janeiro and Bahia. From the latter captaincy came cattle, chiefly from the ranches bordering the eastern shore of the São Francisco. From the littoral and Rio came slaves and a few manufactured articles which tempered the asperities of life in the mining camps.

The same story of hardships and privations that we find in Minas Geraes was repeated in Matto Grosso. In this remote area, which adjoins the present Bolivia on the west, hunger, misery and other calamities were partially allayed when communications were laboriously opened up along the tributaries of the Amazon, or later by means of primitive trails crossing Goyaz to Paracatú in Minas.

The population drawn into Minas Geraes, which was erected into a separate captaincy in 1720, received a new accession through the discovery of diamonds. The presence of occasional diamonds had been detected as early as 1723, but it was not until six years later that an appreciation of their extent and wealth produced such a diamond rush that the gem-bearing district soon harbored a population of forty thousand. It was largely as a consequence of the gold and diamond rushes of the eighteenth century that Minas Geraes to this day contains the largest number of inhabitants of any of the Brazilian states. For, while the wealth in precious metals and stones proved largely ephemeral, the miners stayed on, raised families, and turned to agricultural and pastoral pursuits.

These spectacular developments in Minas Geraes and Matto Grosso naturally had their repercussions throughout Brazil and even in Portugal. Dazzled by the lure of gold, agricultural laborers in the captaincies bordering the littoral deserted the plantations en masse and the contagion sometimes even spread to the owners themselves. The problem of labor in the mining areas at once became acute. The Indians proved to be such wretched miners that Negro slaves became an imperious necessity. They were recruited from every possible source and commanded fantastic prices. The Portuguese colonies in Africa could not cope with this sudden demand, since the comparatively few ships engaged in the traffic were employed for the transport of Negroes to northern Brazil.

The planters of Bahia and Pernambuco, tempted by the high prices offered, sold their slaves and at times even accompanied them to the mines. Agriculture was badly disorganized and the danger of a crisis of under-production became so great that the authorities tried to check the exodus. The local governments and the captains general barred the roads, endeavored to apprehend the slaves and force them to remain on the plantations, and imposed prohibitive taxes on immigration into the mining areas. Such efforts were almost completely sterile. No artificial barriers could stay men dazzled by the dream of suddenly acquired riches.

Certain measures adopted by the government at Lisbon tended in the long run to aggravate rather than to lessen the economic dislocation caused by the discovery of gold and diamonds. To prevent the establishment of industries which might divert labor from employment in the gold placers, orders were issued in Lisbon that all factories or other establishments not essential to the extraction of gold or diamonds should be closed in the mining captaincies. Sugar mills, tobacco plantations, and the like were forbidden. Thus did the crown, naïvely assuming that the mining industry would last indefinitely, stake the prosperity of the new captaincies solely on gold and precious stones. It, therefore, indirectly contributed to the terrible economic crisis which swept over Minas Geraes after the exhaustion of the placers and before agriculture and cattle raising could be placed on a firm footing.

Drastic measures were adopted by the government to suppress smuggling and prevent the concealment of gold dust. In practice they were largely ineffective. Their chief result was to increase the resentment against the authorities at Lisbon and to arouse irritation against the local agents of the crown. This hostility to the government persisted for many years and was skillfully capitalized by the revolutionists in Minas when they launched an unsuccessful movement for independence at the end of the eighteenth century.

One result of the wealth which poured into the treasury from the exploitation of the gold and diamond mines was the consolidation and increase of the royal power. Prior to this time, when the crown was in need of extra revenue or resources, the king had to submit his demands to the parliament or côrtes which might make or refuse the grant. The last meeting of this body took place in

1697, only a short period before the mineral wealth of Minas Geraes was discovered. But thanks to his new source of income, the king could bid defiance to the côrtes, ignore their criticism, and govern according to his own good pleasure. For the new revenues were ample for the king's needs since the crown demanded a fifth of all gold produced, and diamonds, as we have seen, were a royal monopoly.

Although exact estimate of the output of the gold mines is impossible, certain approximations may be hazarded. The following table, which aims to include the gold which was smuggled out of the country or otherwise escaped official control, indicates the amounts in arrobas of 15 kilograms each:

Years	Minas Geraes	Goyaz Matto Grosso	São Paulo Bahia-Ceará
1700-1725	7,500		
1726-1735	6,500		
1736-1751	12,000		
1752-1787	18,000		
1788-1801	3,500		
1720-1801		13,000	5,000
Total	47,500	13,000	5,000

This makes a grand total of 65,500 arrobas or 983,000 kilograms, approximately $600,000,000 or nearly five million contos de réis in Brazilian money of our own day. These statistics extend only to 1801. As regards the output from that day to the present we may easily add some 400 metric tons of gold which increases the preceding total to 1,400 tons, or $840,000,000, that is, more than seven million contos de réis.

According to Eschwege,[10] at the beginning of the nineteenth century, 555 mines were being worked by 6,662 laborers of which only 169 were free and 6,493 slaves. In addition, there were a considerable number of persons who were washing gold on their own account, unconnected with any regular mining establishments. Of these 3,876 were free and 1,871 slaves. This gives us a grand total of 12,409 persons attached in one way or another to the min-

---

[10] In his *Pluto Brasiliensis* (Berlin, 1833).

ing industry. At this period there were no regularly organized companies.

As regards the value of the output of diamonds, statistics are even more unreliable than in the case of gold. Official figures, though honest as far as they go, embrace only a fraction of the activity in the diamond area. The reason is obvious. Diamonds are easy to conceal. Despite the existence of frightful penalties, many were hidden and smuggled out by the slaves. The Negroes became marvelously adept in palming the precious stones or concealing them between their toes, in their wooly hair, behind their ears, or in the folds of their scant garments. On occasion they even swallowed them.

The methods employed in the exploitation and control of the diamond deposits were subject to frequent changes. For a time the magnitude of the discovery and the real nature of the precious stones were not fully realized. It was not until 1740 that anything like a normal administration was set up, and prior to this period no statistics are available. From 1740 to 1771, the government granted contracts for the exploitation of the mines; from 1771 to 1828, the diamonds constituted a royal monopoly under the direct control of the agents of the crown. But under neither system was it possible to check the activities of smugglers and surreptitious workers. To these gentry was given the name of *garimpeiros* (literally "climbers"). Their life of adventure and suffering and the resourcefulness and courage they displayed in their conflicts with the hated mining officials invested them with an atmosphere of admiration and romance. The exploits of some of these daring trespassers are still recalled in the diamond districts and their memory worshipped. The most famous of the *garimpeiros* was a certain Isidoro. After many thrilling adventures he was finally captured and died of hardships and torture in prison. But up to the end he steadfastly refused to divulge the location of the rich gravels which he had discovered.

On the basis of public documents we have the following estimates of the amount of diamonds extracted.

	Carats
Contract period (1740-1771)	1,666,569
Royal monopoly (1772-1828)	1,319,192
Total	2,985,761

Diamonds had also been discovered in Bahia, but by order of the government the mines were shut down. So effectively was the order carried out that the gravels were entirely forgotten until they were rediscovered by the German travellers Spix and Martius in 1822. Within a short time the whole *Chapada Diamantina*, as the diamond-bearing plateau was called, was found to be a very rich area, though never comparable in importance or value to the deposits in Minas Geraes. Diamond-bearing gravels were occasionally discovered in Matto Grosso, Goyaz, São Paulo, Paraná, and elsewhere.

It may not be without interest briefly to carry the story of diamond mining down to our own day. As we have just seen Minas Geraes had yielded almost three million carats up to the abolition of the royal monopoly in 1828. According to Wappäus,[11] this quality approximated 615 kilograms, including stones both lawfully and unlawfully obtained. From 1832, when the mines were definitely thrown open to private exploitation, to our own time the total production of diamonds has risen to nearly 4,000 kilograms, or 3,400 above the figures of 1832. Besides diamonds, properly so-called, large amounts of *carbonatos*, or black diamonds, valuable for industrial purposes, have been exported, chiefly from Bahia.

The Iron Industry in Minas Geraes.—In addition to gold and diamonds, the vast captaincy of Minas Geraes has almost inexhaustible deposits of iron ore in its mountains and valleys. As a result largely of lack of fuel and adequate transportation, this source of wealth has been little exploited. Especially was this true in the eighteenth century when gold and diamond mining was in the ascendant. On the other hand, iron mining could not be totally neglected. As has already been pointed out, some of the Negro slaves had brought over from Africa certain crude methods of smelting iron ore. This knowledge was at once turned to account in the mining districts as the amount of iron required for industrial purposes was comparatively large. It was needed of course for the manufacturing of mining tools but its most important use was for the making of shoes for the beasts of burden. Minas is traversed by high mountains, rugged and stony. The trails and primitive roads over which the pack mules and horses struggled were rough and steep and after the frequent rains muddy and slippery. Here

[11] *Geographia physica do Brasil* (Rio de Janeiro, 1884).

could not be applied the methods used in the north where the beasts of burden were left unshod and their hoofs hardened by the application of molten tallow. When carts were employed the wretched condition of the roads made it necessary to equip the wheels with iron rims or tires.

Growth and Importance of Minas Geraes.—As has already been intimated, life in the early days of the gold and diamond rush was hard and at times cruel. Prior to the establishment of royal authority, every man was more or less a law unto himself. The prizes went to the strongest or most audacious. For something like a decade, life in the mining camps was one long series of tumults, brawls, and even organized feuds or civil wars between the first occupants and the newcomers. In some respects Minas Geraes was not unlike California in the days of '49 with this difference, that the period of disorder was much longer and the manner of life in those days was much more primitive and crude than a century later.

In order to bring some semblance of order out of the prevailing anarchy, the earlier inhabitants of Minas Geraes proclaimed as their chief a certain Manoel Nunes Vianna, a respected Portuguese, who owned a number of cattle ranches on the São Francisco River. He kept things more or less in order and even levied taxes. His was a curious mind to find in this remote wilderness. His leisure hours were spent reading works of the type of St. Augustine's *De Civitate Dei* or editing books on his own account; among the latter one of the most famous was *O Peregrino da America* (*America's Pilgrim*) by Nuno Marques Pereira. But Manoel Nunes had no thought of usurping powers which rightly belonged to the king. His régime was one of transition between utter lawlessness and the establishment of royal authority. When, therefore, the legally appointed captain general arrived in Minas Geraes in 1711 with only fourteen persons in his escort Nunes Vianna handed over his office without the slightest hesitancy and retired to the obscurity of his cattle ranches bordering the São Francisco.

As a consequence of the intense mining activities of the eighteenth century Minas Geraes became, as we have seen, the most populous captaincy in Brazil. The Draconian laws and regulations to which it was subjected might retard, but could not prevent, its development. With augmented wealth and population all the concomitants of civilization naturally appeared. Life became less rude and difficult. Imported luxuries of all sorts found their way into the captaincy. Along with this higher standard of living came a development of intellectual interests. Literature was actively pursued and a school of lyric poets came into existence. The towns grew with such rapidity as to outstrip in population the cities along the littoral. The leading communities were Villa Rica, the capital of the gold mining region, and Tijuco, the center of the diamond industry. The spectacular and artificial growth of these cities, a reflection of the feverish mining activities, is evidenced by the fact that the population of Villa Rica (now known as Ouro Preto) rose to 100,000, only to sink in our own day to barely 8,000 souls. A similar phenomenon is to be observed in the case of Tijuco (now Diamantina); its population of 40,000 in the heyday of the diamond industry has now shrunk to a fifth of its former size. Both are little more than ghost towns, haunted by the shadows of past greatness.

The "Inconfidencia."—The term *Inconfidencia* (literally "lack of confidence") is the name given by Brazilian historians to the revolt which broke out in Minas Geraes against the Portuguese authorities in 1789, an uprising which may be regarded as the premonitory symptom of the movement which led to the complete separation from the mother country some three decades later. The grievances of the Mineiros, as the inhabitants of the captaincy were called, were both economic and political. Taxes in the gold-mining area were numerous and vexatious. The fiscal authorities were extremely arbitrary and redress for illegal or excessive exactions was almost impossible to secure. In the diamond district, the situation was even worse. The whole gem-bearing region trembled and groaned under the terrible sway of the *intendente dos diamantes*, as the chief administrative official was called. Those who infringed in any way the government monopoly were punished with pitiless severity. But no one dared to protest, so discretionary and arbitrary was the power of the *intendente* and so stringent were the penalties imposed by the so-called *Livro da capa verde* (*Book of the Green Cape*), the penal and administrative code of the district.

The fruits of such a system of government were naturally ill-feeling, thinly veiled indignation, and hatred. It is not surprising, therefore, that sentiments in favor of a revolt against what they regarded as an execrable tyranny began to make headway among a number of leading citizens and inhabitants of the captaincy. It is interesting to note that this conspiracy was influenced by the successful revolution in North America against Great Britain. A number of Brazilian students had been following courses in-the famous University of Montpellier in France. One of them, José Joaquim da Maia, afire with enthusiasm for the United States and its independence, wrote in 1786 to Thomas Jefferson, the American minister at Paris, bespeaking the moral and material support of the United States should Brazil throw off the Portuguese yoke. Naturally Jefferson's reply was vague and noncommittal. Though Maia died before returning to Brazil, his comrades learned of his contact with Jefferson and, when relating it to their friends in Minas Geraes and Rio de Janeiro, they found congenial and perhaps too credulous hearers.

The conspiracy had its origin among the intellectual elite of Minas Geraes, including a number of poets and members of the clergy. Some of the conspirators had read widely. In the list of books seized in the library of one of them the French philosophers of the eighteenth century were well represented. The hero of the revolution was Joaquim José da Silva Xavier, nicknamed Tiradentes (literally "Tooth-puller"). Though not the foremost among the plotters in rank or influence he was an enthusiastic republican, a highbred soul, and a devoted apostle of independence and liberty. His duties as a lieutenant of militia took him up and down the captaincy and even to Rio. On his journeys he took with him a copy of the constitution of the United States which he showed to all and sundry, while the burden of his conversation was the necessity of overthrowing the hated yoke of Portugal.

The pretext for the rising, which was scheduled for 1789, was the announced determination of the government to collect certain arrears in taxes, amounting in some cases to very large sums. A number of the debtors, included in the conspiracy, turned against their fellows and denounced the plot and its members to the government. In any case, however, the authorities were certain to learn of it as too many persons were involved in the secret and Tiradentes himself was amazingly indiscreet in his statements. The surprising thing is that the captain general, the Viscount of Barbacena, did not learn of it sooner.

The authorities lost no time in nipping the conspiracy in the bud. The hated orders in regard to tax arrears were rescinded. The leading conspirators were apprehended and thrown into prison. After a trial lasting nearly two years most of the accused were sentenced to exile or imprisonment. Only one, Tiradentes, suffered capital punishment, and perished on the scaffold on April 21, 1792. It was intended that his execution should serve as a terrible example to those insubordinate or ingrateful subjects who dreamed of changing the established order, and the victim chosen was the moral leader of the *Inconfidencia*. The lesson was indeed a lasting one, but not in the sense intended by Portugal. Far from intimidating the colonists it tended to exasperate them. The admirable conduct of Tiradentes during the trial, his nobility and unselfishness in assuming all responsibilities in order to alleviate the lot of his fellow sufferers revealed him as a genuine leader of men. To both contemporaries and posterity he has become a symbol of a noble leader of a great cause. His serene demeanor and his willingness to lay down his life both for his brethren and for the cause of Brazilian independence have given him the aureole of a martyr. In the years which followed, his memory heartened those who opposed the tyranny of Portugal and served to dissolve the ties between mother country and colony. In this sense may Tiradentes be regarded as the precursor of Brazilian independence.

The deep and abiding impression which the conspiracy of Tiradentes left on Minas Geraes is revealed in a more concrete manner. When the movement for the separation of Brazil from Portugal was launched in 1821-1822, the Mineiros insisted that all bonds between the colony and mother country be completely severed and it was only with reluctance that they were willing to associate themselves with the national uprising in Rio when this proved to be not republican but monarchical.

Conditions in Brazil on the Turn of the Century.—Despite the marked decline of gold and diamond production during the last decades of the eighteenth century, the colony as a whole gave evidence of progress. Foreign trade, with a healthy balance in favor of Brazil, steadily grew.[12] The protracted war waged by Great Britain first against the forces of the French Revolution and later against Napoleon redounded to the benefit of Brazil. British command of the sea permitted the Portuguese fleets, both fighting and commercial, to ply at will the Atlantic, now for all intents and purposes an English lake. Exports from Brazil to Lisbon continually increased in volume. As a consequence of a balance of trade in favor of Brazil, exchange rates during long periods remained above par.

This increasing prosperity was accompanied by an ever growing self-reliance on the part of the colonists. At the same time, they became more and more resentful at the domineering and patronising attitude of the metropolis. They felt that Portugal looked upon Brazil as a sort of milch cow, or to change the figure, as a kind of treasure house from which endless revenues could be extracted. This resentment was not allayed by the fact that, by the end of the eighteenth century, the population of the colony had come to equal if not to exceed that of the mother country. Under such circumstances, the Brazilians had come to believe that they were at least as important as their brethren on the other side of the Atlantic. The Portuguese in turn began to be apprehensive of a separatist movement on the part of the colony. Symptomatic of the changing status between Portugal and its trans-Atlantic possession was the increasingly important rôle played by Brazilians in the governing councils in Lisbon and in the direction of the international affairs of the kingdom.

As has already been related, this sentiment of pride and self-sufficiency harks back to the expulsion of the Dutch through the unaided efforts of the colonists. And the conclusion of the struggle with the Dutch was followed by a constant, if at times latent, conflict with Spain. The relentless pressure exerted by settlers and explorers resulting in Portuguese penetration far to the west of the line of Tordesillas has been repeatedly mentioned. We have also seen how the Portuguese gained possession of the larger part of the great Amazon Valley in which the intrepid Father Vieira

---

[12] The exports for 1796, 1800, 1806 were 11,500, 12,600, 14,200 contos respectively. The imports for the same years were 7,000, 15,800, and 8,500 contos respectively. The value of a conto at this time was around $500.

established a whole chain of missions. Finally, we have noted that the Portuguese succeeded in maintaining, for long intervals, a foothold at Sacramento on the northern shores of the Río de la Plata. This amazing success of the Portuguese in pushing their conquests far into the very heart of South America, at the expense of their Spanish rivals, found official recognition in the Treaty of Utrecht of 1715 between Spain and Portugal, and, above all, in the celebrated Treaty of Madrid of 1750 signed by the same powers. In the drawing up of this latter instrument, which brilliantly exemplified the doctrine of *uti possidetis*, the Portuguese negotiator was one of the most famous diplomats of the epoch, the Brazilian Alesandre de Gusmão, a son of Santos.

But the terms of the Treaty of Madrid, advantageous though they were, received further modification in favor of Brazil. The treaty was formally abrogated in 1761 and after interminable debates and much hesitation a new series of clauses was accepted in 1777 and 1778 in the treaties of San Ildefonso; here again was vindicated the doctrine of definite possession. These treaties, also, turned out to be provisional. While their terms were being laboriously carried out in America, Europe fell victim to the long series of wars growing out of the French Revolution and the abolition of the French monarchy. After the Treaty of Basel (1795), Portugal was abandoned by its allies and found itself arrayed against both France and Spain. The kingdom was invaded by the forces of Napoleon and, as will be explained in the next chapter, the prince regent, Dom João VI, transferred the seat of government from Lisbon to Rio de Janeiro in 1808. One of his first acts was to denounce all of the treaties existing between Portugal on the one hand and Spain and France on the other. In this manner all former compromises or adjustments over boundaries disappeared. But the principle of *ulti possidetis* still persisted. It had remained untouched since 1715 as an implicit clause, and from 1750 on as a perfectly distinct and avowed policy.

From this rapid survey of Portuguese-Castilian diplomatic relations, it is obvious that Brazil achieved a brilliant and lasting victory over outworn concepts, inappropriate for the solution of boundary problems arising from the spread of population into unknown areas. In the international life of Brazil this rule of *uti possidetis* has been invariably followed, not only in cases in which it worked out to our advantage but also when it was contrary to our interests.

CHAPTER III

RIO DE JANEIRO, CAPITAL OF THE PORTUGUESE MONARCHY

NOVEMBER 29, 1807, is one of the most memorable dates in the history of Portugal and Brazil. On that day, Dom João VI, regent of the kingdom in behalf of his insane mother, Dona Maria I, sailed out of the Tagus for Brazil accompanied by the royal family and a numerous escort of Portuguese nobles and dignitaries. The seat of the Lusitanian government was about to be transferred from Lisbon to Rio de Janerio. On the following day a French army under Junot entered the capital unopposed. About these events has grown up the legend of a flight pure and simple, and at the same time shameful and cowardly. In reality, the departure of Dom João was in pursuance of a plan worked out after mature deliberation and based on the peculiar conditions then existing in Portugal.

The Transference of the Royal Family to Brazil.—When it became clear that in his life and death struggle with England Napoleon was determined to close Great Britain's access to the continent through Lisbon and Portugal, the fate of Dom João and the kingdom of the Braganzas was sealed. For a number of years, Portuguese diplomacy had been able to ward off this catastrophe. The most effective means employed for this purpose had been a vast system of bribery of the entourage of the emperor, financed chiefly by the products of the diamond mines of Minas Geraes. But finally it became clear that the hostile policy of Napoleon could no longer be checkmated. After Trafalgar, no option was left to the French government but to conquer, or capitulate to Great Britain.

For a time, Dom João believed that the impending danger might be exorcised. Portuguese diplomacy adopted a policy of procrastination, hoping that discussions might be dragged out until the points at issue were forgotten. But Dom João's minister at Paris at length made it clear that a crisis was impending and that the Portuguese monarch was face to face with a terrible dilemma. If he remained faithful to England he would face expulsion from his kingdom. If he threw in his lot with Napoleon he would have to

close Portugal to British influence and join the continental blockade, thus bringing upon himself the hostility of his former ally.
Neutrality was no longer possible and the diminutive kingdom was
in imminent peril of being crushed between the hammer and the
anvil.

The Portuguese were and still are good fighters. Napoleon, a
connoisseur in such matters, esteemed them highly and always
praised the Portuguese Legion. But what chance had tiny Portugal in an armed conflict with France and Spain? As the crisis
drew near, the plan was gradually evolved of transferring from
Europe to South America the capital and government of the
Portuguese realm. The idea was favorably regarded by Dom
João's minister at London, by many of his influential advisers in
Lisbon, and finally by the prince regent himself. Five years later
a somewhat similar plan was adopted by the Czar of Russia: to
retreat before the invader. In this case Father Winter shattered
the French attack on Holy Russia. In the case of Portugal, the
ocean would check and nullify any conquest until a reversal of fate
should come to the aid of the weaker nation.

Yet Dom João hesitated. By nature he was both cunning and
timid. His native cowardice made it difficult for him to follow any
energetic course. Up until the last moment he expected some happy
change in circumstances which would enable him to remain in
Lisbon, for he had a mortal fear of the sea. Yet he had sufficient
foresight and intelligence to order everything to be in readiness
for shipment to Brazil and so well were his orders carried out that
embarcation could take place on a few hours' notice. The details
had, in fact, been perfected with such care that upon landing at
Rio de Janeiro the main bulk of documents, books, archives, and
other government papers were found so well arranged that the
administration of public affairs suffered no interruption or special
difficulties. Yet after everything had been made ready for the voyage, the prince regent delayed his departure and refused to embark until the news reached him that a French army under Junot
was about to enter the capital. It was largely owing to the un-
dignified demeanor of the prince regent during these last moments
of confusion and disorder that the legend arose of a disgraceful
and pusillanimous flight.

It should be made clear at this point that the project of

the transference of the Portuguese court to Brazil was by no means a novelty. In the middle of the sixteenth century, Martim Affonso de Souza, the first royal governor of Brazil, had advised Dom João III to take such a step. When Philip II of Spain contrived, in 1580, to gain possession of Portugal as lawful heir to the kingdom after the death of the cardinal-king, Dom Henrique, his claims were in conflict with those of Donna Catharina, Duchess of Braganza. The Spanish monarch tried to induce her to relinquish her rights by offering to raise Brazil to the status of a kingdom whose throne she should occupy. After the Portuguese restoration in 1640 Dom João IV, threatened by Castile, cast about for allies. One of his schemes was to wed his ill-fated heir, Dom Theodosio, to a French princess, and to place the royal pair on the Portuguese throne, while he himself would establish a Brazilian kingdom in the New World. Finally, after the terrible earthquake in Lisbon in 1755, the great minister of Dom José I, the Marquis of Pombal, broached the idea of abandoning Europe and of creating a powerful empire in Brazil. Thus the French invasion of 1807 called into being a plan already centuries old. From the foregoing it is evident how superficial is the view of those who see in the hegira of the Portuguese court a mere panic-stricken flight.

In any case, the transference of the Lusitanian capital from Lisbon to Rio de Janeiro was a victorious move. The ocean, dominated by the British fleet, proved an impassible barrier to Napoleon's power. With its command of the sea, England, even if vanquished on the continent, could not be really conquered. Whatever the outcome of the Napoleonic wars, the Portuguese monarchy in South America, as Great Britain's ally, would maintain its existence. And should the tide turn against the Corsican, Lusitanian troops, fighting side by side with the English, would help expel the hated invaders from the Portuguese territory. As is well known such a consummation actually came to pass in the Peninsular campaign.

The Reception of the Portuguese Court in Brazil.—Both the court and the government looked forward to their reception in Brazil with considerable trepidation. They were well aware that the colonists were smarting under the humiliations which had been forced upon them by the metropolis. They were not ignorant of the complaints and demands of the colonists, to which such scant attention had been paid. Yet the event belied all their gloomy forebodings. Though the Brazilians had long resented the indifferences, the sneers, and the supercilious superiority of the Portuguese, both monarchy and monarch still enjoyed such great prestige that nothing could mar the immense and heartfelt exultation caused by the presence of the king and the elevation of Rio de Janeiro to the rank of capital of the realm. The loyalty of Dom João's subjects was, to be sure, put to a severe test. They suffered countless annoyances and vexations at the hands of the petty courtiers. This gentry insulted the Brazilians, dubbed them with nicknames, forced them to sacrifice their best dwellings, and imposed upon them almost unbearable expense and discomfort. Yet, despite these and other drawbacks, Rio de Janeiro as well as Brazil in general never forgot the transference of the monarchy from Europe to America and the benefits which this move brought to the former colony. The conceited courtiers and impertinent officials might be despised and hated but the regent was always respected and loved. The populace kneeled along the streets and highways when he passed by and his kindly behavior toward the common people won the hearts of all.

The prince had not been loved in Portugal save by a few intimates. For this his wife, Dona Carlota Joaquina, was partly to blame. She despised her easy-going husband and organized a conspiracy against him, hoping to encompass his overthrow. She was even suspected of plotting his death. Dom João was well aware of these intrigues and he hated and feared her in consequence. Her private life was not above reproach. The royal consorts lived apart and were seen together only on public occasions when the presence of both sovereigns was imperative.

Dom João was captivated by Brazil from the moment of his arrival. He felt himself enveloped by the respect and affection of his subjects. The Brazilians at once realized that in the prince regent they had a true friend, the best and most sensible of all those placed in authority over them. For the first time in its history the country was governed as an autonomous unit and not merely as a source of revenue to meet the needs of the mother country.

Utterly different was the attitude of the Brazilians toward the princess. Dona Carlota Joaquina was generally hated. This antipathy was due in part to her haughty, domineering character, partly to her intense dislike for Brazil, which she made no effort to conceal. Nor did she neglect any opportunity of evincing her true feelings toward the Brazilians, and quite gratuitously humiliated them in public. A single example will suffice. Two cavalry soldiers, riding in front of her carriage, obliged everyone to bow and kneel before the princess as she passed, and whoever refused to comply was slashed or chastized with whips. On one occasion the United States minister, Thomas Sumter, met the princess while she was abroad in her carriage and politely doffed his hat. But the galloping outriders failed to recognize him and were about to lay on with their whips when the diplomat quietly drew a pair of pistols with the intimation that he would shoot them if they advanced a step nearer. This unfortunate contretemps set the whole capital agog; suitable apologies were tendered, and the princess' escort was instructed in future to moderate its zeal.

Despite her domineering manner and unsympathetic personality Dona Carlota possessed certain qualities lacking in her good-natured and indolent husband. She was far superior to Dom João in intelligence, energy, courage, and devotion to friends. She was a born leader of men. Until her death, thirty years later, she was the real chief of the absolutist party, first in Brazil, later in Portugal. To her unscrupulous guidance the most renowned leaders of this party yielded obedience. She fought with unrelenting energy for her political ideal, the restoration and public acknowledgment of the monarchy ruling by divine right. Had she analyzed her sentiments she probably would have given first place to her hatred and contempt for the prince regent. In truth, she never felt herself a Portuguese at heart, and lived and died a Spanish infanta, devoted to the interests of her brother, Ferdinand VII, King of Spain. At the first opportunity she launched a policy of her own against her husband and against the interests of Portugal. We shall later have abundant occasion to observe the part played by this intriguing and unscrupulous princess in the tangled affairs of La Plata basin.

As a ruler, Dom João was regarded by many, including, as we have seen, his wife, as a nonentity. No one heeded his opinions, so he cautiously concealed them and tried to gain the upper hand by postponing solutions, pitting one adviser against another or one minister against his colleague. This last device was easy to follow as the ministers were rarely in agreement. According to the distinguished German geologist and traveler, Von Eschewege, who had been invited to Brazil by the prince regent, the people were wont to compare three of his ministry to three watches: the first went too fast, the second too slow, and the third did not move at all. Thus Dom João's policy of *divide ut imperes* was by no means futile. In most instances, however, the prince regent gained his way by force of apathy or by means of endless adjournments. He won by dividing and wearing out his opponents.

Organization of the Government at Rio.—It is obvious that, once on Brazilian soil, Dom João and his government were confronted with a set of entirely new problems. Prior to the transference of the Portuguese court the colony had existed largely for the benefit of the mother country. The cost of administration had, in the main, been defrayed out of local revenues, with receipts balancing expenditures. But with the migration of the court this balance was naturally upset since the entire burden of the national administration fell upon the Brazilian taxpayers. From Lisbon nothing was to be expected. The French invasion had thrown the whole administrative machinery into utter disorder. Taxes, always in arrears, were in a hopeless tangle. Collection was, of course, out of the question with a French army in possession of most of the country. In fact, funds had to be dispatched from Rio in order to pay the troops fighting against Junot.

On his arrival in Brazil, Dom João found Rio de Janeiro thoroughly colonial in habits and customs. Though it boasted of a population of some 130,000 souls, it knew neither hygiene nor sewerage. No provision was made for clearing the streets or the disposal of refuse. The standard of living, in comparison with European cities of equal size, was low. Life was rather dull and drab. Festivities, not over numerous, were mostly those organized by the religious orders: processions, *Te Deums*, sermons. At rare intervals the viceroys gave receptions. Slaves were the mainstay of all domestic and public services.

The arrival of the Portuguese court wrought a tremendous upheaval in the placid life of the colonial capital. On very short notice, provision had to be made for the housing, subsistence and comfort of several thousand people accustomed to a mode of life far more exacting than that found in Brazil. The most immediate and pressing problem was to find dwellings for the newcomers. In the first flush of enthusiasm caused by the arrival of the royal family, many of the Brazilians opened their homes to their Portuguese guests or even turned over their residences to them. Those less hospitably inclined yielded to the persuasions or orders of the viceroy, the Count of Arcos. In one way or another a roof was thus provided for all of the voluntary exiles. Though there were many grumblings and complaints on the part of both hosts and guests, the necessary adjustments were finally made without leaving any great amount of rancor and bitterness in their train.

Other problems were less easy of solution. The advent of Dom João brought about an abrupt and even dramatic break in the history of Brazil. The most striking evidence of this change was revealed in one of the first acts of the prince regent: the abolition on January 28, 1808, of the old Portuguese monopoly of trade and the opening of the ports of Brazil to the commerce of all friendly nations. Much has been written regarding this measure and those responsible for it have been lauded to the skies. Quite possibly they have been praised beyond their deserts. A moment's thought will show that Dom João could hardly have acted otherwise. After the transference of the seat of government from Europe to South America, Portugal, as a metropolitan power, had ceased to exist. Its soil was occupied by French armies. Navigation and commerce were impossible owing to the British blockade. With Portuguese ports under French control, where should Brazil secure those commodities formerly exported from the mother country? To what market could Brazil now turn? The answer was obvious: Great Britain. And above and beyond these economic considerations was the debt which the Braganza dynasty owed to the British fleet for making possible the removal of the court from Lisbon to Rio.

There were other reasons why trade routes had to be established, not only with Great Britain but also with other friendly powers such as the United States. The government was sadly in need of funds and one of the best means of replenishing the treasury was to levy import duties. The tariff on foreign goods soon came, in fact, to be the chief source of the income of the royal treasury.

Internal Problems and Reforms.—Once installed in his new capital, Dom João's most pressing problem was to make up for lost time and to free Brazil from the heritage of an outgrown colonial economy. He now discovered that his viceroys had not kept him fully informed of the real conditions in Brazil, and in some cases had even deceived him. The halcyon days of the extractive industries—gold and diamonds—were irremediably gone. Agriculture and its corollaries were stifled by lack of credit, and by an absence of adequate legislation, since the one in force was based on false notions regarding the wealth of the mines and their needs and demands. The Brazilians themselves, it was soon discovered, could aid in the solution of more than one difficult problem. Among these most useful local elements were priests, lawyers, and civil functionaries who had studied at the University of Coimbra. Some of them had traveled extensively in Europe and were on the same level of competence as the Portuguese who had accompanied the prince regent on the fleet. In fact they enjoyed one great advantage over these new arrivals: they were familiar with the country.

Dom João embarked at once on his program of reforming existing institutions and of creating new ones, both in Rio and in other parts of the country. As early as 1699, there had been established in Rio a school where questions of defense and fortification were studied. The first nucleus of a future arsenal dates from 1793. The second half of the eighteenth century had witnessed the flowering and early death of many literary academies. Since 1739, two seminaries had supplied a certain amount of training to the clergy and even to public servants. But their program was excessively meager and with the turning of the century they had ceased to meet the needs of the colony.

As has already been pointed out, the year 1808 marks a critical and decisive turning point in the history of Brazil. Immediately upon his arrival, Dom João promoted the establishment of colleges of surgery and medicine in Rio de Janeiro and Bahia. An academy for the training of naval cadets was founded. A royal printing press was set up. During the years 1810 and 1811, a school of commerce and a military academy opened their doors. In 1814, a library, the kernel of our present Biblioteca Nacional, was thrown open to the public. The National Museum and the School of Fine Arts were both created in 1808. For the purpose of improving agricultural methods and of acclimating new plants, steps were taken in 1808 to create our present Botanical Garden. Laws and regulations which hampered industrial activities in the mining captaincies were repealed. Every effort was made to encourage initiative and to release those national energies which hitherto had been thwarted.

One of the gravest difficulties of the period was the absence of credit. Even in normal times Portugal had but little money to give or loan. And now, with the mother country under the heel of the French, nothing was to be hoped for from that quarter. England was absorbed in the prosecution of its wars against Napoleon and granted subsidies only to those countries which aided it in the struggle. But one recourse was left: to issue paper money. In 1808, the first Bank of Brazil was founded. It was an unknown mechanism and had to cope with all the difficulties growing out of ignorance and inexperience. Capital was difficult to secure: it was not until December, 1809, that shares amounting to a hundred contos[1] were sold. Instead of permitting the bank to carry on a normal business, the government was insatiable in its demands for funds to cover all sorts of expenses. The management was not always worthy of praise; in a few instances, it was taxed with dishonesty. On the eve of Dom João's return to Lisbon in 1821, practically all of the notes which had been issued were in the hands of the king, the royal family, the courtiers, and royal functionaries who were preparing to go back to Portugal. This mass of paper money was presented to the bank for gold and silver currency. As a consequence, the cash in the bank fell overnight to 200 contos. The education of the local commercial circles was yet to be made, and it required more than a decade to get accustomed to notes.

The circulation of this paper was hampered by the fact that it was restricted to a comparatively small area, namely Rio, Bahia, and São Paulo. Dom Pedro, the son and successor of Dom João, and the first emperor of Brazil, harbored ill will against the bank and tried to check its growth and activities by every means in his power. The normal demands of business were met without difficulty, but the exactions of the government forced the bank unduly to expand its issues of paper money.

The culmination of twenty years of official hostility finally came

---

[1] Approximately half a million dollars. A conto, it will be recalled, consists of 1000 milréis.—P.A.M.

in 1829 when the legislature passed a bill for the liquidation of the bank. Outstanding notes to the amount of 19,174 contos had to be redeemed. Yet on examination, it was found that this indebtedness was well-nigh balanced by the treasury's debt of approximately 18,301 contos.

This forced liquidation was one of the most glaring faults in the entire financial history of Brazil. In spite of all of its mistakes and blunders, the bank constituted the sole source of credit for the country, and on the whole it had worked in a satisfactory manner. This was proved by the liquidation. Even taking into account the adverse conditions under which this operation took place the shareholders received 90 per cent of their investment. Yet such was the effect of this forced liquidation that for years Brazil lacked a banking institution.

International Difficulties.—Another series of grave difficulties grew out of the intimate political relations existing between Portugal and England. The two nations had been allies since the signing of the Mathuen Treaty of 1703, and this alliance had weathered severe storms. In the interminable struggle between England and Napoleon, Portugal, first through its neutrality and later by throwing in its lot with Great Britain, had proven its solidarity with its ancient friend and ally. England in turn had rendered the Braganza dynasty an inestimable service. The time had now arrived for Albion to claim its reward in the shape of special concessions and privileges in the matter of trade and commerce. In the negotiations which ensued, England was well served by its minister at Rio, Lord Strangford, who through arguments, entreaties, and demands adopted a *big stick policy*[2] toward the unfortunate, trembling, and cowardly regent. Dom João, in fact, had to make a virtue of necessity. As a result of Napoleon's continental blockade on the one hand, and the British orders-in-council on the other, the Atlantic had become for all intents and purposes a British lake where the rule or whim of Great Britain was supreme. Portugal, with its scanty merchant marine and insignificant navy, had to swallow its pride and endure what could neither be cured nor mended.

Taking advantage of this situation, Lord Strangford forced upon Brazil the Treaty of 1810 which laid the basis of an English

---

[2] English in the original.—P.A.M.

commercial preëminence in Brazil lasting almost to our own day. Nominally, the merchant marines of both nations were placed upon the same footing. But in view of the disproportion between the commercial activities of the two countries, this concession proved illusory, especially when it appeared that the British cabinet did not have the legal power to concede to Portuguese ships the favors which Strangford had promised would be extended to them. As if this were not bad enough, Brazil was forced to grant to British imports a lower tariff than that levied on imports from Portugal itself. But the most humiliating concession of all yet remains to be mentioned. Brazil was obliged to extend to its ally a privilege analogous to the old "Capitulations" existing in oriental countries, the celebrated *conservatoria*, which gave to British subjects involved in lawsuits the right to be tried by a special judge, the *juiz conservador*.

In harmony with this privileged position enjoyed by Great Britain, a convention was signed for the creation, by means of a contract, of the first regular packet line between Great Britain and Brazil.

The prince regent had to endure humiliations of still another sort. As a result of the propaganda carried on by Wilberforce, Clarkson, and other English humanitarians, Great Britain abolished its own slave trade in 1807 and then turned its attention to Portugal. In the commercial treaty of 1810 the prince regent agreed to second the efforts of Great Britian by prohibiting his subjects from engaging in the traffic beyond the confines of his African possessions. At the Congress of Vienna, Portugal was forced to give up the traffic north of the equator and agreed to determine by a subsequent treaty the period at which the Portuguese slave trade should cease utterly. Finally, a convention signed in 1817 gave Great Britain the right of search and visit of Portuguese ships operating north of the line and suspected of having slaves on board.

These various treaties, conventions, and agreements with Great Britain were the starting point of endless entanglements and friction which in later years all but led to open hostilities. For it cannot be gainsaid that to some extent Dom João had forfeited Brazil's freedom of commerce by according to England imports an exceptional status. He had impaired the country's sovereignty by permitting foreign tribunals and foreign judges to operate on national territory. In order to place a check on the slave trade, he had permitted the naval forces of a foreign power to seize, judge, and punish the crews of Brazilian ships.

The results of Great Britain's privileged commercial position were not slow to appear. The year 1816, when after the fall of Napoleon conditions should have been normal, may be taken as an example. While the coastwise trade was being carried on by Portuguese vessels, less than half the overseas traffic went to Portugal, and of the remainder more than one half fell to England.

Evidences of Progress.—The reign of Dom João, despite his shortcomings and mistakes, represented for Brazil an era of progress. Production was stimulated by the creation of new markets and of new methods of transportation. Coffee culture had made great strides and along with sugar, hides, tobacco, and some cotton was becoming one of the basic industries of Portuguese America. In 1822, the year following Dom João's departure, the export figures for these commodities were: coffee, 45,644,800 pounds; sugar, 45,-644,800 pounds; cotton, 5,208,000 pounds. The mining industry though in a state of decadence was not without its importance; yet unfavorable symptoms were not entirely absent. A certain economic malaise was evidenced by the fluctuation of the milréis. The tendency on the whole was downward. From a par of 67½ pence the milréis fell to 47 pence in 1822. This drop was the more striking since in the early years of the second decade of the century it had risen above 70 pence. These variations are not to be explained purely on economic grounds; as a matter of fact an equilibrium had been reached in the volumes of imports and exports, each amounting to approximately 8,500 contos. The real cause for the lack of confidence as reflected in the fluctuations of the exchange is to be seen in the political activities of the government. The political commitments in Europe, to be sure, proved no great burden on the treasury since the expenses of Portugal's participation in the Peninsular War were almost entirely met by Great Britain. It was the policy of Brazil in South America—a policy of aggrandizement and intervention—which eventually threw finances into disorder.

Beginnings of Friction in La Plata Basin.—The course pursued by Dom João in his dealings with Brazil's southern neighbors is extraordinarily complicated and can be considered here only in its larger aspects. In truth, not *one* but *three* mutually irreconcilable courses were followed more or less simultaneously in the basin of the Río de la Plata; namely, those pursued by Dom João, Dona Carlota Joaquina, and Great Britain through its minister, Lord Strangford. Cutting athwart these foreign designs on the Platine area were local conflicts of opinions and divided loyalties. Two factions emerged as Spain's grip on the viceroyalty of Buenos Aires began to weaken. One faction, styled the *godos* (literally "Goths") consisted of Spanish-born Castilians. These were the loyalists who remained faithful to Spain through thick and thin. The other faction was made up of *criollos* or creoles, the name given to those of Spanish blood who were born and bred in America. While the majority of the creoles tended to remain loyal to the Bourbons, an increasingly aggressive minority dreamed of independence and eventually raised the standard of revolt against the mother country.

To understand the motives and aims of the Portuguese intervention in La Plata basin, it is necessary to cast a glance at developments in Spain. As early as 1807, Napoleon had determined to bring not only Portugal, but also Spain, within the orbit of his empire. Taking advantage of a disgraceful family brawl between Charles IV and the heir apparent, Prince Ferdinand (later Ferdinand VII), the emperor early in 1808 threw a large army into Spain under Murat. Charles, who had become exceedingly unpopular, was forced to abdicate in favor of his son, after which Ferdinand allowed himself to be lured to the French frontier. At Bayonne, he was bullied by Napoleon into abdicating the Spanish crown and spent the next six years as a prisoner in France. On the vacant throne of the Spanish Bourbons, the emperor placed his own brother, Joseph Bonaparte.

In his seizure of Spain, Napoleon had made one serious miscalculation—he failed to reckon with the Spanish people themselves. The Spaniards would have none of Joseph: they rose en masse against the French and all their works and, though repeatedly defeated by the French armies, they kept up the struggle until the hated invaders were finally driven from Spanish soil.

Naturally, these events in Spain had profound repercussions in

America. The inhabitants of the viceroyalty of Buenos Aires, following the example of the Spaniards themselves, refused to acknowledge Joseph, but pledged their allegiance to the sole lawful heir to the Spanish crown, namely Ferdinand VII. Since, however, Ferdinand was a prisoner of Napoleon, someone must rule in his stead; the question of a regency at once assumed paramount importance.

It was at this juncture that Carlota Joaquina enters upon the scene. The great moment for the Spanish infanta had apparently arrived. As next heir to the Spanish throne during her brother's captivity, her claims to the regency could hardly be questioned. Ambition, family pride, and affection for Ferdinand were compelling reasons for her candidacy. Moreover, her husband, Dom João VI, after the tragi-comedy of Bayonne and the usurpation of the Spanish throne by Joseph Bonaparte, was the natural ally of the "prisoner king." For a time, therefore, he made common cause with the Spanish infanta and directed his ministers to act in accordance with her desires. But despite these ostensible acts in support of his wife's ambitious schemes, he never forgot that his primary obligation was to Portugal.

Dona Carlota was entitled by law to claim the regency and those elements in Spanish America which were incensed at the seizure of the Spanish throne by Napoleon began to look to her for guidance. Especially was this true in the viceroyalties of Buenos Aires and New Spain or Mexico. But in Spain itself, where the movement against the French was directed by a number of juntas acting under the *Junta Nacional de Sevilla,* Dona Carlota's candidacy evoked less enthusiasm, for the daughters of the thoroughly discredited Charles IV enjoyed little popularity. Moreover, the general trend of the public mind in Spain was in the direction of a constitutional monarchy, while the Bourbons were known to be wedded to the principles of absolutism. The reactionary views of the infanta were clearly revealed when, in 1808, shortly after the overthrow of the Bourbons, Buenos Aires sent an emissary to Rio to sound out the princess on the question of a constitutional regency, Dona Carlota not only expelled the envoy from the Portuguese court but denounced him as a rebel to the acting viceroy at Buenos Aires, Don Santiago de Liniers. As the reactionary and absolutist views of the infanta became better known the hopes which she had aroused in many of the inhabitants of Buenos Aires began to fade.

Nonetheless, there was a time when Dona Carlota might perhaps have been proclaimed regent had she presented herself in Buenos Aires. At the outset, Dom João had accorded his permission. Later, however, he withdrew his consent. What were the motives for his refusal? Three principal reasons may be suggested: the fear of the prince regent of being dethroned through the intrigues and hatred of his wife, the apprehensions of the Portuguese courtiers lest they fall a victim to the malicious designs of the infanta, and the tenacious opposition of Lord Strangford to a course which might adversely affect England's South American policy. In each of these reasons was an element of truth, but by all odds the most important was the British veto. Against this Portugal was really powerless. As far as Dom João was concerned, he was more than glad to make a virtue of necessity, for it was in accordance with his real feelings toward his wife.

Whatever hopes Dona Carlota herself may have had of being proclaimed regent at Buenos Aires were rudely dashed by the events of the year 1810, *el año diez* as South American historians call it. This year witnessed the critical point in the agitation for independence. From the Gulf of Mexico to Cape Horn, Spanish America experienced those premonitory tremors which eventually led to the collapse of Spain's mighty colonial empire. In Buenos Aires, the news of the French advance into the Peninsula and the defeat of the Spanish insurgents arrived on May 13. In the tense state of public opinion, this intelligence was sufficient to sever the bonds between the distracted mother country and its colony. On May 25—the birthday of Argentine independence—a great gathering of notables, assembled in the famous "Junta de Mayo," deposed the viceroy who had been appointed by the Spanish Council of Regency and took over the reins of authority themselves. Yet, by a curious anomaly, they kept up the fiction of union with Spain by protesting their loyalty to their "prisoner king," Ferdinand VII. It may be readily understood that the establishment of the "Junta de Mayo" sounded the death knell to the hopes of Dona Carlota Joaquina. To be sure, not all of the viceroyalty of Buenos Aires cut loose from its old moorings. Two provinces—

Paraguay and the Banda Oriental del Uruguay—for a time remained faithful to the Spanish authorities. The former, isolated in the very heart of southern South America, managed to gain its independence, both of Spain and Buenos Aires, in 1811. The latter for a time stood out against Buenos Aires and kept in touch with the infanta.

Though Dom João was not sympathetic, as we have seen, to Dona Carlota Joaquina's dynastic plans, he was not at all unwilling to extend Portuguese sway southward to the Río de la Plata. In order to meet the opposition of Lord Strangford, he was careful to disclaim any intention of furthering the infanta's plan of reestablishing her brother's authority. Rather did he shape his course in accordance with the traditional policy of Portugal, with a view to making the Paraná River and the estuary of La Plata the natural frontiers of Brazil. In so doing, he showed once more that he had misunderstood England's position.

The Spanish system of trade monopoly with its colonies was naturally an obstacle to the development of Great Britain's policy of commercial expansion. Desirous of increasing its trade with Spanish America, Great Britain naturally favored the independence of the Spanish colonies. Its attitude toward Portugal and Portuguese America was of a different order. The Lusitanian kingdom was, in truth, more of a vassal than an ally and if, by successive enlargements, it grew in size and importance, the relations of suzerain and vassal might be altered to the disadvantge of England. Moreover, were Dona Carlota successful in her plans for a regency or were a new kingdom created for her in South America, an endeavor undoubtedly would be made to unite more closely the Spanish and Portuguese possessions in America through a system of matrimonial alliances. Thus, at some future date, the whole continent might conceivably be united into one huge empire. Such a consummation was obviously contrary to British interests.

The Portuguese regent was unable or willing to understand the reasons for British opposition to Portuguese expansion into the Platine territories and was not averse to taking advantage of the existing confusion to further his own dynastic and national interests. For the situation was in truth confusing. Buenos Aires, under an independent government, was now at war with Montevideo which had remained faithful to Spain. In the interests of her royal brother, Dona Carlota was endeavoring to assist with arms and supplies the city of Montevideo, which troops from Buenos Aires were already besieging. In these military operations Dom João saw, or pretended to see, a menace to the Brazilian captaincy of Rio Grande do Sul. In the summer of 1811 he ordered his army, under General Diogo de Souza, into the Banda Oriental, the present Republic of Uruguay. In these troublous times almost anything might happen: there was always a possibility that Portugal could extend its dominion southward to its so-called natural boundary, the Río de la Plata.

But the presence of Portuguese troops in the Banda Oriental was distasteful both to Buenos Aires and Montevideo. Accordingly, on October 20, 1811, the Porteño[3] authorities signed an armistice with the commander of the Spanish garrison at Montevideo and the siege was lifted. With the cessation of hostilities, Dom João no longer had any valid pretext for keeping his army in the Banda Oriental. As a result of pressure from various quarters, including that exerted by Lord Strangford, he was induced to agree to the Rademaker-Herrera Treaty of May 26, 1812, which provided for the retirement of the Portuguese forces to their own territory.

But Dom João was only waiting for a more favorable juncture in order once more to gratify his imperialistic ambitions at the expense of his Spanish-speaking neighbors to the south. The opportunity came in 1816. Events had moved rapidly in the former Spanish viceroyalty of Buenos Aires during the intervening four years. Ferdinand VII had returned to the throne and it was obvious that the fiction of allegiance to a "prisoner king" had come to an end. Accordingly, the Argentines—as we may now call them by way of anticipation—proclaimed the complete independence of their country at the Congress of Tucumán in 1816 under the high-sounding title of the United Provinces of the Río de la Plata. In their desire to include within their control all of the old viceroyalty of Buenos Aires, they came into collision with the Uruguayan *caudillo*, José Artigas, who was endeavoring to free the Banda Oriental from dependence on both Buenos Aires and Spain. He had gained possession of Montevideo as early as Febru-

---

[3] The name given to an inhabitant of Buenos Aires, "The Port" (*Puerto*). —P.A.M.

ary, 1815, and set about vigorously to organize the territory under his control.

The activities of Artigas played directly into the hands of the Portuguese. Dom João, eager as ever to find pretexts for the invasion of Uruguay, could point to the recurrent disorders along the frontier and the attempt of Artigas to bring under his control the so-called "Seven Missions" which the Portuguese considered as forming a part of Rio Grande do Sul. But the real motive of the Portuguese sovereign was to further his imperialistic aims and to attempt once more to extend his dominion southward to the Río de la Plata. Having been assured by the Argentines that they would remain passive spectators in the coming struggle with Artigas, he threw a powerful army under General Lecor, Baron of Laguna, into the Banda Oriental. Artigas was in no position successfully to cope with these seasoned Portuguese troops and on January 20, 1817, Lecor's army made its triumphant entry into Montevideo. By cajolery, flattery, and in some cases bribery, the Montevideans were induced to vote in 1821 in favor of the incorporation of the Banda Oriental into Brazil, the annexed area to be known as the "Cis-Platine Province." In consenting to this step, many of the Uruguayans doubtless felt they were but making a virtue of necessity. Lecor's army was apparently all-powerful. The Argentines had seemingly left them to their fate. Artigas, their great *caudillo* leader, was a fugitive in Paraguay. Yet, morally, this vote was worthless since it had been extorted from a defeated people under the pressure of a foreign army. Nonetheless, it supplied Dom João with a juridical title which lent a certain fictitious legality to this act of spoliation. Dona Carlota Joaquina, now forgotten, had neither part nor lot in this seizure of former Spanish territory. As for England, that country remained silent, biding its time— an attitude little calculated to encourage Portugal in its imperialistic designs.

While these events were taking place the political situation in Europe had undergone momentous changes. Napoleon had been vanquished in 1814. Ferdinand VII now occupied the Spanish throne; he was a typical Bourbon in that during his exile he had learned nothing and forgotten nothing. With his absolutist views unchanged, he determined to combat liberalism wherever he found it and to stamp out ruthlessly the revolt in his American colonies.

Naturally, such an attitude made further revolutions inevitable.

The Congress of Vienna met in 1815. It attempted to settle not only the affairs of Europe but those of South America as well. Brazil was raised in 1815 to the category of a kingdom, on the same level as Portugal, and its frontiers were fixed not only with Spanish South America but also with the French colony of Guiana, which had been temporarily occupied by the troops of Dom João. The slave trade, condemned theoretically by all nations in a grandiloquent manifesto, was now being hard pressed from all sides. Great Britain, in its desire to suppress the traffic, had recourse to methods more and more energetic and violent, a fact which boded no good for Anglo-Brazilian relations. But before this controversy over the slave trade had reached an acute stage, a series of changes occurred which completely altered the status of Brazil and presently led to its complete independence from Portugal. To a consideration of these changes we now address ourselves.

The Return of Dom João to Lisbon.—The elevation of Brazil in 1815 to the status of a kingdom had been ill-received in Portugal, and especially in Lisbon. The prolonged sojourn of Dom João in America had aroused increasing discontent and indignation. The old metropolis could not forget that Brazil had once been a colony over which the mother country exercised undisputed sway. But now, alas, the rôles were reversed, for the capital of the Lusitanian empire was not Lisbon but Rio de Janeiro. As for the king[4] himself, his plight was truly a pitiable one. In Portugal he had lived an unhappy existence, keenly sensitive to the lack of affection of his subjects and a victim of his own cowardice. But in Brazil it was quite different. For the first time in his life he experienced a sentiment of devotion and genuine loyalty. The Brazilians were not ungrateful for the benefits which he had bestowed on the American portion of his domain. He would in fact have been quite content to end his days in Brazil. Well he knew what lay in wait for him in Portugal: cares and anxieties and ruthless conflicts of ambition, while in Rio was quiet, security, the love of his people. His unwillingness to leave is easily understood. Besides the very thought of crossing the sea again filled him with terror.

Not so Dona Carlota Joaquina. She was more than anxious

---

[4] In 1816 the demented queen-mother, Dona Maria, died and Dom João, who had hitherto acted as prince regent, became King Dom João VI.

to leave a country where, without real friends or partizans, she had never felt at ease. The whole milieu was uncongenial. Her attempts to intervene in the tangled affairs of La Plata had proved a fiasco. All her efforts and ambitions seemed thwarted. She could not even be a nuisance to her husband. *"Não é terra de gente,"* [5] she was wont to say. She wept when she landed; when it came time to depart she scandalized the Brazilians by her manifestations of immoderate joy.

In both sections of the Portuguese kingdom the dissatisfaction with existing conditions grew from day to day. Everywhere were premonitions of impending changes. In both Portugal and Brazil the conviction grew that the old absolutist system was ill-adapted to the nineteenth century; the demand for some kind of constitutional government became more and more insistent. The tension first reached the breaking point in 1817 in Pernambuco, where a revolutionary uprising led to the proclamation of a republic. The movement made such headway that for a time three of the northern captaincies were involved. But the rebellion proved premature; the country was still monarchial at heart, and the short-lived republic was crushed by loyal troops from the south.

But the first real breach in the structure of the absolutist monarchy came in Portugal. The existing discontent, to which allusion has already been made, found vent in the constitutionalist revolution which broke out in Oporto in 1820 and quickly spread to Lisbon. The news of this uprising aroused great satisfaction in Brazil. Though loyal to the Braganza dynasty, the Brazilians, like their brethren in Portugal, welcomed the idea of a constitutional régime, and were quite willing for a time to follow the lead of Lisbon. The various captaincies began to elect governing boards of juntas which took over the powers formerly exercised by the captains general. In some instances, when the existing authorities refused to relinquish control, force was applied, but no serious resistance was encountered. As a rule the new governing elements belonged to the most liberal groups of society; in certain cases, notably in Minas Geraes, the tendency was frankly republican, owing to the legacy of Tiradente's abortive conspiracy, the *Inconfidencia*.

Absolutism, however, had deep roots in Portugal. The constitutionalist elements, composed of an aggressive minority, realized

[5] "This is not a country for (civilized) people."

7

their danger. Obviously, a new constitution could not be prepared in a day; meanwhile, they were in danger of being routed by their opponents. To anticipate this menace, they invited the various authorities and persons of influence to take the oath of allegiance to the constitution yet to be elaborated; pending this consummation they adopted as a transitional measure the ultra-liberal Spanish Constitution of 1812. To this document it was also necessary to swear.

The example of the Portuguese constitutionalists was enthusiastically followed in Brazil. The heir apparent to the throne, Dom Pedro, was in the front rank of those who applauded the new turn of events. Not so the king. He hated and feared alike liberals, constitutionalists, republicans, and Freemasons, all of whom he confounded in the same class as "anarchists." But he did not have the courage to resist and *volens nolens*, he took oath to everything demanded of him, trembling in all his limbs, and in one instance fainting from sheer fright.

The most immediate and pressing task was the election of the deputies who were to represent Brazil in the constituent côrtes scheduled to meet at Lisbon. The general tenor of the instructions furnished the deputies may be summed up in the following points: absolute equality, both political and economic, of the two portions of the kingdom; parallel governmental organizations in Brazil and Portugal; alternation in the seat of the government between Lisbon and Rio de Janeiro. But among the Portuguese deputies, embittered and jealous after twelve years of Brazilian supremacy, such views were most unwelcome. The American deputies were rudely received when they entered the constituent cortes, their speeches were treated with ridicule, and their proposals were regarded with contempt. In thus refusing to consider the legitimate demands of their American colleagues, the shortsighted Portuguese deputies were paving the way for the definite and irremediable break between the two portions of the Lusitanian realm.

Meanwhile, Dom João's position was becoming more and more untenable. It was evident that if he expected to exercise any control over the constituent côrtes his return to Europe was imperative; his continued absence, according to his advisers, might bring a catastrophe upon his kingdom. England was particularly insistent upon his return to Europe and even sent a fleet to Rio to convey the king to Lisbon. He refused to return in this manner and invented one pretext after another to delay the voyage. He realized that, once he had left the hospitable shores of Brazil, his days of tranquillity and happiness were gone. His mind, too, was filled with misgivings regarding the future of Brazil, which he loved more than his native Portugal. He had sufficient prescience to grasp the fact that permanent union between the two parts of his kingdom, so disparate in the character of their inhabitants, prospects, and resources, was all but impossible. Too many forces of dissolution were at work and the king dimly sensed that the lusty offspring which had so far distanced its parents would sooner or later become an independent state.

The dreaded day of departure, April 26, 1821, at length arrived. While the queen ostentatiously showed her delight at leaving Brazil the king wept bitterly. He was particularly affected by the parting with his son and heir apparent, Dom Pedro, whom he left as regent. Just before embarking he warned him of the grave changes which he realized the next few months might bring forth. He added that should events turn out as he anticipated and the separation of Brazil from Portugal become inevitable Dom Pedro should place himself at the head of the movement for independence. By such means Brazil might peacefully continue its monarchical evolution as a projection of a greater Portugal under the aegis of the Braganza dynasty.

CHAPTER IV

THE INDEPENDENCE OF BRAZIL; ITS RECOGNITION BY THE "COMITAS GENTIUM"

Dom Pedro.—Who was this new ruler on whose shoulders was to rest the government of the kingdom of Brazil? In 1821, Dom Pedro was twenty-four years of age. He was handsome, bold, inured to hardship, and adept in all sports, a marvelous horseman. He had inherited his mother's devotion to ideals and friendships. He was subject to impulses. He could rise to heights of generosity and heroism, but was quite capable of falling into the opposite extremes. He was clever and intelligent and knew instinctively much more than was suspected by those with whom he conversed. European diplomats, in dealing with him, found him in knowledge of international affairs far superior to all of his advisers with the single exception of Marshal Brant.[1] He possessed a sense of reality and his judgment was good when not influenced by unworthy companions. Frank to the point of rudeness, faithful to his word and loyal to his supporters—as long as they enjoyed his confidence—he was prone to accord undue attention to stories of plots and intrigues against himself. He also lent a too ready ear to accusations against even his most devoted supporters. As a consequence, he could not always be relied upon when it came to carrying out a policy requiring coöperation and mutual concessions.

Dom Pedro was Dom João's favorite son; at all times he was on most intimate terms with his father to whom he was always loyal and devoted. Dona Carlota did not cherish him but centered her affections on her second son, Dom Miguel. Dom Pedro received almost no formal education. He grew up among the servants and hangers-on of the palace. These he dominated by his rank but was in turn ruled by them through flattery and servility. Much of the time he lived in an atmosphere of secret and cowardly accusations and despicable intrigues. In time he came to like these malapert and low-lived fellows who catered to his fancies and

[1] Felisberto Caldeira Brant Pontes, later Marquis of Barbacena, one of Dom Pedro's most able diplomats.—P.A.M.

whims, especially such as found expression in adventures and brawls. As a consequence of his dissolute life and degraded companions he was ill-bred, coarse, and rude, addicted to low jests and practical jokes. These dissolute habits, acquired during his youth, involved him in many disagreeable episodes and eventually contributed to the loss of the respect and esteem of his subjects.

The shortcomings of the young prince, though deplorable, could not obscure his noble qualities. In many of the great crises which he had to meet during the next few years he showed himself to be chivalrous, self-denying, and generous. Happily for himself and Brazil he was a true liberal in the political sense of the term. But brought up in an ambient of absolutism he did not always know how to prove his liberalism. Frequently, he had to choose between his autocratic impulses and his intellectual belief in constitutional rules. This permanent psychological conflict between tendencies and inheritances explains the contradictions and incoherences of his short life of thirty-six years.

Dona Leopoldina.—The wife of Dom Pedro, Dona Leopoldina, was an Austrian archduchess. Although married to Dom Pedro for dynastic reasons, she loved her husband, who, however, was too inconstant fully to requite her affection. In the difficult days ahead she proved, in all matters of state, a devoted collaborator with her husband. This was true both in Brazil and in Europe. Thanks to her father, Emperor Francis I, she was able to make her influence felt in the intimate court and political circles of Vienna. When one recalls the power wielded by the Austrian chancellor, Metternich, the advantage of these connections needs no stressing. In Brazil, to whose independence she directly contributed, her memory is still held in gratitude and affection.

The princess lacked many of those feminine traits which appealed to a man of the type of Dom Pedro. Herself plain in appearance she took little interest in personal adornment. Rather did her predilections lie in the fields of science and she became something of a botanist and geologist. She delighted in riding fiery horses and in taking long rides in the open country. Her charity and kindliness toward those in need were proverbial. On her arrival in Brazil, she felt ill at ease and longed to return to Europe. But as she came to know the Brazilians better and to appreciate their nobler qualities, particularly their desire for freedom and independence from Portugal, she began to love her people and identified herself with them.

The Dawn of Independence.—Meanwhile, tension between Portugal and Brazil steadily grew. The constituent côrtes showed little understanding of or sympathy with the aspirations of the Brazilians. Envious of the development which the former colony had made during Dom João's sojourn in America, it adopted the suicidal course of trying to reduce Brazil to its former status of complete dependence on the metropolis. In pursuance of this policy, the côrtes set about to revoke the various acts which had made possible the progress of Brazil during the preceding decade and a half. This meant in effect the recolonization of Brazil and in some cases the destruction of institutions which had become an integral part of the life of the country. The Brazilian deputies, as we have already seen, were coldly received and their protests and initiatives were disregarded. As news of the supercilious and even hostile attitude of the côrtes reached Brazil it naturally aroused impatience and resentment. These sentiments were greatly intensified when the côrtes committed the blunder of ordering Dom Pedro to return to Europe "in order that he might complete his political education." The real purpose behind this demand was to deprive the Brazilians of a leader to whom they might turn in their hour of need and who might eventually place himself at the head of a movement for independence.

The policy of the côrtes naturally aroused resentment in the heart of the regent. Dom Pedro was the eldest son of Dom João VI. During the latter years of his father's sojourn in Brazil he had indirectly shared in the government of the realm. And now he was treated as a mere boy and taunted with his alleged lack of political maturity. The bitterness and hurt pride of Dom Pedro are clearly shown in the correspondence which he exchanged at this time with his father. He pointed out the stupidity of the members of the côrtes in shutting their eyes to the growth in importance and influence of Brazil in comparison with Portugal. He dwelt on the growing dissatisfaction with the course of events in Portugal and stressed the mounting agitation in favor of independence without or with the coöperation of the regent. Nor did he ignore the wiles and plots of the extremists bent on setting up a republic.

But what could the king do to prepare for the approaching storm? He was terrorized by the liberals whose slightest wishes and demands he obeyed. He trembled for his life and for the poor shreds of power and rank which still remained to him. To all that the côrtes voted or ordered he lent his approval, even though it ran counter to his inmost convictions. He was closely spied upon, his correspondence was violated or confiscated, each act and word was subjected to an implacable and hostile censorship. As a monarch he was less than nothing.

Difficulties of the Regent, Dom Pedro. Organization of the Independence Movement.—Though the life of Dom Pedro was becoming more and more intolerable, he followed the dictates of prudence and forebore showing any resentment at the taunts and insults heaped upon him by certain Portuguese elements both in Europe and in Rio de Janeiro. But as the months passed the situation began gradually to clarify and Dom Pedro came to envision the emancipation of Brazil as a duty which he eventually would be called upon to perform. In reaching this conclusion he was swayed by both patriotic and dynastic motives. Freedom for Brazil sooner or later was inevitable; and it would be consummated with or without his assistance. In case he stood aside and let events take their course, disintegration, pure and simple, was bound to follow. The alternative was to guide Brazil across the uncharted sea into the safe harbor of independence. The glory which comes to the founders of empires might be his; such at least was his dream. But when confronted with the hard reality of events he wavered and finally made public his intention to obey the orders of the côrtes and return to Lisbon. But happily for him, his wife, Dona Leopoldina, saw the political situation with greater clarity and persuaded him to resist. She could hardly have rendered her adopted country a greater service.

Meanwhile, all of the provinces of the south—Minas Geraes, Rio, São Paulo, Rio Grande do Sul, and Santa Catharina—were in a state of ferment. The heart of the kingdom, Rio de Janeiro, throbbed with patriotic fever. Everywhere one thought dominated, one phrase was on the lips of all—Brazil must not lose what had been won. When it came, however, to translating these hopes into realities, difficulties arose. But, whatever the obstacles, the tide of patriotic exaltation was not allowed to ebb. Messengers went up and down the country to keep alive the spirit of autonomy and to arouse even greater enthusiasm. In this campaign the Masonic Order played a prominent part. Among the Masons who especially distinguished themselves were Joaquim Gonçalves Lédo, José Clemente Pereira, Canon Januario de Cunha Barbosa, José Joaquin da Rocha. In addition to this secret organization an important place must be accorded to the *Associação Philotechnica*, a sort of scientific academy, whose guiding spirit was José Sylvestre Rebello, later the first Brazilian minister to the United States.

The chief aim of these organizations was to prevent the departure of the regent for Lisbon. Dom Pedro was besieged from many quarters. From Portugal itself, from the circle of Dom João's intimate friends, the prince regent received confidential advices to remain in Rio and thus save the king, Portugal, Brazil, and himself. Dom Pedro's mind was naturally receptive to such counsels, to which were added those of similar tenor from Dona Leopoldina, and he was gradually approaching a definite decision. But he was unwilling to commit himself irrevocably until he had sounded out the prevailing sentiments of the two great provinces of Minas Geraes and São Paulo. Emissaries were therefore hastily despatched to these provinces in order to collect petitions begging the prince to remain in Brazil. The results exceeded all expectations. These documents, signed by persons of all ranks, including the public authorities, revealed an enthusiastic loyalty to the prince and a practically unanimous opposition to his departure. The only abstentions were in a few municipalities in Minas Geraes where republican ideas, harking back to the days of Tiradentes, still prevailed.

Such an appeal, reflecting as it did virtually all shades of public opinion, admitted neither refusal nor denial. On January 9, 1822, Dom Pedro informed the municipality of Rio de Janeiro, which on this occasion was regarded as the spokesman for the whole country, that "for the good of all and for the general happiness of the nation" he would remain in Brazil. This is the famous *"Fico,"* [2] looked upon by the Brazilians as one of the most memorable events in their national annals. And, in truth, it was a turning point in their history. The Brazilian nation, for the first time articulate, declared its opposition to the unjust demands of a metropolis

[2] Literally "I remain."—P.A.M.

which had arrogated to itself powers it no longer possessed. Independence was in sight; the opening gun in the struggle for freedom had been fired.

The Revolt of the Portuguese Garrison in Rio.—Many obstacles still blocked the path to complete independence. One of these was the Portuguese garrison, amounting to 1,600 troops, stationed in the capital. On learning of Dom Pedro's decision to remain in Brazil, the troops rose in mutiny against the regent in order to enforce the decree of the côrtes and oblige him to embark for Lisbon. From their point of view, their attitude was correct and lawful since the côrtes constituted the highest legal authority in Portugal. But such authority the Brazilians were no longer disposed to recognize. Without perhaps fully perceiving all the implications of the change, the Brazilians had in fact ceased to be Portuguese and behaved accordingly. Acting in concert the population of Rio brought such pressure to bear on the Lusitanian regiments that they were forced to seek temporary shelter on the opposite shores of the harbor. Here besieged and threatened by the artillery, which on Dom Pedro's orders was trained upon them, they agreed to embark and sail to Lisbon though not until nearly a third of their number had deserted to the Brazilians. In mid-ocean they fell in with reënforcements sent by the côrtes to augment the garrison at Rio but these forces were not permitted to disembark and returned to Europe in the same vessels that had brought them.

José Bonifacio.—Events now began to progress at a more rapid tempo. As the first result of his resolution to remain in Brazil, Dom Pedro found himself obliged to choose a ministry, recruited in part from Brazilians in order that these latter might assume their due share of responsibility in the new order. The all-important choice was of course the head of the ministry. Only one who could inspire universal respect and silence undue criticism would be acceptable. In this national emergency, it was agreed both by the regent and the people at large that but one choice was possible, that of José Bonifacio de Andrada e Silva.[3] who was to be known to posterity as the "Patriarch of Brazilian Independence."

Born in Santos of old and honored stock José Bonifacio had

---

[3] See Paul Vanorden Shaw, "José Bonifacio and Brazilian History," in *The Hispanic American Historical Review,* VIII (November, 1928), 527-50.—J.A.R.

received his higher education in the celebrated University of Coimbra. So outstanding were his scholastic attainments that he was appointed professor at Coimbra and secretary of the Scientific Academy of Lisbon. An eminent savant, known and respected in the cultured circles of Europe, he had travelled in almost all of the countries of the Old World and had established personal relationships with its most noted scientists. At two different times, in 1816 and in 1820, his name had been mentioned for important governmental commissions in Brazil. On the first occasion the regency at Lisbon would not permit his departure from Portugal; on the second he himself refused the nomination. But the situation changed radically after the revolution in Portugal in 1820. When juntas were established throughout Brazil in the place of the former captains general, José Bonifacio was elected vice president of the junta of São Paulo and his brother, Martim Francisco Ribeiro de Andrada was appointed secretary of finance. When the various juntas were circularized by Rio on the question of obedience to the anti-Brazilian decrees of the côrtes, São Paulo counselled refusal. The vigorous terms in which this reply was drawn up have been attributed to José Bonifacio himself.

On the difficult problem of the future relationship between Portugal and Brazil his own opinion inclined toward the creation of a dual monarchy, with Portugal and Brazil enjoying the same rights and powers; this is clearly evidenced by the instructions furnished the Paulista deputies to the constituent côrtes of Lisbon. But political conditions were changing with such rapidity that he no longer eyed with suspicion full and complete independence; in fact this might prove the final and acceptable solution.

In the ministry of January 16, 1822,[4] José Bonifacio was undoubtedly the outstanding figure. As events unfolded he revealed the qualities of an organizer, a leader, and a statesman. While not perhaps the first to broach the idea of independence, it fell to his lot to be the founder or, if one wishes, the brains of the movement, first championed on sentimental grounds by the Freemasons of Rio, and later carried forward by the regent and his partisans in the provinces of São Paulo, Minas Geraes, and Rio de Janeiro. In the

---

[4] Brazilian historians are wont to identify ministries by the dates on which they are organized. As frequently the year is omitted this method sometimes results in obscurities.—P.A.M.

final instance, a discussion as to whom belong the exact priority
in the establishment of independence is rather futile. The idea was
in the air, and the country at large, thanks to its progress and
aspiration for better things, was eager for freedom. Not the least
of the merits of José Bonifacio was the fact that he sensed this
national aspiration and was willing and able to take the responsibility of guiding the movement to a successful issue.

Yet he was quick to notice its weak points. For its triumph,
unanimity was essential and Minas Geraes, because of its republican sympathies, might compromise the victory. Even São Paulo
was not without its hostile elements and between the provinces of
the interior and those of the littoral relations were tense. In the
province of Bahia, the capital, São Salvador, was occupied by
Portuguese garrisons which, however, were besieged by the sur-
rounding country in arms. The northern provinces, Maranhão and
Pará farthest from Rio and closest to Portugal, were wavering in
their allegiance to the regent.

At this juncture of events, the suggestion was broached that
there be created a council of representatives (*procuradores*) of
the various provinces of Brazil and on February 16, 1822, Dom
Pedro signed a decree to this effect. The functions of this body
were to be purely advisory and consultative. The provinces in the
south quickly rallied to the idea and appointed their representatives; this was also true of the northern province of Parahyba.
As for the other provinces in the north, Ceará approved of the
council but failed to appoint any members, while Alagoas, Bahia,
Pernambuco, and Maranhão opposed the project.

In March, Dom Pedro undertook a journey through Minas
Geraes. His object was to place himself in contact with the leading
men, to allay their apprehensions in regard to his own plans, to
wean them from their republican views and in general to bring
Minas Geraes into line with the other provinces which supported
the prince regent and favored the independence of Brazil under
the aegis of the Braganza dynasty. The tour proved eminently successful. The regent was greeted with all but universal acclaim and
the loyalty of Minas Geraes seemed definitely assured.

On the initiative of the Freemasons a movement was now launched
to offer Dom Pedro the title of "Perpetual Defender of Brazil."
The regent accepted this title on May 13, the birthday of Dom

João VI. This symbolic act drew still closer the bonds between Dom Pedro and the Brazilians and could well be regarded as an earnest of complete independence from Portugal. Indicative of the new spirit astir was the proposal of Rio Grande do Sul and Ceará that Dom Pedro summon a constituent assembly; the prince replied that he deemed it wiser to wait until the representatives of the various provinces had assembled in order that the opinion of the entire nation might be made manifest. But the Brazilians were in no mood to brook delay when the fate of the whole nation seemed to be at stake. Such was the general anxiety that when three of the provincial representatives—those from Rio and the Cisplatina—had reached the capital, they went into session without waiting for their colleagues and on June 2, 1822, passed a motion urging the regent to summon a constituent assembly. This motion coincided with the wishes of Dom Pedro and the appropriate decree was signed the following day. This was in reality the decisive act in the long process culminating in the separation of Brazil from Portugal. But one step yet remained to be taken; the proclamation of independence.

The news which now reached Brazil from overseas was well calculated to sever the last thread which united the two parts of the Portuguese-speaking world. The côrtes continued its imprudent and provocative attitude toward Brazil. The American deputies were more and more sneered at, insulted, and scorned. When they pointed out the inevitable consequences of the recolonizing measures on which the côrtes was so insistent, the deputies of the former metropolis merely replied: *"Passe muito bem, Senhor Brasil."* [5]

The meeting of the *procuradores* or representatives of the provinces was regarded as an act of rebellion and was promptly revoked by Lisbon. The resistance of Bahia evoked high praise in Portugal and plans were made to send reënforcements. The ministers of Dom Pedro were to be judged in court and henceforth were to be appointed not by the regent but by the Portuguese government. Orders were issued for the accusation and trial of the members of the junta of São Paulo and various others who had defied the commands of the côrtes. As early as August 28, inti-

---

[5] This phrase is translated by Dr. Calogeras as "Fare you well, Mr. Brazil."
—P.A.M.

mations of the tenor of these decrees reached Brazil although the official notification did not arrive until later.

Independence or Death.—Dom Pedro was at this time engaged in a tour through the province of São Paulo similar in purpose to the one undertaken in Minas Geraes earlier in the year. On the arrival of the latest despatches from Lisbon the ministry, under the presidency of Dona Leopoldina, assembled immediately. It was unanimously agreed that the attitude of the côrtes meant nothing less than war. A special envoy carrying the most recent despatches was at once sent to the prince. He was found at Ypiranga, in the vicinity of São Paulo, on September 7, 1822. Dom Pedro seized the despatches, glanced through their contents and at once realized that the time for action had arrived. Waving his hat in the air he shouted "Independence or death." In this dramatic gesture he interpreted the deepest sentiments of the overwhelming majority of the Brazilians; not without reason was September 7 henceforth observed as the birthday of the Brazilian nation.

As has already been suggested, the Freemasons of Brazil had played a not unimportant rôle in the events leading up to the definite break with Portugal. Reference to a few dates constitutes eloquent proof of the intimate collaboration between the Masonic Order and its leaders on the one hand and Dom Pedro and his ministry on the other. As early as August 2, 1822, the prince had been initiated into the Order; shortly afterward he was raised to the rank of grand master, though he did not assume the functions of his new office until his return from São Paulo on September 14. On August 20, the Grand Orient proclaimed, on the motion of Lédo,[6] that the time for the definite and complete separation from Portugal had arrived. The ministers of Dom Pedro resolved to publish two manifestos, one to the nation, the other to the foreign governments. The drawing up of the first was entrusted to Lédo and that of the second to José Bonifacio. Both set forth the reasons why Dom Pedro had decided to remain in Rio de Janeiro and assume the title of "Perpetual Defender of Brazil." Three days later the members of the Grand Orient not only formally adopted the

---

[6] Joaquim Gonçalves Lédo, a prominent Mason, one of the most enthusiastic champions of independence, and director of the patriotic newspaper *O Reverbéro.*—P.A.M.

motion of Lédo but voted that measures should be taken to make it effective throughout the provinces.

The formal acceptance by Dom Pedro of the title of "Constitutional Emperor of Brazil" followed by his solemn coronation, though essential and important, were in reality mere consequences of the declaration of September 7. It is to be noted in this connection that the term empire (*imperio*) in place of kingdom (*reino*) was chosen to indicate the dual source of authority to be wielded by the ruler of Brazil, namely hereditary right and popular choice. Regarding the validity of the second of these sources of power, there could be no possible doubt: the entire nation was stirred to its depths by a great wave of patriotic enthusiasm without precedent in the history of Brazil.

Yet the acclamations were not absolutely unanimous; there were still a number of rifts in the lute of national harmony. The capital of Bahia was still in the hands of Portuguese troops under General Madeira; Pará and Maranhão were still hesitating with an aggressive minority in favor of the côrtes. In the summer of 1822, arms and troops were despatched from Rio to Bahia under General Pedro Labatut who was succeeded later by Colonel Lima e Silva. After an investment extending over twelve months the Portuguese troops were forced, on July 2, 1823, to reëmbark on the fleet anchored in the harbor, and to return to Lisbon. Lord Cochrane, who after distinguished service under the government of Chile had found employment in Brazil, forced the Portuguese garrisons out of the remaining northern provinces. By September, 1823, his mission had been crowned with complete success.

The war of independence in Spanish America had lasted fifteen years; the independence of Brazil was won in as many months. And while Spain's American empire broke into fragments the integrity of Brazil was preserved. This fortunate outcome in the case of Brazil was due chiefly to the transference of the seat of the Braganza dynasty and the Portuguese court to America, to the raising of the former colony to the status of a kingdom, to the decision of Dom Pedro to remain in Brazil and place himself at the head of the independence movement, to the prescience and energy of the statesman, José Bonifacio, and to the consummate skill of Admiral Cochrane. But in almost equal measure, the achievement of independence was owing to the weakness of Portugal, to

the gratuitous taunts and provocation addressed to Brazil, and
to Portugal's ignorance regarding the real conditions of its former
colony, already far superior to the power and wealth of its former
metropolis.

Curiously enough, the last bulwark of Portuguese power in
America proved to be in Montevideo, the capital of the so-called
Cisplatine province. As a consequence of the events which took
place in Rio and São Paulo in 1822, the Portuguese in Montevideo
were divided into two factions, the so-called "Imperialists," or
partisans of the new empire under Dom Pedro I and the "Lusitan-
ians," or those who remained faithful to Lisbon. The former were
strongest in the countryside while the latter, supported by the
cabildo or municipal government, remained in control of Montevideo. The two factions soon came to blows and the "Imperialists"
proceeded to lay siege to the capital. At length, after an investment
of seventeen months, the Portuguese troops, on the orders of the
côrtes, agreed to evacuate the city and return to Lisbon. As a matter of fact the garrison had been so weakened by desertion that
surrender was sooner or later inevitable. With the retirement of
the Portuguese forces from Montevideo on February 28, 1824, no
more foreign troops were to be found on Brazilian soil.

Internal Difficulties Confronting the New Régime.—The Brazilians had freed themselves from the menace of Portuguese control; they now had to face even graver problems of internal reorganization. The burden of government which Dom Pedro's
ministry had to face was all but crushing. Nominally, it was borne
by José Bonifacio and his colleagues; actually, the "Patriarch
of Independence" had to shoulder most of the burden himself. Difficulties of all kinds soon arose. Friction and absence of harmony,
owing to the lack of experience of the ministers and sensitiveness
of the emperor when his own prerogatives were in question, were
perhaps inevitable but it cannot be denied that the vanity and
vindictive spirit of José Bonifacio greatly aggravated the situation. He could not tolerate the criticism of which he was the object
in the Masonic lodges and those who dissented from his own opinions he regarded as his personal enemies. In the case of the emperor,
the affectionate and respectful intercourse of the first days had
given place to suspicion and distruct. José Bonifacio had persuaded
Dom Pedro to exile Lédo, one of the first if not the very first

pioneers of independence, and this remarkable man had barely escaped this affront by fleeing to Buenos Aires. New excesses against his political opponents made continuance of José Bonifacio in the government impossible and on July 12, 1823, he and his brothers tendered their resignation.

Meanwhile, the decree of June 3, 1822, had been put into execution and the constituent assembly had been duly elected. Its first meeting was held on April 17, 1823. Among the deputies were the three Andrada brothers, José Bonifacio, Martim Francisco, and Antonio Carlos. After José Bonifacio's dismissal, the Andradas naturally went into opposition and both in the press and in the assembly carried on an unremitting and at times vicious series of attacks on the government. The English writer, John Armitage, in his famous *History of Brazil* does not hesitate to qualify the opposition of the Andradas as "factious." And it must be admitted that the atmosphere and composition of the assembly particularly favored such attacks.

The first general election in Brazil had sent to Rio de Janeiro a motley crowd of jurists, high dignitaries of the church, country priests, and landed proprietors. Their administrative competence was nil while their capacity for understanding or carrying out the technique of parliamentary procedure was little better. Only a few of the deputies felt at ease in this strange milieu. The majority had inflated notions regarding their own ability and looked down with supercilious condescension on the officials of the government. In this unfortunate attitude was reflected the influence, still persisting, of the abortive conspiracy of Tiradentes and the revolution of 1817 of Pernambuco. Parenthetically it may be noted that this same revolutionary spirit was to flare up again in 1824 in the so-called "Confederation of the Equator," a secessionist movement embracing Pernambuco and adjoining provinces. Although of relatively little importance in the broad sweep of Brazilian history, the revolt occasioned the government considerable embarrassment in its negotiations, then in progress in London, for the recognition of the independence of the Brazilian Empire by Portugal. The suppression of this revolt also proved to be a task of some difficulty.

The Dissolution of the Constituent Assembly. The Granting of the Constitution of 1824.—The slender capacities and lack of experience of the members of the constituent assembly have already been touched upon. While they constituted real obstacles to any constructive achievements, the principal reason for the failure of this body was the deep and bitter antagonism between the ultra-patriotic Brazilians and those who were accused of being in sympathy with Portugal. So high did passions run that some of the foremost champions of Brazilian independence, including Dom Pedro I, were taunted with subservience to Portuguese interests. It is a regrettable fact that the followers of the Andrada brothers were involved in this campaign of villification. The situation, in fact, became so tense that the slightest incident might have caused an explosion. The match which ignited the powder train was finally lighted by an unreasonable attack upon the government for having refused to punish a number of officers who had chastised one of their detractors. Smarting under these insults the officers protested; the emperor sided with them, and deeply wounded in his noble intentions, he ordered the dissolution of the assembly on November 12, 1823. At the same time, he promised to prepare and grant a genuinely liberal constitution. The promise was brilliantly fulfilled and the new constitution, that of March 25, 1834, proved itself to be a monument of political liberalism and well-balanced powers.

Steps Toward the Recognition of the Empire.—After the despatch to the European courts of the August manifesto, José Bonifacio had done little to maintain contacts with foreign governments. Such steps, however, as he took were designed to pave the way for the ultimate recognition of the independence of Brazil. With the official title of consul, but in reality in the capacity of a secret political agent, Correira da Camara was sent to Buenos Aires and Marshal Felisberto Caldeira Brant Pontes, then in London, was accredited as chargé d'affaires. It was also planned to send diplomatic agents of the same category to Paris and Washington. But since these moves were made solely on behalf of Brazil, it was evident that the appointments would become void once independence was proclaimed and the status of the kingdom raised to that of an empire.

An additional word should be said in regard to Brant's activities in Great Britain in 1822. As early as 1805 he had come in contact with the English as a result of certain services he was able to render the naval squadron of Sir Home Popham at Bahia. In this way he came in touch with George Canning, the British secretary of state,

and won his confidence and esteem. The object of his mission in
1822 was to enlist soldiers, to purchase steamers, and to foster a
policy of greater intimacy between the two countries. But unfortunately he was left by the Rio government without either funds or
adequate powers to act. Although Brant drew on his own resources
for his expenses, in the absence of official documents he could accomplish very little.

Influenced by his Austrian marriage, Dom Pedro had sent to
Vienna in 1822 his intimate friend Antonio Telles da Silva Caminha,
whom he later created Marquis of Rezende, on a confidential mission
to explain to his father-in-law, Francis I, as well as to Metternich
the events which had led to the proclamation of independence.
The fact that Silva Caminha had many relatives in the court of
Vienna naturally facilitated his mission.

The Rio government not unnaturally assumed that England
would be unfriendly to the new Brazilian nation because of the
long-standing treaties with Portugal, and it feared also that the
Holy Alliance might intervene in the conflict. The first supposition
turned out to be inexact and the second only partly true since
Austria, largely for dynastic reasons, showed itself friendly to the
new trans-Atlantic empire.

Canning was too well aware of British sentiment and the demands of British trade to oppose the emergence of the new states
of Central and South America. Such areas would constitute valuable markets, open to Great Britain if they were free, closed if they
remained under the monopolistic control of Spain or Portugal.
The English secretary of state was also considering the possibility
of restricting the slave trade through direct agreement with Brazil. But there was no one in London with whom he could negotiate.
He accordingly persuaded Brant to return to Rio in order to
establish contact between the two governments.

He even went further. Lord Amherst, recently appointed viceroy
of India, was about to set sail for Asia in order to take over his
new post. He received orders to pass via Brazil and inform the
de facto government there established that it would be possible for
Great Britain to recognize it, despite Portuguese opposition, if the
new empire were disposed to put an end to the slave trade. Unhappily the special conditions of the country made it impossible
for Dom Pedro and José Bonifacio to accept such a proposal,

however much their personal views might incline in that direction. The matter, therefore, went no further.

Canning, meanwhile, had loyally though confidentially informed Portugal that England was equally a friend of both countries, and that, if the existing tension should eventuate in hostilities between them, the government of His Britannic Majesty would observe a strict neutrality. If, on the other hand, Portugal were disposed to accept the new state of things His Majesty would be happy to coöperate in reaching an agreement agreeable to both parties—all of which reveals the extent to which Great Britain was endeavoring to work on behalf of Brazil and its independence even before the new Brazilian empire had taken any definite steps looking to British recognition.

Great changes were meanwhile taking place in Portugal. The côrtes had become intolerable. The "absolutists," taking their cue from Dona Carlota Joaquina and her son Dom Miguel, launched in February, 1823, a revolution against the now thoroughly hated liberals and against the poor king himself who was accused of being favorable to the côrtes, when in reality he was only its miserable and frightened victim, or to be more exact, its prisoner. In May, the queen and the infante placed themselves publicly at the head of the movement. Dom João, opportunely warned by his friend the Marquis of Loulé, made common cause with the revolution and in this manner was able to preserve his throne. By June the côrtes hed ceased to exist, and its disappearance, far from causing regret, was hailed with satisfaction. The general opinion regarding Brazil was that the separation from the mother country and the proclamation of the empire were merely consequences of the insensate and criminal policy of the constituent côrtes. With the dissolution of this body the results of its actions would likewise disappear and everything would return to its former happy state.

Possibly the king knew better and had some real understanding of the true course of events in Brazil. But as usual he followed the line of least resistance and offered no opposition to the despatch of a "mission of pacification" to Rio. And yet, who knows? Perhaps, after all, something might come of it. Thus with great secrecy was organized and sent to America a political mission headed by the Count of Rio Maior. One of its members, Marshal Luis Paulino, arrived in Bahia sometime before his colleagues reached Brazil. He was detained while the papers which he carried were sent on to Rio. They reached the capital on September 7, 1823, and were promptly turned over by Dom Pedro to the constituent assembly. Arriving as they did when the opposition to Dom Pedro was especially rabid they created an immense sensation. Luis Paulino, who had at length appeared at Rio, was asked if he was authorized to recognize the empire. He replied that he was ignorant of the tenor of the instructions of Rio Maior and that it was necessary to wait for the arrival of the chief emissary whose ship did not enter the harbor until September 20. In response to the query already addressed to Luis Paulino, Rio Maior replied in the negative; he carried no such authorization. Whereupon, the vessel on which he had come was sequestered and the whole mission was obliged to embark on the next packet and sail for Portugal. Such violence was quite unnecessary and redounded to the discredit of Brazil. The government, however, had yielded to popular passion and an overexcited parliament; it was necessary to make concessions to those who had accused the government of favoring Portugal to the detriment of Brazil.

A few weeks later Marshal Brant arrived in Rio. Canning had not weakened in his determination to accept, as regards the independence of Brazil, a *fait accompli*. The Portuguese were in a painful quandary, for they realized that they could not count on the good wishes of their ancient ally in their conflict with their former colony. As a way out of its dilemma, the Lisbon government suggested that the good auspices of the Holy Alliance be invoked. Canning threatened to abandon the peninsular kingdom if such a policy were adopted for it would mean the recognition of a continental supremacy which England would oppose with the greatest energy. At least, urged the Portuguese government, let Austria and Russia have a share in these negotiations. Why? And on what grounds? replied the secretary of state. The presence of Austria might possibly be justified since Emperor Francis I was the father-in-law of Dom Pedro. But no such consideration could be urged as regards Russia.

The Missions to London, Vienna, Paris, and Washington.— Overburdened with international difficulties, the Brazilian government had thus far been somewhat remiss in its efforts to secure recognition of the empire by foreign powers. The arrival in Rio of Marshal Brant directed its attention to this most urgent problem,

From the tenor of Brant's earlier correspondence from England, it was evident that London would have to take first place in all negotiations and that the remaining Brazilian missions would necessarily be guided by the instructions sent to Great Britain. The United States presented another aspect of the problem since, in accordance with the farewell address of Washington, all complications with Europe were to be avoided.

In January, 1824, were drawn up the instructions for the plenipotentiaries, very much alike in substance, but differing in terminology and statement depending on the countries to which they were accredited. The most simple instructions were those furnished José Sylvestre Rebello, who was sent to the United States. Here the problem was of comparatively easy solution. Both the government and the congress of the United States had followed with eager sympathy the independence movement of the South American colonies from its inception in 1810. The name of Henry Clay, thanks to his ardent championship of the struggling dependencies, will never be forgotten in South America. Special missions, such as those of Rodney and Poinsett, had been sent to make a survey of conditions in divers parts of the southern continent, especially the littoral. Under various designations, United States consuls had made elaborate investigations. If recognition remained tardy it was owing to reasons of national and international policy in which South America was only indirectly involved. One of the chief obstacles was Spain's studied delay in refusing to ratify the treaty providing for the acquisition of Florida.[7]

In a sense, the ground had been prepared for the recognition of Brazil by the United States through the presence in Rio during the years 1810-1820 of North American ministers accredited to the court of Dom João VI. The question was, therefore, no new one and in the conduct of negotiation looking toward recognition the good will of the great northern republic was assured. The proof of these happy relations was shown by the speed and facility with which Rebello was able to carry out his mission. Fifty-nine days after his arrival in Baltimore, the empire of Brazil was officially acknowledged as an independent nation by President Monroe, on May 26, 1824. The United States was the first power to welcome Brazil into the comity of nations.

---

[7] This treaty was not ratified by Spain until 1819.—P.A.M.

In Europe, on the other hand, the problem was much more complex. A number of the powers had complaints or grievances against Brazil, or scores to settle. The envoys of Dom Pedro had to tread warily and display great tact and skill in dealing with the chancelleries of the Old World. In the case of England, the first stumbling block would be the question of the slave trade, to whose abolition the British Government was irrevocably committed. Another possible difficulty was the succession to the Portuguese throne. To Great Britain it was also a matter of considerable concern whether Portugal, its chief foothold on the continent, was in the friendly hands of the liberal Dom Pedro or in those of his brother Dom Miguel, the instrument of Metternich and the Holy Alliance.

As for Portugal itself, the problem of the succession to the throne was of capital importance. Brazil refused to consider any status short of complete independence. Dom João VI and his ministry insisted on the elimination of the possibility of Dom Miguel's ever assuming the crown of Portugal. Who then would succeed Dom João since Dom Pedro's fate seems indissolubly linked with the new Brazilian empire? Then, too, there was the thorny problem of defining the reciprocal situation of Brazilians and Portuguese in both countries. Last but not least was the baffling question of indemnities and the adjustment of the national debt. But before any of these questions could be considered, it was necessary that Portugal give up its determination, on which it apparently was adamantine, of reëstablishing the situation as it had existed before the declaration of Brazilian independence.

As was to be expected, the negotiations on these difficult points were initiated and prosecuted in London with Austria and England playing the rôle of mediators. Unfortunately, these two powers were far from being in entire agreement. Great Britain maintained its traditional point of view of sympathy with the aspirations of the newly liberated states. The rôle of Austria was that of a buffer. Without taking any initiative itself, that country strove to conciliate opposing points of view and to prepare the ground for a settlement acceptable to both parties. But in carrying out this policy Austria sounded a discordant note in the concert of the Holy Alliance since Russia was strongly prejudiced, in the name of legitimacy, against all movements for independence and a fortiori against any and all constitutions. Prussia tended to rally to the point of view of Russia. France, bound to a degree by the treaties imposed upon it after the defeat of Napoleon, and involved in the consequences of the unhappy invasion of Spain carried out at the behest of the Holy Alliance, hesitated and wavered in its policy touching the recognition of the new American states.

The position of Austria was somewhat embarrassing. With its commitments in the Balkans and its difficulties with the Italian Carbonari, Austria felt it to its advantage to maintain a close solidarity with the other members of the Holy Alliance. On the other hand, the emperor, Francis I, father of the wife of Dom Pedro, could not but sympathize with the cause of Brazilian independence. Even Metternich may well have been beguiled by the possible advantages of placing Brazil in Austria's debt while at the same time undermining England's dominant position in Portugal, the eternal protegé of Great Britain.

In any case, it cannot be denied that the services rendered Brazil by Austria were of the first importance. On the one hand, Metternich strove to create an atmosphere of moderation in Lisbon by insisting on the need of prudence and harmony in dealing with the Brazilian question. On the other hand, within the heart of the Holy Alliance itself, he checked impulses which otherwise would have been directed to the crushing of the independence movement in Brazil. For such reasons the name of the Austrian chancellor should be remembered in Brazil with gratitude, whatever may have been the psychological or political basis for his actions. At all times he revealed himself as a powerful and skillful advocate of the cause of our country.

London, Center of the Negotiations in Europe. Canning, Felisberto Caldeira Brant Pontes.—Canning, the British secretary of state for foreign affairs, was beyond all doubt the guiding spirit of the entire debate, yielding the palm to no one. But a place of almost equal prominence must also be accorded to the chief of the Brazilian negotiators, Marshal Brant. This diplomat, raised to the nobility with the title of Marquis of Barbacena, appears as an outstanding figure in both the foreign and domestic policies of the reign of Dom Pedro I.

Hardly were negotiations initiated in London before they ran into an impasse. Portugal demanded the submission, pure and simple, of its former trans-Atlantic colony. Little by little the strenuous efforts of Canning induced both groups of plenipotentiaries to allow the questions of Brazilian independence and Portuguese sovereignty temporarily to rest in abeyance, the discussion to be confined to the ways and means for restoring pacific and stable relations. Brant had turned over to Canning a memorial embodying the demands and pretensions of Brazil. The English secretary of state utilized this as a basis of his own memorandum to which he added the points insisted upon by Portugal. After a long and at times acrimonious debate the document was sent to Lisbon for submission to the Portuguese government. Here it was condemned in its entirety and a counter-proposal was drawn up and forwarded to London. As an evidence of the wide distance separating the two points of view, it is sufficient to point out that while Canning and Brant advocated the recognition of Brazilian independence by Dom João VI, the new proposal advanced by the former metropolis included the reëstablishment of royal sovereignty over Brazil. It was clear that further debate could serve no useful purpose nor was there any likelihood that two points of view so diametrically opposed could possibly be reconciled. After a number of diplomatic incidents, both in America and Europe, the *pourparlers* in London came to an end and negotiations were broken off.

At this juncture Canning decided to take matters into his own hands. He ordered Sir Charles Stuart, a well-known and competent diplomat and former ambassador in Paris, to proceed to Lisbon and explain to its former ally that Great Britain found itself constrained by its own interest to recognize Brazilian independence and that Stuart himself was about to leave for Rio de Janeiro for this purpose. He added, however, that he preferred to despatch Stuart on this latter mission only after Portugal had accepted what was patently a *fait accompli*. After long discussions on this point, the Lisbon foreign office capitulated and Stuart set out for Rio, accredited not only as the British but also as the Portuguese plenipotentiary.

This is not the place to rehearse the negotiations which took place after Stuart's arrival in Brazil. The envoy had received from Dom João personally such wide and discretionary powers that he might act as he thought best for the interests of Portugal, but at whatever cost he was to secure a definite treaty of peace. Stuart made full use of these extraordinary faculties and after long and arduous controversies over both the conditions and the wording of the treaty an agreement was reached and the instrument was signed August 29, 1825.

Brazil had won a complete and spectacular triumph. In both the preamble and Article I of the treaty "His Most Faithful Majesty . . . recognizes Brazil to be in the category of an independent empire, and separated from the kingdoms of Portugal and Algarves." Nothing was said of the slave trade: this problem was to be settled by subsequent agreement. Nor was the succession to the Portuguese crown mentioned. The Brazilian constitution permitted such succession under certain determined conditions, but the Portuguese laws remained unchanged. The door was thus left open to the fulfillment of Dom João's wishes that he might have as his successor the first emperor of Brazil. But such an arrangement rested upon a most uncertain basis and many were the doubts and misgivings voiced at the time. The failure of the treaty of 1825 definitely to settle the problems of the Portuguese succession was later to prove the cause of infinite difficulties.

Immediately after the ratification of this treaty, the remaining European and American powers hastened to extend their recognition to the new empire.

Despite the success of Brazilian diplomacy, the treaty of 1825 by no means met with universal approval. Political passions were running very high and those elements opposed to the government launched a vicious and bitter attack on the financial conventions attached to the treaty, particularly to the assumption by Brazil, to the extent of two million sterling, of the debt of the Portuguese monarchy. These attacks did not disappear even after the government had convincingly demonstrated the wisdom and justice of its procedure. Much of this factious opposition was due to the friends and followers of the Andradas. In fact, the seeds of distrust sown at this time soon ripened into a deep hostility against the emperor and his counsellors, a hostility which even survived the abdication of Dom Pedro six years later.

CHAPTER V

COMPLICATIONS IN LA PLATA BASIN; GROWING DISCONTENT; ABDICATION OF DOM PEDRO I

Dom Pedro Abdicates the Portuguese Throne.—Scarcely had the problems of recognition been settled by the treaty of 1825 before new difficulties arose. On March 10, 1826, Dom João VI died and the question of the succession to the Portuguese crown demanded immediate solution. The old king, as well as his ministers in Lisbon, had made all their plans for the coronation of Dom Pedro, although serious objections might be raised, and were in fact raised, against the legality of such a move. The emperor himself harbored doubts on this point. Nonetheless, he accepted the legacy, and took a number of important steps to secure the succession. He granted a constitution to Portugal, proclaimed a general amnesty, and abdicated in favor of his daughter Dona Maria da Gloria, who should espouse, as soon as she was of marriageable age, her uncle Dom Miguel.

All of these arrangements turned out to be ill-considered. In reaching out for the Portuguese crown, if only for his daughter, Dom Pedro had stirred up a veritable hornets' nest. The upshot was a legitimist and absolutist revolution against the pretensions of Dom Pedro and the coronation of Dom Miguel as king of Portugal. As we shall see later, both Brazil and the emperor could not escape being involved in these complications although the empire as such had everything to gain by keeping free from Portuguese entanglements. Needless to say these events had their repercussions in Rio de Janeiro and especially in the Brazilian parliament.

Hostilities Between the Emperor and the Chamber of Deputies.—In dealing with this period of Brazilian history one must never forget that the constitution and the parliamentary system were innovations in the Brazilian empire. Dom Pedro, though a liberal by instinct, was a complete tyro in all that had to do with government and legislation. He interpreted and put into practice constitutional clauses as if he were an absolutist ruler. On the other hand, the leaders of parliament, complying with their duty, endeavored to lay the foundation for a true cabinet government with ministerial responsibility. Had real bonds of sympathy and mutual good will existed between the executive and legislature some kind of understanding and *modus operandi* might have been reached. With rare exceptions, however, everything conspired to widen the gulf between Dom Pedro and his legislators. The dissolute life of the emperor; the debased character of many of his most intimate friends and counsellors, almost all of whom were Portuguese; the increasing lack of confidence which harked back to the opposition of 1823; the terms of the financial convention of 1825 which were regarded as unjust to Brazil and too favorable to Portugal; the alleged incompetency of the government in handling various international questions—all of these factors, including a number of minor ones, had tended to separate the sovereign from the deputies. In the senate, in which were to be found almost all of the protagonists of independence—men who had collaborated with Dom Pedro in the trying days of 1822 and 1823—hostility against the executive was much less in evidence. Of the accusations levelled against the monarch, both in the chamber and in the senate, the most persistent and the most damaging was the charge that he had sacrificed the interests of Brazil to those of Portugal—a flagrant injustice, this, but such is the logic of human ingratitude. Unfortunately, the conduct of the emperor had on many occasions apparently confirmed his detractors in their opinions.

The government's conduct of foreign affairs frequently appeared suspect to the two houses of parliament. Sir Charles Stuart, the British minister, had on various occasions exceeded his instructions, and was replaced by Robert Gordon in 1826. The agreements signed by Brazil and Great Britain in the matter of commercial intercourse and eventual cessation of the slave trade had aroused much anxiety, as it was feared that their effects on commerce and agriculture would be disastrous. By the terms of the treaty, ratified March 13, 1827, the year 1830 would be the last year in which slaves could be legally imported;[1] after that date such traffic would

---

[1] The treaty of 1827 ratified verbatim the Anglo-Portuguese agreements of 1817 and stipulated furthermore that at the expiration of three years after the ratification of the treaty the slave trade should cease utterly. The chief provisions of the agreements of 1817 had to do with the right of search granted to British cruisers and the establishment of mixed commissions at Sierra Leone and Rio.—P.A.M. [See Lawrence F. Hill, "Abolition of the African Slave Trade to Brazil," in *The Hispanic American Historical Review*, XI (May, 1931), 169-97.—J.A.R.]

be considered as piracy. These stipulations deeply wounded public opinion for they permitted Brazilian sailors to be judged by foreign tribunals according to British laws.

In the treaty of commerce nothing was accomplished by way of abolishing the odious privilege of the *conservatoria*, save the promise to abandon it when, in the opinion of Great Britain, Brazilian legislation would offer adequate guarantees to British subjects. In the case of the treaty with France, ratified March 19, 1826, there existed certain clauses of a perpetual character. It is only fair to add, however, that this is the only instance in which the Brazilian government was guilty of such a monstrous error. In the remaining international agreements the duration of the clauses was from six to fifteen years.

The ill will of parliament was exacerbated by the fact that all of the agreements or treaties were sent to the assembly[2] after ratification, thus effectively annulling any parliamentary coöperation. The legislators regarded this practice as a gross breach of courtesy. As might be expected, the situation developed into a veritable impasse; the government refused to modify its practices and the assembly declined to take official cognizance of the treaties. One may readily understand the ill will which grew out of these differences between the legislature and the executive. It was not until 1831, after the abdication of Dom Pedro and the advent of the regency, that true theory of the collaboration of the two powers was observed and followed, and even then the practice had to be sanctioned by special legislation.

A still further cause of suspicion and distrust was the practice of silence and secrecy adopted by the executive in the conduct of public affairs. Parliament demanded annual reports (*relatorios*) on the activities of the various departments of the government, but the ministers evinced reluctance in carrying out this constitutional mandate. On this point, however, they were forced to yield, and within a short period adopted the practice of sending periodical reports to both branches of the assembly.

The "Cisplatina."—Quite apart from the causes of friction which we have just analyzed, the Brazilian parliament had many reasons for anxiety and apprehension. Of these causes the most im-

---

[2] The joint session of the senate and the chamber of deputies.

portant was the insurrection that had broken out in the Cisplatine province.

It would be hard to imagine anything more artificial than the union, brought about in 1821 by Portuguese arms, between Brazil and the Banda Oriental del Uruguay. Three centuries of intermittent warfare between Spain and Portugal protested against the establishment of the troops of Dom João VI on the left bank of the Río de la Plata in 1817. Yet at first blush the moment for the absorption into Brazil of this section of the former viceroyalty of Buenos Aires seemed not ill chosen. Spain, the former mother country, was powerless as regards its former Platine colonies. Buenos Aires, torn by internal dissensions and without resources, was in no position to expel the Portuguese invaders from a territory which was now regarded as its own. And in the Banda Oriental itself the situation in 1817 might well have seemed equally hopeless. Yet, there were many in Uruguay who had refused to despair. They had pinned their hopes on Artigas, who was opposed to the rule of both the Portuguese and the Porteños. This hero, the greatest glory of Uruguay, fought for the principle of absolute autonomy. For a time he was victorious but finally was defeated by treachery. During his entire career he nobly merited the admirable title by which he was greeted by his devoted followers—"*el protector de los pueblos libres*" ("the protector of free peoples").

All of the inhabitants of the Platine basin had one sentiment in common: the horror inspired by the troops of the Portuguese general, Lecor. They did not possess the means, however, of putting an end to their sufferings; the Lusitanian kingdom possessed such prestige and such an abundance of resources that effective resistance was hopeless. But little by little the situation of the opposing groups began to change. The Portuguese revolution of 1820, the intemperate actions of the constituent côrtes, the return of Dom João to Lisbon in 1821, the growing difficulties between the two sections of the Portuguese realm—all undermined the power and influence of the Braganza dynasty.

After the declaration of independence, as we have seen, Brazil had to cope with grave disorders in Bahia and Maranhão. In Uruguay, as has already been pointed out, the army of occupation was divided into two factions: the Portuguese section obeyed Dom

Alvaro da Costa and the orders of the côrtes; the other, the Brazilian part, adhered to General Lecor and the new empire. The
Portuguese sympathizers were besieged in Montevideo by the forces
of Lecor. But the côrtes resolved to abandon the country and with
the evacuation of the Portuguese garrison the troops of Lecor
entered Montevideo without opposition.

At this juncture the Uruguayans despatched envoys to Buenos
Aires to ask for assistance in expelling the Brazilians. Don Juan
Antonio Lavalleja, the head of the mission, immediately recognized
that nothing was to be hoped for from this quarter despite the
community of sentiment existing among the inhabitants of both
banks of La Plata. The Porteño government was too weak to resort
to arms and its chief, General Martín Rodríguez, confined his efforts to the attempt to secure by diplomatic means the withdrawal
of Brazil from Montevideo and the transference of the city to the
United Provinces of the Río de la Plata. After his failure in Buenos
Aires, Lavalleja sought support in other quarters, especially in
the present Argentine provinces of Santa Fe and Entre Ríos. He
received promises and a certain amount of effervescence developed
along the shores of the Paraná River, but it soon died down.

Meanwhile, in October, 1823, the cabildo of Montevideo addressed a noble appeal to the Brazilian empire and the constituent
assembly imploring them to order the recall of the imperial troops.
Such withdrawal, declared the message, would permit the Cisplatina and its people freely to manifest their wishes, and their decision, irrespective of its character, would be unanimously and
loyally accepted. No attention was paid to this appeal.

In Buenos Aires the excitement was intense. Uruguay, whose
fate now hung in the balance, had once been a part of the former
viceroyalty; the *Orientales*, as the inhabitants of the Banda
Oriental were called, were one in blood and language with the
Porteños who could not look with indifference on the suffering and
oppression of their brethren across the Plata estuary. They were
only waiting a favorable opportunity to come to their aid.

At this juncture a new and most important event occurred.
Castlereagh, the bulwark of legitimacy and metropolitan rights,
committed suicide. Overnight, as it were, the conduct of foreign
affairs in Great Britain passed into the hands of George Canning.

No longer was England's foreign policy to be conducted in accordance with the wishes of the ultra-conservative, the High Tories. Under Canning, the views of British commercial and trade circles gained the ascendancy and henceforth the revolted colonies and not their mother countries were to receive the unqualified support and sympathy of Great Britain. Obviously, this new orientation in British policy was distinctly favorable to the hopes and desires of the peoples living on the shores of the Río de la Plata. That a new spirit was astir was realized at once in Buenos Aires and Montevideo; it was even sensed by the Brazilian ministers accredited to London and Vienna.

These changes coincided with the complete failure in Rio of the mission from Buenos Aires. Don Juan Valentín Gómez, the envoy chosen by General Martín Rodríguez, remained for several months in the capital of the empire. But his efforts and arguments, though able and judicious, made no headway against the bad faith and evasive replies of the Rio foreign office. In April, 1824, he was forced to return to Buenos Aires with a courteous but decisive refusal to all the Argentine demands.

The curtain had been rung down on another act of the Cisplatine drama. The hour for diplomatic negotiations had passed. The campaign to liberate Uruguay from its invaders would have to draw its strength from the filial love and spirit of sacrifice of its own sons. Lavalleja realized that the moment for action had arrived and he launched forthwith his crusades for freedom. His decision was not uninfluenced by the memorable victory of Ayacucho in Peru, which on December 9, 1824, delivered a mortal blow to Spanish rule in America.

The Uruguayan chieftain found aid and encouragement in Buenos Aires. To hearten his fellow patriots and to prepare them for impending events he despatched to the Banda Oriental a young colonel whose name was later to ring through the continent, Don Manuel Ortíz de Rosas.

The Cisplatine Campaign.—On April 19, 1825, a day famous in Uruguayan annals, a troop of thirty-three horsemen headed by Lavalleja crossed the Paraná River bound for Uruguay. These were the famous "thirty and three," immortalized in history and romance. This handful of soldiers, numerically insignificant, symbolized the freedom of Uruguay and in them was incarnated the soul of their country. Immediately reënforcements, both men and horses, began to pour into their camp.

Skirmishes with the Brazilian forces soon took place with the advantages generally on the side of the liberators. Local *caudillos* who had made a virtue of necessity by submitting to foreign masters, realized that a new day had dawned. Seizing their lances they galloped away in search of their former companions and old allegiances. Such a one was Don Fructuoso Rivera, one of the protagonists of Uruguayan independence and later president of the republic. From the opposite shores of La Plata estuary came arms, ammunitions, and resources in a steady stream. To assure the continuance of this invaluable aid, Lavalleja summoned at the town of Florida a congress of representatives from various sections of the Banda Oriental. On August 25, 1825, this assembly voted the incorporation of Uruguay within the United Provinces of the Río de la Plata and declared null and void all of the existing treaties with Portugal and Brazil. The act of August 25 was, in effect, a declaration of Uruguayan independence, at least as far as Brazil was concerned. News of action of the congress aroused tremendous enthusiasm in Buenos Aires and throughout Argentina; the feeling was all but universal that the Uruguayans should not be left unaided in the approaching conflict with the Brazilian empire.

The emperor as well as his ministers fully appreciated the gravity of the situation created by the campaign of Lavalleja and his followers. As early as June the Brazilian government despatched to Buenos Aires a squadron with instructions to request, or if need be, demand explanations regarding the aid furnished by the United Provinces to the insurgents in Cisplatina. The first half of June was expended in fruitless discussion between the commander of the squadron and the minister of foreign affairs, Don Manuel José García, one of the great figures in Argentine diplomacy.

In well-informed circles in Rio there were no illusions regarding the precarious position of Brazil. Our diplomats in Europe were instructed to request Canning to exert his influence with the Buenos Aires government to the end that a damper be placed on the bellicose zeal of the Porteños. The replies from London were most disconcerting; in this question, Great Britain, far from being favorable, showed itself to be hostile to Brazilian designs and rallied to the point of view of the Porteños and Uruguayans as regarded the evacuation of the Banda Oriental by the forces of Lecor.

Reports from the south were equally distressing. First came the news of the action taken at the congress held at Florida with the vote in favor of union with the United Provinces. Then arrived accounts of the Uruguayan victories of Rincón and Sarandí over the Brazilians. The last straw was the report that on October 25, 1825, the constitutional congress of the United Provinces of the Río de la Plata had voted in favor of the union and incorporation of Uruguay. War was inevitable. A great wave of national pride and indignation swept away all opposition. Through an imperial decree of December 10 war was formally declared.

A worse moment for the declaration of hostilities could hardly have been chosen. The present war was not looked upon as a logical corollary of the expansionist movement of the Brazilian people. It was not an example of the fulfillment of "manifest destiny." Rather did it represent a continuation of the imperialist policy of Dom João VI. As such it was not popular and Dom Pedro was accused of preferring the Portuguese heritage of conquest to the true national interest of harmony and peace with Brazil's southern neighbors.

While the war clouds were gathering in the south, Brazil was threatened with serious complications on the west. As a consequence of the patriot victories at Junín and Ayacucho over the Spanish forces operating in the highlands of Peru, the region known in colonial days as the Audiencia of Charcas was erected into the Republic of Bolivia, named after the great Venezuelan revolutionist, Simón Bolívar. But the local governor of the Bolivian province of Chiquitos remained royalist in sentiment and sent an emissary to the adjacent Brazilian province of Matto Grosso begging the imperial authorities to take his province under their protection until the king of Spain was in a position to reconquer his viceroyalty of Peru. This proposal was accepted; Brazilian troops marched to Chiquitos and took up their quarters there. Were the government of Rio to lend its sanction to such an invasion it would be tantamount to inviting Bolívar to lead his army across Bolivia for the purpose of conquering Brazil. The results of such a campaign might well have been disastrous for the empire. The appearance of Bolívar on Brazilian soil would have served as a direct and powerful incentive to the sporadic but dangerous republican agitation which was especially strong in the north, the theater of the revolutions of 1817 and 1824. It is conceivable, too, that the powerful Masonic Order, which thus far had supported the empire, might have thrown its influence on the side of the republicans. Fortunately, the government carefully weighed all of these eventualities and despatched orders to Matto Grosso for the withdrawal of the Brazilian forces from Bolivian territory.

A more real and tangible threat to Brazilian designs on Uruguay was the policy of Canning. From the despatches of both the Brazilian and Portuguese ministers in London, it appeared that the cabinet of St. James was contemplating the transformation of Montevideo into a kind of Hanseatic city under the protection of Great Britain. That which Sir Home Popham was not able to accomplish in 1806, namely, the establishment on the margin of La Plata estuary of an English naval base dominating the South Atlantic, the new plan would make possible. We may say, by way of anticipation, that this plan, which failed in 1825 as regards the Platine area, was successfully carried out in 1833 in the Falkland Islands lying off the extreme southeastern coast of Argentina. The occupation of these islands was another proof of the prevision so characteristic of English diplomacy and so often justified by later events. In the present case, for instance, the Falklands were utilized as a base by Admiral Sturdee when in the fall of 1914 he destroyed the fleet of Count von Spee.

The Brazilian Aspect of the Problem.—Throughout the war with Argentina the Brazilian higher command frequently proved incompetent. A blockading squadron was sent to the entry of the Río de la Plata but the admiral was lacking in aggressiveness, while his ships were unsuitable for the navigation of the shallow waters of the estuary. Lecor, who commanded the land forces, remained completely inactive and it never occurred to him to coördinate the land operations with those of the fleet. As a result of this state of affairs, the naval operations were of necessity indecisive, although the Brazilian sailors were not lacking in courage. Owing, however, to the draft of the ships, the Brazilians were seldom able to come to final grips with their opponents who when worsted found asylum in their shallow harbors. But the greatest blunder was to leave undisputed the free passage from one bank of the estuary to the other. As a result of this negligence, the United Provinces were allowed to locate their training camp on Uruguayan territory, an arrangement of the utmost value to them in the prosecution of the war. As will be explained later, the blockade gave rise to number-less protests from neutrals and involved Brazil in serious inter-national complications.

A few privateers, with letters of marque issued by the United Provinces, harassed Brazilian shipping and caused great annoy-ance and ill-will in the provinces fronting the littoral.

The Brazilian troops were insufficent in number, ill-fed, ill-paid. They lacked practically everything: uniforms, ammunition, foot-wear, arms. The number of cavalry was inadequate. To bring order out of this confusion, Marshal Brant, now Marquis of Barbacena, was appointed commander-in-chief. In the course of the ensuing campaign he revealed high qualities as an organizer and strategist. Unfortunately, he was no tactician. This grave shortcoming was revealed in the Brazilian defeat of Passō do Rosario, or as the Argentines calle it, Ituzaingó, on February 20, 1827. In this, the most important engagement of the war, Barbacena failed to main-tain sufficiently close contact with his troops and did not make the most of the gallantry of the officers and men.

The battle of Ituzaingó was followed by a lull in the campaign. Such minor engagements as took place had no military significance. The United Provinces were financially exhausted and on the verge of bankruptcy. Though not so badly off, Brazil was in a sore plight, for it was struggling with the gravest budgetary difficulties. But its greatest handicap was the general unpopularity of the war.

In both houses of parliament were heard harsh and pitiless criticisms of both the government and Marshal Brant. Nor was Dom Pedro himself spared; he was suspected of trying to weaken the Brazilian forces in order to further Portuguese plans for the reconquest of Brazil. Fantastic and unjust as these charges were they, nonetheless, influenced the public mind and increased the pre-vailing lack of confidence. Everywhere the complaint was voiced that the emperor was more interested in Portugal and his daugh-ter's crown than he was in Brazil. By a curious irony of fate, at the very moment when these absurd accusations were being bandied about, Dona Carlota Joaquina and the Marquis of Chaves were fomenting a legitimist insurrection in Portugal and Dom Miguel in Austria was promising anything and everything in order to return to Lisbon, where one year later, in April, 1828, he was to betray his brother's confidence and snatch from his niece and bride the crown he had sworn to defend.

Peace Negotiations.—Disorganization in the United Provinces had reached such a pass that Don Manuel García, minister of foreign relations, set out on a special mission to Rio in order to negotiate peace at any price. The conclusion of hostilities was in his opinion a matter of life or death. García reached the Brazilian capital early in May, 1827; on the twenty-fourth of the same month the peace treaty was signed. By the terms of this instrument, despite the Brazilian defeat at Passō do Rosario or Ituzaingó, Cisplatina remained in possession of the empire.

Great Britain, whose ministers in Rio and Buenos Aires had mediated between the belligerents, accepted the treaty, although in reality it was a mortal blow to its plan of converting Montevideo into a British protectorate. But in Buenos Aires the terms of the treaty signed by García aroused great indignation. The opposition in fact assumed such violent form that Don Bernardino Rivadavia, the head of the government, felt himself obliged to disavow his envoy. García, he declared, had violated both the letter and the spirit of his instructions. He even deemed it his duty to resign his high office as president of the republic.[3]

The manifesto published by him on this occasion, though reflecting the patriotism and nobility of its author, reveals at the same time Rivadavia's painful realization that he was abandoning a post of danger. The president, in fact, found himself impaled on the horns of a frightful dilemma: he could neither carry on a war nor negotiate a peace. He did not have the resources to finance another campaign nor sufficient public support to enable him to sanction a treaty acceptable to Brazil. As a consequence he resigned. Yet, after all, had he but known it, there was a way out

---

[3] Rivadavia, the head of the Unitarian party and one of the ablest of Argentine executives, took this step not merely because of the fiasco of the García mission but also owing to the refusal of the various provinces to accept the Unitarian constitution of 1826.—P.A.M.

of this impasse despite all the difficulties involved; his successor, General Dorrego, followed it in 1828.

The news of the rejection of the treaty by Buenos Aires caused general stupefaction in Rio de Janeiro. The country was sick and tired of carrying on an extremely unpopular war. The supply of volunteers was practically exhausted; the depleted ranks of the army were filled through the impressment of soldiers in the towns and cities on the occasion of public gatherings or festivities. Nothing was better calculated to increase the public discontent than this violent and arbitrary method of securing recruits. In fact, the conflict had badly disorganized the labor situation in the interior of the country and had created a veritable economic crisis. In governmental and parliamentary circles the signing of the treaty had brought a feeling of intense relief, and no one felt disposed to assume again the burdens which had been so joyfully relinquished. So general was the discontent that a number of German mercenaries in Rio Grande do Sul, ill-paid or in many cases unpaid, mutinied against their officers and were put down only with great difficulty. Some of them even went over to the enemy. As if these domestic difficulties were not enough, bad news from Portugal added further anxieties to the sorely tried empire. Dom Miguel had definitely thrown off the mask which he had worn for a number of years and from his exile in Vienna declared his intention of assuming the Portuguese crown.

From all sides came intimations and suggestions that the time was ripe for the cessation of hostilities. England and France, in veiled terms to be sure, let it be understood that they did not intend any longer to tolerate the grave inconveniences they were suffering in the Platine area, especially from the Brazilian blockade. Rio Grande do Sul showed signs of restlessness and republican propaganda began to raise its head—a forerunner of the storm which was to break over Brazil in the years 1835-1845. Rio de Janeiro could not remain unmoved by such grave warnings.

The Peace Treaty of 1828.—Dom Pedro's objections to any peace treaty which might diminish the territorial patrimony inherited from his father began to weaken. A new embassy from Buenos Aires reached Rio in August, 1828, and on the twenty-seventh of this month a new agreement was concluded. On this date, the Republic of Uruguay was born into the comity of the free states of America. By the terms of the treaty Brazil agreed to evacuate Cisplatina. The United Provinces agreed that the liberated territory should not be incorporated into their confederation. Both nations accepted the independence of Cisplatina, presently to be metamorphosed into the "República Oriental del Uruguay," and pledged themselves to act as guarantors of the freedom of the new state. In taking this step they fell in with the wishes of Canning and with the objective of his policy. For the first time in an international treaty appears the freedom of navigation of the rivers which serve as boundaries of the contracting states.

The Reverend Richard Walsh in his book published in 1828 informs us that "the end of the war was received with general disappointment and great discontent." [4] Certainly the parliamentary opposition made the most of the treaty of 1828 to undermine the government. Dom Pedro became more unpopular than ever. The loss of esteem of his subjects was increased as a result of the death of Empress Leopoldina in December, 1826, and it was rumored that her demise had been precipitated by her grief at the licentious life led by her husband. After her death the scandal growing out of his intimacy with the celebrated Marchioness of Santos took on even greater proportions.

The Blockade of the Río de la Plata.—Another cause of the growing difficulties in which the young empire was involved was the blockade of the Platine estuary. This measure, which was determined upon in 1825, was almost ludicrously inadequate. Walsh says in this connection: "The declaration of the blockade embraced a coast of twenty leagues of latitude, and the whole force available for carrying it out amounted to one corvette, two armed brigs and some gun-boats, a force which would not suffice to guard Buenos Ayres alone."

No means were available for making the blockade effective. Instructions were frequently altered and the commanders charged with their execution as frequently ignored them. So great were the abuses and so many rules were violated in the matter of reprisals and the capture and sale of prizes that the envoys of England, France, and the United States daily laid before the Brazilian government the protests of their citizens whose rights had been flouted. But Dom Pedro's ministers were all but powerless; orders

[4] *Notices of Brazil* (2 vols., London, 1828).

duly sent to the blockading squadron were disobeyed; legislation
on the means of enforcement was lacking; and claimants, both the
private owners of crafts and cargoes, as well as the ministers of
their respective countries, saw their grievances put off from day to
day. The imperial government realized perfectly that these protests were legitimate but it found its hands tied. In September,
1827, a law was passed designed to remedy the worst of these
abuses but there was little or no agreement between the government
and the protestants regarding its interpretation.

Finally France lost patience. Admiral Roussin on July 6, 1826,
sailed into the harbor of Rio to force the government to meet
the claims of French citizens. The United States and England also
lodged protests. The naval demonstration of Roussin was perhaps
unnecessary and it deeply wounded the national pride of the Brazilians. Yet so insistent and in the main so just were the protests
against the breaches of international law committed by the blockading squadron that the government formally admitted itself to
be in the wrong and undertook to amend the existing commercial
treaties and rules of the blockade so as to meet the demands of the
protesting powers. Although these belated acts of justice helped
to relieve the international tension, the responsibility for all of
these unpleasant occurrences was laid at the door of the ministry
and the emperor. Everything was enveloped in an atmosphere of
suspicion and distrust.

*Juridical and Administrative Organization of the Empire. The
Slave Trade. Attempts to Foster Immigration.*—The foreign
complications which fill such a large place in the reign of Dom
Pedro I should not blind us to the constructive work carried on in
the general assembly during the same period. One of Brazil's crying needs was a juridical organization of its own. Theoretically,
the legislation of Portugal should have ceased to apply to Brazil
on April 25, 1821, but in the absence of law codes of our own such
a step was impossible. The necessity of continuing to follow the
Portuguese codes, as a purely transitional measure, was formally
recognized by the law of October 20, 1823. A great step forward
in the juridical life of Brazil was the creation, in September, 1828,
of the Supreme Court of Justice (*Supremo Tribunal de Justiça*),
resulting in the abolition of old tribunals based on Portuguese
models. In 1830 was put into force the new criminal code.

In all that had to do with national economy the slave trade played a rôle of the first importance. The Anglo-Brazilian treaty of 1826, which fixed 1830 as the last year in which slaves could be legally imported, was looked upon by virtually all Brazilians as a terrible, impending menace to the agricultural life of the country, the basis of the nation's prosperity. Every effort was exerted, therefore, to augment the number of slaves which might be imported within the remaining years of grace. It has been conjectured that during the last years of the legalized traffic the annual importation fluctuated between sixty to eighty thousand.

Despite the relative ease with which Negro slaves could be introduced during the reign of Dom Pedro I, and despite, too, the profits involved in the traffic, some efforts were made to stimulate white immigration into Brazil. The obstacles, however, were formidable. Apart from the difficulty, not to say impossibility, of securing white laborers who would work side by side with the slaves on the plantations, there was the vast stretch of ocean between Brazil and Europe, in comparison with the relatively short distance separating Brazil from the teeming coasts of Africa. Then, too, the land itself was too savage and the isolation of the settlers too absolute to incite European immigrants to cross the Atlantic in order to open up farms in the jungle or in the virgin forest. Nonetheless, a few colonies were established under Dom João VI and Dom Pedro I, but their prospects were by no means encouraging. One of these, founded in 1812, was located in the province of Espirito Santo. Another, called Dona Leopoldina as an act of homage to the future empress, was founded in 1817, on the banks of the river Peruipe, in southern Bahia. Nova Friburgo, established by Swiss peasants in 1819, was located in the Organ Mountains not far from Rio de Janeiro. Forquilhas and Torres, in Rio Grande do Sul, dating from 1826, and São Leopoldo, established two years earlier in the same province, became prosperous and promised a bright future. Their inhabitants were almost all Germans. São Leopoldo counted, as early as 1828, six thousand souls. Almost all of these settlements still exist and today are thriving towns or cities. In Santa Catharina the first attempt goes back to 1827, while in the case of São Paulo we have the colony of Santo Amaro founded in 1828-1829.

As a general rule these colonists had come to Brazil as mercenary soldiers and only later were settled on allotments of land granted by the government. This method gave rise, on various occasions, to very disagreeable incidents: riots, uprisings, veritable rebellions which had to be put down by force. This was the case with the German regiments, who were the first mercenary troops to arrive, and also with the Irish who came in 1828 with Colonel Cotter. In the case of the Germans, the pretext for the uprising was the excessive punishment inflicted on one of the soldiers; it is quite possible, however, that the revolt had some connection with the tumults in the south growing out of the Cisplatine campaign. As for the Irish, Colonel Cotter had promised more than he could carry out. When he reached Brazil with 2,400 immigrants from Cork no preparations had been made for their reception. Their sufferings and privations were intense; barely four hundred were finally located in Ilhéos in southern Bahia; as many of the remainder as survived returned to Ireland famished and ruined.

These unhappy occurrences brought most unfortunate results in their train. For many years they effectively prevented all immigration to Brazil. They also served to reënforce the opinion that only Africa could supply the needs of Brazilian labor and that such man power must necessarily be servile. It is only fair to add that, accustomed as they were to slavery, even the best-intentioned statesmen could not comprehend the essence of free labor, namely voluntary consent on the part of the workman. Nicolau Pereira dos Campos Vergueiro was one of the most eminent of these public men interested in questions of immigration. Later he pointed out the way of solving the labor problem on the great coffee plantations of São Paulo by means of a joint partnership between landowners and free settlers—the so-called *parceria* system. Yet this same Vergueiro, in 1830, secured the passage by the assembly of a law providing for a complicated system of contracts which in their essence were little more than disguised slavery. In the case of laborers bound by such agreements, the slightest infraction might give rise to an arbitrary and brutal intervention by the police, often followed by jail sentences. The final solution of these baffling labor difficulties was to come later as a consequence of social progress and a better understanding of the economic and human factors involved. In such matters laws and politics could in the long run accomplish very little.

Evidences of Progress.—In spite of the unfavorable conditions to which allusion has been made, the rhythm of progress and development of Brazil showed no interruption. In 1828 the imports of commodities exceeded more than fifteen million dollars in value, balanced by exports of approximately the same amount. In the same year, excluding coastwise traffic, 470 ships entered the harbor of Rio. Of these 266 flew the British flag and 151 that of the United States. The chief agent of progress had been the Bank of Brazil which supplied credit for ordinary commercial operations. But in 1829 was committed, as has already been pointed out, a very grave error, by the passage of a law which provided for the liquidation of the bank.[5] This step was the result of political animosities, exaggerated rumors of dishonest management, and a campaign to cast discredit on the institution. As we have already seen, the stockholders received back 90 per cent of their capital despite the unfavorable conditions under which liquidation took place. For a number of years no bank existed in Brazil with the result that credit operations were rendered most difficult and complicated.

While the volume of business revealed a sound and steady increase, national finances went from bad to worse. Proof of this assertion is to be found in the steady drop in exchange. The milréis was assumed to be at par $67\frac{1}{2}$ pence. In 1830, exchange in Rio fluctuated between $21\frac{1}{2}$ and $24\frac{3}{4}$ pence; in Bahia, between 26 and $33\frac{1}{2}$; in Maranhão, between 39 and $48\frac{1}{2}$; while in Recife it remained more or less stabilized at $51\frac{7}{8}$. These great differences in exchange among the different financial centers in Brazil were owing in large part to the absence of normal means of communication along the coast; in Recife, for instance, the milréis was worth nearly twice its value in Rio de Janeiro.

In general, this wretched financial situation is to be explained on three different grounds: the bad management of public finances; the war with Portugal and the hostilities in northern Brazil and in Cisplatina; and the issue of copper money. This is not the place to embark on a detailed discussion of these monetary problems. We have already published a special work on this subject.[6] Here we shall confine ourselves to a brief résumé of the facts.

---

[5] *Cf.* above p. 58.

[6] *Politique Monétaire du Brésil* (Rio de Janeiro, 1910).

Excessive issues of paper money, as is always the case, had expelled all gold and silver from the market and the only metallic currency in circulation was copper, minted at a face value far higher than its commercial price. The coins were crudely made and easily counterfeited. A double fraud was perpetrated: the government began to issue excessive quantities of this money in order to benefit by the difference between its face and intrinsic value; private individuals collected or imported copper disks, similar in appearance to the legal ones. So badly made were these coins that it was quite impossible to distinguish between the genuine and the counterfeit. At length things reached such a pass that it was necessary for the treasury to call them all in, the true with the false. The operation was wound up in 1837 at a cost of some 35,000 contos. This epidemic of both genuine and counterfeit copper coins naturally fostered speculation, upset prices, and threw the whole monetary system into confusion.

Contest Between the Emperor and the Legislature.—On the mind of the emperor all criticisms had the same effect: he considered them attacks on the majesty of the throne. He failed to distinguish sincere and able criticism growing out of parliamentary discussions from mere bursts of passionate opposition or ill-will. If his ministers dissented from his views, he promptly dismissed them and appointed as their successors men more amenable to his will. The resentment of the legislature and public opinion at these methods naturally served to strengthen Dom Pedro in his absolutist convictions. As the Brazilians acquiesced less readily than the Portuguese in the emperor's theories of government, Dom Pedro tended to choose his counsellors among the latter; this practice lent color to the belief that he was giving the empire a second place in his affections.

During these years, the members of the legislature had learned much. At first the parliament did not realize how numerous or effective were the powers vested in it by the constitution. As a result it was led more often by passion than by reflection. But after a lapse of four or five years it found itself, so to speak; and in all emergencies and crises it appeared to better advantage than the emperor. While Dom Pedro remained a victim of his emotions, parliament was guided more and more by reason and the true interests of the state. It was characteristic of the emperor that he violated quite unconsciously constitutional rules and parliamentary privileges. Ill-will on both sides all but led to an open break. On one occasion, while standing at the window of his palace, Dom Pedro openly insulted the representatives of the nation as they passed by.

His aversion to the legislature was only equaled by his predilection for the army. He may almost be said to have lived with his troops. Naturally, the army became suspect to parliament and the latter missed no occasion to weaken the army in order to diminish the power of the emperor. Even up to our own day, Brazil has suffered from the consequences of this impolitic and ill-conceived course of action. The mistakes committed during the unhappy Cisplatine campaign are partly to be explained by this lack of cooperation between the army and the legislature.

For all practical purposes the budget did not exist. Dom Pedro was wont to give direct orders to the treasury for the payment of such and such expenses, for which in many cases no legal authority existed. Nominations within the competency of the ministers were made by the emperor himself without regard to results of such a deplorable practice.

The strained relations between the executive and the legislature were of course well-known throughout the provinces. The accounts were even exaggerated as a result of the versions relayed by the representatives to their constituents. So great was the tension that when Dom Pedro closed the last session of the first legislature, instead of delivering the customary speech reviewing the achievements of parliament, he merely declared: "The session is at an end."

It was in this atmosphere of profound hostility to the emperor that the second legislature was elected. The charges made by both sides were exaggerated or distorted by passion. The government was saddled with responsibility for everything, even for those acts to which Dom Pedro had been opposed and whose origin had been in parliament itself.

The "Aurora Fluminense."—Meanwhile a new, and as events proved, a salutary element was injected into the troubled situation. In 1827 appeared a newspaper with the title of *Aurora Fluminense.*[7]

---

[7] The adjective "Fluminense" which appears frequently in Brazilian history is derived from the Latin word "river" (*flumen*), an allusion to the name of Rio de Janeiro, or "River of January."—P.A.M.

Its aim was a clear and serene discussion of facts, as opposed to the insults and taunts which hitherto had formed the stock and trade of political controversy. The public was wearied of sterile polemics and the influence of the new journal at once became marked. Its proprietor, Evaristo Ferreira da Veiga, a bookdealer, shared the political convictions of Senator Vergueiro, one of the most able public men of the period. Owing in part to this association the new journal strongly reënforced the conservative elements in Brazil, and within a short time there was created a nucleus of serious, energetic, calm, and foreseeing political leaders, equidistant from demagoguery and absolutism—a group to which Brazil owed the most eminent services during some of the most difficult moments of its constitutional life.

In 1830, thirty-three newspapers were published throughout the empire; of this number only eleven supported the government. In the opposition press were journals favoring both a federation and a republic. Such ideas were premature; had they been realized at this time both national unity as well as internal peace would have been shattered. Vergueiro and Evaristo were fully alive to those perils and exerted all their efforts to avoid them. Nobly did they fulfill their self-appointed task.

The ascent of Dom Miguel to the throne of Portugal was followed by the persecution of the partisans of Dona Maria da Gloria. Of these supporters of the daughter of Dom Pedro I some fled to Brazil, but the majority sought voluntary exile in London from whence they proceeded to the Azores where the young queen had a large circle of adherents and her authority was respected. Dom Pedro, as father and legal guardian of Dona Maria, could not avoid taking a hand in events in Portugal. Unfortunately, as he became more and more absorbed in these dynastic and family complications, he tended to neglect purely Brazilian interests. So at least it appeared to many Brazilians and bitter was their resentment. As a natural reaction, Dom Pedro was tempted to fall back upon his Portuguese subjects to the exclusion of Brazilians from his circle of intimate friends and advisers. There were times when not a single portfolio was held by a Brazilian.

The New Mission of the Marquis of Barbacena.—Deeply concerned with the fate of his daughter, Dona Maria da Gloria, Dom Pedro decided that he would place her under the protection of her

grandfather, Francis I, emperor of Austria. With this end in view
he sent her to Europe in June, 1828, under the escort of Barbacena.
The departure took place shortly before the news of Dom Miguel's
usurpation reached Brazil, and it was not until the royal party
arrived at Gibraltar that this act of treason became known. Since
Francis I was the protector of Dom Miguel, Barbacena naturally
abandoned the idea of conveying the twelve-year-old princess and
affianced bride of Dom Miguel to Vienna. Accordingly, he and
Dona Maria went on to London where Barbacena exerted every effort to secure the acknowledgment by Great Britain of the princess'
sovereign rights. Success finally attended his endeavors. To him
Portugal owes much: the legal government of Dona Maria, the
freedom of her person, and the maintenance of the liberal Portuguese constitution.

Barbacena had been entrusted with a further and equally delicate
task—to find a bride for the emperor. Here, too, he was successful and when he returned to Rio de Janeiro on October 16, 1829,
he brought with him not only Dona Maria da Gloria but also Dona
Amelia de Leuchtemberg, the second empress of Brazil.

For a few months the internal political situation in Brazil took
a turn for the better. The Andrada brothers, back from exile and
reconciled with Dom Pedro, pointed out to him the dangers with
which the monarchy was faced and urged him to appoint a genuinely Brazilian cabinet. Barbacena gave the same advice and was
promptly entrusted with the task of carrying it out.

Unsuccessful Attempt at Constitutional Government.—Thus
was formed the ministry of December 4, 1829. It was Barbacena's
intention to organize a truly parliamentary government. To this
end he obtained the emperor's promise to abstain from any violation
of the constitution and, with much greater difficulty, contrived to
ship off to Europe a group of Dom Pedro's secret and irresponsi-
ble advisers, a veritable "kitchen-cabinet," which, recruited from
the lowest quarters of the palace of São Christovão, had dominated
Brazil. For a time Dom Pedro tried to abide by his promises but
he could not resist the temptation to carry on correspondence with
his former Portuguese and absolutist counsellors. This gentry,
still smarting under the contumely heaped upon them by Barbacena, neglected no opportunity to poison the mind of the emperor
against his minister. So well were these intrigues carried out, and

such a ready ear did Dom Pedro lend to these calumnies, that Barbacena, on October 4, 1830, resigned from office. Such gains as had been made during his incumbency were irretrievably lost. Dom Pedro soon slipped back into his earlier and vicious methods of governing. For a time, to be sure, a number of Barbacena's colleagues remained in the ministry but without the inspiration and guidance of the marquis they could accomplish little or nothing and one by one they left office, their places being filled by persons of utter insignificance.

Among these new political figures was included Deputy José Antonio da Silva Maia, whose reëlection to parliament by Minas Geraes was necessary if he were to remain in the ministry. For Dom Pedro such reëlection was a question of honor. He, therefore, set out for Ouro Preto, the capital of the province, to aid Silva Maia by every means in his power.

Increasing Difficulties of Dom Pedro.—In embarking on this tour through Minas the sovereign failed to remember that in this province, always independent in its attitude and still influenced by the traditions of the *Inconfidencia* conspiracy, the dominant spirit was liberal and even republican. In the elections of 1829, governmental support was a poor augury for any candidate. A new factor at this time contributed to the unpopularity of the emperor. In São Paulo an Italian exile, Libero Badaró by name, owned a newspaper in which he freely voiced his own advanced opinions. He favored the French revolution of 1830 and defended students who had been accused and punished by the legal authorities for the type of trivial offenses of which students are guilty the world over. Badaró attacked the local judge himself through the columns of his paper; feeling ran very high; the offending journalist was assassinated, and the judge was accused of being responsible for his death. He was tried on this charge in Rio but was acquitted on the ground that his guilt had not been proven. The events of the trial had been followed with passionate interest from one end of Brazil to the other. In the popular mind the judge had been freed by an order of the government. In no part of the empire did these unfortunate events produce a deeper impression than in Minas Geraes. The true sentiments of the *Mineiros*[8] were made abundantly clear to the emperor during his electioneering

---

[8] The name given to the inhabitants of the province of Minas Geraes.

tour. In the same cities and towns where in 1822 he had been received as a divine being by the kneeling populace, the bells of the churches tolled as masses were being held for the repose of the soul of the liberal Badaró, murdered by official absolutism.

The emperor returned to Rio with the determination to abdicate. His American mission was finished. Nothing held him any longer on this side of the Atlantic. All his thoughts were now directed toward his daughter and her cause. His first visit to Minas revealed to him the greatness and extent of Brazil and the impossibility of governing it from Portugal. The second supplied abundant evidence that the country rejected his method of government.

He was coldly received in Rio. "*Viva o Imperador, emquanto constitucional,*" [9] was the acclamation which resounded on all sides. A bloody conflict took place between his adherents and opponents; these brawls took the name of *Garrafadas* from the large number of *garrafas* (bottles) employed as weapons in the frays. These clashes might have assumed serious proportions but for the quick wit and intelligence of Evaristo da Veiga, the proprietor of the *Aurora Fluminense.* Through the columns of his paper, Evaristo urged the Nationalists to wear as a signal of unity and solidarity the green and yellow national cockade. The hint was followed; in a few hours these emblems of patriotism appeared on hats, coats, and garments. The appearance of the national colors not only acted as a sedative to national and political passions but it had the practical advantage of enabling the Brazilians to count themselves. So numerous were they that their opponents either remained silent or sought cover.

A self-appointed group of twenty-four known as the "*Aurora Fluminense,*" with Senator Vergueiro at their head, decided to submit to Dom Pedro a clear alternative: to obey the constitution and the laws and to forbid his followers to use violence, or face the certainty of deposition. To this warning Dom Pedro vouchsafed no reply. Plans were now made to submit a bill to the house of deputies declaring the emperor deposed. The sponsors of this project also advocated the abolition of the monarchy and the proclamation of a republic. Both Vergueiro and Evaristo were

---

[9] The meaning of this phrase is of course, "Long live the emperor provided he abides by the constitution."—P.A.M.

opposed to such a move, and their opinion, though not without a struggle, prevailed. The project, for the time being at least, was dropped.

In the army were many Brazilians, both among the officers and in the ranks. Volunteers had been numerous. Soldiers and civilians fraternized freely. It was evident that the emperor could no longer count on the unconditional support of the army.

Abdication of Dom Pedro I.—Even at this critical juncture Dom Pedro might perhaps have saved the situation through the appointment of a ministry which commended itself to public opinion. He took a certain step in this direction when he called together a new cabinet on May 19, 1831, consisting for the most part of moderates. But none of the new ministers was a member of parliament and his failure to consult the legislature was regarded as a further breach of the constitution. Dom Pedro now completely lost his head. On pretexts which were regarded as frivolous, he dismissed the ministry of March 19 and appointed on April 5 as their successors men who were not only known to be died-in-the-wool absolutists but also were reputed to be anti-Brazilian in sentiment. As the news of this further violation of the constitution was divulged popular excitement became intense. Rumors began to circulate that the freedom of the press was to be abolished. As if impelled by some occult and mysterious force, great throngs began to congregate in the Campo de Santanna, now known as the Praça da Republica. Everywhere troops fraternized with civilians. Dom Pedro, now thoroughly alarmed, sent a message promising to obey the laws. It was trampled under foot by the infuriated populace. Three justices of the peace repaired to the palace of São Christovão where in the name of the people they demanded that the emperor recall his former ministers. The only answer was a flat refusal.

It was the beginning of the end. The desertions began in the imperial palace itself. As the troops departed to join the demonstrators in the Campo de Santanna Dom Pedro remained alone with his family. There was no violence or lack of respect. It was a case of the quiet but unanimous rejection, on the part of the nation, of absolutism and all that it implied.

On April 7, 1831, the emperor abdicated and forthwith departed for Europe with the members of his family. As his successor he named his son, Dom Pedro de Alcantara, then less than six years of age. From this day forward Brazil was to be governed exclusively by Brazilians.

1825

CHAPTER VI

THE PERIOD OF THE REGENCY, 1831-1840

Organization of the Regency.—With the abdication of Dom Pedro I liberalism apparently had won an undisputed victory. Events were to show however that even after the departure of the emperor absolutism had its numerous votaries. The many elements which might profit by absolutism could be counted upon to oppose the smooth functioning of a constitutional regime and to strive for a return of the old system. But the first months after Dom Pedro's departure revealed on the part of those entrusted with the government of Brazil a laudable attitude of self-denial and a real appreciation of national needs. Nicoláu Pereira dos Campos Vergueiro was the spiritual leader and Evaristo da Veiga his right-hand man. The constitution contained no provisions applicable to the present crisis, for none of the relatives of the deposed emperor had reached the age of thirty-five, the limit fixed by the constitution for the assumption of the regency. Some new device must, therefore, be found to solve this dilemma. A provisional regency was elected from among the members of parliament, the choice falling upon the Marquis of Caravellas, the principal author of the constitution, upon Senator Vergueiro, and upon General Lima e Silva, chief of the forces whose coöperation had permitted the revolution of April 7, 1831, to pass off without bloodshed. Rio de Janeiro might well pride itself on its inhabitants, who at this critical juncture displayed admirable calm and forbearance. There were no insults, no acts of violence, no taunts at the absolutist or anti-Brazilian Portuguese from whom the population had endured so much.

An amnesty was at once declared. On June 14, 1831, parliament voted a law regulating the powers of the regency; the bitterly debated question of the approval of international treaties was solved by a provision declaring that they were to be submitted to parliament prior to their ratification. On June 17, the permanent regency was elected. Its members were Costa Carvalho (later Marquis of Monte-Alegre), João Braulio Muniz, and General Lima e Silva.

Constitutional reforms came next. There existed a strong sentiment in favor of increasing the rights of the provinces in harmony with the general tendency toward converting Brazil into a federation. On October 12, 1832, preliminary legislation to this end was sanctioned: the next legislature, in accordance with existing provisions, was empowered to reform the constitution. The most important reforms envisaged were the creation of provincial legislative assemblies, the abolition of the council of state, and substitution of a single regent for the triple regency.

The senate was regarded as a reactionary body; here were to be found all of the old absolutist counsellors of Dom Pedro I. In the liberal minority Barbacena, Vergueiro and Caravellas figured prominently. It was the general opinion that the majority, fearful lest Brazil be converted into a federation, would refuse to vote for the proposed constitutional reforms.

Four groups struggled for political control: the absolutists, the republicans, the constitutionalists, and the so-called "*commodistas.*" This last group was dubbed the "snails" by popular wits because of their haste in withdrawing into their shells or disappearing whenever any danger threatened. So great was the mutual distrust among the various groups that the slightest incident raised the political passions to fever heat.

Father Diogo Feijó, a liberal priest with republican leanings, an outstanding figure who later, as we shall see, was regent of the empire, served at this time as minister of justice. He was convinced that the aged José Bonifacio, appointed by Dom Pedro I as tutor and guardian of his little son, the future Dom Pedro II, was conspiring to secure the return of the emperor. It is beyond cavil that the Andradas as a whole favored this step. On this account, Feijó proposed the dismissal of the tutor; the chamber accepted the proposal but the senate rejected it.

The minister of justice possessed an energy and drive which led him to brush aside legality when he felt the higher interests of the state were in jeopardy. He went so far as to plan the elimination of the senate in the elaboration of the preliminary law on the constitutional amendments. But this proposal encountered unexpected opposition in the chamber of deputies, especially from Honorio Hermeto Carneiro Leão, the future Marquis of Paraná, one of the most eminent, judicious, and liberal statesmen of Brazil.[1] This deputy caused the project to be dropped, as both unconstitutional and revolutionary. Partly as a consequence of his eloquent pleas the senate itself agreed to pass the preliminary law, but Feijó was forced to resign. There were now passed in rapid succession through both houses of parliament laws dealing with constitutional amendments, the national guard, and the code of criminal procedure.

The decade following the abdication of Dom Pedro was indeed the storm and stress period of Brazilian history. The agitation of the public mind was profound and was inspired by many causes. The fear of absolutism was one of the most deep-seated. In July, 1831, in the capital itself Feijó had been obliged to quell a number of riots by the employment of armed forces. Pernambuco remained disturbed until 1835. As late as 1837 Pará was the theater of sanguinary disturbances which at the outset were instigated by republicans but later degenerated into simple outlawry. Only with great effort was peace restored in the distracted province. Agitation continued in Maranhão until 1832, in Amazonas until 1833, and in Ceará until 1834. Minas was relatively free from these disturbed conditions, although a military revolt occurred in Ouro Preto in 1833.

The Additional Act (Acto Addicional).—The parliament which assembled in 1834 was one of the most important in the whole history of Brazil. Its most immediate and pressing duty was to vote on the constitutional reforms known as the "Additional Act" which had been proposed during the preceding legislature. After a heated debate, it was decided that the reforms should be voted by the chamber alone, without the consent of the senate.[2] The amendments to the constitution adopted on August 12 by the Additional Act included the abolition of the council of state, the provision that, in the absence of an adult heir to the throne, a single regent with a term of four years should be selected by electoral

---

[1] The distinguished historian, Dr. Oliveira Lima, once told the editor of the present work that he considered Paraná the outstanding statesman of the empire.—P.A.M.

[2] The decisive argument in this debate was that only the deputies could vote for the reform as they alone had received the necessary mandate from their electors at the last election. The members of the senate were not elected but appointed for life.—P.A.M.

colleges in the provinces, and finally the creation of provincial legislative assemblies with a large degree of autonomy, in place of the existing councils whose functions had been very restricted.

Obsessed by the fear of absolutism and anxious to obtain the maximum degree of independence, the framers of the Additional Act had gone to excessive lengths in the matter of decentralization. The principal author of the reform, the great Bernardo Pereira de Vasconcellos, was quick to note this defect. As a matter of fact, the objectionable clauses had been incorporated contrary to the prudent advice and opinion of the special commission appointed to study and draft the law. But, as already intimated, the specter of absolutism and the panic fear of the return of Dom Pedro I caused the majority of the Brazilians both in and out of parliament to lose all sense of proportion.

In reality the deposed emperor never remotely considered returning to Brazil; at no time did he authorize his partisans to invoke his name. Finally, on September 24, 1834, Dom Pedro I died and the intrigues and agitation fomented by the "party of the restoration" automatically ceased. Unfortunately, however, the excesses of the Additional Act remained to plague for many years the public life of Brazil.

Bernardo de Vasconcellos.—The deplorable effect of these excesses had been clearly foreseen by Bernardo de Vasconcellos. The concessions made to the provinces were much too extensive. Instead of contributing to the unity of the country these reforms had released centrifugal forces which made possible or even encouraged secession. Nothing had been clearly defined regarding the respective powers of the provinces and those of the central government.

As a result of the ambiguities and uncertainties of the Additional Act progress was paralyzed. The yearly messages of the executive and the annual reports of the various ministries repeatedly demanded that the offending sections be reformed or at least that their intent be made clear. Only by such means could the agitation and anxiety which prevailed throughout the country be checked.

This crisis came at a most delicate moment in our national life. For three years the government of the triple regency, though conservative in character, had been obliged to cope with the intrigues and propaganda carried on by the absolutists in favor of Dom

Pedro's return. The death of the former emperor in 1834 was followed by a gradual lessening of the tension in public life. The heat of political passions little by little began to cool. A few, though very few, privileged minds now began to detect premonitions of a new era, a period of calm in the fevered quest for greater liberty. It is to the eternal credit of Bernardo de Vasconcellos that he perceived this phenomenon and acted accordingly. For a time he was a leader without followers. But presently other eminent Brazilians rallied to his cause and a new party, conservative in the best sense of the word, came into being. This new group occupied a middle position between autocratic reaction and exaggerated federalism. That such a restraining influence was needed admits of no possible doubt. After the passage of the Additional Act any further advances toward federalism would have been madness, for the unity and integrity of Brazil were at stake. But it required both balance of judgment and serenity of spirit to resist the seduction of specious but sterile theories and the reiteration of such shibboleths as liberty, liberalism, federalism.

Here lay the greatness of Vasconcellos. Here also is to be found the explanation of the savage attacks levelled against him and the accusation of "treason" on the part of his former co-workers. But strong in his own convictions he remained unwavering in the support of his new political ideal. The need of a firm policy was at this time the more necessary as the country was a prey to internal dissensions. The executive, as is inevitably the case with provisional and temporary regencies, was weak and inefficient. Under such circumstances the prime obligation of any government is the maintenance of order. This salutary truth Vasconcellos clearly saw and to the best of his ability strove to put into effect.

Diogo Antonio Feijó, Regent.—It will be recalled that the Additional Act provided for the election of a sole regent for a term of four years, in place of the provisional triple regency. On April 7, 1835, Diogo Antonio Feijó was elected and on October 12 assumed office. His choice reflected that feeling for order and that need of energy which were latent in the minds of the majority of the thinking Brazilians throughout the empire. The electors saw in him that same powerful and energetic statesman who as minister of justice had put down anarchy in Rio de Janeiro in 1832. One of his chief supporters was Evaristo da Veiga, whose friends and partisans had led the political campaign. Bernardo de Vasconcellos and Honorio Hermeto Carneiro Leão, on the other hand, were opposed to him.

Unfortunately, Feijó was not the same man he had been in 1832. He had suffered his first attack of paralysis a week before he assumed his duties as regent. Despondent and in poor health, he apparently cherished no hopes of improving the conditions of the country. Despite his energy he lacked confidence in his own forces. He looked at the world through dark glasses. A most curious figure, this priest, and one entitled to respect. He was entirely without pretense. His life and character were exemplary; he cared nothing for distinctions or rewards; he was the incarnation of honor and patriotism. He had but one ideal: order and obedience to law. Passionately wedded to his own opinions he was unable to understand or to do justice to opinions which differed from his own. This shortcoming twice wrecked his career: in 1832, when he unsuccessfully tried to secure the dismissal of José Bonifacio as tutor of the boy-emperor; and in 1837, when he attempted to maintain in power a ministry to which the majority of parliament was opposed. In both instances, rather than yield, he preferred to resign office. It was this inability to look facts in the face, to realize that the methods which he employed as minister of justice in 1832 were not applicable in parliament five years later, which accounted for his disagreement with Vasconcellos and Carneiro Leão, both statesmen of great mental power and political acumen.

Tumults and Disorders in Pará.—In 1832, the province of Pará was the theater of mutinies and disturbances. The central government, weak at the time, tried to arrive at an accommodation with the rebels. This attitude merely encouraged the leaders of the revolt which now took on republican leanings. Under the direction of Colonel Felix Antonio Clemente Melcher, Pará defied the imperial authorities. Defeated and imprisoned in the last weeks of 1834, Melcher was liberated by his followers, who after a carnival of murder, proclaimed him president of the province. But his rule as president was short-lived. After being deposed by one of his supporters, a certain Pedro Vinagre, he was brutally murdered by a new set of rebels. The assassination of Melcher ushered in an era of even greater disorder and violence. In Rio de Janeiro, counsels were divided and the government seemed powerless to cope with the problem. It was at this juncture that Feijó assumed power. The regent acted with his usual vigor; he followed the only course possible if the imperial authority was to enjoy any respect. Troops in sufficient force were despatched to the disaffected region and the insurrection was ruthlessly crushed. Such drastic actions were justified, for the revolt had degenerated into an orgy of violence in which criminals, thieves, and murdering gangs of half-breeds terrorized the province. Martial law was proclaimed and remained in effect until the leaders of the revolt had been apprehended, condemned, and punished. By 1837 peace was restored.

The Beginning of the Revolt of the "Farrapos."—Much more serious than the rebellion in Pará was the civil war which for a number of years raged in Rio Grande do Sul. This, the southernmost province of the empire, was conterminous with Uruguay and the Argentine Confederation. Owing to the long protracted conflicts on both sides of La Plata estuary, as well as to the similarity of environment, customs, and modes of living, all of the inhabitants of these southern regions had certain traits in common. Perhaps the dominating characteristic was the love of a wide autonomy which would offer them liberty of movement and opportunity to solve their local problems free from outside interference. They regarded a loose federation as the type of government best calculated to meet these needs. Artigas had personified this trend of political thought. It was not until the government of Buenos Aires refused to accept this federalist ideal that the Uruguayans insisted upon complete separation from their neighbors across the Río de la Plata.

During the Cisplatine campaign, a certain affinity of views had existed between the *Rio-Grandenses*[3] and the Uruguayans. The first, though loyal to Brazil, could not but regard with sympathy the struggle of their neighbors for freedom. After the treaty of 1828, creating the Republic of Uruguay, ties, old and new, continued to exist. Leaders and *caudilhos*[4] participated in joint raids on alien territory. Don Fructuoso Rivera, Don Manuel Oribe,[5] and

---

[3] The inhabitants of Rio Grande do Sul are thus designated by the Brazilians. —P.A.M.

[4] Defined by Dr. Calogeras as "chiefs of armed bands with political aims." The Spanish equivalent is *"caudillos."*—P.A.M.

[5] These heroes of Uruguayan independence were the first two presidents of Uruguay.—P.A.M.

others on the southern side of the boundary had among their friends and relatives on the Brazilian side such notables as Marshal Sebastião Barreto, Colonel Bento Manuel Ribeiro, Colonel Bento Gonçalves da Silva, and many others.

Political questions and issues on one side of the frontier had their inevitable repercussions on the other. No study of the Platine basin can be accepted as valid, at least from the historical point of view, which fails to take into account the fact that at this epoch the region constituted a political-geographical unity, in which conventional boundaries did not isolate populations one from another. In both countries were to be found common friends and foes, allies and adversaries, and their influence was not confined within legal bounds but passed beyond the frontiers. As soon as a revolution, a revolt, or an uprising occurred the leaders cast their eyes across the boundary where they were certain to receive aid and support as often as they asked for them. Such sentiments lasted for a great many years and even today are not entirely extinct or forgotten.

Contrary to what took place in Pará, both the contending factions in Rio Grande do Sul drew their support from the best elements of the province. In the weak hands of President Fernandes Braga, the local administration had allowed the reins of government to slacken. He was charged with being reactionary. His opponents, consisting of the so-called liberal party led by Colonel Bento Gonçalves da Silva, strove by every means to secure provincial autonomy. Public opinion ran high and on September 19, 1835, the conflict of ideals and interests led to an armed clash between the partisans of the president and those of Bento Gonçalves. The next day Bento Gonçalves called to arms the national militia,[6] and on the twenty-first marched into Porto Alegre, the capital, from which the president had incontinently fled.

These events coincided with the inauguration of Feijó as regent and he was immediately confronted with the problems growing out of the revolts in Pará and Rio Grande do Sul. In the case of the northern province, where the rebels were no better than armed mobs, he put down the rebellion pitilessly, as we have already seen.

---

[6] Bento Gonçalves had been appointed by the regency commander of the national guard of the province but Fernandes Braga refused to recognize this order. The militia, however, as in the present instance, accepted the authority of Bento Gonçalves.—P.A.M.

But the situation in the south was quite different. Here the regent had to cope with certain political principles, with which to be sure he could not compromise, but which he would have regarded as commendable had they not been so premature. Moreover, he had to deal with respectable and high-minded leaders, mistaken perhaps, but animated by genuine ideals.

In a letter to the Marquis of Barbacena, who was then in London, the regent wrote of his utter helplessness when faced with the situation in Rio Grande do Sul. All his efforts were concentrated on the suppression of the revolt at Pará; no resources remained for the south; agitation was gaining throughout the entire country; he was fearful of committing some error of judgment which might affect the prestige and credit of the government.

A new president of the province was appointed, José de Araujo Ribeiro. He not only possessed skill and tact but had the advantage of having friends and relatives among the best families in Rio Grande. It was hoped that he would prove an emissary of peace and harmony but at the outset, at least, his errand proved a failure. The inauguration of the new president was to take place in the presence of the provincial assembly. This body, the first chosen in accordance with the terms of the Additional Act, was in its majority opposed to the former president, Fernandes Braga, and was under the control of Bento Gonçalves. From various intimations which reached him Ribeiro was convinced that the deputies would not permit him to assume office. In reply to a number of indiscreet queries addressed to him by the deputies, he stated that he would assume his new duties immediately in the city of Rio Grande where he was then staying, and not in the capital, Porto Alegre. The assembly, as a consequence, suspended him from his functions. These events took place early in 1836.

War was now inevitable. Fortunately for the government, Ribeiro's appointment had the great advantage of detaching the ablest military leader from the ranks of the rebels, namely, Bento Manuel Ribeiro. This *caudilho*, a friend and relative of the president, remained faithful to him through thick and thin. The situation now began to improve. Porto Alegre was reconquered. In a number of scattered engagements the legal troops were victorious.

It was obvious that if Ribeiro were to remain in command of the situation he would need the full support of the central government.

But for motives that are not entirely clear Feijó hesitated, and then dismissed the president. This act aroused such a storm of protest in the province that Ribeiro was reinstated twenty days later. His hold on the province was strengthened by a flotilla of gunboats which entirely commanded the navigation of Lagoa dos Patos and the rivers tributary to it. Bento Gonçalves, the chief of the rebels, was not only obliged to abandon his attack on Porto Alegre but to retreat before the columns of Bento Manuel. Unfortunately, these successes could not be maintained. On September 10, 1836, at Seival the rebels won an important victory over the imperial troops and were so puffed up with their success that on the following day they proclaimed the "Republica Rio-Grandense." They set about to organize their government and chose Bento Gonçalves as president. But since the latter had been taken prisoner his place was provisionally filled by José Gomes Vasconcellos Jardim.

Federalism Rather than Separatism.—It would be incorrect to say that separation from the empire was a crucial point of the rebels' program. In the government which they set up no changes were made in existing laws, save as they affected the officers charged with enforcing them. In the innumerable protests made to the imperial authorities the idea of an eventful return to the empire was never impugned but a grant of autonomy for the province was always stoutly demanded. When eventually peace was concluded in 1845, the all-impelling motive was the common danger which threatened Brazil on the part of the Argentine Confederation. Federalist, rather than secessionist, the Rio-Grandense Republic was above all fighting for the preservation of its local liberties.

The republican troops never constituted an organized army. They excelled in guerilla warfare and harassed and worried their adversaries by their incessant movements. As Rio Grande do Sul was essentially a pastoral country there was an inexhaustible supply of horses, a basic requisite for raids and cavalry engagements. Troopers came and went as the spirit moved them. They assembled when convoked by their leaders; they fought, dispersed, or pursued the enemy, according to events and orders. At the utmost their numbers never exceeded six thousand. Of artillery there was almost none, perhaps twenty cannon, captured for the most part from their enemies.

The government was a replica on a small scale of that of the empire. The system of administering justice was faulty. The judges were temporary and too greatly under the influence of the military. The rebel organization could not have survived if Feijó, ill-advised, had not committed the gross error of definitely dismissing Araujo Ribeiro from the presidency in the first days of 1837 when almost the entire province was subject to the authority of the regency. And to enhance the gravity of the blunder, the dismissal of the president and his withdrawal from Porto Alegre was interpreted as an act of punishment and an evidence of distrust. This treatment of a man whose services were worthy of the highest praise is a serious blemish on the reputation of Feijó.

An immediate and deplorable consequence of the elimination of Araujo Ribeiro was the abandonment of the imperial cause by Bento Manuel. When this powerful *caudilho*, filled with indignation, and losing all sense of proportion, passed over to the rebels, the situation at once took a turn for the worse and the republicans little by little regained the territories they had lost. Feijó, at his wits' end, was unable to cope with the situation. He appointed president after president, at intervals of only a few weeks. Now his choice was a soldier, now a political negotiator. Disorder was everywhere rampant. The imperial message, read at the opening of parliament in 1837, reveals the utter despair and discouragement of the regent.

The Resignation of Feijó.—He asked for more troops but parliament turned a deaf ear. In fact the regent could count on no assistance from the legislature. The opposition was in the ascendancy, at least in the chamber of deputies. In addition to Honorio Hermeto Carneiro Leão and Bernardo de Vasconcellos, the leaders of public opinion were opposed to the politics and methods of the regent. The staunchest supporters of Feijó recognized that he did not know how to hold his friends, so harsh and unprepossessing were his manners. His religious convictions were tinged with old Portuguese regalist ideas. If carried to their logical end, these convictions would eventually have led to a separation from Rome and the creation of a national and Gallican church—to a schism, in fine. Needless to say such a tendency encountered the hostility of the overwhelming majority of the best minds and of the greatest statesmen in Brazil.

Feijó refused to admit the possibility of summoning Vasconcellos to the head of affairs although the votes and decisions of parliament all pointed in that direction. The regent admitted the brains but abhorred the character of the eminent Minas deputy whose private life was far from being exemplary. "A book to be read and tossed aside," Feijó once said of him. The ill-will against the regent, both in and out of parliament, now reached its height. As a crowning misfortune, his counsellor and most influential friend, Evaristo da Veiga, had died in May, 1837. At length Feijó read the handwriting on the wall and realized that his position was no longer tenable. He might perhaps have saved himself had he been willing to seek the collaboration of Vasconcellos, but to such a step he was unalterably opposed.

Pedro de Araujo Lima. Regent.—On September 19, 1837, Feijó resigned his office which, in accordance with the constitution, was provisionally taken over by the minister of empire (*ministro do imperio*),[7] Pedro de Araujo Lima, who on the following April was duly elected regent and later received the title of Marquis of Olinda.

The first move of Araujo Lima was to carry out the precepts of parliamentary government and organize a cabinet with Bernardo de Vasconcellos as chief. There now definitely emerged a new principle: ministerial solidarity. With a full understanding of his duties to the dynasty and to the Brazilian people, Araujo Lima conscientiously played the rôle of a constitutional monarch. Secure now in the support of parliament, the government asked for and received the grant of supplies which had been refused to Feijó. The policy of conciliation had failed in Rio Grande do Sul; another course was now adopted, that of crushing the rebels by force. Difficulties had increased, since the prisoners, among whom was the president of the so-called republic, Bento Gonçalves, had contrived to escape and the entire province was now aflame with revolt. Once again Bento Manuel defeated the imperial forces. Discouraged, the central government again had recourse to conciliatory

---

[7] A position similar in other countries to that of minister of the interior or of home affairs.—P.A.M.

measures and on January 1, 1839, offered a general amnesty. Very few of the republicans consented to lay down their arms. Instead of checking the conflagration such expedients were looked upon as evidences of weakness and the passions of the contending forces flamed higher than ever. Porto Alegre was again invested by the enemies of the empire.

Uncertainty and Hesitation of the Government.—During the years 1838-1839, the prospects were indeed gloomy. The government proved to be extraordinarily unhappy in its choice of representatives in the various provinces throughout the empire. In Rio Grande do Sul, the president, Elisiario de Brito, did not show himself in any sense equal to the occasion and only contrived to make a bad situation worse. Finally, the minister of war set out for the disaffected province, in order to inform himself *in situ* regarding the military and political developments. As aide-de-camp he took with him a young man whose fame was later to resound throughout Brazil. Major Lima e Silva, later marshal, baron, count, marquis, and finally, duke of Caxias, was a few years later to achieve the distinction of pacifying the south and of bringing the seemingly interminable rebellion to an end. On the present occasion he studied the problems and secured information and data which later were to prove invaluable.

The visit of the minister of war at first seemed to be quite barren of results. The activities of the republicans increased rather than diminished. They even advanced northward into the province of Santa Catharina, seizing on July 22, 1839, the little port of Laguna. They now set up an ephemeral republic and elected a "president." Four months later, however, a combined attack by land and sea dislodged the invaders and drove them back into Rio Grande.

Once more the regency committed the gross blunder of dividing its authority, bestowing upon an officer of the army command of the troops and turning over to a lawyer the civil administration. As if to make the error irreparable, the official selected was General Manuel Jorge, worn out by long years of service and on this account almost incapable of any decisive action. The lack of understanding between the military and civilian representatives was complete and operations came to an end. This condition of inertia lasted until March, 1840.

Yet one ray of light penetrated the gloom which seemed to be settling over Rio Grande do Sul. Bento Manuel, one of the most astute and intelligent among the rebel leaders, had come to realize that his position was growing precarious. In the ranks of the republicans he was only *one* of the numerous generals and as such he could hardly expect successfully to compete with his rival Bento Gonçalves. Thanks to the enormous resources at the disposal of the empire, the insurrection in Rio Grande was bound sooner or later to be crushed, with disastrous results to himself. He would be well advised, therefore, to renew his former allegiance. As early as July, 1839, he made public his determination to abstain from all military action. A year later he wrote to the president, who represented the imperial government, offering on behalf of himself, relatives, and friends, to abandon the insurgents in return for a grant of amnesty.

To add to the difficulties of the regency there was a recrudescence of revolutionary activity in the north. During the years 1839-1840 the province of Maranhão was the theater of an extensive uprising known as the *Balaiada,* from the name of its leader, Ferreira Balaiada. Serious though this revolt proved, it was largely the work of disorderly elements such as escaped convicts, brigands, cattle and horse thieves. When it came to crushing this rebellion, the regency for once was happy in its choice of commanders. On December 20, 1839, Lima e Silva set out for Maranhão with the combined authority of president of the province and head of the military and civil authorities. He took possession of his post February 7, 1840. The criminals and bandits were ruthlessly tracked down, laws were once more enforced, and order at length prevailed. The future Duke of Caxias was beginning to reveal those extraordinary qualities which later raised him to the highest military post in the empire.

Vital Necessity for a Strong Government.—Behind the recurrent disorders there were two fundamental causes: the discredit into which authority had fallen and the tendency toward secession. Both causes vindicated Vasconcellos' foresight when, in 1836, he proclaimed the necessity of a genuinely conservative policy.

The different regencies, necessarily provisional in character, lacked the strength and prestige of governments organized on a normal, constitutional basis. Depending as they did on elections they fostered ambitions and exacerbated existing rivalries. The Additional Act, due to its inherent faults and dubious wording, stimulated provincial ambitions and encroachments on the imperial authority. It paralyzed the activities of the central government, the administrative machinery frequently came to a standstill, and the evil at times assumed such proportions that general laws were abrogated by the provincial assemblies. Under such conditions a dangerous weakening of the cohesive powers of the empire was all but inevitable, and in such soil the seeds of secession could easily take root.

At this point reference must be made again to the decisive rôle played in this critical period by Bernardo de Vasconcellos. He had rendered his country signal service by removing certain flaws in the original draft of the constitution. It was now his good fortune to prevent the Additional Act from becoming a menace to Brazilian unity. First as deputy and later as senator, he intervened in the debates regarding the interpretation of the Act. Representing the views of the conservative party he demanded that the powers of the provincial assembly be clearly and adequately defined and that the central authority should not be unduly curtailed. His opponents, on the other hand, were in favor of an excessive federalism which would, in the judgment of the conservatives, make for the disunion of Brazil. Vasconcellos' views finally prevailed and on May 12, 1840, the law interpreting the Additional Act was voted and sanctioned.

Influence of the Platine Political Parties in the Rebellion in Rio Grande do Sul.—Allusion has already been made to the interpenetration of political factors on both sides of Brazil's southern boundary. This situation was pregnant with serious consequences whose ultimate issue was to be the Brazilian intervention in the Río de la Plata area and war against the Argentine Confederation, culminating in the defeat of the Argentine dictator, Rosas, at Monte Caseros in 1852. Our immediate concern, however, is to make intelligible the developments which took place in the Platine basin during the decade from 1830 to 1840.

As was pointed out earlier, the various factions contending for power in Rio Grande had their partisans and allies on the Uruguayan side of the frontier. Conflicts and skirmishes in which Uruguayan interests suffered were inevitable. In Montevideo the conviction was general that the Brazilian government fostered and abetted these troubles. The sad truth is that Brazil could not confess the lamentable but simple fact that the central government of the empire was powerless in Rio Grande do Sul when it came to dealing with the exalted partisans of local autonomy. The latter, directed by Bento Gonçalves and his friends, supported by every means in their power the Uruguayan revolutionists, moved as they were by motives of personal friendship, family bonds, and tacit alliances. There was a good military reason too. The success of any campaign depended upon cavalry and Uruguay was better provided with horses than Rio Grande do Sul.

In 1830 Uruguay elected its first president, Don Fructuoso Rivera, for a term of four years. But shortly after his inauguration, Rivera had to contend with a rebellion fomented by Lavalleja, the famous leader of the "Thirty-Three" who had raised the standard of Uruguayan independence in 1825. In his contest with Rivera, Lavalleja secured supplies of all kinds, especially food stuffs and cavalry, in Rio Grande. The Uruguayan government naturally protested, for it seemed obvious that the imperial authorities had either connived at this breach of neutrality or were unable to repress it. In either case, the ultimate responsibility rested with Rio, but because of the weakness of the regency the government was powerless to enforce its neutrality decrees.

In 1835 Don Manuel Oribe, another hero of Uruguayan independence, succeeded Rivera. He had been selected by his predecessor and elected through his influence. But once in the saddle Oribe treated his former protector with scant consideration. Rivera was relieved of his important position as commander of the army (*Comandancia general de campaña*) and his advice was neither asked nor followed. The inevitable happened. In 1836 Rivera launched a rebellion against the government of Oribe.

Developments in another quarter now complicated the situation. On the further side of the Río de la Plata a new star was in the ascendant. Don Juan Manuel Ortiz de Rosas, the idol of the gauchos and leader of the so-called federalists, had gained control of the Argentine Confederation. His opponents, the unitarians, were hunted down ruthlessly and to escape his clutches most of them had sought exile. The best brains and ablest leaders of the unitarians found refuge in Uruguay where they organized the Unitarian Committee of Montevideo (*Comité Unitario de Montevideo*). Among their number was General Lavalle, one of the heroes of the Spanish American wars of independence.

These unitarian exiles represented a most important element in Uruguay, since they constituted a picked body of troops, in many cases the mental and moral elite of Argentina. They were some 14,000 in number and the total population of Uruguay at this time did not exceed 75,000. Rivera took them all under his protection and enrolled them in the regular Uruguayan army.

Rosas looked upon this act as an insult and Rivera became his personal enemy. But the Argentine dictator had other grounds for animosity. Despite the fact that the government of Buenos Aires had solemnly agreed to respect the independence of the Republic of Uruguay, Rosas' secret hope was to bring the east bank of the Uruguay under his control and to reunite all the former portions of the old viceroyalty of Buenos Aires. Such a task would be facilitated if Uruguay were rent with factional strife and civil war. To this end Rosas now bent his efforts.

Party Alliances in the South.—Thus, two groups were formed: one consisting of Rivera with the Argentine Unitarians; the other, Lavalleja (and later Oribe), Rosas, and the insurgents of Rio Grande do Sul. Between the two, the Brazilian government officially maintained neutrality and attempted before the outbreak of hostilities in the South to restrain Bento Goncalves and his friends from furnishing aid to the Uruguayan exiles who were scheming for the overthrow of President Rivera.

But when Rivera raised the standard of revolt against President Oribe great changes had occurred. Oribe had become a friend of Rosas and of Lavalleja. He was the recognized leader of the *Blancos*, or "Whites," one of the two traditional parties of Uruguay.[8] The position of Rivera, the leader of the *Colorados* or "Reds" soon became critical. But Buenos Aires was not primarily interested in the mere substitution of one chieftain for another.

---

[8] The designations *Blanco* and *Colorado* came from the white and red ribbons by which the partisans of Oribe and Rivera were distinguished at the battle of Carpinteria, fought in 1836. Both parties have persisted to the present day although the *Blancos* are officially known as "Nationalists."—P.A.M.

The all-important consideration was to keep Uruguay in such a position of weakness and dependency that the Porteños might exercise effective control whenever they desired.

At length, in September, 1827, Rivera was decisively defeated, and was glad to escape with his life and a handful of companions into Rio Grande do Sul. A few months earlier, Araujo Ribeiro had been dismissed from the presidency of this province; Bento Ribeiro, furious at the affront inflicted upon his relative and friend, had abandoned the imperial forces and thrown in his lot with the insurgents. He was presently joined by the Uruguayan exile Rivera who coöperated with him in the ensuing campaign. From now on the grouping of forces in La Plata basin was as follows: Rivera, the Argentine unitarians, and the Rio Grande insurgents sided together; Oribe, Rosas, and Lavalleja constituted the opposing party. Rio de Janeiro endeavored to remain netural, but its natural tendency inclined it to favor the second group, which after all represented legal authority. This disposition of Brazil was strengthened by a step taken at this juncture by the Uruguayan president. Oribe, eager to have his country profit by Brazil's internal dissensions, had sent an emissary to Rio in order to negotiate a treaty definitely fixing the boundary between Brazil and Uruguay. This boundary had been provisionally agreed upon in the treaty of 1828; Oribe proposed that the limits of 1777 be accepted, a solution greatly to the advantage of Uruguay. Feijó and his cabinet were willing to accept such an arrangement but parliament, indignant at such weakness on the part of the executive, voted down the government's proposal.

French Blockade of Río de La Plata.—The next year witnessed another shift in the political scene. Rivera once more invaded Uruguay and on June 15, 1838, decisively defeated Oribe's forces at the Battle of Palmar. On October twenty-fourth the president submitted his resignation to the national assembly and on March 1, 1839, Don Fructuoso was elected the president of Uruguay for the second time. In his contest with Oribe, Rivera had secured aid from an unexpected quarter. For reasons that were on the whole trivial—maltreatment by Rosas of certain French subjects —the government of Louis Philippe had instituted a blockade of the Río de la Plata and had entered into a compact with the Argentine Committee of Montevideo, which was acting in behalf of the unitarian party, to wage war on the Argentine dictator. This compact had little to recommend it, for France was supporting by subsidies and naval aid a cause which was not its own and in which it had little real concern. As was to be expected Rivera joined the coalition against Rosas. Despite the defeat of his ally, Oribe, Rosas continued the struggle. He represented the cause of American freedom and liberty against the invasion of groups of Argentines subsidized by French gold. His triumph was complete. He was respected, even in Europe, as the defender of the continental autonomy of both Americas. The French ministry, headed by Soult, at length recognized the ineptitude of its diplomacy in the Platine basin and the fool's part that it had been playing. The French naval forces abandoned the blockade, a formal apology was tendered Rosas, and a treaty was signed on October 29, 1840, which put an end to the conflict. On the following day the French ships fired a salute in honor of the Argentine flag. Shortly afterward Rosas put down the various rebellions fomented in Argentina by the Montevideo committee. Oribe, serving under Rosas as an Argentine general, commanded the federalist troops.

A curious situation had developed. Rosas, the governor of the province of Buenos Aires, towered above his allies and completely overshadowed his opponents. He had triumphantly defended the cause of liberty and independence. A new phase had arisen in the history of the continent. Rosas now indulged in the dream of incorporating Uruguay into a larger Argentina having the same boundaries as the old Spanish viceroyalty of La Plata. Rivera, in turn, harbored the aspiration of constituting a greater Uruguay, embracing the former Cisplatina, the Argentine province of Corrientes (lying between the Paraná and the Uruguay), and the Brazilian province of Rio Grande do Sul. But the Brazilian revolutionists in the South, though bound by treaty with Rivera, had no intention of breaking completely with Brazil; they were much more intent upon local autonomy than they were on separation from the empire. A perfect comedy of errors.

Proclamation of the Majority of Dom Pedro II.—Coming events cast their shadows before. Rumors of these various plots to dismember the empire eventually reached Rio de Janeiro and increased the longing for peace and order and for a government capable of maintaining national unity. There was a growing conviction, especially among the liberals, that the regency did not possess the prestige and authority necessary to bring these interminable conflicts and civil wars to an end. As early as 1839, Feijó, the two surviving Andrada brothers, Hollanda Cavalcanti, and many other liberals had come to the conclusion that one of the most efficacious means of repressing internal disorders would be the immediate coronation of the young emperor. He had not reached the legal age, to be sure, but this difficulty might be met by special legislation. One of the most intimate friends of Feijó, Senator Alencar, proposed in April, 1840, that an association be formed to further this plan. The idea met with favor; a political club in support of the majority of the emperor was organized, and adhesions poured in not only from those liberal elements opposed to the government but even from a number of conservatives. In the speech from the throne, delivered on the opening of the legislature of 1840, the question of the declaration of the majority of the emperor was raised and on May thirteenth of the same year a bill was introduced setting aside the constitutional provisions relative to the age in which the emperor would assume full power.

But the government, caught by surprise, was averse to any precipitate action. Three conditions would have to be met if the movement were to be crowned with success: the acquiescence of the young Dom Pedro, a favorable vote of parliament, and the sanction of public opinion. By sounding out the Andradas and Deputy Pinto Coelho, a relative of Dom Pedro's tutor, the Marquis of Itanhaén, it was learned that the emperor would consent to an immediate declaration of majority. The people at large were enthusiastically in favor of such a move. As for the parliament, it was difficult to ascertain the predominating sentiment but it was obvious that there existed a strong current in favor of immediate action. Honorio Hermeto, always in the forefront when it was a question of upholding the law and the constitution, came out in favor of what was after all the only legal course, namely to submit the whole matter to the voters at the next general election. But this proposal had one serious drawback: it was logical and it was legal but it ran counter to the excited passions of the moment.

The first clash in parliament on the question of the emperor's majority arose in connection with the reply to the address from the throne. In the senate, those in favor of the proposed step were defeated by two votes; in the chamber, by fifteen. The liberals were exultant, for such a narrow defeat presaged ultimate victory. They now redoubled their efforts in public meetings, in parliament, and in political clubs. They also enjoyed the inestimable advantage of being supported by public opinion.

José Clemente Pereira, one of the patriarchs of Brazilian independence, a supporter of the government, a man who enjoyed great respect and whose opinions carried much weight, declared in the senate that the immediate coronation of the emperor was a national necessity even if it did violence to the constitution. The Marquis of Paranaguá, likewise one of the founders of the empire, and president of the upper house, publicly expressed similar opinions. The government now realized that only energetic measures could prevent its defeat. An urgent invitation was addressed to Bernardo de Vasconcellos to accept the portfolio of the empire, in order that he might be in a position to crush any revolutionary attempt to crown the emperor at a date earlier than that permitted by the constitution. Bernardo was not the man to recoil from responsibilities and he accepted the heavy burden. Like the overwhelming majority of his party, he had come to realize that sooner or later Dom Pedro would have to assume the functions of supreme ruler. The only disagreement was over the date. The liberals favored the latter part of July; the conservatives wished to stave off this event until December second. Vasconcellos foresaw that a liberal triumph would mean loss of power to himself and his followers. He was anxious therefore to utilize the dwindling conservative majority to secure the passage of a number of preliminary laws before the declaration of Dom Pedro's majority. He was especially desirous of the creation of a new council of state[9] which, established at the initiative of a conservative government, might serve as a stronghold of his party.

All of Bernardo's efforts to stem the tide proved futile. The liberals foresaw the ruin of all their plans should Vasconcellos remain in office. The Andradas, whose violent temper was well known, headed the opposition. With the aid of their friends, they interrupted and finally broke up the sitting of the lower house. A mob, in which liberal deputies figured prominently, invaded the senate

---

[9] This body had been originally created by the constitution of 1824 but it had been abolished by the Additional Act.—P.A.M.

and turned the upper house into what was virtually a revolutionary convention. Vasconcellos resigned as a protest against such violence and subsequently declared, in a manifesto addressed to the nation, that he considered his nine hours' ministry the most glorious event of his public life. From a strictly partisan or party point of view this attitude was perhaps intelligible but it certainly could not be justified from the point of view of a statesman. At the most Bernardo could only hope to delay for a few months a consummation which the majority of the nation ardently desired.

A passionate appeal was now directed to the boy-emperor, imploring him to consent to save the country by immediately taking over the reins of power. A commission was appointed to convey this message to the imperial palace of São Christovão. With great dignity the fourteen-year-old Dom Pedro[10] received the parliamentary commission and retired to deliberate. The regent, Pedro de Araujo Lima, explained to His Majesty that it had been the intention of the government to pave the way for the proclamation of the emperor's majority in the first days of December. But in view of the existing conditions Dom Pedro must decide for himself whether he should adopt the course planned by the government or decide on an immediate assumption of power.

"I wish it at once" ("*Quero já*"), was the imperial reply.

Nullo adversante, in the phrase of Tacitus, Senhor Dom Pedro II on the twenty-third of July, 1840, entered upon the exercise of his functions as ruler, and his personal reign began.

---

[10] Dom Pedro II was born on December 2, 1825.

CHAPTER VII

POLITICAL AND ECONOMIC PROBLEMS UNDER DOM PEDRO I AND THE REGENCY; THE SLAVE TRADE

BEFORE continuing our narrative history of Brazil, it seems wise to consider in some detail the most important political and economic crises which the empire had to face from its creation in 1822 to the accession of Dom Pedro II in 1840.

The Emergence and Development of the Parliamentary System. —The meeting of the first parliament, in 1826, represented a great step forward in the constitutional life of Brazil. Both deputies and senators were, with rare exceptions, men of calaber and ability. On the other hand, the great majority were necessarily men without experience or training in public affairs. Yet such were their achievements that they may well deserve the title of fathers of their country. They were the real founders of Brazilian nationality. Constitutional Brazil was of their making.

In laying the foundations of the constitutional and legal structure of the empire, the members of parliament came into open conflict with the executive. The truth of the matter is that Dom Pedro I, despite his good will and liberal views, was incapable of honestly playing the rôle of a constitutional monarch. From the outset the executive and the legislature clashed on the interpretation of the constitution. The struggle began at the very first meeting when the assembly rightly insisted on being considered and treated as one of the powers of the state and was successful in carrying its point.

The prestige of parliament was further increased when it imposed upon the members of the cabinet the duty of presenting annual reports. The collaboration of both houses in ratifying treaties, though flouted by Dom Pedro I, was enforced immediately after the abdication of the first emperor. Under the regency the parliamentary system was definitely established. Feijó, autocratic and dictatorial, was as we have seen little disposed to follow the behests of a parliamentary majority. Yet Bernardo de Vasconcellos in 1837 forced the old and venerable priest to resign office and from then on the parliamentary system was never successfully challenged.

This same quickening of national life was to be seen in the juridical and administrative organization of the country. The old Portuguese legislation had been provisionally adopted by the empire on the establishment of independence but such an arrangement was necessarily unsatisfactory, for Brazil needed laws of its own, adapted to its peculiar conditions. Brazilian jurists, largely self-trained, at once addressed themselves to the task of drawing up the necessary codes. In 1830, the criminal code was promulgated and two years later the code of criminal procedure.

In 1827 two faculties of law were established in São Paulo and Recife respectively. The same year saw the founding of an astronomical observatory in Rio de Janeiro. Naturalization of the Portuguese who had been residing in Brazil since independence was voted. Legislation was passed dealing with the responsibility of ministers and secretaries of state. Provision was made for the setting up of primary schools in each district and town. The administration of justice was organized; a supreme tribunal was created and rules for its procedure were published in 1828. The organic statute of the provincial councils was put into execution; the postal system was formally organized and greatly expanded; public works of all kinds were stimulated; municipal councils took on a new lease of life. The freedom of the press was regulated in 1830. The national militia was created in 1831. The schools of medicine were expanded in 1832. A general law dealing with naturalization was voted in 1833. In 1837 regulations were adopted designed to increase the efficiency of the army. In fine, the constitutional, political, and administrative life of the empire was placed upon a satisfactory and stable basis thanks in part to the amendments to the Additional Act of 1834 and the Interpretative Law of 1840.

The Economic and Financial Situation.—Efforts were also made to put the finances of the country on a firmer foundation. During the decade from 1830 to 1840 the treasury was reorganized; the public debt was funded and its service regulated; a sinking fund was created. Yet these salutary measures were insufficient to prevent the financial difficulties caused by excessive expenditure and the mistaken policy in regard to the currency.

The excessive issuance of copper coins, discussed in an earlier chapter[1] had, in accordance with Gresham's Law, driven out of the country practically all gold and silver money. Circulation consisted of paper currency and copper coins, both depreciated, as was evidenced by the rise of exchange. Moreover, the amount of money in circulation was excessive in comparison with the value of production. As a consequence, the cost of living increased, expenses rose to new heights, and no great expansion of commerce or exports was possible.

Mining activity was afflicted with a serious depression almost amounting to a collapse. The basic reason was the exhaustion of all but the deeper mines, the exploitation of which required great outlay of capital. But this fact was less obvious at the time and, on the supposition that the parlous condition of the mining industry was owing to excessive taxation, the government reduced this burden from 20 to 5 per cent. The local circulation of gold dust was tolerated. Later all restrictions were lifted and the use of unminted gold was permitted in all transactions, including payment of taxes. But all of these measures were powerless to exorcise this monetary crisis whose ill effects were felt by all. The slave trade, which was very active during the last years of legal importations allowed by the Anglo-Brazilian treaty of 1826, demanded large sums for its financing. The disastrous 5 per cent loan of 1829, sold to bankers at fifty-two, was a heavy burden on the treasury.

The parliament struggled to find a way out of this dilemma, but without success. The only measures proposed were the further issue of paper money, a new fixed rate of exchange, or a combination of both. In 1833 a new currency law was passed, arbitrarily fixing the par of exchange at 42 2/10 pence. Such legislation revealed a complete ignorance of economics and monetary problems; it was passed under the pressure of the moment, due to the desire to bring to an end the violent fluctuations of the milréis. Its results were nil; the quotations of the milréis continued to fall.

The population was nevertheless increasing; and commerce and production during the regency began to show a promising advance. From 1822-1834 to 1839-1840 the value of imports had risen from 36,337 contos to 52,358 contos; that of exports from

[1] See above, pp. 58, 59.

33,000 to 43,192 contos.[2] This improvement helped to arrest the drop in the quotation of the milréis which was finally kept between 26 and 31 pence. Inquiries were made by the authorities among responsible financial circles and opinions were tendered. Eventually these suggestions were taken into account when the law of 1846 fixed a new parity of the milréis at 27 pence.

The Commercial Treaties.—One of the greatest obstacles to the freedom of taxation was to be found in the treaties negotiated by the recently founded empire during the period from 1826 to 1829. Through these instruments commercial freedom, liberty in tariff matters, the power of carrying out a sound and consistent economic and fiscal policy had been gravely impaired. From the very first parliament had opposed these treaties and that for two reasons: the menace to the rational exploitation of the natural wealth of the country which it detected in these instruments, and the implied violation of the constitution when these treaties were ratified without parliamentary sanction.

The duration of these treaties was from six to fifteen years, with the exception of the French agreement, which unhappily contained a number of perpetual clauses. None of the remaining instruments was supposed to extend beyond 1842, but in the case of the English treaty its expiration was postponed two years by means of arguments based on chicanery.

Everyone complained of these conventions. The ministerial reports stressed the fact that they were entirely useless to the country. Parliament, as we have just seen, opposed them since they hindered the collection of taxes necessary for balancing the budget. Public opinion looked upon them as both unnecessary and inequitable. Worst of all were the French and English treaties, the former on account of its perpetual clauses, and the latter because of the preposterously low import duties of which Great Britain was the sole beneficiary. An added cause of resentment against the United Kingdom was the so-called *conservatoria* privilege, which gave the subjects of His Gracious Majesty residing in Brazil the right to be tried by one of their own judges (*juiz conservador*). The Brazilians smarted under these exceptions which, tolerated by Portugal since 1450, were resented in America by the touchy descendants of the old peninsular metropolis.

---

[2] It may be recalled that a conto consists of one thousand milréis.—P.A.M.

It was expected by the Brazilians that the adoption in 1832 of the code of criminal procedure—a striking monument of juridical science and liberalism—would remove the most galling of these anomalies, that of the *juiz conservador*. Clause VI of the treaty with Great Britain had accorded Brazil the right to demand its abolition as soon as an acceptable substitute, which would offer equally satisfactory guarantees to British appellants, was available. But the British Government made it abundantly clear that it had no intention of abandoning this privilege, guaranteed by the treaty of 1827. Brazil repeatedly insisted in its demands, which reflected the general desires of the nation. The British Government finally ceased to reply to our appeals, just and well-founded though they were. This was a great mistake on the part of the Palmerston-Aberdeen Cabinet, for the intransigent and insupportable attitude of Great Britain greatly embittered relations between the two countries. No other recourse was left to Brazil save to wait until the treaty expired. Other problems were also involved in this diplomatic controversy, especially those concerned with the administration by British consuls of the estates of British subjects who died in Brazil intestate.

Another grievance was the 15 per cent import duty to which British goods were subject. The Brazilian government, quite erroneously, deemed itself bound to apply this low tariff to all goods passing through the customhouses, whether they were of British origin or not. It was thus estopped from levying adequate duties on such non-British imports as wines, brandy, oil, and vinegar, the tariff on which should have been a most important source of revenue. It was not until the Marquis of Barbacena, then on a special mission to England, explained to the Rio cabinet its rights in this matter that Brazil regained its freedom in the making of its tariff. But even then British imports constituted an odious exception to such liberty of action until the commercial treaty of 1827 finally expired in 1844.

The Slave Trade.—As was pointed out in an earlier chapter,[3] Brazil had signed, in 1826, a treaty with Great Britain providing for the final abolition of the slave trade at the expiration of four years. The treaty was signed under the pressure of circumstances. England's sympathy and support might be essential to the interests

---

[3] *Cf.* above, Chapter V.

and even life of the newly born empire. But in the opinion of the
overwhelming majority of the Brazilians the treaty was little short
of a disaster; were its terms to be carried out a death-blow would
be inflicted upon the agriculture and incipient industry of the
country. For three centuries slaves had constituted the only form
of labor and had been the basis of the material progress of Brazil.
White labor, at least on the plantations, was almost non-existent;
such whites as were employed acted as superintendents or overseers. With the high death rate among the Negroes and mulattoes,
the problem of the maintenance of an adequate *main d'oeuvre*
might prove exceedingly difficult if the source of supply for additional Negro labor were cut off. And in four years, that is in
1830, such a catastrophe was due to arrive. A general feeling of
stupor and despair invaded the mass of the landowners and pro-
ducers, who constituted at this time the leading class in Brazil.
The instruction of these men in economics was less than rudimentary and they failed to realize that servile labor was in the
long run neither productive nor cheap. To be sure a few exceptions
were to be found among public men who were close students of
political economy and public wealth. These men, some of whom
were political leaders, were fully aware of both the iniquity of the
slave trade and of the eventual necessity of its abolition, but they
were only a handful in number. Their followers refused to accept
their views and clung tenaciously to the conviction that both the
slave trade and slavery were essential to the very existence of the
empire. Time alone could be counted upon to modify this all but
unanimous belief.

The slave trade at this time could not be raised to the dignity
of a party issue; conservatives and liberals looked upon it in the
same light. Leaders of both parties, who endeavored to cope with
the evil, found themselves deserted by their followers who availed
themselves of the most effective type of opposition—mere inertia.
Slavery at this period was almost regarded as a national institution which few undertook to justify because no justification was
needed. The great landowners (*fazendeiros*) and their depend-
ants virtually controlled the country. It was they who elected the
deputies and senators, from whose files in turn were recruited the
members of the cabinet. Party leaders and politicians, if they

hoped to maintain their influence, necessarily had to take into account the views of their constituents and followers.

The situation was paradoxical. Many of the foremost political leaders and responsible members of the government expressed themselves in favor of the abolition of the slave trade and of the strict adherence to the relevant treaties with Great Britain. But they spoke as isolated individuals and when as government officials they tried to enforce the laws and treaties they could find neither help nor support among the mass of the Brazilians.

England never succeeded in grasping this peculiarity of our political life. Brazil was far from being on the economic or ethnic level of Western Europe; its mentality was still a primitive one, swayed by impulses and instincts. A long period was necessary before exact and scientific notions regarding the real character of servile labor could make any headway among the rank and file of the people. To assist the Brazilians in rising to a broader and truer grasp of these problems, great skill and tact were essential. But in these qualities Great Britain was sorely lacking. Though convinced that they were the champions of a cause that was essentially liberal and Christian, Palmerston and Aberdeen created difficulties of all kinds, and complicated rather than simplified the solution of the questions at issue between England and Brazil. While it cannot be denied that pressure from Great Britain was a factor in the suppression of the slave trade, the action of British cruisers in entering Brazilian waters in pursuit of suspected slavers hindered rather than helped the Brazilian authorities in putting an end to this ignominious traffic.

Conditions in Brazil Favorable to the Slave Trade.—Almost without exception public opinion was favorable to the importation of Negroes. The orders issued by the government and its representatives against the traffic were either disobeyed or were carried out with such ill-will and delay that they proved quite ineffective. The reasons for this failure have already been suggested: the hostility between those who would loyally carry out the treaty stipulations and the solid compact mass of the *fazendeiros*, that is, virtually the entire nation.

Great Britain had spent many years and expended much effort to put an end to the slave trade in which its own subjects had been engaged. But the leaders of the great campaign against the traffic —such men as Wilberforce and Clarkson—were not content until this monstrous evil had totally abolished. Spurred on by these and other reformers and supported by public opinion at home, Great Britain insisted that the Brazilian traffic should come to an end at the expiration of the four years contemplated by the treaty of 1826. Experience was soon to demonstrate that under conditions as they then existed in Brazil this interval was much too brief. For Great Britain, the traffic represented a mere fraction of its commercial and economic activity in the West Indies, while in the case of Brazil the whole economic life of the empire was apparently at stake.

As has already been intimated, the peculiar difficulties of the problem were not understood in England and the disobedience and delay of the local authorities and the ill-will of time-serving functionaries were attributed to the duplicity of the imperial government. It was on such false assumptions that British action was predicated. Palmerston and Aberdeen taxed Brazil with bad faith, when in reality the government was powerless to force obedience on the *fazendeiros*. Yet, how could the Brazilian ministers confess such impotence? It would have been equivalent to flouting the very conventions to which Brazil affixed its signature.

Conflicts Over the Interpretation of the Treaties.—On the other hand, the treaty of 1826 was not always respected by Great Britain itself. The treaty had been justified on the ground that it was an instrument for the abolition of a traffic in Negro slaves, in which the mortality as a rule rose to 30 per cent of the human cargo, all to the accompaniment of frightful atrocities. But, in carrying out the terms of the treaty, the British cruisers were guilty of grave irregularities in the seizure and disposition of prizes. Two tribunals had been established, one in Sierra Leone and the other in Rio de Janeiro. The first being close to the source of the slave supply dealt with the great majority of cases, passing on the legality of the capture of the alleged slavers by the British cruisers. A Brazilian commissioner was supposed to take part in these proceedings but during long periods this officer was absent. But even under these conditions, the tribunal ruled that many ships had been unlawfully captured and were to be returned to their owners who were to receive a suitable indemnity. But the

British Government in many cases paid no heed to these judgments; neither were the ships returned nor the money paid, despite the undeniable fact that the British judges themselves had often condemned the excessive and unwarranted zeal of the British cruisers.

It is easy to understand that such procedure evoked violent protests throughout Brazil. And since every opportunity to increase the labor supply was regarded as legitimate, the man in the street was led to regard the policy of Great Britain as a violation of Brazilian sovereignty and an unendurable form of tutelage. But this growing tide of resentment produced not the slightest effect on the policy of Great Britain, which if anything became more harsh and unyielding.

As the British cruisers continued their arbitrary seizures of Brazilian ships and their violation of Brazilian territorial waters the hatred against the successive British cabinets became more and more intense.

The Rio government proposed to indemnify Brazilian citizens who had suffered losses through the excessive zeal of the British by utilizing sums due English subjects growing out of the unlawful seizures made by the Brazilian blockading squadron in the Río de la Plata. But the London government refused to entertain such an offer. The real aim of Great Britain was to bring about the suppression of the traffic by making the situation hopeless for the shipowners. But the methods employed proved ineffective. The slavers were able to circumvent the British cruisers by various ingenious stratagems with the result that the slave trade assumed larger and larger proportions. The great mistake made by Great Britain was to attempt to solve the difficulties by compulsion rather than by coöperation. And the efforts of the English were particularly inopportune as they were exerted at a time when public opinion in Brazil was undergoing a profound modification.

The Birth of a National Movement Against the Traffic. Measures Presented to Parliament.—As the result of discussion and debate the number of those convinced of the economic disadvantages of the slave trade steadily grew. In parliament efforts were made to discover ways and means of finding a substitution for slave labor. Most of the suggestions broached at this time, though admirable in intention, were inadequate and impracticable.

It could hardly have been otherwise. Brazil in the thirties and forties was scantily populated, without roads, without harbors, without hygiene, and under the constant menace of Indian tribes and epidemics. Yet some of these abortive efforts to cope with the evils of the traffic are sufficiently interesting to deserve a brief mention.

In 1830 only a few thousand slaves were imported and these under the flags of Portugal and France. Steps were taken to re-export these Negroes to Africa, either to the newly founded Republic of Liberia or to the domains of the petty chieftains who had sold them to the traders. From the United States, curiously enough, a few Negroes found their way into Brazil. They were all free Negroes, who had been deceived and seduced by promises and presents. Many of them fell victims to a plot designed by unscrupulous importers. They were cleared through the customhouse as freemen, but were subsequently captured and sold into slavery. It was necessary hastily to vote a law for the punishment and suppression of this crime; such an act was sanctioned on November 7, 1831, and regulated by a decree of April 12, 1832. This legislation provided that all Negroes who landed on Brazilian soil became *ipso facto* free. Importers of slaves were fined and obliged to return the Negroes to Africa. But these stipulations could not be carried out; the African chieftains refused to take back these Negroes and refund the payments they had already received.

Despite the fact that England expressed approval of the law of 1831, the excesses committed by the British cruisers showed no signs of diminution, and the anger and indignation of the Brazilians steadily mounted. The Rio government offered to reëxport freed slaves to the British colony of Sierra Leone but met with a refusal. The Brazilian cabinet returned to the attack in 1834. It submitted to parliament a bill appropriating money for the repatriation of the Africans who had entered Brazil illegally. The deputies, now thoroughly aroused against England and its policy of repression, voted down the proposal. It was evident that any measure which could be construed as a concession to Great Britain was quite unacceptable.

Despite these sentiments regarding the slave trade and its abolition the opinion gained ground that the slaves constituted a dangerous element in the population. Frequently *fazendeiros* or overseers were assassinated, in many instances the victims of the frightful vengeance of slaves who had been tortured or punished without just cause. Attempts were made to cope with this peril by making punishments more severe and by enforcing strict regulations on the bearing of arms. But the menace remained and fear of outrages and even insurrections on the part of the slaves was never entirely absent.

New orders were issued for the apprehension of smugglers and Negroes illegally imported. Such Negroes, technically free by the law of 1831, were distributed by the government among well-known *fazendeiros*, who were required to pay them regular wages; or else they were put to work on public roads or buildings. But the safeguards thrown about these freedmen were in practice exceedingly lax. Moreover, the expenses incurred by the government for the wages and protection of these Negroes proved a considerable burden. Little by little these freedmen, either through carelessness or design, became so mixed with the slaves that it became impossible to separate them.

The government now cast about for other means of solving the perennial problem of an insufficient labor supply. The most promising solution seemed to be the establishment of colonies of European immigrants.

New Mission of the Marquis of Barbacena.—The Marquis of Barbacena, who was at this time in Europe on a special mission, was entrusted with the task of discovering prospective immigrants to Brazil. During the year 1836 he sought them both in England and Switzerland. His quest proved a bootless one. He also tried to secure England's consent to a treaty providing for the union of the British and Brazilian fleets for the suppression of the traffic. Failure again dogged his steps; the cabinet of St. James had much more faith in its own cruisers, free to roam the Atlantic at will, than in diplomatic instruments and promises.

Yet the idea of substituting white free labor for Negro slaves would not down. In 1835 there was established in Brazil a colonizing society (*Sociedade Colonizadora*) for the purpose of protecting the immigrants who had recently arrived in America. Something was accomplished: from June, 1836, to January 31, 1839, it contrived to aid 2,508 of these colonists.

In 1836 a new aspect of the question appeared in the shape of a curious bill presented by Deputy Henriques de Rezende, based on a careful and detailed analysis of the conditions peculiar to the slave trade. The worst horrors of the passage across the Atlantic occurred on the smaller ships, which were greatly in the majority. From documents prepared at Sierra Leone and from information sent to Lord Palmerston by his agents at Rio it developed that 90 per cent of the prizes weighed less than 400 tons; in general they fluctuated between 60 and 240 tons, with ships of 150-180 tons representing a fair average. This small tonnage was a result of the peculiar conditions under which the traffic had to be conducted. The smaller ships were easier to navigate, were more obedient to sail and helm, were less easy to detect than larger craft, could navigate in shallow waters or across bars where the cruisers did not dare to venture, and, finally, could make their way into rivers and inlets where free from pursuit they could discharge their human cargo and safely escape to the open sea during the hours of darkness. Rezende believed that if Brazilian custom officials were forbidden to clear vessels under 400 tons a mortal blow would be dealt the Negro traders. Such was the intent of the bill which he presented to parliament. Unfortunately, however, like so many other measures dealing with the slave trade during the thirties and forties, the bill was never enacted into law.

Such in general was the parliamentary situation when in 1837 Barbacena returned from Europe. The marquis determined to tackle once more the apparently insoluble problem of the slave trade. So marked was his influence and so great was the respect which he inspired that the British minister in Rio received instructions from Lord Palmerston to present to the Brazilian statesman the compliments of the cabinet of St. James on his initiative in undertaking this tremendous task.

It was Barbacena's opinion that the law of 1831, which declared that all slaves imported into Brazil were *ipso facto* freed, had proven a failure. At first, the contraband trade in slaves had been unimportant, as means had not yet been contrived to escape the law. But presently, at strategic points on the coast, slave depots were founded where the Negroes received instruction in the rudiments of Portuguese. Brokers and leaders of slave convoys greatly increased in number. They visited the various fazendas in order to tempt the landowners to purchase their human merchandise. And as this machinery for the illegal importation of Negroes was perfected the traffic began to assume much greater proportions. Especially was this true for the years 1834-1837.

Usually the traders could count on the support and protection of the *fazendeiros*, who were naturally anxious to enlarge the cultivated portions of their lands. This sentiment can hardly be condemned, based as it was on the needs of local economy. It was the unwillingness or inability of Barbacena to recognize the complicity of the plantation owners which rendered the results of his reform nugatory. For, while the marquis planned to inflict all kinds of fines and dire punishments on the slave traders engaged in transporting the Negroes from Africa to Brazil, he allowed the brokers and *fazendeiros* to get off scot-free. Thus a premium was placed on the ingenuity of the merchants who were clever enough to elude the vigilance of the cruisers and to land safely their human cargoes. Here lay the fatal blunder in the proposed bill.

When years afterward, in 1850, Eusebio de Queiroz immortalized his name by drafting and enforcing a law which brought the infamous traffic to an end, this defect was avoided. With this exception the ideas of Barbacena were closely adhered to by his illustrious successor and constituted the heart of the measures finally adopted. It is our duty to insist upon these details, for even in Brazil the contribution of Barbacena to the final settlement of this vexatious problem is but little known and appreciated.

When Barbacena's measure was submitted to the senate, it met with a hostile reception. The sponsors of the abolition of the traffic were indignant at the immunity enjoyed by the slave brokers and the purchasers; the supporters of the slave trade condemned the fines and other restrictions inflicted upon the traders who were unlucky enough to have their ships captured. Parliament hesitated in coming to grips with the subject and contended itself with the discussion of certain ancillary problems such as the establishment of colonies, the liberation of Negroes who had been brought fraudulently into the country, etc., yet, despite the recurrent interest in European immigration, not more than twelve thousand colonists had been introduced in the twenty years prior to 1840.

The Project of Senator Vergueiro. The Parceria.—The very

year in which the majority of Dom Pedro II was proclaimed, a decisive step was taken toward furthering the introduction of free labor in Brazil. This time the initiative came not from the government but from a private individual. Senator Nicolau Vergueiro, the statesman who guided the nation through the difficult days culminating in the abdication of Dom Pedro I in 1831, brought in a number of white settlers on a partnership contract known as the *parceria*. The method was first tried with a few scores of Portuguese who were settled on his fazenda of Ibicaba. By the terms of the agreement, the landowner advanced to the colonists the expenses of the voyage, the cost of installation, and such funds as were needed for living expenses until the first paying crop was marketed. These loans bore a low rate of interest, and were repaid out of the laborers' earnings. They formed a first charge on the gross value of the crops. Net profits were equally divided between the owner and the colonists; the latter were permitted to have a few cattle and small plots of ground of their own. As time went on this system was perfected but its broad outlines remained unaltered. It became, in fact, the normal type of partnership and coöperation between *fazendeiro* and colonist. Within ten years, no less than sixty thousand immigrants had settled in São Paulo under these conditions. The best proof of the success of the system is to be seen in the fact that when the immigrants became wealthy and possessed land of their own they followed it in the case of laborers introduced by themselves.

The name of Vergueiro is almost forgotten today—an example of the normal ingratitude of men. To recall it is but an act of simple justice, for our country owes much to him. On two different occasions he blazed for Brazil the trail that it was to follow: in 1831, when he prevented the empire from dissolving into a congeries of petty and insignificant republics; and in 1840, when he evolved a satisfactory solution of the labor problem through white immigration working on a basis of a free partnership with the landowners.

The Mechanism of the Slave Trade.—It was many years before the reforms of Vergueiro attained their full realization. Meanwhile, the agricultural development of the country had as its normal consequence an increase in the importation of Africans despite its flagrant illegality. At this point we may pause for a moment to consider the machinery employed in the carrying out of this infamous traffic. Great Britain through its consular and diplomatic authorities had thrown out a veritable network of observers, both in Africa and Brazil, who reported to the Foreign Office a vast body of information relative to the slave trade. This mass of data, condensed and classified, was made public through the annual *British and Foreign State Papers*, the *British Sessional Papers*, and special reports. It is therefore possible for the historian to reconstruct the history of Brazilian slave trade even in its most minute details. The vigilance of the British began on the coast of Africa, accompanied the slavers on their voyage across the Atlantic, and extended even into the remote areas of our own country. No phase of the traffic escaped the attention of the British cruisers or the British agents; ships, crews, cargoes, brokers, merchants, abettors, localities which served as depots and distributing points of this human freight—all were objects of careful scrutiny.

The determination and persistence of Great Britain were equaled only by the ingenuity and cunning of the slavers. Despite the abominable character of their activities one cannot but admire the perfection to which they had brought the mechanism of the slave trade. The Spanish shipyards furnished the swiftest vessels and were the slavers' chief source of supply. The markets located on the African littoral displayed an amazing rapidity and precision in supplying the slave ships with their human cargoes. The question of flag was of paramount importance. Owing to the conventions in force, it was regarded as unsafe to fly the Brazilian colors; thus, up to 1840, the emblem of Portugal was the one most employed. In 1837, 76 ships set out from Rio de Janeiro and of these 71 sailed under the Lusitanian banner; in the same year, 92 ships arrived in Brazil, of which 89 claimed to be Portuguese. In 1838 and 1839, all of the ships engaged in the traffic sailed under the Portuguese flag. The year 1840 brought a change; of the 35 ships which set sail from Rio, 27 carried Brazilian colors. Of 15 ships arriving at the Brazilian capital in 1843, the distribution according to flags was as follows: United States, 6; Portugal, 3; Brazil, 2; Spain, 1; Hamburg, 1. This constant changing of flags was of course designed to embarrass the British cruisers in their efforts to apprehend the slavers on the high seas.

When the slave ships approached the South American coast

they took advantage of a vast system of warning signals which enabled them to enter ports and anchorages without molestation. Under the guise of fishing craft a great fleet of boats, canoes, and *jagandas*,[4] went far out to sea. Here, scores or even hundreds of miles from land, they made contact with the *tumbeiros*,[5] and supplied them with information regarding suitable landing places, the location of the patrolling forces, the condition of the market, and other items of interest. If the slaver approached the coast during the night he was guided by beacons and fire signals; if he arrived by day he was aided by conventional signs of one kind or another. The favorite landing section was the strip of coast between Cabo Frio and Santos: north and south of this area disembarkments were exceptional. The choice of landing place was dictated by the proximity and absorptive capacity of the markets of central Brazil and the facilities afforded by local accomplices. The extent of this complicity, in which government officials themselves were involved, is evidenced by the fact that Negroes were landed in the rear of the customhouse of Rio, and on the beaches of Botafogo and Copacabana, both well within the city limits and almost under the guns of the fortresses of São João and Santa Cruz.

These maneuvers, which flagrantly violated existing treaties, did not escape the watchful eyes of the British observers. On the basis of their reports, the cruisers redoubled their vigilance. The results of these increased activities were to be seen in the rise in the price of slaves. Negroes who formerly were sold at 88 milréis each now brought 200 milréis; insurance increased from 15 per cent to 50 per cent. The number of slaves illegally imported had gradually risen from a few thousand to 46,000 in 1838. But when the new instructions furnished the cruisers by the British admiralty came into operation the number dropped to less than 10,000 in 1841.

As was intimated earlier in the present chapter, a change in the popular attitude toward slaves began to make itself felt in the forties. The Negroes came to be regarded as a dangerous element in the population, a menace to the lives and safety of their masters. A further change is also to be noted, not unrelated to

---

[4] A peculiar Brazilian craft not unlike an outrigger canoe.—P.A.M.
[5] Literally "floating coffins," a name given to these ships in Angola.—P.A.M.

this fear of slave uprisings. When importations were numerous it seemed cheaper to use up the slaves quickly and fill their depleted ranks with recruits from the more remote and savage tribes of Africa. But when the supply began to lessen, it was found to be more humane as well as more profitable to treat the slaves with greater kindness, and to take steps to lengthen their life span as well as to increase their birth rate.

Predominance of Portuguese Interests in the Traffic.—Another interesting phenomenon to be noted at this time was the growing realization that the chief participants in, and beneficiaries of, the traffic were not Brazilians but Portuguese and Spaniards. As early as May 19, 1835, this fact was alluded to in a communication addressed by the House of Commons to the king of England. The natural resentment caused by the activities of these foreigners was further increased when the Brazilians became convinced that they were being exploited by Portuguese greed. It was not the *fazendeiros* but the dealers in human flesh, the brokers and middlemen, who encouraged the traffic. It was people of this ilk— Portuguese in the great majority—who played up incidents, aroused patriotic resentment against the alleged excesses of the British cruisers, and lost no opportunity to envenom the relations between Brazil and England. Anticipating a little, it may be pointed out that in 1850 out of the 38 or 39 prominent slave dealers and importers 19 were Portuguese, 12 Brazilians, 2 Spaniards, 2 Frenchmen, 2 North Americans, 1 English, and 1 Italian. The slave trade required large sums for its financing and the greater portion of the capital came from Portugal. That country supported and protected such activities to the extent of conferring titles and decorations on the chief participants in the traffic, even after the great minister of justice, Eusebio de Queiroz, had put into effect the law of 1850 which brought the slave trade to an end.

The antipathy between Brazil and Portugal was of course nothing new. Its origin goes back to colonial days and it was greatly accentuated during the crisis of independence. And now the Brazilians, who had insisted on the severance of every bond which formerly bound them to the Portuguese, suddenly discovered that the slave trade brought in its train two consequences—equally disagreeable to contemplate. The profits went to the sons of the

former mother country while the risks, annoyances, and humiliations all fell to the lot of the Brazilians themselves. Two of the most
conspicuous sponsors and beneficiaries of the traffic about 1839 were
the Portuguese consul in Rio de Janeiro, João Batista Moreira,
and his collaborator in this nefarious enterprise, the governor of
Angola in Africa, Admiral Noronha.

When the Brazilians came to realize that they were being used
as cats' paws by Portuguese speculators and that their natural
reluctance to abolish the traffic was skillfully exploited by unscrupulous oversea traders for their own personal advantage, a
profound reaction took place. At any cost this shameful solidarity
with the old metropolis must be broken. In the domain of laws,
politics, and international relations the divorce was complete; that
the only existing bond should be the slave trade was unendurable.

What pressure from England had been powerless to exact, this
wave of anti-Portuguese sentiment was able to accomplish. Partly
on this account, the importation of the Africans declined, though
it would be idle to deny that the heightened activities of the English
cruisers contributed to the same end. By and large, the *fazendeiros*
had come to the conclusion that the slave trade, with all its sinister
concomitants, sooner or later was doomed. Though total suppression had to wait until the turning of the half century, by 1840
it was evident that the days of the traffic were numbered.

Intellectual Activity.—We have just seen that anything that
smacked of subordination to Portugal was intolerable to the Brazilians. This sentiment, strongest in the domain of politics and
finance, was reflected in the literary productions of the epoch.
During the first two and a half centuries of colonial history, the
mentality of Brazil was closely moulded on that of the metropolis.
Symptoms of literary and intellectual independence began to appear in Bahia by 1730. But it was not until two decades later,
in Minas Geraes, the rich captaincy of gold and diamonds, that the
local soul began to reveal itself. The pride of being Brazilian now
appears; the scenery, fruits, flowers of Brazil are described; incidents, or even noteworthy events of colonial history, supply the
material for productions in both poetry and prose. Thus, the latter half of the eighteenth century witnessed the flowering of the
so-called *escola mineira.*[6] Its output consisted of poems, pamphlets,

---

[6] *I.e.*, the literary school of Minas Geraes.—P.A.M.

and political satires in which flows a rich vein of local color, here and there tinged by hostile feelings toward Portugal, but not sufficiently differentiated from the traditions of the mother country to deserve the title of a truly national literature. As was perhaps to be expected, the poets of Portugal held the literary productions of the colony in slight esteem and regarded them as of little importance.

The year 1830 represents the point of departure of a new phase in our intellectual life. Profoundly influenced by the emergence of the romantic school in Europe the poets and prose writers of Brazil broke with the past and inaugurated a period of literary autonomy; such at least is the view of some of the critics and historians of our literature. Other scholars speak of a period of reform in which romanticism forms the bridge between the old and the new. But whatever characterizations may be employed, all investigators are agreed that the year 1830 ushers in a new literary epoch.

Progress is revealed in all types of production, from political pamphlets such as the *Aurora Fluminense*, to works of fiction and historical research. In 1838 was established the Brazilian Historical and Geographical Institute (*Instituto Historico e Geographico Brasileiro*) which during its existence of nearly a century has rendered the cause of historical investigation inestimable services.

During the thirties and forties our literature was characterized by the emphasis placed on local sentiment, local thought, and Brazilian points of view. To be Portuguese, or to be inspired by Portuguese models, was a poor passport to public favor. "Indianism" and "Americanism" were increasingly stressed in poetry and romance. Thus, in the case of literature as in the case of politics and law, the motto was "Away from Portugal." And this liberating, moral force found new expression in both the intellectual and esthetic life of Brazil.

CHAPTER VIII

PROGRESSIVE PACIFICATION OF INTERNAL STRUGGLES; PLATINE PROBLEMS; EQUILIBRIUM OF POWERS; MONTE CASEROS.

The "Journée de Dupes."—The declaration of the majority of Dom Pedro II was indubitably a *coup d'état*. In this stroke of policy the whole nation was, as it were, implicated. Although it had been engineered by the liberals against the conservatives, both parties had been agreed on the essential point—the necessity of the measure. They differed chiefly on the question of the date and opportuneness of the step. Paradoxically enough the immediate effect of the enthronement of the young emperor was disappointment in both political camps. The conservatives found themselves elbowed from power, despite the fact that some of their most noted leaders had contributed to the success of the *coup d'état*. The liberals, though triumphant over their traditional opponents, found their victory monopolized by two small groups within their party, important groups to be sure, but not representative of the party as a whole.

The "Cabinet of the Majority," [1] as it was called, counted among its six members two pairs of brothers, the two Andradas and the two Cavalcantis, and on this account it was looked upon as an oligarchy bound together by a kind of family compact. A fifth minister, Aureliano de Souza e Oliveira Coutinho, an able statesman with an engaging personality, was suspected of too close intimacy with the advisers of Dom Pedro. The last of the six, who outlived them all, Antonio Limpo de Abreu, was the only minister thought to be in his proper place. This cabinet owed its existence to the chain of events culminating in the proclamation of the majority of Dom Pedro; its members really held office by virtue of the part they had taken in this unconstitutional movement.

Antonio Carlos.—The outstanding personality in this group was Antonio Carlos Ribeiro de Andrada Machado e Silva. He was eloquent, patriotic, liberal, erudite, capable, and Brazilian to his fingertips. In the Portuguese côrtes of Lisbon in 1822, he was

---

[1] The cabinet remained in power from July 24, 1840, to March 23, 1841. —P.A.M.

the leader of the Brazilian delegates. But unhappily for him and for his country he cared more for glory than for coherence of ideas and conduct, and for this reason his influence in the Brazilian Constituent Assembly of 1823 was detrimental rather than salutary. As was pointed out in an earlier chapter,[2] he and his two brothers, José Bonifacio and Martim Francisco, aroused such dissension in the assembly that, in spite of their eminent services in the cause of independence, they were exiled to France.

Unfortuntely, Antonio Carlos possessed no notion of administration; he hesitated when duty called for action; though sincerely liberal in his outlook he was, nevertheless, inspired by party views and interests. His incapacity was clearly revealed in his handling of the rebellion in Rio Grande do Sul which had been raging for five years. As minister of the interior (*imperio*) it was his duty to crush this subversive movement. With the best of intentions he imagined that he could bring this civil war to an end without further bloodshed. But in his attempt to come to some agreement with the rebels he merely weakened the position of the government still further. His bungling and hesitation prolonged the revolt for another half decade.

The authority of the empire in Rio Grande do Sul was at this time represented by General Soares de Andrea, a valiant soldier who had already put down rebellions in the two provinces of Pará and Santa Catharina. It was Andrea's method to attack the rebels with all the strength and vigor at his command. At the same time, he was disposed to lend a ready ear to any honest and sincere offers of submission. He never forgot that the struggle was one between brothers of the same blood.

It was the obvious duty of Antonio Carlos to extend to the delegate of the imperial government in the theater of the struggle all possible support and coöperation. Instead, he accepted letters from rebellious chieftains with whom he entered into *pourparlers* without reference to Andrea. The latter was not the man calmly to endure such disloyal and discourteous treatment and he at once tendered his resignation. The authorities appointed to take his place proved unequal to their task. As a consequence of their policy of weakness and concession, they lost all prestige and became the laughingstock of the rebels. Their utter incapacity finally

[2] *Cf.* Chap. IV.

became so evident that the government was obliged to dismiss them. This act was followed by the resignation of the cabinet after a brief existence of eight months. Naturally this political crisis in Rio greatly redounded to the advantage of the revolutionists in the south.

The Restoration of Authority.—Happily, conditions in Rio Grande do Sul were not typical of the situation in the empire as a whole. The advent to power of the young emperor—though he was but fifteen years of age—brought to an end the instability and inherent weaknesses of the various governments that had held power during the regency. We have already seen that the revolution in Pará had been put down as early as 1837. Peace was restored in Bahia the following year. Normal conditions prevailed again in Santa Catharina in 1840. Then came the turn of Maranhão, where in 1841 order was reëstablished by Colonel Lima e Silva, who for this service received the title of Baron of Caxias, the first of a long series of honors, ending with his promotion to the rank of Duke of Caxias[3] on his retirement from the Paraguayan War. It is to be noticed that, in the case of all these seditious movements, permanent separation from the empire was never advocated. The insurgents repeatedly stated that they would reunite with the common fatherland as soon as the emperor had attained his majority and taken over the reins of power. The only serious element of disintegration was the interminable revolution in Rio Grande do Sul. Yet even here, with rare exceptions, the leaders of the rebellious factions intimated that they would return to the fold of the empire if certain local conditions were met.

Resignation of "The Cabinet of the Majority."—As has just been pointed out, the prestige of the cabinet of August 22 had been sadly impaired by its bungling and ineffectual attempts to put down the rebellion in Rio Grande do Sul. But the real cause for the fall of the cabinet is to be sought elsewhere. We have already seen that the liberals were responsible for the time and circumstances of the *coup d'état* of 1840. On the other hand this had its origin, and found its chief support, in the vast body of conservative opinion which feared that the policy of the regency, as reflected in the amendments to the Additional Act of 1834, would

---

[3] Caxias was the only holder of this title in the entire history of the Brazilian empire.—P.A.M.

bring the empire to the verge of dissolution. The liberal cabinet of August 22 found itself, therefore, in a rather anomalous position. As liberals they felt bound to oppose the current of conservatism which had really been responsible for their advent to power. But as the months went on the strength of the conservatives steadily increased. The attempt of the minister of the interior, Antonio Carlos, to secure by pressure and fraud the election of deputies and other officials belonging to the liberal party aroused general indignation. The wind blew now from another quarter; everywhere arose the demand for the reinforcement of authority, which had been seriously impaired by the liberal experiments since the abdication of Dom Pedro I.

Here we may descry the real cause for the resignation of the "Cabinet of the Majority" which took place on March 23, 1841. Parliament, which represented the country, was overwhelmingly conservative in complexion. This fact was amply demonstrated when it passed two important laws in harmony with the point of view of the conservatives. The first, that of November 23, 1841, created the council of state, and was designed to serve as check on hasty and ill-considered action by both the executive and parliament. The second, passed December 3 of the same year, emended the code of criminal procedure, and aimed at making violations of the law more difficult.

As a consequence of these developments, the liberals found themselves ousted from the inner councils of the government. A new crisis, however, was approaching. The year 1841 was the last year of the fourth legislature; the "Cabinet of the Majority," fully aware of the precariousness of its position, left no stone unturned to secure the return of a liberal majority in the next chamber of deputies. This was one of the gravest accusations made against Antonio Carlos and his friends. And as a matter of fact such a complaint was well founded. The elections were characterized by a violence and utter disregard of law and morality unprecedented in the history of Brazil. Even if one discounts the exaggerations and bitter complaints of the defeated candidates, the truth of most of the charges of fraud, corruption, and pressure is beyond question.

On January 1, 1842, the chamber of deputies was legally dissolved although it had not completed its preparatory sessions.

The fury of the liberals knew no bounds. They had been greatly disgruntled with the laws of 1841; the dissolution of the chamber caused them to lose all sense of moderation. Under the leadership of the greatest names of the party, they launched organized rebellions in Minas Geraes and São Paulo. In the latter province, Feijó and Vergueiro were the most prominent leaders of the seditious movement.

The Mission of the Baron of Caxias.—The Baron of Caxias was entrusted with the task of restoring order in the revolted provinces. In June, 1842, the uprising was crushed in São Paulo. In August of the same year Minas was pacified. Respect for the law and the constitution was restored and the ringleaders of the revolutionary movements were tried and condemned. With the single exception of Rio Grande do Sul peace once more reigned in the empire. The prestige of both the government and the emperor was enormously enhanced. Dom Pedro was at length able to initiate a reign characterized by tranquility and progress.

Victory of Rosas in the Politics of La Plata.—Unfortunately, Brazil's relations with the countries bordering on the Platine estuary were far from satisfactory and as time went on they tended to grow worse rather than better. As we have already seen, the situation in Uruguay and Argentina was intimately related to the chronic rebellion in Rio Grande do Sul. The dominant figure in Platine affairs was at this time the Argentine dictator, Juan Manuel de Rosas. In his attempt to extend his authority over the regions formerly embraced in the old viceroyalty of Buenos Aires he was confronted, as was explained in an earlier chapter,[4] by a coalition in which figured the Uruguayan leader Don Fructuoso Rivera, the Argentine unitarians, and through Rivera, the rebels in Rio Grande do Sul. Don Manuel Oribe, elected president of Uruguay in 1835 through the influence of Don Fructuoso, soon broke with his former sponsor and protector. Defeated by the *colorados*, as the supporters of Rivera were called, he abandoned the presidency in October, 1838, and went over bag and baggage to Rosas who appointed him a general in the federal armies though he affected to treat him as legal president of Uruguay. In 1840 Rosas emerged victorious from the protracted controversy with the government of Louis Philippe which had culminated in the

---

[4] *Cf.* Chap. VI.

French blockade of Buenos Aires. The prestige of the Argentine dictator now rose both in America and Europe. His position was indeed a strong one: politically, because he symbolized the cause of freedom and independence; morally, owing to his resistance against foreign invaders working in concert with the Argentine unitarians subsidized and aided by French arms and gold. These glories belong not to Brazil but to Argentina and on this account are passed over with only brief mention.

The enemies of the dictator of Buenos Aires now included Rivera, the remnants of the unitarians who had sought asylum in Uruguay, certain elements in the Argentine province of Corrientes hostile to Rosas, and always, behind Rivera, the Rio Grande insurgents, although these latter did not actively participate in the invasion of Argentina. From 1838 on there existed agreements between Don Fructuoso and the republicans of Rio Grande, at first secret, later embodied in solemn treaties. In Brazil, with the exception of those dissident elements hostile to the empire, public opinion generally inclined toward the Argentine dictator because of his noble and inspiring resistance to French demands.

After a defeat of the coalition of the provinces of northern Argentina Rosas turned to the suppression of the disturbances along the Paraná littoral, and this congenial task was entrusted to Don Manuel Oribe, now fighting as we have seen under Argentine colors. Rivera's situation now became critical. It had been his hope to detach the provinces of Corrientes, Santa Fe, and Entre Ríos from the Argentine Confederation and unite them with a Greater Uruguay. In spite of his reluctance to divide his army he could not abandon his partisans in these provinces now that they were threatened by Oribe, the "right arm of Rosas." At the head of some eight thousand men he advanced into Entre Ríos to meet his enemy and rival.

Defeat of Don Fructuoso Rivera.—The encounter took place at Arroyo Grande in Entre Ríos, on December 6, 1842. The battle proved to be a decisive one in the history both of Argentina and of Uruguay. Both armies were about equal in size,[5] but owing possibly to dissensions in the ranks of Rivera, the latter suffered an over-

---

[5] According to the Uruguayan historian, Hermano Damasceno, *Ensayo de Historia Patria* (Montevideo, 1923), p. 568, the forces of Oribe numbered 14,000 men as opposed to some 7,000 of Rivera.—P.A.M.

whelming and irremediable defeat. Only with great difficulty was he able to escape to Uruguay. His grandiose plans for the erection of a Greater Uruguay collapsed like a house of cards. For the space of a decade until the defeat of Rosas at Monte Caseros in 1852, Argentine soil was undefiled by foreign invasion.

Despite the great victory of Rosas' general, the situation of the Argentine federalists, financial as well as moral, was replete with difficulties. The unitarian committee of Montevideo was carrying on a tremendous campaign of propaganda against its adversaries, a campaign in which the truth was so blended with calumny as to give the civilized world the impression that in Buenos Aires existed a veritable reign of terror and that throughout Argentina assassination, pillage, vengeance, and cruelty held high carnival. The belief was sedulously fostered abroad that the whole life of Argentina was dependent on the commands or whims of Rosas, carried out ruthlessly by an association of bandits, the *Sociedad Popular Restauradora*,[6] commonly known as the *Mazorca*.[7]

Exaggerated Character of the Campaign Against Rosas.—The campaign against Rosas was carried on by means of pamphlets, newspaper articles, and books.[8] The propaganda included both North America and Europe in its scope and was successful to the extent that it created the impression that Argentina was groaning under a monstrous and hideous tyranny. Both American and European ministers accredited to Argentina protested against the calumny. In pointing out the falsity of such charges they stressed the fact that their numerous compatriots residing in Argentina were prospering and enjoying the benefits of peace and progress. Statistics were published on the steadily mounting wealth of the country. Documents were divulged which made clear that among the victims of the terrifying list of proscriptions were to be found the casualties on both sides in the civil wars, and even these were

[6] The adjective "Restauradora" refers to Rosas' claim to be the "restorer" (*restaurador*) of the laws of Argentina.—P.A.M.

[7] The term literally means an ear of corn, one of the emblems of the organization. In the popular mind, the origin of the term was frequently alluded to as "Mas-horca," *i.e.,* "more gallows."—P.A.M.

[8] The most famous of these books was the classic work of D. E. Sarmiento (later president of Argentina), known as *Facundo, o Civilización y Barbarie* (first edition, Santiago de Chile, 1845).—P.A.M.

exaggerated. Numerous persons who were supposed to be assassinated were living in perfect health and tranquillity. Nothing availed to stem the tide of these slanders and to this day Rosas is in the popular mind considered as the vilest of cutthroats.

The *Sociedad Restauradora* included many preëminent citizens of the capital; it is possible that a few desperadoes and partisan fanatics were to be found within its ranks. When political passions run high, as they did when Rosas was fighting on the defensive, there is always a mob or criminals who emerge from the *bas-fonds* of society, ready to commit the worst excesses, without either the order or sanction of responsible authorities. Such was the case during certain crises under the dictatorship of Rosas.

The honor of history requires that these defamatory judgments be revised. Without doubt the period was a cruel one, but crimes of violence were committed by opponents as well as by supporters of the Argentine dictator. As a basis for these slanders against Rosas we may detect the partisan hatred of his opponents, the *ôte-toi de là que je m'y mette*, the envious spirit of small-minded enemies who were incapable of emulating his achievements.

To be sure Rosas was no sweet-mouthed, weak-handed ruler. In character he was strong-willed and unflinching, cruel as were all men of this same ilk in this period of Argentine history. Yet he was perhaps less hard-hearted than many of his opponents and was disposed to prevent human suffering whenever possible. But he was above all a statesman, a man of ideas with the will power and strength of character to put them into execution.

Those chiefly responsible for the atmosphere of exaggerations and calumny of which Rosas was the object were the members of the unitarian *Comisión Argentina* of Montevideo. Among them were to be found men of the highest intellectual attainments who with rare courage and self-sacrifice were enduring the hardships of exile for the sake of their ideals. They were blinded, however, by partisan passion. From one point of view, they might even be looked upon as traitors to their country, since they summoned foreign invaders and accepted French gold in order to advance their selfish aims as members of a political group. Rosas on the other hand was defending the liberty, independence, and self-respect of the confederation.

Renewed Attempts at Anglo-French Mediation.—We have al-

ready seen that Rosas' enemies signally failed to bring the dictator
to time by means of the French blockade. So spectacular in fact
was Rosas' victory that the government of Louis Philippe tendered
humble apologies and the French fleet saluted the Argentine flag
in 1840. But the foes of the dictator refused to admit defeat. They
now struck a new note: Anglo-French mediation, if judiciously
employed, might bring to an end the troubled situation in the
Platine basin and settle once for all the vexed question of the navigation of the rivers. The first attempt was made in 1841, only to
encounter a round refusal on the part of Rosas. In the following
year another effort was made on the joint initiative of England
and France. Again the dictator rejected the proposal; in partial
explanation he stressed the impossibility of reaching an agreement
with Rivera. The Anglo-French reply delivered in November, 1842,
was in the nature of a threat; if their offer was refused the would-
be mediators might have recourse to other means to enforce the
peaceful navigation of the rivers.

This new aspect of the problem, fraught with the possibility
of war with the two greatest powers in Europe, filled Rosas with
apprehension. At this critical juncture, he cast about for allies.
In spite of his suspicion of the empire he entrusted his plenipotentiary in Rio de Janeiro, General Tomás Guido, with the
mission of negotiating an offensive and defensive treaty with
Brazil. The imperial cabinet was disposed to look with favor on
these overtures. Caxias, then in Rio Grande, advised his government to make terms with one of the Platine belligerents, preferably
Rosas, since Rivera inspired no confidence; he had in fact only
recently signed a treaty of alliance with the rebels of Rio Grande
do Sul.

Distrust of Rosas in Brazil.—The agreement was at length arrived at between the representatives of Argentina and Brazil and
was signed by the emperor in March, 1843. Meanwhile, the attitude of Rosas had undergone a change as a result of Rivera's
defeat at Arroyo Grande. The projected Anglo-French intervention was no longer menacing, and indifferent to the fact that he
was offering a gratuitous insult to Brazil, he refused on behalf of
the confederation to ratify the Rio convention. The alleged motive
or pretext was the absence in the document of any reference to the

presidential powers of Oribe, which Rosas affected to consider as legal.

In reality the Argentine dictator was swayed by three dominant sentiments or rather prejudices the consequences of which were all but fatal to Argentine diplomacy. As has already been pointed out, Rosas harbored the illusion that he might be able to reconstruct the former viceroyalty of Buenos Aires. To this end, reannexation of Paraguay and Uruguay was of course indispensable. It was on this account that he welcomed every opportunity to intervene in the former Banda Oriental and secure a foothold on the left bank of the Uruguay. Intensely personal in his political appraisals, he hated Rivera, partly because he did not trust him and partly because the Uruguayan president cherished ambitious plans for the erection of a Greater Uruguay through the incorporation of the Argentine provinces of Entre Ríos and Corrientes. These were the two motives which led him to favor Oribe, over whom, besides, he exercised a great personal ascendancy. Realizing how useful Oribe might be as a pawn in the high political game which he was playing in the Platine basin, Rosas forced the Uruguayan *caudillo* to retract his voluntary resignation as president of Uruguay. By alleging that Oribe and not Rivera was the lawful executive of the small republic he found a more or less plausible pretext for lending Oribe Argentine troops for the invasion of Uruguay and for the siege of Montevideo. As has already been intimated, Rosas was quite out of sympathy with the Brazilian empire which he accused of harboring plans of conquest on both sides of La Plata estuary.

Rejection of the Brazilian-Argentine Treaty.—Had the treaty just negotiated with Brazil been put into effect, the independence of Uruguay would have been strengthened and both Rivera and Oribe would have been eliminated. All hope of the annexation of the Banda Oriental by Argentina would have vanished. The chief beneficiary of this changed situation would be Brazil whose prestige would be enhanced far beyond the desires of the Argentine dictator. Yet in refusing to ratify the treaty negotiated at Rio, Rosas was guilty of a serious blunder. In signing this instrument, Brazil harbored no ulterior motives, but merely wished to remove a constant source of trouble and conflict on one of the most exposed points on its frontier. The proof of this was later to be seen in the treaty of the Triple Alliance of 1851 against Rosas and the special convention between Brazil and Uruguay directed to the same end.

In 1843 Brazil admired Rosas and believed that he merited confidence. After the rejection of the treaty—regarded as a gratuitous affront to our country—the ill-will of the Argentine dictator toward Brazil was patent to all. The empire from now on merely followed a natural and logical course when it took steps to avoid being involved in further complications and difficulties with its southern neighbors. Had the treaty been ratified by the Argentine dictator in all probability order would have been reëstablished within a very short time and thus would have been avoided those causes of friction which finally led to war in 1852. Argentine historians aver that in the last years of his rule Rosas was convinced of this fact and regretted his errors. But repentance came too late.

The battle of Arroyo Grande had shattered the Uruguayan army and in February, 1843, the victorious Oribe, followed five months later by the Argentine general, Urquiza, invaded Uruguay, and with an army of 17,000 initiated the famous siege of Montevideo. As against this horde, the Banda Orinetal assembled some 6,000 troops to defend the capital and placed an approximately equal number in the field under the orders of Rivera. The defense of Montevideo itself was in the hands of Joaquín Suárez, president of the senate.

Repercussion of These Events in Rio Grande do Sul.—By no one were the developments in the Platine basin followed with keener interest than by the Baron of Caxias. He realized that on the whole they would make for the pacification of Rio Grande do Sul since they resulted in the weakening of the allies of the rebels. When Caxias reached Porto Alegre, he took over both the presidency of the province and the command of the imperial troops. Approximately a third of the province was in the hands of the insurgents, though by means of cavalry raids they were able to spread terror far and wide. They occupied Cacapava, Piratiny, Alegrete, and a number of other small towns in the interior. All of the coast with its important cities remained faithful to the empire.

As has been noted elsewhere, practically all of the fighting was done by the cavalry and in this respect the insurgents enjoyed a distinct advantage as they had an unlimited supply of horses at their disposal. In the matter of supplies, their Uruguayan allies— Rivera and his companions—furnished them with munitions, food-stuffs, and even mounts, when these were necessary. In return for these favors, Brazilian volunteers from Rio Grande crossed over into Uruguay to swell the ranks of Rivera who was also supplied with artillery by his Brazilian sympathizers. The greatest single advantage enjoyed by the republicans of Rio Grande was the mobility of their cavalry. Their troops did not much exceed 6,000 men but they could count on some 20,000 horses.

The new commander-in-chief arrived at a critical moment in the campaign. He took over his new duties on November 9, 1842, less than a month after the disaster of Arroyo Grande had shattered, at least temporarily, the forces of Rivera. This changed situation in Uruguay necessarily affected the plans of Caxias. The threatened invasion of Uruguay by the army of Oribe might be a means of cutting off the supplies being sent to the Rio Grande rebels by their ally Rivera and should, therefore, be encouraged. But one great difficulty must be overcome; Brazil's unswerving international policy was to side only with lawfully constituted governments and from the point of view of the empire Rivera or his representatives constituted the only legal authority in the Banda Oriental. With Oribe, therefore, as an aspirant to the presidency of Uruguay, it was impossible to treat. But fortunately for Brazil, Oribe was also an Argentine general, subordinate to Rosas, with whom, as recognized dictator of Buenos Aires, Brazil felt entitled to negotiate.

This course Caxias recommended to his government, which ordered its diplomatic representatives to proceed accordingly. Such an understanding distinctly redounded to the advantage of Rosas and his satellite Oribe, and after a brief interval the situation of the contending parties in the Platine basin was completely reversed. The Argentine province of Corrientes, under the governorship of Don Joaquín Madariaga, in pursuance of the orders of Rosas, proceeded to sell cavalry to the Brazilian forces and to disarm rebels who fleeing from the imperial army sought refuge on the right banks of the Uruguay or Río de la Plata. Complications continued for a time in Uruguay where Rivera was able to hold his own against the partisans of Oribe. But in 1843 Urquiza, the governor of the Argentine province of Entre Ríos crossed the Uruguay River with reënforcements. During the next two years, Rivera contrived to avoid a decisive engagement with these superior forces; but on March 27, 1845, his army was cut to pieces at India Muerta and he was obliged to take refuge in Brazil. During the years 1843 and 1844 the greater part of the Republic of Uruguay was under the effective control of Oribe and Urquiza.

Plan of Caxias.—On taking over his command, the Baron of Caxias had a carefully matured plan: to carry on the campaign with energy, while having as his goal the genuine pacification of the province; to dry up all the insurgents' sources of supplies in the Platine republics, while diverting as many of these supplies as possible to the use of the legal troops; to purchase cavalry absolutely indispensable in warfare of this type in neighboring sections of Uruguay and the Argentine Confederation. Such were the chief features of his plan. He was able to carry them out thanks to official agreements between Rio and Buenos Aires and as a result of the orders transmitted to Oribe by Rosas. By these methods he fought the rebellion with its own favorite weapons— an adequate cavalry and an inexhaustible supply of horses. He was relentless in his pursuit of the disbanded rebel detachments, giving them no opportunity to reassemble their forces. He also brought to his task leadership superior to that of his opponents, a better knowledge of tactics and strategy, and an unequaled prestige. Finally, the insurgents were practically without infantry and their artillery was indifferent in quality and amount. As a consequence, they were unable to derive any permanent advantage from their momentary successes.

Bento Manuel, the only imperial general who had consistently fought the insurgents up to his desertion to the rebel cause in 1837, repented of his action which in large part had been the result of personal pique. He publicly declared his loyalty to the empire, requested an amnesty, and asked permission to reënter the imperial army. His request was granted and he proved a tower of strength to the commander-in-chief. So thoroughly in fact did he justify the confidence reposed in him that his column became the most important in Caxias' army, and included almost twice as many troops as that commanded by the baron himself.

Rent by internal dissensions, the republicans found themselves in desperate plight; the enthusiasm and energy of the first years of the war were rapidly evaporating; their capacity for resistance had all but vanished. By the end of 1843 they had lost possession of the cities and towns which they had formerly occupied in the interior. Foodstuffs and other supplies began to give out. To escape capture they were obliged to wander in small detachments through the less accessible portions of the province, but even here they were ceaselessly harassed by the flying columns of the imperial army. In 1844 the active and indefatigable campaign of Caxias resulted in their final discomfiture and defeat. The few who escaped sought refuge in the interior in small groups of thirty or forty horsemen but even these were eventually captured or dispersed.

Pacification of Rio Grande do Sul.—Completely discouraged, the insurgents now began to plead for an amnesty, at first without any great amount of sincerity, but with greater insistence as the extent of their defeat became more obvious. This change of heart was accompanied by a wider vision. The events taking place in the Platine republics foreshadowed grave misunderstandings and conflicts of interest between Brazil and Argentina. Once more, to use the English phrase, it was proven that blood was thicker than water; in spite of all that had been said and published against the empire during the course of the revolution, the insurgents came to realize that they were sons of a common fatherland, now in danger of attack or aggression at the hands of foreigners. The last word on the unhappy, long drawn-out revolution was said on March 1, 1845, when peace was signed and Rio Grande do Sul was reincorporated into the majestic unity of the Brazilian empire.

The Mission of Sinimbú to Montevideo.—Though the empire was at length freed from internal dissensions, the situation in the Platine basin was far from reassuring. From the despatches of Brazilian agents in Montevideo and Buenos Aires, it was apparent that renewed Anglo-French intervention was imminent. It was also clear that the sentiments of Rosas toward Brazil—as evidenced by his rejection of the Treaty of 1843—were far from cordial. Storm clouds were piling up on the southern horizon. It behooved the empire to follow events with the utmost care and take such measures as were necessary to protect the nation from sudden attack. In the middle of 1843 the Rio government despatched Cansansão de Sinimbú on a special mission to Montevideo. His most important duty was to keep the Brazilian foreign office informed of developments both in Uruguay and Argentina. His task was by no means a simple one. Montevideo, as we have seen, was undergoing a prolonged siege by the combined forces of Oribe and Rosas. The position of Brazil, as regards the beleaguered capital, was a most thorny one. Officially, the empire was bound to recognize and support the acting authorities; that is, President Rivera and his followers the *Colorados;* on the other hand it was thanks to the correct attitude of Rivera's adversaries, the besieging troops of Rosas and Oribe, that Caxias had been able to put down the rebellion in Rio Grande do Sul.

The real desire of the empire, as is proven by all the documents —even the most confidential—in our archives was effectively to guarantee the independence of Uruguay, in harmony with the obligations imposed by the Treaty of 1828, and to assure the pacification of this republic under a government acceptable to the general mass of the population. Such a policy was the more justified since any conflicts in Uruguay, as we have repeatedly observed, had an enormous repercussion on the province of Rio Grande do Sul. Districts adjacent to the boundary were kept in a constant state of turmoil as a result of raids and theft of cattle and crops, usually to the accompaniment of loss of life. But in attempting to uphold the independence of Uruguay, Brazil ran directly counter to the aims of Rosas, intent on recreating the old viceroyalty of Buenos Aires.

The nine-year siege of Montevideo presented certain unusual aspects. Oribe did not attempt to destroy the capital, but merely aimed at reducing it through starvation. He refrained from any bombardment and gave similar orders to the Argentine fleet. Commodore Purvis, who commanded the English squadron, refused to allow any fighting in waters adjacent to the city and was supported in this determination by the ministers of England and France. These diplomats pointed out that Montevideo was not fortified and should therefore be regarded as an open city. Rosas refused to accept this point of view and on April 1, 1843, officially blockaded the port. As a belligerent, he was well within his rights and finally, after considerable desultory discussion, both the English and French governments accepted his contention and ordered their respective fleets to recognize the legality of his action.

Such was the situation when Cansansão de Sinimbú reached his post. At the very outset of his mission he committed a blunder by declaring that he would not recognize the blockade. As soon as this *gaffe* was known in Rio, efforts were made to repair this error; Sinimbú was instructed to recognize that the Argentine fleet was acting quite within its legal rights. Unhappily, the initial mistake of the Brazilian diplomat had already produced its effect. The relations between Buenos Aires and Rio de Janeiro, already tense, now reached the breaking point. Our minister at the Argentine capital, Duarte da Ponte Ribeiro, received his passports from Rosas after a caustic exchange of words and notes. The ill-will between the empire and the confederation steadily mounted.

In reality the Argentine blockade did little harm to Montevideo. Rosas did not possess the requisite technical means to make it effective. The foreign naval forces anchored in the roadstead of the Uruguayan capital refused to permit any decisive operations. The chief conflicts took place on land but even here everything conspired to reduce results to a minimum. Oribe, though fighting under Rosas' orders, could not forget that he was an Uruguayan, and he avoided as much as possible the destruction of lives and property. The actions of the local representatives of the various powers tended to restrict the theater of hostilities.

The Abrantes Mission to Europe. Its Failure.—The imperial government foresaw a long struggle, followed perhaps by an indecisive peace. If only because its own commercial interests were in jeopardy, it was extremely desirous to see normal conditions restored in the Platine basin. It was evident, furthermore, that Europe itself was suffering serious losses as a consequence of these interminable conflicts. Finally, as one of the signatories of the Treaty of 1828, it was the duty of the Brazilian government to remove these hindrances to the development of the Republic of Uruguay, whose independence was seriously threatened by the plans of Rosas and his satellite, Oribe.

Such were the reasons for the mission of the Viscount of Abrantes to Europe in the fall of 1844 and the winter of 1845. From the confidential despatches found in the archives of the Brazilian ministry of foreign relations, it is abundantly clear that his instructions required him to consult the governments of Great Britain and France—the nations most directly interested in the problems of the Río de la Plata—on the following points: I. The guarantee of the independence of Uruguay; II. A similar undertaking in the case of Paraguay; III. The adoption of measures best calculated to bring to an end the war between the Argentine Confederation and the Republic of Uruguay.

In regard to the first two points Abrantes encountered no difficulty. Both the English and the French governments rallied to the Brazilian point of view that the independence of both Uruguay and Paraguay must be maintained and guaranteed. The two European powers, furthermore, agreed that Rosas was deserving of praise for his administration of the internal affairs of Argentina and that his removal from power would result in an era of chaos and civil war. Great Britain and France were struggling for first place in the foreign commerce of the Platine basin as well as for a preponderance of influence, and neither power was inclined to have confidence in the other. They were disposed, however, should a joint intervention be decided upon, to make of Montevideo a free port open to fleets of all nations, and as a necessary corollary they desired the free use of the rivers of the estuary. They were willing to leave Rosas in undisputed possession of the Argentine Confederation as then constituted provided he would listen to reason. But should he persist in his intransigent attitude the powers were agreeable to the creation of a new and independent state consisting of the Argentine provinces of Corrientes and Entre Ríos. As regards Brazil, the British and French governments were on the whole favorably disposed but they evinced no enthusiasm for assuming any risks on its behalf. Both powers were willing to utilize their fleets in the event of hostilities with Rosas but they made it clear that they would not supply any troops for fighting on land. These obligations would devolve on Brazil in case it were invited to participate in the intervention.

Such a proposal was little calculated to appeal to Brazil. Were an intervention of the type proposed to take place the most difficult, costly, and hazardous part would be the land campaign. On this account Abrantes judged such an arrangement entirely unacceptable and in this view he was supported by the Brazilian ministry. Besides, was the tri-partite intervention possible or desirable? Yes, said Paris. No, replied London.

On being approached by the imperial envoy, Aberdeen (the British secretary of state for foreign affairs) replied with an absolute frankness, which at times bordered on rudeness. Twice Great Britain had proposed mediation to Rosas, which the latter had refused; a third rebuff was undesirable. As to a program of joint intervention, Her Majesty's government felt it would be imprudent to attempt to enter into an agreement with Brazil, since the first condition of such a policy was a perfect and constant understanding between the two cabinets. To its regret, England was forced to admit that no such understanding existed.

The allusion is patently to the difficulties growing out of the slave trade. And in all candor it must be confessed that the claims of international honesty, justice, and humanity were on the side of England, however ill-timed, clumsy, and devoid of real knowledge of Brazil's internal situation the British acts and arguments might be. But this aspect of the problem will be considered later.

Argentine and Uruguayan writers point to this refusal of Great Britain to enter into an agreement with the empire as an evidence of the distrust on the part of Europe of Brazil's intentions in the Platine controversy. This is an error. There was no disagreement on the solutions proposed. As has already been suggested, England's attitude was entirely conditioned by Brazil's delay in extinguishing the slave trade and the resultant state of unhappy relations between the two countries.

As a consequence of the failure of Abrantes' mission, the empire remained absolutely neutral during the ensuing Anglo-French intervention. Such a position was the more easy for Brazil to assume since by 1845 the revolution in Rio Grande do Sul was completely subdued and the heightened activity of the British cruisers had aggravated, if such were possible, the tension between London and Rio de Janeiro.

Failure of the Anglo-French Attempt at Mediation.—The manner in which Guizot and Palmerston had planned the intervention condemned it to a ridiculous failure. At this period the life of Argentina and its economic perspectives had not transcended, to any appreciable extent, its local frontiers. As a consequence a naval blockade, though it might cause no end of inconvenience, could never strike a decisive blow. Such a blow could only be given by land and the absence of the empire from the list of the belligerents reduced the bellicose activity of the blockading fleets to little more than a spectacular parade.

The immediate antecedents to the Anglo-French intervention may be briefly sketched. In April, 1845, there arrived at Buenos Aires Mr. Gore Ousley and Baron Deffaudis, plenipotentiaries respectively of Great Britain and France. They requested Rosas to suspend the siege of Montevideo pending the negotiation of peace. Rosas refused to accede to this request and insisted in turn that England and France recognize the Argentine blockade of the Uruguayan capital. The two ministers retorted with an ultimatum demanding that Rosas withdraw his forces from the territory and waters of Uruguay within eight days. On the dictator's refusal they asked for their passports and crossed over to Montevideo.

The English and French squadrons now broke up Rosas' blockade and captured his fleet. But this easy triumph only served to align the population of Argentina more solidly behind the dictator. Throughout Europe and America popular sympathies were on the side of Rosas. This was true even in Brazil, where it was recognized that the type of intervention envisaged by Abrantes and by the Rio de Janeiro cabinet was quite different from the one actually put into effect. The aim and hope of the Brazilian government had been to put an end to the disturbed conditions in the Platine basin without altering the political situation in Buenos Aires and without infringing on Argentina's territorial sovereignty. But by their capture of the Argentine fleet and their violent seizure of the rivers the two European powers had done these very things; more specifically, they had deprived Argentina of the control of internal navigation of its own territory. This could only be construed as an act of aggression.

The almost ludicrous failure of Ousley and Deffaudis to establish peace or to bring Rosas to terms spurred the intervening powers to new efforts. In the summer of 1846 a special plenipotentiary, Thomas Hood, accomplished nothing. In May of the following year new ministers appeared on the scene: Lord Howden and Count Colonna Walewski. But instead of acting in concert, each followed an independent course in accordance with the instructions received from his home government. They did contrive, however, to arrange an armistice with Oribe, but the authorities at Montevideo refused to accept it. Howden then ordered the British fleet to raise the blockade, a course which was not followed by his colleague, Walewski. The French continued to blockade the Argentine ports and the French minister maintained relations with the unitarian refugees in Montevideo. On the withdrawal of Howden, the Frenchman exercised a veritable protectorate over the legal government of the Uruguayan capital.

In March, 1844, arrived a new mission headed by Robert Gore and Baron Gros, the envoys respectively of Great Britain and France. In carrying out their mission, they entirely ignored Rosas and treated with Oribe, and the authorities of Montevideo under the presidency of Don Joaquín Suárez, the leader of the *Colorados*. In reality, however, Oribe was only a puppet in the hands of the Argentine dictator. A single incident will make this clear. Oribe had expressed his willingness to come to an accommodation with Suárez but from Buenos Aires came orders couched in brutal terms to continue the siege. Whereupon Oribe ate his own words and accepted Rosas' commands without demur. This was one of the worst blows which his prestige has suffered, for it made clear to all the world that he was not acting as the chief of a Uruguayan political party but as a simple Argentine soldier at the beck and call of Rosas.

By this time everyone was sick and tired of this interminable war. The French squadron suspended its blockade; in 1848 the mission headed by Gore and Gros retired ingloriously from American soil. But a body of French marines remained in Montevideo and their chief, Admiral Leprédour, received orders from Paris in 1849 to reopen negotiations. This time the French representatives treated with Rosas and Oribe, to the entire exclusion of the government of Montevideo. But the treaties thus drafted were rejected by the French Parliament. Once more Leprédour opened negotiations, and as a proof of his sympathy with the French defenders of Montevideo he sent reënforcements to the extent of 1,500 men, a step which he did not even mention to Don Joaquín Suárez. This was tantamount to the abandonment by France of the cause of the *Colorado* party.

Dominating Position of Rosas in the Platine Basin.—The resistance of Rosas to European aggression had won for him an almost unanimous popularity in his country. Even the great San Martín, one of the two protagonists of Spanish American independence, from his self-imposed exile in France wrote to the Argentine dictator, applauding his conduct and offering him his services. A revulsion of feeling took place in England where public opinion now swung over to the cause of Rosas. France, isolated and powerless in the Río de la Plata, was becoming a laughing-stock both in Europe and America.

The unhappy plight of France was largely of its own making. France was the victim of its own policy of backing and filling—eager to intervene in Platine affairs, yet unwilling to adopt the only means which would have made intervention successful. In Paris itself this distant expedition had become unpopular. Publicists, such as St. Marc Girardin, in widely-quoted and influential articles, showed how selfish and unjust France's policy in regard to Argentina had been. Thiers and his friends tried vainly to persuade the government to despatch a genuine military expedition supplied with adequate resources.

The February Revolution of 1848, which swept the government of Louis Philippe from the throne, brought the French intervention to a definite conclusion. In America itself certain new factors appeared which had to be taken into account in any appraisal of the situation in the countries bordering on the Platine estuary.

The Reaction in Brazil to the Menace From La Plata.—Although European intervention had come to an inglorious end, the relations between Argentina and Brazil tended to become worse rather than better. While the Brazilians may have approved Rosas' proud defiance of the two greatest powers of Europe, they soon came to discover that he was a most uncomfortable and even dangerous neighbor. Early in the fifth decade of the century premonitory symptoms of the approaching conflict between Argentina and Brazil began to accumulate. Rosas' newspapers accused, insulted, and threatened Brazil. As was pointed out earlier in the present chapter, the clash with our minister, Duarte da Ponte Ribeiro, apropos of the refusal of Sinimbú to recognize the blockade of Montevideo, caused a break in diplomatic relations. On both sides were bitter complaints and manifestations of ill-will.

The mission of Abrantes to Europe added fuel to the fire. Rosas affected to see in the activities of this Brazilian diplomat the incentive for the Anglo-French blockade, in spite of the essential difference between the aim of Brazil, intent only on the restoration of order, and the rôle adopted by the European powers. Buenos Aires entirely forgot that the Anglo-French intervention had been decided upon even before Abrantes arrived in Europe.

When in 1847 the Memorandum of Abrantes to Aberdeen was made public the Argentine representative in Rio de Janeiro, Don Tomás Guido, demanded of the Brazilian cabinet an explanation of the tenor and conclusions of this document. In its official reply the Rio foreign office set forth the reasons why Brazil considered Oribe an intruder in the affairs of Uruguay and its desire, for its own sake, to have the civil war on the Rio Grande frontier brought to an end. No policy of aggression was involved. The government of Uruguay had proposed an offensive and defensive alliance. This overture the empire had declined, precisely because it would have led to war, a consummation which on no account Brazil desired. For this reason, the empire had maintained a strict neutrality during the Anglo-French intervention.

At this posture of events, economic factors began to exert their influence. The forces of Oribe invaded Rio Grande, stealing cattle, killing or maiming the inhabitants, both *fazendeiros* and peons. It was not a question of mere forays. In 1850 it was currently said that no less than 800,000 head of cattle had been stolen over an area of 600 square leagues. Veritable armed incursions took place, sometimes on a large scale. As a result of Oribe's legislation on branding, it was almost impossible to prove theft even when the stolen cattle were located.

The request of the imperial cabinet that these laws be amended met with a curt refusal on the part of the Uruguayan authorities, coupled with protests against alleged invasions of the Banda Oriental by Brazilian cattle rustlers. As a matter of fact, incursion into Uruguayan territory had taken place; the owners of the decimated herds had united and organized armed bands for the recovery of their stolen property. Their chief was Colonel Francisco Pedro de Abreu, Baron of Jacuhy, one of Caxias' outstanding officers in the last revolution in Rio Grande do Sul. All of this was well-known and the object of common debate and discussion in local assemblies and even in parliament. Public opinion supported the victims of these frontier aggressions. The exasperation of the Brazilians was further increased through the pretension of Rosas to represent Oribe and Uruguay in the diplomatic controversies which arose over these border incidents. As in duty bound and in accordance with international law, the Rio cabinet refused to admit the pretensions of the Argentine dictator. Whereupon Rosas' minister, Guido, demanded his passports and on September 30, 1850, diplomatic intercourse between the two countries was suspended.

The Impending Conflict. Urquiza.—The hour for the final reckoning with Rosas was now approaching. Brazil had premonitions of the coming storm and in due time had taken measures to meet it. As rapidly as the inadequate means of communication would permit, Rio Grande was put on a war footing. The number of troops concentrated in the province rose from 16,000 in 1851 to 24,000 in 1852. Repeatedly, over a period of years, Brazil had been urged to intervene in the Platine basin but had insisted on remaining neutral. But the time had at length arrived when intervention, painful as it might be, could no longer be avoided. In taking this step the empire was impelled by two powerful motives: self-protection in the case of Rio Grande do Sul, and the maintenance of the independence of Uruguay in accordance with the Treaty of 1828.

The person chiefly responsible for this impending crisis was the Argentine dictator. Rosas' life of unceasing toil and his insistence on personally regulating even the most minute affairs of state had little by little undermined his tremendous energies. After nearly twenty years of uninterrupted labor—for he had been head of the state since 1831—with every nerve and fiber strung to the utmost tension, his incomparable mental and physical organism was beginning to give way. His most friendly biographers point to 1848 as the critical year when the symptoms of his approaching breakdown became evident. At the first signs of his waning powers, rifts began to appear in the political fabric which he had so painfully and ruthlessly built up during the past two decades. When the dictator was in the plenitude of his power, his enemies within Argentina did not dare to raise their heads and such dissensions as existed were kept beneath the surface. But now murmurs were heard that Rosas' dictatorship had outlived its usefulness. The first voice of protest came from Entre Ríos and Corrientes and was uttered by General Justo José de Urquiza, the governor of the former province. In this fertile region between the Paraná and Uruguay rivers Urquiza enjoyed enormous prestige and had an immense following. He was one of the dictator's best generals, fearless and intelligent; unlike his superior he did not nurture that unrelenting hatred toward his adversaries which caused Rosas to be the most feared of men.

After the defeat of Rivera at India Muerta in March, 1846, Urquiza had crossed the Uruguay to put down the opponents of Rosas in the province of Corrientes. In one of the first skirmishes, a local chieftain of the Madariaga family fell into his hands. Through him as intermediary, the general entered into relations with the brother of his prisoner, Don Joaquín Madariaga who was governor of the province. The upshot of this meeting was the negotiation—contrary to the express orders of Rosas—of two treaties. One, made public, placed Corrientes under the sway of Buenos Aires; the other, secret, proclaimed the neutrality of Corrientes in the war which Rosas was carrying on against Uruguay. Only the public treaty was submitted to the dictator. He rejected it out of hand on the ground that it did not stipulate the unconditional surrender of his adversaries.

In November of the same year, Urquiza was sounded out by the government of Montevideo as to his willingness to mediate between the belligerents. The general replied in the affirmative, but his action was promptly disavowed by Rosas who declared that the governor of Entre Ríos had been guilty of a serious blunder in thus exceeding his authority.

Much against his will, but in pursuance of the pitiless orders of Rosas, Urquiza reopened hostilities with Corrientes and in 1847 defeated the provincial forces at Vences. The insistence of the Argentine dictator was to cost him dear. The irritation of Urquiza against Rosas, already great, was vastly increased by the ruthless manner with which he treated the interests of Entre Ríos. This fertile province had made great progress under the enlightened administration of Urquiza and its exports through the port of Rosario de Santa Fé, the only river port left open by the dictator, had steadily grown in importance. But in August, 1847, Rosas ordered the closing of Rosario and selected Buenos Aires as the only outlet for the products of the province. Two years later he forbade the dispatch of currency to Entre Ríos in accordance with his determination to concentrate all of the circulating medium in the capital of the confederation.

By 1849 the public indignation of the inhabitants of Entre Ríos against the dictator of Buenos Aires had risen to a fever heat, and as the months wore on the tension between Rosas and Urquiza increased rather than diminished. The imminence of the rupture was revealed in the spring of 1851 when Urquiza's newspapers omitted from their front page Rosas' famous slogan "Death to the savage Unitarians" (*"Muerte a los salvajes unitarios"*) and launched an appeal for peace and reconciliation.

The only rejoinder of Rosas to this affront was to stigmatize Urquiza and his supporters as "anarchists."

But the appeal from Entre Ríos awoke echoes in the hearts of all the thinking elements in the regions bordering on the Río de la Plata. In Montevideo, Urquiza's change of front was lauded by the press. In Brazil, it received the enthusiastic support of the imperial cabinet. In harmony with the new point of view, Andrés Lamas, the Uruguayan minister in Rio, and one of the most notable of the paladins in the crusade against Rosas, proposed the slogan for the campaign: "Among the Uruguayans, neither conquered, nor conquerors."

The Eve of the War.—Events now moved rapidly. On May 29, 1851, was signed in Montevideo a treaty of alliance between Entre Ríos, Corrientes, Uruguay, and Brazil. As early as December 25, 1850, there had been signed a treaty between Paraguay and Brazil, providing for the free navigation of the Paraná River, the Argentine stretches of which had been closed by Rosas.

Exhausted by the long war with Rosas and Oribe, Uruguay was sorely lacking money, arms, and ammunition. Through the agency of Ireneu Evangelista de Souza, later Baron and Viscount of Mauá, and one of the outstanding men of the Brazilian empire, the imperial cabinet loaned to the little republic the sums necessary for the purchase of arms and the payment of troops. But of even greater importance than the implements of war was the striking

change in the spirit and morale of the Uruguayans. The alliance
with Brazil and Urquiza, with its promise of freedom from the
perpetual menace of Rosas, the offer of amnesty to Uruguayans
of all political complexions provided they would join the army of
liberation—all proved fatal to the *Blanco* cause. So numerous were
the desertions that the army of Oribe dwindled to a handful of
troops which had been supplied by Rosas. Seemingly the sun of
the *Blancos* had definitely set in Uruguay.

In the great campaign against Rosas it was expected that the
army of the allies would be commanded by an Uruguayan. Partly
as a token of reconciliation, General Eugenio Garzón was appointed commander in chief. Unfortunately, he died in December
and the leadership naturally devolved upon Urquiza.

On July 19, 1851, began the crossing of the Uruguay River.
Shortly afterward, Oribe capitulated; without an army no other
course was open to him. On October 8, Urquiza, in agreement with
the government of Montevideo, signed with the defeated *Blanco*
leader a treaty of peace which finally brought to an end the unhappy fratracidal war among the Uruguayans. The treaty was
really worthy of the occasion. The good faith of both parties was
recognized by the adoption of the formula: "There will be neither
victors or vanquished (*no habrá vencidos ni vencedores*)." So complete was the reconciliation that Oribe and his family were permitted to remain undisturbed on his estate at Paso del Molino in
the vicinity of Montevideo.

Invasion of Argentina by the Allies. Victory of Monte Caseros.—
The military campaign was now launched in earnest. In January,
1852, a combined force of some 28,000 men recruited from
Uruguay, Brazil, Entre Ríos, and Corrientes invaded the territory
of the Argentine Confederation. With the first shock of war the
real weakness of Rosas' system was manifest to all. The population
at large, weary of the hard yoke of the dictator, had no stomach
for fighting. The battalions and squadrons on which Rosas had relied simply disintegrated; some surrendered to Urquiza, while even
those troops which nominally remained loyal to Rosas proved unreliable. Only one serious engagement took place. On February
3, 1852, was fought the decisive battle of Monte Caseros near
Buenos Aires, in which Rosas suffered an overwhelming defeat.

When he saw that the game was up the dictator fled to the capital, and under the protection of Robert Gore, the British minister, sought exile in England.

Thus ended Brazil's campaign for the overthrow of Rosas. With the removal of the hated dictator, a certain political equilibrium or balance of power was now possible and a new and better era dawned for the nations of the Platine basin.

CHAPTER IX

THE ABERDEEN BILL; THE ABOLITION OF THE SLAVE TRADE; GENERAL PROGRESS OF BRAZIL

Recrudescence of British Hostility.—Brazil's difficulties with its southern neighbors, which we have analyzed at some length in the preceding chapter, were increased by the strained relations with Great Britain. These grew directly out of the slave trade. They help explain the empire's neutrality from 1845 to 1850 in the conflict raging in the basin of La Plata. Since 1847 England had been inclined to look with much greater favor on the pretensions of Rosas. Had Brazil allowed itself to be drawn into conflict with the Argentine Confederation it might expect to suffer even stronger pressure from British cruisers intent on suppressing the slave traffic. This was no imaginary fear. In 1851 England showed itself hostile to the proposed Brazilian alliance with Rosas' opponents. A few years earlier it could have exercised strong pressure upon Brazil by an increased activity of its cruisers. But in the early fifties the Brazilian government had deprived Great Britain of this possible weapon by taking on its own initiative effective steps for this suppression of the infamous traffic. Hence, the British cabinet found nothing to reply to the imperial government's rejection of any hint of abandoning its allies.

But prior to 1851 the grievances of Great Britain were real and substantial. We have already seen that the existing treaties relative to the slave trade had been systematically disregarded by the Brazilian authorities. There were good reasons for this. In many instances, the leaders of the two political parties, the liberals and conservatives, were virtually powerless. The great landowners, for whom a constant supply of new slave labor was regarded as a necessity, and the slave traders, who saw their lucrative business menaced by the suppression of the traffic, were naturally hostile to the treaties. Since from these classes was recruited the bulk of the electoral body, the government was forced to acquiesce in a situation which it was all but powerless to remedy. But as we come to the forties of the last century a new spirit was astir. Little by little the Brazilians began to realize that the traffic was becoming more of a menace than a benefit. Their patriotic sentiments were outraged by the discovery that while the Brazilians had to support the inconveniences and odium of the traffic, it was the owners of Portuguese ships and Portuguese capitalists who were the chief beneficiaries.[1]

Before leaving this subject, we may cite one more instance of the official indifference to the violation of the law. After crossing the Atlantic the slave ships with their wretched cargo were frequently brought into the bay of Rio de Janeiro or convenient inlets in the vicinity. So tolerant were the officials that landings even took place behind the customhouse, in the vicinity of the forts at the entrance of the bay, or on the beaches of Botafogo and Copacabana within the municipal limits of the capital. After debarcation the slaves were usually placed in large compounds or depots. Here they were taught a smattering of Portuguese, and given elementary instruction in the tasks which awaited them. Four of these compounds were reported to have at various times as many as six thousand Negroes awaiting sale. Though the location of these depots were of course well-known, no attempt was made by the government to abolish them.

The laxity of the Brazilian authorities in the matter of the traffic was equaled only by the pertinacity of the British Government. Again and again England, in its campaign for the suppression of the slave trade, had lodged vigorous protests with the imperial government. But often its actions were tactless; England did not scruple to violate on its own account existing treaties, and thus weaken its moral authority. A note sent by the Brazilian minister of foreign affairs, Paulino José Soares de Souza (later Viscount of Uruguay), to the British envoy in Rio in January, 1844, included among the grievances of the imperial government the landing of armed marines, the overhauling of Brazilian ships in territorial waters, and, in general, gross disrespect for the sovereignty of a friendly nation. These proceedings not only wounded national pride, but also led the populace to sympathize with and countenance the actions of the slave traders. As measures designed to suppress the traffic, the effect was nil; rather did they tend to increase it.

---

[1] Dr. Calogeras might well have added to the offending Portuguese, citizens of the United States. The participation of North Americans in this traffic is clearly brought out by Professor Lawrence F. Hill, *Diplomatic Relations between the United States and Brazil* (Durham, 1932), Chap. V.—P.A.M.

The Aberdeen Bill.—Yet, when all is said and done, it cannot
be denied that Brazil was shamefully remiss in meeting its international obligations and in living up to the treaties which had been
signed with Great Britain. Lord Aberdeen, the British minister
of foreign affairs, was therefore fully justified in taking the steps
necessary to put an end to this scandalous state of things. On
August 8, 1845, was passed by the British Parliament the famous
bill which bears his name. In effect, it empowered the British
Government to take unilateral measures to cope with a traffic whose
suppression had hitherto been supposedly the joint concern of
Great Britain and Brazil. By virtue of this new law, Brazilian
ships engaged in the slave trade might be taken as prizes and
brought for trial, not before the mixed Portuguese-British
tribunals, but before British admiralty courts.

The act aroused a tremendous hue and cry in Brazil. Glossing
over the shameful disregard of treaties and iniquitous commerce
in human flesh, Brazilian official protests confined themselves to
mere juridical technicalities. But popular protests went much
further. The sovereignty of the empire was treated with contempt;
foreigners were aiming to rule the country, acquiescence in the
British policy of aggression was tantamount to a betrayal of the
fatherland—such were the popular charges hurled at Great
Britain. As may readily be imagined, those who were immediately
interested in the traffic did everything possible to add fuel to the
fire and to place the action of Great Britain in an odious light.

For a time they were successful. Their skillfully devised propaganda still further inflamed public opinion. Far from declining,
the traffic grew by leaps and bounds. In this regard statistics are
eloquent. In the early forties the number of Negroes illegally imported averaged twenty thousand or less per year. After the passage of the bill the numbers rose as follows:

1845	19,453	1848	60,000
1846	50,324	1849	54,000
1847	56,172	1850	23,000

The significance of the last figure will be explained in a moment.

The Final Abolition of the Traffic.—We may now consider the
steps which brought to an end for all time this infamous traffic.
The conservatives had come into power on September 29, 1850, 48
under the Marquis of Olinda. Their advent aroused distrust and

misgivings in the British Government. Were they not the representatives of the great landowners, those most interested in the maintenance of the traffic? The apprehension, though natural, was in reality quite baseless. As events turned out, it was to the Olinda cabinet that the honor fell of removing the greatest stigma ever attached to Brazil.

The person chiefly responsible for this achievement was the minister of justice, Eusebio de Quiroz Coutinho Mattoso da Camara. He felt, as did the rest of the cabinet, that the definite settlement of the slave trade problem could be staved off no longer. In order to expedite matters he adopted, as the basis for new and drastic legislation, the draft prepared by Barbacena in 1837 to which were added a number of amendments designed to meet the criticisms of the original project, which was so loosely drawn as to put a virtual premium on the astuteness and ingenuity of the slavers. The chief aims of these modifications were to strengthen existing laws regarding clandestine debarcations; to make the punishments really effective and workable by reducing their penalties which hitherto had been so Draconian that they could not be enforced; to try all cases, not before juries composed of landowners where acquittal was almost certain, but before special tribunals created *ad hoc*; and finally to require all owners of ships sailing for Africa to put up a bond covering the value of the vessel and possible cargo, said bond to be forfeited if the ship was found to be engaged in the traffic. In fact the law was drawn with such care that no loopholes were left either for the traders or their abettors.

For a time the fate of the bill hung in the balance. It was England, curiously enough, who was chiefly responsible for this uncertainty. England's failure to appreciate the honest efforts of Brazil gravely jeopardized the success of the measure. Palmerston and Aberdeen, convinced that Brazil was simply following its usual dilatory tactics, decided in 1850 to order the British cruisers to invade Brazilian territorial waters, including ports, rivers, and bays, and seize all ships fitted for the slave traffic, even under the very guns of Brazilian forts.

These highhanded acts, for which the British minister at Rio, James Hudson, was held largely responsible, gave the Brazilian cabinet much concern. It was feared that hostilities might break out at any moment; in fact a number of clashes did occur, notably in Paranajuá. Some of the cabinet urged that it would be well to suspend the actions of the new law, in order to avoid the impression that Brazil was acting under compulsion. But on second thought it was decided to go forward. It was rightly felt that the settlement of a great moral issue, in which motives of humanity bulked so large, should not be balked by the error of a single individual or by the opposition of a minority of the cabinet.

The law, known as the Lei de Eusebio de Queiroz, was formally sanctioned on September 4, 1850. Everything now depended on its execution. Here again, figures speak more eloquently than words. In 1850, imports of slaves fell to 23,000 (about two-thirds of the yearly average for the period 1843-1849); in 1851, the number decreased to 3,287; and in 1852, the total number imported barely reached 700. During the next four years, two attempts were made to land slaves, but the Negroes were practically all captured and set free. The infamous traffic became a thing of the past.

Were we to sum up the factors that contributed to the suppression of the slave trade we should at once have to admit that England played a rôle of the first importance. It kept the question ever to the fore and gave the Brazilian government no rest. On the other hand, England sinned grievously through excess of zeal and want of tact. By wounding the pride of a sensitive nation, it actually gave a new lease of life to this infamous traffic in human flesh, as is abundantly proven by the statistics already quoted. And when it came to the final and definite suppression, we have seen that the drastic measures adopted by Brazil in 1850 owed nothing either in their elaboration or enforcement to Great Britain. The efforts were Brazil's and to Brazil belongs the credit.

Freedom of Navigation of the Rivers. The Decree of 1866.[2] We now address ourselves to a question of an entirely different order: the freedom of navigation of the rivers of Brazil. As practically all of these streams had their upper reaches in countries other than Brazil, the problem was naturally one of international concern. Although the problem was by no means a new one, for reasons which will presently appear, it became acute after 1850.

[2] On this subject *cf.* Hill, *op. cit.*, Chap. VIII; and P. A. Martin, "The Influence of the United States on the Opening of the Amazon to the World's Commerce," in *The Hispanic American Historical Review*, I (May, 1918), 146-62.— P.A.M.

The history of freedom of navigation of international water-
ways is a curious one. In 1748 Austria had demanded the opening
of the River Scheldt and won its point by an act passed in 1792
by the French National Convention. In the same manner, by a
treaty between The Netherlands and France negotiated in 1795,
the doctrine was applied to the Rhine and a number of other
streams. In 1815, the Congress of Vienna adopted as a general
rule the freedom of international rivers. In 1826, however, England
opposed the application of this rule to the St. Lawrence River.
The United States was quick to protest and demanded that there
be applied the same principles which had led France in 1763 to
open the Mississippi to English ships; the same principles, in fine,
which had forced Spain to give up its attempted monopoly of the
same stream, and subsequently led the United States to throw open
its waters to the use, in times of peace, of all nations.

In the present instance, the attitude of Brazil was absolutely
inconsistent. In the case of the Paraná, the upper reaches of which
lay in its territory, Brazil protested against the policy of the
dictator Rosas of closing the lower reaches to all but Argentine
ships. But when it came to the Amazon, and its tributaries, the
upper portions of which drained Perú, New Granada, Ecuador,
and Bolivia, Brazil insisted on the maintenance of a rigid monopoly
for itself.

It was natural that these republics, anxious to have an outlet
to the Atlantic, should demand the right to navigate the Amazon
throughout its entire length. But Brazil affected to see dangers
and inconvenience in granting such permission—this, despite the
fact that after the overthrow of Rosas in 1852 both the Paraná
and Uruguay rivers were thrown open freely to navigation by the
Argentine Republic.

In the long run, Brazil's position was of course untenable.
Pressure was brought to bear on the government from various
quarters. In 1853-1854 the United States minister, William
Trousdale, engaged in a long correspondence with the Rio foreign
office, looking to the signing of a treaty in which the opening of
the Amazon to United States ships should be accorded as a natural
right. The theory was rejected by the imperial cabinet. It was
then submitted to the council of state which handed down its

opinion in January, 1856. The majority advised that Brazil enter into *pourparlers* with the interested riverine countries, but only after the settlement of pending boundary controversies. Since Brazil had difficulties of this sort with practically all its neighbors, this course was tantamount to shelving the question indefinitely. As for England and France, any action must be suspended until the limits of Brazil with British and French Guiana had been settled. Then, and then only, might the imperial government throw open the navigation of the Amazon to all flags, under conditions at that time to be determined.

This intransigent attitude could not be maintained indefinitely. Public opinion began to veer toward a more liberal policy. The writings of Lieutenant Matthew Fontaine Maury, who had been carrying on a violent campaign in the United States in favor of the opening of the Amazon, became known in Brazil through translations as early as 1853. His views were reënforced by the publicist, Tavares Bastos, who in a series of essays entitled *Letters of a Hermit* (*Cartas do Solitario*) made an impassioned plea for freedom of navigation. A number of eminent public men, including Francisco Octaviano and Sousa Franco, lent the movement their support. The minister of foreign affairs, in his report for 1864, stressed the urgency of such a measure. The success of the long-drawn-out campaign was now in sight. Antonio Coelho de Sá Albuquerque, in charge of the foreign office, commissioned the distinguished jurisconsult, Nabuco de Araujo, to draw up the final decree which was signed on December 7, 1866. It provided that after September 7, 1867, the Amazon should be free to the merchant ships of all nations as far as the frontiers of Brazil. Of the tributaries, the Tapajós was to be open to Santarem, the Madeira, to Borba, and the Rio Negro, to Manáos. The Tocantins, which strictly speaking is not a part of the Amazon system, was to be opened to Cameta, and the São Francisco, lying entirely outside the Amazon basin, to Penedo. The navigation of tributaries, only one bank of which was Brazilian, was to depend on agreements and treaties negotiated with the nations in question, and eventually of course on the settlements of pending boundary controversies. In the solution of this aspect of the problem, Brazil followed a consistent policy, summarized years afterward by the Baron of Rio

Branco[3] as follows: When a river traverses the territory of two or more countries, freedom of navigation for the owner of the upper section depends upon a previous agreement with the owner of the lower reaches, such agreement to be based on full reciprocity.

Economic Progress of the Empire.—At this point we shall leave for a moment our narrative account to consider the economic and social progress of the empire. From the cessation of revolutionary agitations in 1845[4] to the outbreak of the Paraguayan War in 1864 we find two of the most prosperous and fruitful decades in the entire history of Brazil. The revolutionary spirit had become extinct. Vexatious constitutional questions had been settled. Public life from now on was to find expression in the press (which enjoyed complete freedom), in parliament and other public gatherings, and in elections. The inhuman and un-Christian slave trade, which had cast a merited stigma on Brazil, was a thing of the past. A definite political equilibrium had apparently been reached in the troubled affairs of La Plata basin. The stage was set for a releasing of national energies on a grand scale.

Economic changes of great import were impending. Up to this time, Brazil had been under the influence of a state of economy which the Germans call *Naturwirthschaft*.[5] The spirit of enterprise was all but non-existent. Profits from pastoral industries were invested almost exclusively in land and cattle; profits from agriculture, in land and slaves. Hazard might well play a large and decisive part in such enterprises. The black laborers might be decimated by epidemics or herds wiped out by pestilence; in either instance such a calamity might spell ruin for the owner, as both slaves and land stock had been purchased on credit. The debt remained, while the possibilities of repayment were swept away. Catastrophes of this order, which were of not infrequent occurrence, had greatly contributed to the revulsion against the slave trade on the part of the landowners. There was a growing conviction that some means must be found both to increase production and to lessen its cost. The human factor was of course of

---

[3] Brazil's most eminent minister of foreign affairs under the republic (1902-1912).—P.A.M.

[4] An apparent exception is the revolution in Pernambuco in 1848. On analysis however, this is seen to be little more than an explosion of party dissensions, of purely local significance.

[5] Literally "nature economy."

prime importance. Without an adequate supply of labor an increase in output was impossible. The slave trade had proven, as we have seen, to be both costly and inefficient. The answer was white immigration.

We have already noted the partnership system as devised by Senator Vergueiro. Something had been accomplished. Credits were voted and associations were formed for the purpose of increasing the number of immigrants. But until 1850 the total number had been small. All told something like 19,000 were to be found in "colonies" supported by the government on private estates. But with the turn of the half century the immigration movement grew by leaps and bounds. For the years 1855-1862, the average was 15,000. In 1866, the number had risen to 40,000. For the period 1817-1849, the number of colonial nuclei did not exceed twenty. From 1850 to 1867, fifty-four new ones sprang to life. Prior to the middle of the century, white labor was practically non-existent. After the abolition of the traffic it took on a new lease of life. Manual labor, formerly stigmatized as something vile, became honorable.

The financial structure of the empire was vastly strengthening during the same period. In 1846 a new currency law was voted. Parity was fixed at 27 pence the milréis. Partly through the efforts of the Baron de Mauá—whose widespread economic activity will be discussed later—a large number of local banks were established not only in the capital but in such relatively remote localities as Ceará, Maranhão, Bahia, and Pará. All of these establishments supplied an impetus to commerce; some of them even had the right of issuing paper money. Since this faculty might easily lend itself to abuses, a special law was passed limiting this right to a single bank of issue. But owing to the disastrous repercussion in Brazil of the world crisis of 1857 and the failure of a number of institutions of credit following the collapse of the great banking firm of A. J. Souto & Co. in 1866, all existing banking laws were abrogated and there was once more put into effect the pernicious system of official issues of paper money by the treasury. As early as 1862 the metric system was officially adopted although it did not come into general use until a decade later.

This quickening of economic life naturally was reflected in increased emphasis on transportation. Navigation naturally took the lead. From 1839 to 1874 the number of voyages under the Brazilian flag increased by 50 per cent; under foreign flags, by 101 per cent. The increase in tonnage for the same period was 130 per cent in domestic, and 414 per cent in foreign ships. The use of steam grew slowly. As late as 1859 commerce was confined almost exclusively to sailing craft; even in 1875 only 29 per cent of the ships were steamers. Nonetheless, through Mauá's efforts steam navigation on the Amazon and its tributaries was inaugurated in 1850. Three years later, due to the efforts of this public-spirited capitalist, a company was launched to supply gas illumination to Rio de Janeiro.

The first railroad was constructed in 1854 through the efforts of Baron de Mauá. It was fourteen and one-half kilometers in length and extended from the port of Mauá, at the extreme western end of the harbor, to Raiz da Serra, at the foot of the escarpment over the rim of which was located the beautiful summer capital of Petropolis. Considering the difficult character of the country and the fact that population was in general restricted to a fringe along the Atlantic littoral, the latter years of the empire could show a creditable increase in railroad construction. The figures for 1864, 1875, and 1889 (the last year of the empire) are 475, 1801, and 9,584 kilometers respectively.

Similar progress is to be noted in the extension of the telegraph system. At first the telegraph was a mere optical contrivance, but as early as 1852 the first electric machines were employed. The extension of the service was now rapid: 187 kilometers in 1864; 6,286, in 1875; 18,925, in 1889. It was not until 1874 that the first submarine cable was laid; here, as in so many other fields of economic progress it was Baron de Mauá who took the initiative.

No less remarkable was the increase in trade and commerce during the years in question. For the fiscal year 1846-1847, imports had totaled 55,740 contos,[6] and exports, 52,449. Five years later the figures had risen to 76,918 and 67,788 contos respectively. For the fiscal year 1858-1859 they had climbed to 127,722 and 106,805 contos respectively. During twelve years they had registered an increase of something like 150 per cent. It will be noticed that in the last year mentioned imports had more than balanced exports;

---

[6] A conto at the then prevailing rate of exchange was worth something over $500.—P.A.M.

from then on there was a steady rise in the favorable balance of
trade for Brazil. Thus, for the fiscal year 1874-1875 imports
amounted to 167,549 contos and exports, 208,494 contos. We have
already noted that the par of exchange had been set at 27 pence.
While it was found impossible to hold the milréis at all times at
par, the range of fluctuation was kept within close limits. During
the period 1850-1864, the lowest point reached was 23½ pence;
the highest, 29½. Most of the time it remained around 26.

Advance of the Empire in Other Fields.—Progress during this
period was by no means confined to the economic domain. It was
also evident in all fields of social development, especially legislation. The commercial code and its regulations is a case in point.
Though sanctioned as early as 1850, it stands today as a monumental work with the hallmark of ripe statesmanship and knowledge of juridical science. Other legislation of immense significance
was passed at approximately the same time. We have already
stressed the importance of the law of 1850 suppressing the slave
trade. Laws governing the incorporation of companies were enacted in 1849 and amended and supplemented in 1859 and 1860.
The various ministries which were in office during the fifties[7] were
responsible for most of these beneficent activities which wrought
transformations in almost every domain of national life. These
activities included legislation or decrees dealing with public lands,
taxation, railway administration, reforms in the organization of
the army and navy, commercial tribunals. The whole educational
system also engaged their attention. Improvements were made in
the organization not only of the elementary and higher schools,
but likewise of the schools of law and medicine. Nor were other
important national interests neglected. Reforms and changes were
made in the imperial, civil and diplomatic service, banking organization, boards of public health, the stock exchange, the rights
and privileges of foreign consuls in Brazil, and a host of other
matters. Efforts were also made during this period to settle Brazil's numerous boundary controversies, vexatious legacies of the
Portuguese and Spanish colonial periods. Since, however, these
difficulties were not finally solved until a half century later under

---

[7] This was especially true of the ministries of September 29, 1850 (Marquis
of Olinda); of September 6, 1853 (Marquis of Paraná); and of May 4, 1857
(Marquis of Olinda).

the republic, we may more conveniently leave them for later discussion.

Literary Movements.—The forward march of Brazil during the middle decades of the nineteenth century was also evident in the field of literary endeavor. Here we may use as our guide the *History of Brazilian Literature* published in 1925 by the eminent critic Ronald de Carvalho.[8] The period between 1836 and 1870 reveals a progressive awakening of national consciousness. Romanticism displays four separate trends in poetry. Gonçalves de Magalhães, later Viscount of Araguaya, comes first with an inspiration that was fundamentally religious. Next, Gonçalves Dias, drawing his inspiration directly from nature, reveals himself to be a sincere and authoritative interpreter of the Brazilian milieu, under the influence of strong pantheistic convictions. Alvares de Azevedo is the chief of a peculiar school in which irony, sadness, and doubt are perhaps the distinguishing features. Castro Alves, a poet with a heart close to the people, vibrating with emotion, filled with ideals and noble enthusiasm, revolted at the social injustice he saw about him. He was the paladin of liberty and generosity—a rebel against prejudices.

Our great novelists drew their inspiration and their themes from the colorful history of Brazil and its native races. Indianism and the history of colonial days captivated José de Alencar. Joaquim Manoel de Macedo and Manoel Antonio de Almeida found the settings for their novels in colonial times and the early years of the empire. Bernardo Guimarães and Alfredo de Taunay were the first to explore in their writings the mysterious and vast hinterland of Brazil.

At this period only one notable historian calls for mention—Francisco Adolpho de Varnhagen (Viscount of Porto Seguro), who remains over the lapse of years our undisputed historian on the colonial period. Other names which bulk large in Brazilian historiography, such as Capistrano de Abreu and Oliveira Lima, do not come until later.

The drama lagged far behind the novel. But one name, that of Martins Penna, needs be recalled. He essayed to interpret the life of the humble and under-privileged.

In general, it may be said that these decades witnessed a pro-

---

[8] *Pequena Historia da Literatura Brasileira* (Rio de Janeiro).

found change in the orientation of our literature. It became, as it were, nationalized. The influence of the Greek and Latin classics became less. Themes and models were more and more chosen from Brazilian life. European influence, however, continued to exert tremendous influence. The foreign language, culture, and civilization most prized in Brazil were those of France. French was commonly spoken by the educated classes. French textbooks were used extensively in all of the higher schools. The successive French literary movements of the nineteenth century had their repercussions in Brazil and, despite the increasing predilection for national themes and motifs, found their imitators. The writers who possibly had the greatest influence were Chateaubriand and Victor Hugo.

English and German literature, insofar as they were known or studied, came to the Brazilians through French translations. Sir Walter Scott and James Fenimore Cooper were greatly admired and had their followers among novelists and poets. Byron also enjoyed considerable popularity. Goethe and Schiller found a more limited circle of readers. In the southern provinces of the empire there were naturally some intellectual and literary contacts with the Platine republics. Spanish was currently understood and read and, in the limithrophe regions, spoken. Latin was taught in all of the secondary schools and familiarity with classical writers was widespread among persons of cultivation.

It cannot be too often repeated, however, that such imitation of foreign models as existed had ceased to be servile. It may even be said that this appreciation of the literature and thought of other countries contributed to that intellectual ferment which eventually made the literature of the empire more nationalistic and more Brazilian.

CHAPTER X

THE PARAGUAYAN WAR

General Considerations.—The Paraguayan War, which lasted from 1865 to 1870, was the one military struggle of major importance in which the empire became involved.[1] In comparison, the Platine invasions of Dom Pedro I and the campaigns against Rosas ending with the dictator's defeat at Monte Caseros were little more than skirmishes. Before the Paraguayan War was over, both the resources and the man power of the empire were subjected to a severe strain. Brazil's victory turned out to be a hollow one. In fact, the consequences of the war were not unrelated to the waning of the empire and the overthrow of the Braganza dynasty in 1889.

It does not fall within the scope of this history to take up in detail the causes of this conflict. In fact, responsibilities for the war are still matters of dispute and controversy among South American historians. We shall limit ourselves to setting forth impartially and objectively the part played by Brazil in this struggle. Only brief allusions will be made to the military events. Rather shall we stress the course of Brazilian diplomacy during the anxious months which led up to the outbreak of the war. Some mention will be made also of the chief actors in the drama: López, Mitre, Caxias, and others.

Anarchical Conditions in Uruguay.—The elimination of Rosas in 1852 did not at once bring peace to the distracted countries bordering on La Plata. Argentina was to wait for a full decade before being able to perfect its national organization. During much of the time the nation was rent by a schism between the city and province of Buenos Aires on the one side and the Argentine Confederation on the other. Though freed from the nightmare of absorption by Rosas, the little republic of Uruguay was still torn by the ambitions of rival factions of the *Blancos* and *Colorados* and for a number of years was a prey to an intolerable anarchy.

[1] The literature on the Paraguayan War is immense. A satisfactory introduction to the subject may be found in *The Origins of the Paraguayan War*, by P. H. Box (Urbana, Ill., 1927), Chap. VII of Hill, *op. cit.*, and Chap. XIV of J. F. Rippy, P. A. Martin, and I. J. Cox, *Argentina, Chile and Brazil since Independence.*—P.A.M.

During the space of the four years from 1852 to 1856, the unhappy country had been the victim of three revolutions, as many dictatorships, and two provisional executives. It is unnecessary to add that during these seemingly interminable struggles foreign interests were gravely jeopardized. Brazil, Uruguay's neighbor on the north, was the worst sufferer.

The imperial government was careful to show no preferences in these internal conflicts in Uruguay. It adhered to a strict neutrality and officially maintained diplomatic relations with the government in power at the time. This had also been true in an earlier period. The Brazilian authorities had treated successively with Rivera, Oribe, and the defenders of Montevideo as long as they wielded lawful authority. It is an absurdity to speak of such or such party as being the friends or protegés of Brazil. But in the distracted republic of Uruguay opinions ran quite the contrary. Each group in power begged for the empire's assistance; and its sentiments toward its great northern neighbor depended on the extent to which such aid was forthcoming.

Thanks to the wider perspective and the greater knowledge at our disposal, these erroneous opinions are no longer held. With virtual unanimity, historians of the present day acknowledge that the real aims of Brazil were liberal and unselfish. Even those who in the past have criticised and censured the imperial policy in the Platine countries have recanted and generously avowed their mistakes. In recent years the Brazilian archives have been thrown open and confidential documents have been published. It is no longer possible to doubt the sincerity of the government of Rio, either in its pretensions or in its acts.

Growing Friction Between Brazil and Uruguay.—We may pass over in silence the tangled history of Uruguay from 1852 to 1864. But if we are to understand the subsequent actions of Brazil, it is essential to consider in some detail the grave difficulties which had accumulated on each side of the Uruguayan-Brazilian frontier. Here the situation, especially in the southern portion of the province of Rio Grande do Sul, was difficult in the extreme. Border raids and disorders of all kinds had become almost endemic. Many Brazilians possessed lands in Uruguay adjoining their own properties in Rio Grande. Hostilities chiefly took the form of cattle raiding by the Uruguayans across the border, accompanied not infrequently by brawls and murders. The dwellers of Rio Grande do Sul have always been known as a fiery and touchy lot. This petty warfare aroused them to fury. Their only property—cattle —was at stake. Their lives were in jeopardy. Their lands were overrun and pillaged. It has been estimated that no less than 800,000 head of cattle were lost to the Brazilians in raids which extended over some six hundred square leagues of grazing land.

Complaints poured in to Rio. The ministry made fitting diplomatic representations at Montevideo but there existed no machinery for obtaining justice in a country torn with civil war. For this reason the imperial government did not insist too strongly on its legitimate demands. It is not surprising that under these circumstances retaliation began to take place. As noted in the preceding chapter, small bands of Brazilians crossed the frontier to recover their own cattle and to seek revenge for the outrages they had suffered. The Montevideo government was not slow in protesting in its turn to Rio de Janeiro; their protests became even stronger when the Brazilians, goaded to dispair by the apathy of local authorities, took matters more and more into their own hands. They organized regular military *commandos* under the general leadership of the Baron of Jacuhy, who had been one of the ablest officers of Caxias during the war of the *Farrapos*.

The situation was thus going from bad to worse. The imperial government felt constrained to adopt more energetic measures if for no other reason than to forestall the possibility of a rebellion in its southernmost province. Finally, in April, 1864, it sent a special mission to Uruguay under Deputy José Antonio Saraiva for the sole purpose of arriving at a satisfactory and durable understanding with Brazil's southern neighbor.

At first blush it would seem that circumstances were favorable to a permanent settlement. Uruguay's international status in recent years had become more secure and no longer was aggression feared from the other side of the Platine estuary. Since 1862 Argentina had been governed by one of the greatest of its presidents, Bartolomé Mitre, a former unitarian and an exile under Rosas. He was entirely opposed to any attempt to extend the hegemony of Buenos Aires over Uruguay and had as his aim a general pacification of the Platine republics. He desired also to be on the best of terms with Brazil in whose loyalty he had the utmost confidence. In fact, his attitude was one of the determining factors in the despatch of the Saraiva mission. Finally, Saraiva himself was the personification of honor, moderation, and the spirit of justice. He much preferred to attain his ends by suasion rather than force. In fact, so highly rated were his qualities that in the latter years of the empire he soared, as it were, above parties, and was even sometimes called the "vice emperor."

Unfortunately, any hopes which Saraiva might have cherished of redressing the legitimate grievances of Brazil or of bringing internal peace to Uruguay were largely nullified by the advent to power, on March 1, 1864, of the president of the Uruguayan senate, Atanasio C. Aguirre. He was a violent partisan, whose political ideas did not extend beyond the horizon of blind party loyalty. He was willing to resort to any measure to keep himself and his satellites in power. Such was the man with whom the imperial envoy had to deal. As already intimated, Saraiva's instructions were to secure the redress of past wrongs, the punishment of the guilty, and indemnity for the losses suffered by the inhabitants of Rio Grande do Sul. He was authorized, if he saw fit, to present these demands in the character of an ultimatum with the threat of reprisals if they were not complied with. But he much preferred to use persuasion rather than threats.

On May 12, 1864, he presented his credentials to Aguirre and six days later sent a most courteous note stating the object of his visit. The answer was a rude and intemperate reply, infused with partisan animosity. Saraiva, with the utmost courtesy, demolished the arguments of the Uruguayan executive and reiterated his demands. He still withheld any mention of the ultimatum.

He was still awaiting a reply to his second note when, on June 6, the Argentine minister of foreign affairs, Rufino de Elizalde, and Edward Thornton, British minister to Argentina, arrived at Montevideo with the object of proffering their good offices to Aguirre. It was the wish of all of the diplomats in Buenos Aires that the domestic dissensions in Uruguay should cease as soon as possible. Saraiva felt very hopeful that, with their aid, he could bring the Uruguayan government to listen to reason. Together they waited upon the president and after lengthy discussions agreed on a formula of conciliation designed to put an end to bloodshed and restore peace to Uruguay. Saraiva rightly felt that such an agreement would greatly facilitate the settlement of Brazil's claim. The formula was made public on June 10.

General Venancio Flores, leader of the *Colorados*, and bitter opponent of Aguirre, was then consulted and agreed to abide by the formula provided the president consented to the incorporation of a number of *Colorados* in his ministry. The protocols were then submitted to the Uruguayan government and accepted. But at the last moment, when it came to presenting the documents to Flores, it was discovered, to the amazement and indignation of the mediators, that Aguirre had incorporated conditions in frank contradiction to the formula which had been agreed upon. Further negotiation proved fruitless and on July 3 Flores was informed of Aguirre's action. The *Colorados* were furious at the president's breach of faith and the civil war, which had ceased during the course of negotiations, broke out with renewed bitterness.[2]

Once again Saraiva delayed the accomplishment of his mission. He repaired to Buenos Aires in order to despatch a detailed account of recent events to Rio de Janeiro and demand definite instructions. Even then he did not close the door to the possibility of eleventh hour negotiations. The reply of the Brazilian government was categorical. Saraiva was instructed to grant Aguirre a short time in which to meet the Brazilian demands in full; should he still refuse, the imperial envoy was to present the ultimatum and announce that reprisals would at once be enforced.

The War With Uruguay.—On August 4, 1864, the ultimatum was presented. The Uruguayan minister of foreign affairs returned it as unacceptable and proposed arbitration. Such a proposal could not be entertained by the empire as it meant protracting still further a debate which had already lasted many years. Too long had the good faith of Brazil been trifled with. On August 30, Uruguay broke diplomatic relations with the empire. Even then hostilities were slow in beginning. In order to allay any fears regarding the ultimate plans of both Brazil and Argentina, Saraiva, on the eve of his departure from Buenos Aires, signed with Elizalde a declaration that whatever the future had in store the independence of Uruguay would be respected.

---

[2] An account of these events from the Uruguayan point of view is given by H. D. (Herman Damasceno) in his *Ensayo de Historia Patria* (Montevideo, 1923), 5th ed., p. 659.—P.A.M.

From the foregoing it seems clear that the responsibility for the war which broke out between Uruguay and Brazil rests largely with the stubborn leader of the *Blancos*, President Atanasio Aguirre. But this does not tell the whole story. Refusal to accept Saraiva's demands was based on something more fundamental than the hostility of a single individual. The underlying cause that led the president and his cabinet to reject all peace proposals was the deep-seated distrust which they had of both the Brazilian Empire and the Argentine Republic. The first power they suspected of harboring designs of conquest; the second, of plotting to alter the internal situation in Uruguay. We have already alluded to Brazil's complete innocence of any oppressive designs against its southern neighbor. As for Argentina, it was quite true that President Mitre was a friend of the *Colorado* chieftain, Venancio Flores. But from this it did not follow that Argentina was exerting its influence to bring about the overthrow of the *Blanco* president, Aguirre. Throughout this difficult period of negotiations, President Mitre and his minister of foreign affairs, Elizalde, acted in absolutely good faith, and had as their sole aid the pacification of Uruguay. At the present time, with the archives thrown open and all the facts known, we may judge these events with a greater degree of serenity. Even Uruguayan historians, who once criticized and accused Argentina and Brazil, have come honestly and nobly to confess their errors.[3]

The Intervention of Paraguay.—While the sincerity and good faith of Brazil and Argentina may no longer be questioned, unfortunately, the same may not be said regarding the *Blancos* and their intrigues in the Argentina provinces of Entre Rios and Corrientes, and in the Republic of Paraguay. The testimony of contemporary pamphlets and the instructions and reports of diplomats leave no possible doubt on this score.

The mention of Paraguay introduces us to a new element in the complicated history of the Platine republics, and if we are properly to understand the rôle which this land-locked nation was about to play in South American affairs we must go back a

[3] Dr. Calogeras, in believing that agreement has been reached on the causes of these dissensions which led to the Brazilian intervention in Uruguay and eventually to the Paraguayan War, is much too optimistic. Many of the *Blanco* historians, *e.g.*, Dr. Luis Alberto de Herrera, still incline to the traditional point of view.—P.A.M.

few decades and glance at its history since the early years of the nineteenth century.

In the latter days of the colonial period Paraguay, once the preserve of the Jesuits, was a province of the vice royalty of La Plata. But with the coming of independence, Paraguay broke away from the leading strings of Buenos Aires and in 1811 set itself up as a separate state. In a few years, however, it fell under the control of the dictator, Dr. José Gaspar de Francia, who until his death in 1841 remained the undisputed master of the country. This gloomy despot has found few defenders. Thomas Carlyle, to be sure, made him the subject of a rather flattering essay, but really knew little about his hero. Francia was not only despotic but wantonly cruel. He took delight in watching the executions of his adversaries, whom he condemned to death on the shallowest of pretexts. Delation existed everywhere, even among members of the same family. The Paraguayan people, largely Guaraní in blood, inured to blind and passive obedience under the Jesuits, were so much plastic material in his hands. The dictator became known as *El Supremo* and was looked upon by the superstitious Guarinís as the vicegerent of God upon earth. During the course of his long rule they became somber, silent, and fanatically devoted to their leader. His authority, whether direct or delegated, was never questioned. History offers few parallels of a people more willing to sacrifice itself to its ruler.

On the other hand, Francia has one great service to his credit. He kept Paraguay free from foreign entanglements. He well knew that his country was too weak to achieve victory in any clash with its neighbors and he, therefore, made every effort to keep Paraguay isolated. He wished Paraguay to be forgotten until its people were in a position to make its influence effective. Consuls or ministers he neither received nor sent. The Paraguay and Paraná rivers which were the only means of communication with the outside world, were closed to navigation. The country was encompassed by a kind of Chinese wall.

A partial exception to this policy of exclusion was to be seen in Paraguay's relation to Brazil. During the troubled years 1824-1826 the empire feared serious complications with both Argentina on the south and Bolivia on the west. The southernmost province of Cisplatina (the present Uruguay) could hardly expect to face so many possible battlefronts with success. At this juncture Paraguay might well serve as a sort of buffer state, and in 1824 and again in 1826 Brazil sent envoys to Paraguay with the object of inducing Francia to maintain an unswerving neutrality. Such missions were easy to carry out since they fell in with Francia's own sentiments. Their real importance lay in the fact that they were tantamount to a recognition of the independence of Paraguay. However, an official communication to this effect was not despatched to Paraguay until 1842, a year after Francia's death. In 1841 Brazilian diplomats were again accredited to Asunción and almost continually represented the empire until the outbreak of the Paraguayan War in 1864.

Francia was succeeded in 1841 by a well-to-do planter by the name of Carlos Antonio López. The new ruler of Paraguay was a violent and coarse-grained despot but happily he had little of Francia's cruelty in his make-up. Though he insisted that the Paraguayans yield to him the same blind obedience they had shown to his predecessor life became more tolerable. He opened contacts with the outside world. He received a number of foreign envoys, especially from Brazil, as we shall see in a moment. His two sons he sent abroad to be educated: Benigno, to Rio de Janeiro, and Francisco Solano, to France. Paraguay at length became a member of the South American family of nations.

Allusion has just been made to the diplomatic relations between Paraguay and Brazil. Though initiated under Francia they took on greater proportions under the first López. On the whole they were cordial, largely because Paraguay harbored deep-seated suspicion of the Argentines who had never forgotten that the landlocked republic had once formed part of the old viceroyalty of La Plata. In 1845 the Buenos Aires government went so far as to protest against Brazil's formal recognition of Paraguayan independence the preceding year. A long series of conventions were negotiated between the governments of Rio de Janeiro and Asunción—1844, 1845, 1850, 1856, and 1858. All but the first were ratified. During this whole period Brazil made it clear that Paraguay enjoyed the full sympathy of the empire in its resistance to the designs of Argentina. Only for the years 1853-1855 was this harmony interrupted owing to differences in regard to the free navigation of the Paraguay and Paraná rivers.

Francisco Solano López.—The elder López died in 1862 and was succeeded by his son Francisco Solano. It is exceedingly difficult to find anything good to say of this man. His early outlook on life was not so dissimilar to that of Francia and López I. Everything prepared him for the life of an absolute autocrat. The lives, the honor, the possessions of his subjects he looked upon as his own and disposed of them as suited his fancy. The slightest attempt at disobedience was visited with death.

His career falls into two epochs: his early life up to the death of his father, and the period of his dictatorship. We have just seen that he was sent by his father to be educated in France. Here he led a life of idleness and debauchery. On his return to Paraguay he brought with him as his mistress a certain Alisa Alice Lynch, the divorced wife of the famous French naturalist, Quatrefages, and a famous Parisian demi mondaine. Her influence was in every respect bad. Her power over López was all but complete. She had two dominating ambitions: to be married to López and to see him play a decisive and dramatic part in South American politics. Only the second of these ambitions was gratified, and that in a manner to cause her name to be execrated. Her greed for riches was incredible; it led her to commit veritable crimes. Her natural sadism and hardness of heart turned her on occasion into a virago. Some of López's most atrocious crimes were committed at her suggestion.

After his military defeats López's worst qualities were accentuated. He took to hard drinking. He fell victim to a sort of blood lust; in this respect he has been compared to Nero. He gloried in the torture of his enemies, alleged or real. Before his death many of his friends and devoted supporters were sacrificed to his homicidal mania. The testimony of all foreigners—English, Germans, Italians, Americans—living in Paraguay at the time is unanimous on this point. The most lenient and charitable hypotheses are that he was insane, or that the few drops of Indian blood in his veins brought on, under the strain of war, an atavistic outburst of ancestral cruelty.

Let us now turn to a consideration of the public career of this Paraguayan dictator. History would seem to show that there is a kind of insanity, a delusion of greatness, if you will, which at some stage in their career, is apt to take possession of those entrusted with the destinies of people. In South America, Simón Bolívar harbored grandiose dreams of empire and in the end plowed the sea. On a smaller scale, Dom João VI and Dom Pedro I likewise nurtured imperialistic ambitions which finally came to naught. Rosas, the Argentine dictator, met the same fate. Now came Paraguay's turn. Everything points to López's ambition to erect a Greater Paraguay by absorbing the Republic of Uruguay and the Argentine provinces of Entre Ríos and Corrientes. Thus would the little land-locked country become a great Atlantic power with Montevideo as its capital.

Such a program was indeed bold and daring and under certain conditions not entirely without the bounds of possibility. To carry it out would entail the crushing of Uruguay, the dismemberment of Argentina, and possible hostilities with Brazil, whose interests would almost certainly be jeopardized. Only a political and military genius could hope to encompass such a task. Certainly Francisco Solano López was not such a genius. It was the great error of the *Blancos* of Uruguay not to have grasped the inferiority of the Paraguayan dictator and not to have seen that his triumph would have sounded the death knell of Uruguayan independence.

The full story of the relations of the *Blancos* of Uruguay and the dictator López has not yet been told. The chief facts, however, are reasonably clear. We have already seen that Uruguay harbored deep, though in reality, groundless suspicions of both Argentina and Brazil. Under these conditions, it was but natural that Uruguay should cast about for allies. The then little-known Paraguay might serve such a purpose. In 1862 the government of Montevideo dispatched to Asunción one of its ablest diplomats, J. J. Herrera. He arrived at Paraguay shortly before the death of the elder López. He was instructed to ascertain the aims, interests, and international problems of Paraguay. But as events turned out, it was not a case of sovereign powers meeting on an equal footing. Rather was it a case of a vassal entreating the good will and protection of an overlord. This desire to secure the favor of Paraguay went so far as to offer it the island of Martín García, lying at the La Plata estuary, and in those days, the key of all the navigation on the Paraná and Uruguay rivers. The unconscious humor of the situation lay in the fact that it was not Uruguay's to give as it was in the possession of Argentina.

The younger López, who was being groomed for the succession to the dictatorship, dissembled and feigned indifference. As a matter of fact, an alliance with the *Blancos* of Uruguay would fit in admirably with his plans. But he was careful not to go so far as to commit himself by a treaty with Uruguay, though he promised when the time came to help the Montevideo government by deeds, not words, and this promise, as we shall later see, he tried to fulfill. His real idea was not to allow himself to be fettered by any kind of bonds with a country which he eventually intended to conquer.

The younger López might flatter himself that he had brought the *Blancos* well within the orbit of his ambitious plans. But his designs did not stop here. He hoped, as we have seen, to dismember Argentina, at least to the extent of detaching the fertile and prosperous province of Entre Ríos from the confederation. The key to the situation was Justo José Urquiza, the ex-president of the republic and the victor over Rosas at the Battle of Monte Caseros in 1852. Subsequently, Urquiza had clashed violently with General Mitre, by whom he was decisively routed at the Battle of Pavón in 1861. But Mitre had shown moderation in his hour of triumph and had allowed Uriquiza to resume the governorship of his native province of Entre Ríos. Nonetheless, Uriquiza was far from friendly to Buenos Aires and to Mitre's friends, especially the leader of the Uruguayan *Colorados*, Venancio Flores. López had accordingly some justification for counting on Urquiza as a possible ally and eventually a victim. He was to reckon, however, without his host. Urquiza was no statesman. Rather was he a *condottiere*, the last that Argentina may show. He possessed a certain natural astuteness and was certainly not devoid of patriotism. He did not intend to betray the Argentine Confederation. He might not be unwilling at a favorable juncture to overthrow the government of his enemy Mitre and put himself in his place. But the wily López felt that he might use Urquiza as a convenient tool and then cast him aside. The Paraguayan dictator was about to play a very dangerous game which ultimately was to be his undoing.

In the light of the foregoing, the action of Aguirre, the *Blanco*,

Uruguayan president, in flouting the Brazilian-Argentine mediation is somewhat more comprehensible. Treacherous and disloyal his action was but it was based on a certain amount of shrewd calculation. He was convinced that if it should come to a crisis with Brazil he could certainly count on the support of López and should Argentina become involved, on that of Urquiza. He had received assurances from the minister of foreign affairs, J. J. Herrera, his former envoy to Paraguay, that Paraguay would mobolize in the event of hostilities with the empire (thus protecting Uruguay from the rear) and that Entre Ríos under Urquiza would join the war on the side of the Uruguayan *Blancos*.

Admiral Tamandaré.—It was at this juncture, when the atmosphere was heavy with intrigue and suspicion, that Brazilian diplomacy committed a capital error. It is obvious that a successful handling of the tangled affairs of the Platine republics required consummate skill and tact. Saraiva, as we have seen, possessed such qualities to an unusual degree. In fact, the appreciation with which he was held in Argentina paved the way for the understanding that eventually grew into the Triple Alliance of 1865. It will be recalled that after the breakdown of the negotiations with the *Blanco* president, Aguirre, he left Montevideo for Buenos Aires in September, 1864. His place was filled in December by another diplomat of outstanding ability, José Maria da Silva Paranhos, later the Viscount of Rio Branco, whose brilliant achievements we shall take up in detail when we come to discuss the abolition of Negro slavery. But between September and December the management of Brazilian affairs in the Platine basin had fallen into the hands of the admiral of the imperial fleet, Baron of Tamandaré. As a naval commander, he was one of the most striking figures of the empire. He was a gallant old salt, fiery as brimstone, true as steel, bravest of the brave, courting rather than shunning danger. He lived to a very old age. Up to the very day of his death he clung to many of the habits acquired in his days as a midshipman. His bed was nothing but wooden boards; his pillow a wooden block. His patriotism and devotion to the emperor took on the proportions of a legend. For these and other reasons he was highly esteemed and his advice and counsel carried immense weight. Unfortunately, he judged everything from a purely military viewpoint. Forthright in all his actions, he was suspicious of lawyers and negotiators. He could conceive of no conflict, diplomatic, military, or naval, in which Brazil did not emerge victorious.

In accordance with the ultimatum delivered by Saraiva, he at once began to exercise reprisals against the Montevideo government. On October 20, 1864, he signed with Flores, the leader of the *Colorados*, the secret agreement of Santa Lucía, in which the Brazilian demands received full recognition. From this time on, Flores became the protegé of Brazil and its faithful ally. The Brazilian occupation of the country now began in earnest. As early as October 16 imperial forces under General Menna Barreto entered the department of Cerro Largo and seized the town of Melo. In November, Tamandaré's fleet in close coöperation with Flores laid siege to the important port of Paysandú on the Uruguay River. The town continued to hold out until January 2, 1865, when it surrendered to the combined forces of Tamandaré and Menna Barreto. The two Brazilian commanders, aided by Flores, then turned their attention to Montevideo, the capital.

In visiting reprisals on Uruguay, Tamandaré certainly went too far. On the other hand, it cannot be denied that his action met with the full approval of the majority of the inhabitants not only of Rio Grande do Sul but also of Rio de Janeiro. The average Brazilian was infuriated with the taunts and duplicity of the Uruguayan *Blancos*.

Councillor Silva Paranhos.—Fortunately, the conduct of affairs soon passed into the more competent hands of Silva Paranhos who arrived in Buenos Aires as Brazilian plenipotentiary on December 2. More politic and farseeing than Tamandaré, he cast about for means to bring hostilities to an end. Opportunity came when Aguirre's term of office ended on February 15, 1865, and he was succeeded by Tomás Villalba, president of the senate. The new Uruguayan executive at once asked the Italian minister to beg for peace. Under the general auspices of Paranhos an agreement was reached only five days later. The peace convention of February 20 included provisions for a general amnesty, a provisional government presided over by Flores, elections at the earliest possible moment, restitution of confiscated property, and perhaps most important of all, acknowledgment of Brazilian claims.

Outbreak of the Paraguayan War.—Hostilities between Brazil and Uruguay were thus brought to an end by the Convention of February 20, 1865. But the importance of this act was completely dwarfed by events which had already occurred in Paraguay. The impossible had happened. Like a thunderbolt, the news descended upon Rio that on November 11, 1864, the dictator López without warning had captured the Brazilian steamer *Marquiz de Olinda* as it was leaving Asunción for the interior of Brazil, had taken prisoner Colonel Carneiro de Campos, the new president of the province of Matto Grosso, and had seized various official documents, as well as remittances to the provincial treasury. The amazement of the Brazilians at this outrage was equaled only by their indignation. The entire country, without distinction of party or class, demanded that this affront to the national honor receive its just punishment.

Passions aroused by a seemingly gratuitious attack on national dignity render difficult an objective judgment of these events. But truth and equity demand that we make an honest attempt to fathom the motives of López at this time. In justifying his actions, the Paraguayan dictator alleged that the occupation of the Uruguayan town of Melo by the Brazilian troops in October, 1864, constituted for the Paraguayans a *casus belli*. Such a statement is absurd on two grounds. In the first place, the Brazilian-Uruguayan difficulties were no concern of López. Secondly, the occupation of Melo stood well within the legal activities of campaign of reprisals being carried on by the imperial government against Uruguay, after all efforts at conciliation had broken down.

The truth of the matter is that López knew well what he was doing. He realized fully that the wanton seizure of the *Marquiz de Olinda* would precipitate war with Brazil but he had, as he thought, counted the cost. And it must be owned that, if in the furtherance of his ambitious plans, he chose to throw down the gauntlet to the largest country of Hispanic America the moment was not ill-chosen. In Uruguay, he felt that he could count on the alliance of the *Blancos;* in Entre Ríos, that of Urquiza. As for Brazil itself, he hoped to make short work of its army. And in truth it must be said Paraguay was in a strong position. López had early realized the possibilities of building up a powerful army out of the docile and obedient Paraguayans. His task had been greatly facilitated by the steps which his father had taken in strengthen-

ing the military defenses of Paraguay. The elder López, fearful
of the designs of Rosas, had secured from Brazil professional
soldiers to drill his army and engineers to build defenses to protect
the access to the Paraguayan sections of the Paraguay and
Paraná rivers. In fact, it was Brazilian technical skill which made
possible the erection of the great fortress of Humaytá ("the
Gibraltar of South America") at the confluence of these two
streams. Brazilian diplomats have been severely taken to task for
failing to realize the future menace involved in thus aiding
Paraguay to fortify itself. Such criticism really has no basis.
Under the elder López, relations between Paraguay and Brazil were
most cordial. Even the plans of the younger López for the creation
of a Greater Paraguay did not necessarily menace Brazil. The
best of the Brazilian diplomats did not have the gift of omniscience.

Now that hostilities had actually broken out between Paraguay
and Brazil, the formidable character of López's military machine
became more evident. As early as November, 1864, he had
80,000 troops trained and equipped. A few months later this
figure rose to 100,000. On the other hand, Brazil had only 17,000
troops; half were dispersed throughout the empire, half fortunately, concentrated in the province of Rio Grande do Sul. The
largest number Brazil ever had in the field during the whole course
of the war was 68,000 (in April, 1866). It will be seen that this
fell far below the highest figures for Paraguay.

Had López chosen to remain strictly on the defensive, he could
have bade defiance to his enemies almost indefinitely. But this did
not comport with his plans for the expansion of Paraguay and
for the maintenance of what he rather pretentiously called "the
equilibrium of La Plata." Accordingly, when the *Blanco* leader,
Aguirre, called upon him to attack the Brazilian forces from the
rear and thus force them to raise the siege of Montevideo, he complied with alacrity. But one serious obstacle stood in the way of
the realization of this project. The Argentine territory of Mis-
siones and the provinces of Corrientes and Entre Ríos lay between
Paraguay and its two enemies. To come to the aid of the hard
pressed *Blancos* it was necessary then to cross Argentine territory. Permission was asked of President Mitre and was naturally
refused. It was then that López committed what was probably the
greatest blunder of his career. Disregarding Mitre's prohibition,

the Paraguayan dictator threw his troops into Corrientes, flagrantly violating the neutrality of Argentina. As was to be expected, President Mitre promptly declared war. Thus López found himself engaged in hostilities with the two foremost nations of South America. In defying the Argentine government he had counted on Urquiza's promised coöperation. But things fell out differently. By February the *Colorado* chieftain, Flores, thanks to the support of the Brazilian army, was the recognized head of the Uruguayan government. To Paraguay's two enemies was now added a third. On May 1, 1865, was signed by Brazil, Uruguay, and Argentina the Treaty of Triple Alliance, by which the Allies, as we may henceforth call them, agreed not to lay down their arms until the power of López had been destroyed.

The Rôle of Urquiza.—The violation of Argentine neutrality and the signing of the Treaty of Triple Alliance naturally gave Urquiza pause. Had he at an earlier date revolted against Buenos Aires, and received aid from López, he would have been able to invoke precedents and discuss the legitimacy of his action; but under the present conditions with foreign troops on Argentine soil his unwritten understandings with the Paraguayan dictator, if put into effect, could only be regarded as treason. For after all Urquiza's state of Entre Ríos was still officially a member of the Argentine Confederation. Besides as a *condottiere*, chiefly concerned in feathering his own nest, he realized that with the defeat of his old allies the *Blancos* in Uruguay, López's chances of victory had become more remote. Discretion at this juncture was surely the better part of valor.

Urquiza therefore refused to move, and thus, in a sense, betrayed everybody. But the Brazilians, taking no chances, determined to render him harmless. Though he was far from being poor Urquiza's love of riches was insatiable. General Osorio (later the Marquis of Herval) was well acquainted with this foible, and he determined to exploit it to the full. The imperial army was greatly in need of cavalry. The Brazilian commander proceeded to buy up virtually all of the horses available in Entre Ríos, amounting to some 30,000. This meant in effect the disarming of the province, for the followers of Urquiza, though extraordinarily able riders, constituted an indifferent infantry. Thus was the great *caudillo* of Entre Ríos virtually eliminated as a factor in the war.

Mistakes and Miscalculations of López.—At the very beginning of the war, López committed a number of capital military blunders. Instead of holding his troops behind the Paraguayan frontier where the rivers formed an admirable protection he divided his forces and launched an offensive both in the north and the south. Both were failures. The invasion of the Brazilian province of Matto Grosso, undertaken in December, 1864, though it caused much property damage, served no possible military end. Equally unsuccessful was his southern offensive. One portion of his army, after seizing the Argentine port of Corrientes, was defeated in the battle of Yatay, August 17, 1865; the other section contrived to capture the Brazilian town of Uruguayana but was forced to surrender on September 18 of the same year. Nor was this all. Epidemics probably took as heavy a toll among the troops as actual fighting. Dr. Cecilio Baéz, the ex-president of Paraguay, in a recent publication[4] declares that at the end of 1865, before the allies had invaded the republic, López's first army of 64,000 men had ceased to exist.

Equally unfortunate was López in his initial naval campaign. On June 11, 1865, at Riachuelo on the Paraná River, not far from its junction with the Paraguay, his fleet was almost totally destroyed by a Brazilian squadron under Admiral Barroso. It is interesting to note that a full year before the victory of the Austrians over the Italians at Lissa ramming tactics were successfully employed by the Brazilian commander.

As the only feasible approach to Paraguay was by the rivers— in fact the Paraguay River may be regarded as a great fortified corridor through which all vessels had to make their way to reach Asunción, the Paraguayan capital—the Brazilian navy necessarily played a significant part in the struggle. Its most important duty was to destroy or silence the powerful shore batteries which had been erected by López at strategic points, and from which the ships were subjected to a devastating cross fire. Of the various engagements, in many of which the Brazilian fleet covered itself with glory, the most famous was the passage on February 19, 1868, of the great fortress of Humaytá—"the Gibraltar of South America."

This is not the place to discuss the military aspect of the War

---

[4] *Resúmen de la Historia del Paraguay* (Asunción, 1910).

of the Triple Alliance as it does not fall within the scope of our task, which is an account of the historical formation of Brazil. It may be merely pointed out that after three years of unceasing effort and many sanguinary engagements, Asunción was occupied by the Allies on January 5, 1869. With the remnants of his army, López fled into the interior, to the accompaniment of unspeakable atrocities. He was finally run to earth and shot down by a common soldiers at Cerro Corá near the Brazilian frontier on March 1, 1870.

Courage, daring, heroism were to be found in both armies. Brazil, Argentina, and Uruguay may be proud of their soldiers. But equal homage must be accorded the sons of Paraguay. Bold and obedient, suffering without wincing under the hardest strains of war, they fought, won, or died with utter fearlessness and absolute devotion to their country. When offered quarter, they refused, on the ground that they had no orders to accept it. The esteem and admiration they inspired in Brazil were only equaled by the horror caused by López's insane and wanton cruelty, and his atrocious and monstrously selfish disregard of his people's welfare and interest.

The war produced two great strategists. The first was the Duke of Caxias, whom we have already met as commander of the imperial forces in the rebellion which in the thirties and forties devasted Rio Grande do Sul. And now in the much greater struggle of the Paraguayan War he was made commander-in-chief of the allied forces after the retirement of President Mitre. The second strategist was Caxias' successor, the son-in-law of Dom Pedro II, the Comte d'Eu, who during the very difficult last stages of the war commanded the allies in the so-called campaign of the Cordilleras. Lesser commanders, of great ability and capacity for sacrifice, were to be found in all four armies. And as for the common soldiers, no words of praise are too high.

Shortly after the flight of López, a provisional government was set up in Asunción. With it Brazil and Argentina signed a preliminary treaty of peace on June 20, 1870, to which Uruguay adhered on August 1 of the same year. But agreement as to the final treaty was hard to reach. The difficulties arose, not from Brazil, but from Argentina. Weary of fruitless diplomatic bickerings, the empire finally, in January, 1872, signed with Paraguay four different treaties dealing with peace, boundary limits, extradition, and commerce and navigation. The boundaries were those always claimed by Brazil under the *uti possidetis* rule. There remained, however, difficulties of interpretation and other matters with Argentina which were finally not cleared up until the Buenos Aires Conference of 1876.

The Paraguayan War and South American Public Opinion.—Before we definitely leave the Paraguayan War, a few general considerations are perhaps in order. During the course of the struggle, public opinion in South America generally favored Paraguay. There was felt to be a general affinity on the part of the Spanish-speaking republics with a country whose language and institutions were similar, a country which was the victim of an attack by a great alliance, of which the most important member was the Portuguese-speaking empire of Brazil. The immense disparity in territorial extent and armed forces between Paraguay and its enemies was sufficient in itself to arouse sympathy for the small, land-locked republic. This situation López was quick to exploit by adroit and lavishly-paid propaganda and publicity. Only gradually was the real character of the struggle made manifest.

From the first the Allies alleged that they were fighting not against the Paraguayan people but against their dictator, López. This conviction rested on the fact that López was the cause of all of the difficulties they had to face and that as long as he was at the head of the government no permanent peace was possible. On this point the Allies were adamant; they would be content with nothing less than the banishment, imprisonment, or elimination of the Paraguayan ruler. Hence the rejection by Mitre of López's peace overtures at Yataity-Corá in September, 1866; hence, too, the refusal of Brazil to entertain an offer of mediation made by the United States early in 1867.[5]

The results of the war were deplorable. The adult male population of Paraguay was all but exterminated. The war bore heavily on the empire as well. The casualties amounted to some 33,000; the expenditures to 600,000 contos (approximately $300,000,-000). Yet all is not on the debit side of the ledger. From the three

---

[5] On this subject *cf.* the detailed discussion by Hill, *op. cit.*, Chap. VII.—P.A.M.

occasions in which Brazil intervened in the La Plata basin[6] there have resulted a closer intercourse and a better understanding between Brazil and its former allies or enemies. Transitory bitterness, distrust, and ill-will gradually gave way to a real appreciation based upon reciprocal knowledge. And with the passing of López and his insane ambition the greatest threat to peace in South America was removed.

[6] In 1851-1852 for the overthrow of Rosas; in 1864-1865, on behalf of the Colorados in Uruguay; and in 1865-1870 for the overthrow of López.—P.A.M.

CHAPTER XI

EVOLUTION OF POLITICAL PARTIES; FIRST STEPS IN NEGRO EMANCIPATION; THE RELIGIOUS QUESTION; THE WANING OF THE EMPIRE

THE LATTER years of the sixties and the opening years of the seventies constitute a period of extreme importance in the historical evolution of Brazil. The explanation of this phenomenon is to be sought partly in the results of the Platine wars, this quite apart from their military and international aspects. These struggles, particularly the Paraguayan War, profoundly affected not only the evolution of the various political parties but also the political development of the empire as a whole. Especially was this true of the propaganda in favor of a republican as opposed to the imperial régime. We have already pointed out that republican sentiment existed to a greater or less degree of intensity—according to locality—in the first days of the empire, but that its influence registered a marked decline after the abdication of Dom Pedro I in 1831. The revolution in Rio Grande do Sul in the thirties and forties should not deceive us. Despite appearances to the contrary, this movement did not aim at separation from the empire or the overthrow of imperial ideas. Rather was it to be regarded as a local struggle, of great violence to be sure, whose object was a greater degree of local autonomy.

New Political Horizons.—Following the conclusion of the Paraguayan War republican ideas flared up again; and this time they were never to be extinguished. From 1864 to 1870 there were revealed with increasing clearness the loss of prestige of the dynasty, the tacit opposition of the army and navy, and the growing coolness between the monarchy and the clergy. The factors in this transformation were but few and simple. The first was to be found in the imperial constitution itself. In addition to the classic tri-partite division of power into the executive, legislative, and judicial, there was provided in the Constitution of 1824 a fourth power designed to harmonize the other three, namely the so-called moderative power. And this faculty, the key to the whole political system, was incarnated, so to speak, in the person of the emperor himself. We may, therefore, pause for a moment to consider in greater detail the qualities and characteristics of the chief of the state.

The Emperor.—Legally and morally, the emperor was forced to intervene in the daily march of public affairs; the result was that he could not avoid taking a stand and making decisions in the conflicts of party and other interests. The result was to draw upon himself the hostility and imprecations of those groups he was forced to oppose. Such a situation was apt to develop with each change of ministry and the advent, almost by rotation, of another party to power. The ill-will of the "outs" was invariably visited upon the emperor, while the "ins" felt no particular gratitude when they found themselves entrusted with the government. After a certain amount of this kind of rotation all of the groups had at one time or another found themselves in opposition, and all had found occasion to criticize, frequently quite unjustly, the chief magistrate of the nation.

Moreover, the personality of the emperor was such that he never placed the slightest obstacle to the expression of the ill-will of his detractors. As a philosopher, he possessed the highest civil virtues. He devoted his whole time to the welfare of the country, but he was much less concerned with currying the favor of individuals. He deserves to be considered as a veritable *redresseur de torts*, a sort of ancient Roman censor. Not all found this rôle of the emperor to their liking.

Tolerant by nature, Dom Pedro II permitted criticism, insults, and even calumnies to run their course unchecked, and their authors suffered no penalties, however outrageous their attacks. He never defended himself. As an honest man with a clear conscience he considered himself immune to the shafts of his detractors. Always careful to avoid offending public opinion, he utilized his great influence to guide his country and its representatives in the way of solving all public problems for the greatest good of the community as a whole. He never permitted the slightest attack on the dignity of Brazil. When in 1863, the English diplomat, Christie, showed himself offensive, Dom Pedro II broke relations with Great Britain, and only renewed them after official excuses had been tendered by the British Government. During the Paraguayan War no one felt more keenly than he the affront committed by López against Brazil. He devoted himself heart and soul to providing the army and navy with the necessary supplies and equipment. Such intense labor was very exhausting. At the beginning of the war he was a man of forty with a powerful physique and full of life; five years later, he had the appearance of an old man, white-haired and decrepit.

His habits were simple and without formality. He was a philosopher and a savant, whose favorite occupation was studying and reading. Sincerely devoted to the army and navy, he never completely understood them, nor did he arrive at a full appreciation of their political and social rôle in the development of the modern state. For this reason it is frequently alleged that he was unsympathetic toward the army. Such a view is inaccurate. On the other hand, there is ground for the belief that he was not interested in its growth and expansion in times of peace. From this point of view Dom Pedro was a pacifist.

He had no favorites nor would he tolerate sycophants. He listened to and respected all opinions. Counsel and advice he accepted, if he considered them worthwhile. His full confidence he granted to few persons, but he gave everyone a chance to reveal himself; never did he permit himself to be influenced by blind sympathies or by baseless suspicions. His life, both public and private, was above reproach. Before everything he placed duty and devotion to the state. It may be said that he was the best, and at the same time the first, sincere, republican of Brazil.

Such moral traits and characteristics explain many things; among them the mixture of sorrow, affection, and respect, which filled the soul of the people and its rulers, when the force of circumstances, more powerful than the wishes of men, obliged the newly born republic to exile the entire imperial family to Europe.

Public opinion, especially abroad, gave him great concern. In the imperial court, in keeping with the old Portuguese tradition, existed the custom of kissing the hand (*beija-mão*). In 1871, on the occasion of his first voyage to Europe, he noticed that such a token of respect had become obsolete, and he at once abolished it in Brazil. He was at all times a firm believer in the abolition of slavery, and never missed an opportunity to reveal his sentiments in this regard. There were not lacking ministers of state who, shocked by his tendencies to liberate his own slaves and others belonging to the state, respectfully suggested that he should desist from such a course, since he was a sovereign of a state in which slavery existed as a legal institution. To such arguments he gave no heed. During his sojourn in Rio Grande do Sul in 1865 he came in contact with a number of the leading figures in the political and intellectual life of Argentina and Uruguay, and was quick to note the general repulsion inspired by the existence of slavery in the empire. It would seem, in fact, that as a consequence of such contacts his convictions were strongly reënforced that Brazil must be freed, if only gradually, from the stigma of slavery.

Thanks to his exalted position as head of the state, and the possession of the notable qualities we have already enumerated, the influence of Dom Pedro was very great and continued to increase from day to day. In his youth he had gained his apprenticeship in public affairs under the direction of, and in coöperation with, the founders of the empire; little by little as these men passed off the stage of history the emperor quietly but effectively assumed many of the prerogatives and faculties they had once exercised. Thus gradually but quite naturally he became the *primus inter pares* of the great public figures in Brazil. Although the list of such statesmen is an imposing one there are few in the seventies whose abilities could measure up to the emperor's; São Vicente, Cotegipe, Rio Branco, Zacharias, Paulino José Soares de Souza, Caxias at once come to mind. In the eighties were such outstanding political figures as Souza Dantas, João Alfredo, Affonso Celso, Lafayette Rodrigues Pereira. But above them all, thanks to his experience, his seniority in the office of statesman, and his incessant activity, was to be found the emperor.

In maintaining his preëminence, Dom Pedro could count on one all-important factor, that of time. While everything changed about him, he was always at his post as commander of the ship of state. Nothing tends to reënforce authority more than duration and permanence. The ability to bide his time, coupled with endless patience, was not the least of Dom Pedro's hallmarks as a great ruler.

Party Evolution.—At this point a word should be said regarding the evolution of political parties in Brazil. The period of the fifties and sixties represented perhaps the most rapid changes in the party organizations to be found during the entire reign of

Dom Pedro II. Aside from the perturbations of the regency, the long civil war in Rio Grande do Sul, and the momentary flare-up in Recife in 1848, little had occurred to modify the general desire for peace. In 1853, Honorio Hemeto Carneiro Leão, Marquis of Paraná, succeeded in consolidating into a single party, the so-called party of conciliation (*concilação*), all of the outstanding members of parliament of the country, provided they were genuinely liberals or conservatives. At his death in 1856 this political orientation, slightly tinged with conservatism, had acquired such prestige that it lasted until 1859. At this latter date a sort of party disintegration set in which became accentuated in the year following.

In 1861 the chamber of deputies contained three party groups: conservatives, divided into extremists and moderates; and the liberals, forming a single bloc. In 1862 an entente known as the League (*Liga*) was consummated between the moderates and liberals. This new grouping came into power under the name of the progressive party (*partido progressista*). Such a juxtaposition of divergent elements contained in itself the seeds of dissolution and revealed symptoms that on the first occasion the party would break up into liberals and conservatives. The various ministries became increasingly liberal in tone. But the progressive party remained in power five years (1863-1868) during which period the dominant figure was a severe and austere liberal, Senator Zacharias de Góes e Vasconcellos.

Largely owing to the press of foreign affairs, no grave problems engaged the attention of the parliament at this time. The abolition of slavery and the intervention of the army in politics did not come until later. As a consequence, the old party formulas and slogans began to lose their meaning, and republican propaganda made its appearance. It was destined steadily to grow in power and influence up to its definite triumph in 1889.

As has already been pointed out, Dom Pedro had returned from Rio Grande do Sul deeply impressed by the disrepute which in the unanimous opinion of civilized nations slavery was bringing upon the empire. In thinking thus the sovereign was by no means alone; a few years later Silva Paranhos pointed out to the senate how much he had felt this moral pressure, exerted by foreign countries, and that, during the course of the conflicts in the Platine basin, more than fifty thousand Brazilians had returned to their homes with the same impression. The moment had arrived, therefore, frankly to face and to solve the whole problem of abolition.

The movement had already been launched on a limited scale by a few thinkers in parliament, on the bench, in scientific associations, and in the press. But these were isolated cases—sentinels of an apparently lost cause. The difficulties to be overcome did not spring from any open hostility, but rather from a complete popular apathy and indifference. It was the general conviction that the institution of slavery was the keystone of the whole structure of Brazilian economy, and that it was entirely impossible to remove it without letting loose upon the nation the scourge of ruin and racial civil war.

The Law of "Free Birth." The Viscount of Rio Branco.—In the sixties, however, the problem took on new and different aspects. The emperor himself entered into the conflict and despite the checks placed upon him by his official position, he did not hesitate to make clear his own opinion. He contributed subscriptions designed to liberate slaves so that they might be enrolled in the armies engaged in the Paraguayan War; he instructed some of the ablest statesmen in the empire to make a careful study of the subject and report on the best means of solving it. Thanks to his initiative, the conviction gained ground that the paramount duty of the moment was to devise means whereby all children born of slave mothers should henceforth be free.

In this matter his principal adviser, both from the legal and political point of view, was Pimenta Bueno, later Viscount and Marquis of São Vicente. The president of the council, the Marquis of Olinda, refused to admit that such an explosive question was even open to discussion. Zacharias, his successor in 1866, was no friend of São Vicente and was in quite a different political camp. Thus he was fully disposed to yield to the will of the emperor and with all of his strength he championed the idea of emancipation when the question was submitted to the council of state. His views were reënforced from an unexpected quarter. During the last days of his ministry the French Emancipation Committee wrote a letter to Dom Pedro, destined to become famous, urging him in the name of humanity to abolish slavery in Brazil. In its reply, dated August 2, 1867, the government stated that abolition was simply a question of time and opportunity, and would receive due consideration after the conclusion of the Paraguayan War.

The emperor and the government were thus bound by a solemn promise to take some definite step in favor of abolition. But there still remained a long and weary road to travel before any measure of this sort could count on general support. The powerful *fazendeiro* class was convinced that its whole livelihood and prosperity were at stake. Among the members of the council of state the feeling was general that it was the part of wisdom not to open this Pandora's box. But the attitude of the emperor and the ministry made it impossible to shelve the question; and the minority pointed out that further procrastination was useless, since sooner or later the question would have to be faced. Zacharias, the prime minister requested Senator Nabuco de Araujo,[1] a profound and vigorous political thinker, an eminent jurisconsult, and the intellectual leader of the liberal party, to draw up the draft of a bill looking toward gradual emancipation.

In August, 1868, his labor was finished. It represented a marked progress over the five earlier projects of São Vicente; with certain amendments it continued to be the official project of the council of state. To such an extent was this true that when Silva Paranhos, Viscount of Rio Branco, urged upon parliament the adoption of the law, it was the draft approved by the council of state, that is the plan of Nabuco, which was submitted. The outstanding feature of the project was the provision that all children born of slave mothers should be free. One modification, in theory very important, was embodied in the bill as finally enacted; the option accorded the slaveowner either to utilize gratuitously the services of the *ingenuos*[2] up to the age of twenty-one, or to receive a grant from the government of 600 milréis for each *ingenuo* provided he were turned over to the state at the age of eight. But in practice it turned out that almost

---

[1] He was the father of Joaquim Nabuco, the famous abolitionist, whom we shall meet later. The younger Nabuco has written a magisterial biography of his father entitled *Um Estadista do Imperio: Nabuco de Araujo, sua Vida, suas Opiniões, sua Epoca* (3 vols., Paris, 1900). It is probably the best single work on the empire which we possess.—P.A.M.

[2] This word, for which there is no exact equivalent in English, refers to the children of slave mothers, who were legally free in accordance with the law of September 28, 1871.—P.A.M.

without exception the slaveowners chose to avail themselves of the services of the *ingenuos* up to the age of twenty-one.

Such were the chief provisions of the famous law of September 28, 1871. Henceforth, no one might be born into slavery in Brazil; this was but the natural complement of the law of 1850 by Eusebio de Queiroz, abolishing the traffic. In this manner, the institution of slavery had received its death blow as the two sources of its existence had been destroyed: the traffic and natural increase. Even if at a later time no further legislation had been passed, slavery could not have endured much beyond the life time of the slaves then living—at the most thirty or forty years. As a matter of fact, it did not last as long as this; immediate abolition took place in 1888.[3]

Influence of the Military in Politics. The Duke of Caxias.—We now approach one of the most discussed and thorny problems in Brazilian history: the rôle of the military in politics. The manner in which the army and the government worked at cross-purposes, to the ultimate discomfiture of both, is perhaps best revealed in the conflict which arose over the Duke of Caxias, the most famous soldier in Brazilian history. The imperial constitution permitted the election to parliament of officers in active service; this was a great mistake, since it invariably led to conflicts between military duty and party discipline. It was a concession granted the military at the time of Brazilian independence from Portugal. Among the senators from Rio Grande do Sul had figured since 1845 the greatest soldier of the empire, Marshal Luiz Alves de Lima e Silva, Marquis and later Duke of Caxias. Throughout his glorious career he was uniformly successful on the field of battle. He was a staunch conservative and twice was minister and president of the council. His opinion carried great weight in conservative circles and after his election to the senate he eagerly threw himself into party discussions. As a result, his political enemies were numerous and active.

Zacharias, it will be recalled, was prime minister or president of the council in 1866. He was fully cognizant of the fact that Caxias was the only general capable of meeting and solving the

---

[3] On this whole subject, *cf.* the article by the translator of this book entitled "Slavery and Abolition in Brazil," in *The Hispanic American Historical Review*, XIII (May, 1933), 151-96.—P.A.M.

immense difficulties of the Paraguayan War. The Brazilian army contained many officers well fitted to command troops and lead them bravely into battle; but the empire possessed but one strategist, and that was the marquis. On the other hand, there were two obstacles, both serious, which caused Caxias to hesitate in accepting the post of commander-in-chief. The ministry of Zacharias was liberal, and the minister of war, Angelo Muniz da Silva Ferraz, the future Baron of Uruguayana, was a personal enemy.

It is obvious that between the minister of war and the commander-in-chief, a constant and intimate coöperation was essential. Under the unhappy circumstances then existing, it was evident, that either the soldier or the civilian must yield. As Caxias was quite indispensable, Ferraz had to abandon his post—this, despite the fact he was one of the ablest public men in Brazil, capable of holding any of the cabinet positions, or for that matter all of them. The purely political differences between the prime minister and Caxias were much more easily settled. Both realized that the issues of the war far transcended distinctions between conservatives and liberals. On October 19, 1866, Caxias was formally appointed commander-in-chief of the Brazilian forces.

Unfortunately, the act brought no truce to party conflicts. Even in the most critical days of the war, dissensions showed no sign of abating. The partisan press published the wildest and most improbable rumors; it criticized unmercifully the operations in Paraguay, and did not scruple bitterly to offend Caxias himself.

The tasks confronting the commander-in-chief were indeed tremendous. Up to the time of his appointment, the conduct of operations had been characterized by great indecision and disorder. When combats took place, victory usually fell to the lot of the Allies, but the guiding hand of an energetic commander and a real strategist was lacking. Moreover, the situation of the army was very delicate. Brazil was already supporting the chief burden of the campaign, both as regards resources and men. Flores feared a revolution led by the *Blancos* of Uruguay, and after the first unsuccessful attack on Curupaity in 1866 was obliged to return to Montevideo. Mitre, the commander-in-chief of the Allies, was hampered in his mission by disturbances in Argentina, and did not show himself to be a great army commander. He was forced to return to Buenos Aires to put down uprisings. Tamandaré and Inhaúma, the admirals of the Brazilian fleet, had no confidence in the republic and hesitated to use their fleets to their full efficiency because of their fear of lukewarm support or even treachery on the part of the Argentines. Mitre on his part accused the admirals of inertia at a time when the maximum effort was essential. General Osorio (Baron, and later Viscount and Marquis of Herval), one of the bravest of the brave, retired to Rio Grande do Sul alleging illness; but, in reality, neither he nor General Marquis de Souza (the future Count of Porto Alegre) approved of Mitre's generalship.

With the advent of Caxias, everything took on a new lease of life. Chiefs who had withdrawn from the field of combat returned to it; sailor and soldiers, officers of all ranks, eager to show their fighting spirit, pleaded for a general advance. Especially was this the case when the journey of Mitre to Buenos Aires in 1864 brought Caxias to the supreme command of the Allies. But even after the president's return to the Paraguayan battlefields on August 1, 1867, he gave the Brazilian general full liberty to direct operations. Under the command of Caxias, there began a period of great intensity in the conduct of the war. But in spite of these herculean efforts, the press of Rio attacked Caxias without mercy, accusing him of inaction in face of the enemy. Finally, on January 14, 1868, Mitre returned once more to Buenos Aires, and Caxias came to assume definite command of the allied armies.

The general was tireless in carrying out his duties, and did not allow himself a moment of repose. He was in personal command of an army of 50,000 men, which for the time was very large. He undertook reconnaissances himself, and was to be found in the thick of the battle like a young officer. At the bridge of Itororó, in December, 1865, though an old man of sixty-five, weakened by ill-health, he emulated the heroic action of Bonaparte at Arcole and, sword in hand, led his troops across the bridge swept by shrapnel, after three generals had been laid low by deadly, even mortal, wounds.

Such was the man whom the partisan press, small-bore politicians, and armchair strategists accused of being weak, lazy, and quite incapable of coping with the difficulties of the situation.

It has been the sad lot of the Brazilian army never to have been understood by civilians, and especially by the political parties. Safe in their homes, or installed in comfortable berths in the ad-

Calogeras in for military

ministration or parliament, these self-appointed critics have been prone to discuss, approve, or accuse the actions of soldiers, whose tasks, self-sacrifices, and achievements they are unable to measure or even fully to comprehend.

Though a conservative, Caxias had been selected and appointed by a liberal ministry, as he was the only strategist whom Brazil possessed. The most elementary sense of justice and duty would demand that the ministry aid him with all of its strength and make every effort to supply him with the resources needed to accomplish his difficult task. In place of such coöperation, the liberal press carried on a campaign of suspicions, malicious insinuations, and downright calumnies against the marshal. Deputies and senators vied with each other in accusations and criticisms which merely revealed their own incompetency.

Through private correspondence and newspapers, Caxias was fully informed of all of these miserable intrigues, tolerated, if not fomented surreptitiously by the friends of the ministry. Wounded to the quick by these unworthy attacks, and realizing that he was not receiving the support to which he was entitled, he tendered his resignation. As a reason he alleged his poor health (as a matter of fact he was gravely ill) but in a personal letter to the minister of war he made clear the real motives for this act. It was obvious that either the ministry with Zacharias at its head or the commander-in-chief of the Allies would have to retire to private life. As the services of the marshal were simply indispensable, it was the ministry which eventually had to yield.

This Caxias "affair," as we may call it, has given rise to bitter and protracted commentaries in practically all accounts of the period, and constitutes one of the outstanding episodes in the history of the empire. Unhappily, the true situation was understood by few contemporaries and the violence of party prejudice has tended to perpetuate the confusion.

At the time the real character of the problem was not made clear to the members of the council of state, to whom Zacharias presented all of the relevant documents. The prime minister declared that Caxias was mistaken, that his own confidence in the marshal never wavered, but inasmuch as it would be quite impossible to replace him, and harmony between the higher command

and the government was essential, the entire ministry would present its resignation.

The members of the council of state unfortunately regarded the crisis from a single angle—a ministry overthrown by pressure of the army. The attacks on Caxias' honor, and the disloyalty shown the commander-in-chief failed entirely to influence them, blinded as they were by the hypertrophy of party feeling. The situation was rendered the more delicate from Zacharias' assertions that he never had the slightest intention of casting aspersions on the ability of the marshal. His conscience in these matters was, he alleged, entirely clear. The inference was obvious. In resigning, the ministry was simply yielding to force.

The real truth of the matter is that Zacharias was never a statesman, despite his intellectual and moral endowment. During his whole public life he was dominated by a single idea—his party and its interests. Everything, including principles, he subordinated to this end. In making this statement, there is no danger of being taxed with exaggeration; the proofs exist. As we pointed out earlier in the present chapter, he championed wholeheartedly before the council of state the emancipation project subsequently embodied in the law of 1871; his own personal convictions were in favor of the measure. Despite this fact he fought it with every means at his command when it came before the senate merely because it was presented by the conservative party, by the ministry presided over by José Maria da Silva Paranhos, later known as the Viscount of Rio Branco. It is not fair to say that he encouraged attacks on Caxias. But what was almost as bad, he crossed his arms and permitted his political friends to attack the old soldier. His duty, however, was clear as the light of day. It was to defend and support the marshal by every means in his power, since he had already accepted the collaboration of the great conservative chieftain, knowing full well that his services were absolutely indispensable.

His vanity wounded to the quick, Zacharias closed the door to any possibility of reconciliation with Caxias—this, despite the unanimous opinion of the council of state that the resignation of the cabinet under the existing circumstances was both necessary and desirable. But the prime minister and the other members of the cabinet did not wish to resign leaving the impression (which they themselves had created) that they were yielding to pressure from the military. To this end, they invoked a pretext: the choice of a senator, which they criticized and refused to approve. As is well known, the appointment to membership to the upper house of parliament was an exclusive prerogative of the emperor. The matter dragged for six months, from February 20 to July 16, 1868, greatly to the prejudice of the cabinet, for the public was well aware of the real cause of the crisis.

Even after his resignation Zacharias, resentful and vindictive, created further difficulties. The liberals had a majority in parliament and included in their ranks a number of leaders who could very easily and logically have taken his place. But when Dom Pedro, after accepting the resignation of the cabinet, sought according to custom the advice of Zacharias as the choice of his successor, he refused to collaborate with the emperor. This was tantamount to declaring that the liberals did not have suitable timber for the post of prime minister. As a consequence, the conservatives were called into power, in direct defiance of parliamentary usage. For this anomalous situation, Zacharias alone was responsible. But the liberals, as was natural, took great offense. Instead of accusing Zacharias and themselves, as the persons responsible for the disaster suffered by their party, they launched a chorus of accusations against Dom Pedro, an attack which was led by the ex-prime minister himself. The political atmosphere became exceedingly tense. The resentment of the liberals went so far that many of their more exalted members deserted their party in order to form the nucleus of a group of militant republicans. This whole episode had a lasting effect on public opinion. It is no exaggeration to say that from the fall of Zacharias dates the first symptoms of the disintegration of the monarchical structure. The empire was from now on the object of attacks by the monarchists themselves, by disgruntled and dishonest politicians, and by political intriguers intent only on their own advancement.

Decline of Monarchical Sentiment.—This is not a prophecy made after the event. As early as 1868, Senator Nabuco de Araujo, the spiritual mentor of the liberals, indicated to his coreligionists the great error which they were committing: the campaign against the empire, he pointed out, removed still further the possibility of their return to power, and at the same time strengthened the forces of their political opponents, first the conservatives, and ultimately the republicans.

The mileposts in this political evolution may be noted at this point; most of the names mentioned in this summary we shall meet later. As early as 1862, the progressive party had advocated a series of reforms aiming to decentralize the government and bestow upon the ministers of state the responsibility for the acts of the moderative power, hitherto an exclusive prerogative of the emperor.[4] This was, in effect, a move designed to curtail the powers of the ruler as the moderate power was, in the words of the constitution of 1824, "the key to the entire political organization." In 1866 the liberals carried on a press campaign for the abolition of both the moderative power and the life tenure of senators. The dismissal of Ferraz and the appointment of Caxias, as already noted, only served to strengthen these demands. After the resignation of Zacharias in 1868, the radicals were already occupying a halfway post between a monarchy and a republic. On December 3, 1870, was launched the famous "Republican Manifesto," with its demand for the abolition of the empire. In the new party were to be found the names of a number of advanced liberals, including Saldanha Marinho, Quintino Bocayuva, and Aristides Lobo. These men served as a link between the aspirations of 1870 and the achievements of 1889. In São Paulo in 1871 the so-called convention of Ytú paved the way for the launching two years later of another republican manifesto, signed by Prudente de Moraes and Campos Salles, in the fullness of time both presidents of the republic.[5] In 1876 São Paulo sent to parliament the first republican deputy, and in 1877 a group of three republicans was elected to the provincial assembly.

During these years the liberals had become convinced that the functions of the moderate power should be exercised by the president of the council (or prime minister) following the example of Great Britain. For the republicans, the problem presented

---

[4] The moderative power had as its chief attributes the nomination of senators, the convocation of the general assembly (the chamber and senate) whenever the good of the empire might require it, the dissolution of the chamber of deputies, the appointment and dismissal of ministers of state, and the granting of amnesties.—P.A.M.

[5] During the years 1894-1902.

itself under a different guise. They had no reason to favor the transferring of the moderative power from the emperor to the ministry with the consequent strengthening of the parliamentary system. With their eyes fixed on the republic, in whose advent they believed implicitly, they preferred that the balance of power remain with the executive until the time when a president might be substituted for a monarch. They were, in other words, wedded to the idea of the presidential system, which, adumbrated in the republican manifesto of 1870, was fully realized on the overthrow of the monarchy in 1889.

The latent hostility between the army and the civilian leaders, especially during the conflict between Caxias and Zacharias, has already been mentioned. The breach between these two groups tended to widen in the seventies and eighties. It was some time before Dom Pedro himself became involved in this unfortunate situation. At first the emperor was rightly regarded as the sincere defender of the army. But after the Paraguayan War the conviction grew that he was according scant heed to the needs of the army and that he did not grasp the true rôle which military institutions should play in the social and political life of the country. Such a charge was true to the extent that Dom Pedro considered a number of national problems much more important than the welfare of the army. In any event, these attacks on the empire and its chief, at first confined to a number of the higher officers of the army, eventually came to include a number of ardent and even fanatical younger officers. What was still worse, most of these became hostile to the whole system of hereditary rule and were ready to welcome the advent of a republic.

The foundations on which the empire rested were further weakened by an unhappy conflict between the government and certain elements of the clergy. To this, one of the major events in the history of the empire, we shall now briefly address ourselves.

The Empire and the Church.—Friction between the ecclesiastical and civil powers dated back for many centuries, even before the reformation. In France, the university and parliament, *i.e.*, the courts of justice, were long considered the theological advisers of the sovereign, and continuously invaded the sphere of competency of the government of the Church. In Spain, Philip II discussed with the Pope questions of dogma and discipline, as if he himself were the administrator of things spiritual. The same thing happened in Portugal; the advent to the throne of King José I with his minister Pombal indicated the highest point of development of this tendency of the civil power to invade the rights of the Church.

As a matter of fact, there existed for many years entire areas of public activity in which ecclesiastic legislation could only be executed through the agency of the civil power. A potential conflict was thus ever pending between two sources of authority: revelation and material force. From their very nature, regalism and Gallicanism, whether in France or Portugal strove to extend their authority. The Church never altered its position, but found itself constrained constantly to fight for its freedom against the encroachments of the civil power.

When Brazil achieved its independence the relations between Church and State were those which had long existed in the mother country, Portugal. Although the constitution of 1824, exceedingly liberal for its time, permitted complete freedom in matters of faith, Catholicism remained the official religion. In the years between 1827 and 1838 there had arisen a serious conflict on such matters as the celibacy of the priesthood and the rights of the clergy. Taken by and large, however, these thorny questions were handled with care and discretion by the successive ministries, which were anxious to maintain good relations with the Holy See.

Nabuco de Araujo, minister of justice from 1854 to 1857, furnished an instance of this type of coöperation in his reforms of the convents in which the religious life and discipline had suffered great relaxation. He went so far as to prohibit the admission of novices, as a preliminary step to the general reform of the religious orders. It turned out, however, that a measure that was intended to be merely provisional remained in effect almost up to the end of the monarchy. In fact, the novitiate was not reestablished until 1888 by Ferreira Vianna, on the eve of the republic. That it was not the intention of Nabuco permanently to prohibit the admission of novices is beyond all doubt; his own religious convictions and declarations are sufficient proofs. In 1857

Calogeras is very conservative

he reënforced a disposition of the Council of Trent by abolishing appeals to the crown in cases where the bishops had pronounced suspensions or interdicts *ex informata conscientia.*

Unhappily, such discretion and prudence were not always observed. Not infrequently members of the imperial cabinets evinced a lack of judgment in ecclesiastical matters or even took a certain pleasure in promoting dissensions; the result was an almost continuous undercurrent of irritation between the religious and civil powers.

The point of departure of this type of Brazilian regalism was the right claimed by the imperial authorities to sanction the promulgation of ecclesiastical ordinances originating with the Holy See. No act issued by the Pope or the Curia could be carried out in Brazil if it had not been confirmed by the *placet* of the imperial government. The Church obviously could never officially admit such a doctrine, yet in practice it was forced to make concessions. According to the constitution of 1824, the clergy formed a separate recognized class closely bound up in the general organization of the empire. For this reason, Rome tolerated, even if it did not approve, the temporary necessity of civil interference in purely ecclesiastical matters.

From this strange and hybrid situation arose innumerable difficulties. Dogma necessarily was held to be beyond the competency of the state, but even here, the civil power tended steadily to encroach upon this purely ecclesiastical domain. If the movement continued unchecked but one result was possible: the subordination of the Church to the State.

Under these conditions, a conflict of some sort was inevitable. It finally came over the practical question of the place of the Masonic Order in the religious and political organization of the empire. This order had played a rôle of exceptional importance in the days of independence. It organized the movement and directed the successive governments from 1810 to 1825 in the Spanish colonies and from 1821 to 1823 in Brazil. Aside from these patriotic endeavors, it found scope for its activities in mutual aid, deeds of charity, and the encouragement of liberal aspirations on the part of its members. It was something quite different from the strenuous activities of French and Italian lodges (such as the

Carbonari), in which ideas of liberty were mingled with professional conspiracies and anti-religious propaganda.

In the early decades of the empire innumerable priests belonged to the Masonic Order, even taking the higher degrees. The situation was nonetheless anomalous. More than once the Holy See had condemned the Masonic Order in general. After the revolutionary wave which swept over Europe in 1848, in which the influence of the Order is beyond question, these condemnations became more severe. One special reason for this increasing severity was the activity of the Masons in the states of the Church, activities which did not cease until the abolition of the temporal power of the papacy in 1870.

While these conflicts were raging in Europe, the Brazilian lodges were enjoying absolute peace. Their energies were devoted to philanthropic and charitable ends. Sooner or later, however, they were bound to run foul of the Church. The various apostolic condemnations of the Masons and all their works could in the long run suffer no exceptions. On the other hand the papal sentences were couched in general terms and wide latitude was allowed the bishops in carrying them out. For these and other reasons, the Orders were allowed to remain in peace for the first half century of the empire.

An acute situation suddenly developed in 1871. In honor of the Rio Branco emancipation law, the lodges of Rio de Janeiro held a great festival in which a Catholic priest delivered a sermon in terms which strongly smacked of Masonry. It was published in the newspapers under his signature. Though taken to task by the bishop, the offending priest refused to deny his Masonic sympathies. Faced with such indiscipline, the bishop suspended his recalcitrant subordinate both from the pulpit and the confessional.

This episode was little more than a mere canonical rule exercised by the ecclesiastical authorities for the maintenance of the internal and spiritual discipline of the clergy. Something infinitely more serious was to follow. In April, 1872, the Masonic lodges of Rio, in a general assembly, resolved on an attack on the Brazilian episcopate and summoned the united forces of Masonry to hostilities against the Church. The gravity of this move was immeasurably enhanced by the fact that it was counselled by none other than the Viscount of Rio Branco, who was both prime minister and grand master of the Masonic Order in Brazil.

There can be no possible doubt that the responsibility for the outbreak of hostilities rested with the Masons. From north to south newspapers, pamphlets, lectures all conspired to create an atmosphere of suspicion and ill-will. Their attack was chiefly directed against what was called the intolerance of the Church, which, it may be truthfully said, was interested only in maintaining the proper discipline and orthodoxy of the clergy. The Bishop of Rio, D. Pedro Maria da Lacerda, who had originally condemned the offending undisciplined priest, bore all of these criticisms with the utmost patience, in spite of the new provocations to which he was continually subjected; there is even reason to believe that his attitude of sufferance was carried too far. Rumor had it, however, that he was merely following the counsels of the papal internuncio, D. Domenico Sanguigni.

D. Vital and D. Antonio de Macedo Costa.—On May 24, 1872, took place the installation of the new Bishop of Olinda, a Capuchin friar by the name of D. Vital Maria Gonçalves de Oliveira. He was regarded by the liberal elements with suspicion, and was freely accused of being ultramontane. Against him the Masons unleashed a virulent campaign of defamation. The bishop silently began to institute reforms in his religious family, in which movement he was followed by all of his clergy save two fathers, who refused to abjure their heretical views. He did not meet with equal success in the case of the brotherhoods (*irmandades*), a type of benevolent institution which operated under a kind of mixed constitution, both civil and religious. Some of the members had Masonic sympathies, and they lodged objections to the expulsion from their ranks of a number of their brethren who had fallen under ecclesiastical censorship, owing to their affiliation with the Masonic Order.

The bishop, nonetheless, persisted. He suspended the two offending priests and ordered the members of the brotherhoods who were Masons to withdraw; those who refused to obey were threatened with excommunication. One of the brotherhoods refused to recognize this order, and on January 5, 1873, was suspended. Others followed. In Pará, the bishop, D. Antonio de Macedo Costa, on March 25 of the same year, took similar steps.

The action of the two bishops was the signal for the outbreak of the most serious religious conflict in the entire history of the empire. Though it was the Church which had been attacked, it probably would have supported this trial in silence if the Masons had not attempted to invade the sphere of purely ecclesiastical activities. On the other hand, it must be said in all candor that the Church would have been well advised had it been a little less intransigent in its attitude. But it is difficult to hazard an opinion since such problems, in which the spiritual element plays a large part, are hardly amenable to the judgment of outsiders.

D. Vital, as well as the Bishop of Pará, defended the cause of orthodoxy, and the papal decrees dealing with Masonry with sincerity and with the strength of their faith. Were they, however, under the existing circumstances, acting in the best interests of the Church in taking up the gauntlet thrown down by the Masons? This will always remain a matter of opinion. But on one point all are agreed: they acted quite alone. Neither the Archbishop of Bahia, the primate of Brazil, nor the other bishops rallied to their support. D. Domenico Sanguigni, the papal internuncio, at all times counselled peace and moderation.

When the Holy See was called upon to express its judgment, it naturally approved the doctrine of the two bishops, as the eternal doctrine of Rome. It did not fail to point out, however, that such a course in the present instance might be taxed with imprudence. Errors so inveterate and widely diffused could not be suddenly eradicated through a single impulse. And as a matter of fact it is not entirely clear just why the two bishops felt constrained to adopt such a belligerent attitude at this time. A greater degree of patience and charity might in the long run have been more efficacious.

D. Vital and D. Antonio were extraordinary men, the glory and pride of the Brazilian clergy, wise, modest, filled with love for their neighbors, Christians in the fullest sense of the word. Since the proclamation of the empire fifty years previously, no question in connection with the Masons had arisen. As has already been intimated, Masons were to be found everywhere, in all classes, among the clergy as well as the laity, God-fearing and devout. It is abundantly clear that the belligerent tendencies of the sect in Europe had not crossed the Atlantic, or if it had crossed the ocean, had expended its energies in the struggle for independence throughout all of America. Why, then, had the bishops adopted a course which broke so diametrically with tradition? It has been charged that they were young and inexperienced, that they were consumed with a zeal for martyrdom for their faith, that they wished to call attention to themselves. But an examination of the evidence would seem to show that such charges were unfounded and perhaps unjust. It is possible that the two bishops, educated in French seminaries, approached the question of Brazilian Masonry with preconceived ideas, that they analyzed a purely local situation in the light of French experience, and that their suspicions were not justified by the past history of Brazil.

The brotherhoods suspended by D. Vital appealed to the crown, which insisted in turn that the matter be laid before the council of state. Summoned before this body to explain his acts, the bishop refused to defend himself. His statement on this occasion was limited to a single sentence: "Omitting any observation on the innumerable inexactitudes contained in the said summons, I limit myself to informing you that such an appeal is condemned by various dispositions of the Church."

In its majority, the council of state adhered to the theory of regalism. Offended by the refusal of D. Vital to recognize its competency, the council forthwith ordered the offending prelate to lift within fifteen days the interdict under which he had placed the brotherhoods. The bishop flatly refused to obey and denied at the same time the right of the government to interfere in his spiritual functions. A similar attitude was adopted by the Bishop of Pará. The minister of the interior, João Alfredo, carried to the supreme tribunal of the empire the accusations against D. Vital and D. Antonio. The Bishop of Olinda defended himself by quoting from the gospel, *"Jesus autem tacebat."* The Bishop of Pará contented himself with a statement almost as brief: "I have no other recourse but to appeal to the justice of God." Under these circumstances, the action of the government was a foregone conclusion. On February 21, 1871, D. Vital was condemned to four years' imprisonment at hard labor and on July 1, D. Macedo Costa received the same sentence. The emperor commuted the sentence into simple imprisonment.

With this nominal triumph of the government, the magnitude of the blunder which had been committed began to appear in its true light. The situation had really remained unchanged. The bishops had not revoked the interdicts. The ecclesiastical officials, canonically nominated by them, followed the same procedure. Civil law and official orders appeared ridiculous when it was discovered that legal violence was powerless in the face of conscience and religious beliefs. It was the old story of the futility of the persecution of ideas and religious convictions.

As might have been anticipated, this conflict, which for a time shook the empire to its foundations, brought about a sharp alignment of opposing forces in the higher sphere of Brazilian life. More and more it became evident that in the final instance it was a case of Brazilian Gallicanism as opposed to the universal Church. As has already been intimated, the majority of the Brazilian statesmen, beginning with the prime minister himself, were regalists. The emperor both from dynastic tradition and personal conviction shared their views. Hence he considered the procedure of the bishops a grave offense against the crown. It was for this reason that he was much more intent on the punishment of the bishops than was the prime minister himself—this despite the fact that the Viscount of Rio Branco was grand master of the Masonic Order.

In passing, it may be noted that the Masons who had been so largely responsible for the outbreak of this unhappy dispute suffered an immense loss of prestige and influence long before the conflict had run its course. In fact, they were more or less forgotten as the question took on wider proportions and it is not too much to say that the Order gradually reverted to the comparative obscurity from which it had been lifted by its patriotic exertions during the days of independence.

During the initial phases of the strife, the whole affair was looked upon by the government as something exclusively Brazilian and as such was simply a matter of domestic policy. But as time wore on, it became increasingly clear that, inasmuch as the Catholic hierarchy was involved, Rome could not be permanently ignored. When at length the regalists were forced to admit this axiomatic truth they did so with ill-grace and secret reservations. Confronted with what was virtually an impasse, the government finally decided to send a special mission to Rome with instructions to induce the papacy to take steps to prevent the extension of the

conflict. At the same time, the mission received peremptory orders
not to embark on a discussion with the Holy See of any of the
fundamental issues involved unless it were absolutely necessary;
in such an event the mission should insist on the point of view of
the empire. It was in effect a mission, not of peace, but of war.
And a circumstance really fatal to the success of the mission was
the fact that the government insisted that the trial of the bishops
be carried on while these delicate negotiations were in progress.

The Mission of Baron Penedo to Rome.—Baron Penedo, the
Brazilian representative, was a competent lawyer and an experienced diplomat. For this reason he did not carry out his
belligerent instructions. Rather did he use every effort to settle the
conflict by pacific means, without wasting time in discussing the
official points of view on questions of dogma or ecclesiastical
discipline in which the Holy See obviously would never admit the
rule of the laity when it ran contrary to its own. Penedo preferred
to emphasize the propriety and necessity of restoring religious
peace in the empire. Although his explications and assurances were
somewhat vague, the Holy Father had reason to believe that the
trial of the bishops would be dropped in the event that negotiations
with the papacy were satisfactory. With this idea in mind, he
ordered Antonelli, the cardinal secretary of state, to send a letter
to the bishops reminding them that, though they were right in
theory, the means which they had employed were not deserving of
equal approval as they were lacking in prudence. The interdicts,
therefore, should be raised, and since complications were to be
foreseen if Masons were to be excluded from the brotherhoods,
special rules and regulations were to be devised to meet the
situation.

Hardly had Penedo left Rome when news reached the Pope of
the imprisonment of D. Vital. The result may easily be imagined.
Pius IX took the matter as a personal insult, and made the affair
of the bishops his own. He revoked the letter written by Cardinal
Antonelli and protested solemnly against the sufferings imposed
on his sons in Brazil and against the violations of sacred ecclesiastical immunities. And the just indignation of the papacy
was shared by the entire clergy of Brazil; from now on the cause
of the bishops, for the vast majority of the Brazilians, became the
cause of God, of the Holy Father, and the Church in general. The

whole country fell victim to grave religious dissensions and there seemed no way of emerging from this crisis as long as the condemnations stood. Under the circumstances but one solution was possible: to recognize the mistakes that had been committed and to capitulate.

This was done. On September 17, 1875, the imperial government granted amnesty, and by this act of political wisdom and good sense brought this grave incident to a close. The Church had won a resounding triumph over its persecutors. But the religious sentiments of the Brazilians had been stirred to their depths. During the entire history of the monarchy no question had so wounded the national conscience. None had such deplorable and lasting results, none so weakened the loyalty to the empire.

Capistrano de Abreu, our greatest historian,[6] records a characteristic phrase of D. Pedro Maria da Lacerda, Bishop of Rio de Janeiro. Early in the morning of November 16, 1889, the bishop was crossing the large square in front of the imperial palace. He observed unusual activity, sentinels at the doors, soldiers everywhere. In reply to his queries he was informed that the republic had been proclaimed the previous evening and that Dom Pedro and the entire imperial family were detained in the palace. "Exactly as he did with the bishops," was the comment of the prelate.

In the collective pastoral of the Brazilian episcopate of March 19, 1890, on the separation of Church and State, written by the Bishop of Pará, D. Antonio de Macedo Costa, appears a clarion note or pean of victory. "The throne disappeared . . . and the altar? The altar stands!"

Increasing Disintegration of the Empire.—Before concluding this chapter we may attempt a brief summary of the forces which in the critical decade from 1866 to 1875 completely changed the aspect of Brazilian public life. As we have seen, the personality of the emperor, hitherto regarded as above and beyond party conflicts, became a subject of general discussion. Both of the great traditional parties successively attacked the "inviolable and sacred" person of the emperor, although the imperial attributes to which they took exception had their sanction in the constitution itself. Apparently they failed to realize that proceeding in

[6] This view is not shared by all Brazilian students; many would be disposed to accord Varnhagen or Oliveira Lima first place.—P.A.M.

this manner they were sapping the very foundations of the state. It was inevitable that Dom Pedro's prestige and authority should decline when the throne became the object of attack by its own supporters. The monarchical parties thus shamelessly revealed their political incapacity. They mutually destroyed each other when they revealed themselves as unable to carry out their party programs. The liberals proposed reforms which they never succeded in carrying out; the conservatives, noting this situation, took these same proposals, which they formerly had opposed, and put them into practice. Cynicism could hardly have gone to greater length. With the exception of a number of eminent personalities, both groups were concerned only with courting favor with the sovereign, to whom they abased themselves for the purpose of gaining political power. Fortunately for the country, the sovereign was Dom Pedro II, a model *gentleman*,[7] possessed of character and the highest civic virtues.

As has just been suggested, the plans and programs of the liberals suffered demoralization, and many members of this party gravitated more and more toward the camp of the republicans; at least this was true to the extent that they accepted many of the aims of the latter: federalization, abolition of the council of state, abolition of the life senate, extinction of the moderative power. The conservatives, belying their name, had shown themselves incapable of defending the property rights of the slaveholding class; nay more, they actually were responsible for the passage of the "free birth" law in 1871. When they were accused of betraying the very class whose interests they were supposed to safeguard they threw the blame upon the emperor.

The army, convinced as we have seen that it was the object of neglect, found its grievances unheeded by the two great parties. It assumed that this indifference to its demands reflected the attitude of the monarch; in fact, the politicians affirmed—perhaps again in order to shift responsibility—that Dom Pedro II was profoundly apathetic in such matters. The military gradually came to the conviction that the whole monarchical system was inimicable to their interests.

The religious question we have discussed at length, but its im-

---

[7] Dr. Calogeras here used the English word.—P.A.M.

portance must once more be noted in any summary of the causes of the waning prestige of the empire.

A certain malaise began to spread throughout the empire. Public opinion, in so far as it was articulate, tended to divide into two large currents. The majority of both parties—between which there was little to choose in regard to ideals—had become frankly opportunist. Though they had lost their pristine confidence in the throne, they still rallied about it on the theory that their own interests were involved. On the other hand, a small but active minority openly attacked the institution of monarchy, skillfully utilizing the weapons originally forged by its own defenders. Their number grew at an alarming rate. Its personnel was recruited from the left wings of the traditional parties, from the great landed proprietors and slaveowners, from disgruntled officers of the army, and finally from the clergy, still bitterly incensed at the action of the empire in the question of the bishops.

The first fissures began to appear in the imperial edifice.

The last days of the monarchy had dawned.

CHAPTER XII

THE FINAL ABOLITION OF SLAVERY; THE MILITARY QUESTION; GROWING DISAFFECTION; FALL OF THE EMPIRE

WHILE THESE grave events, so significant in our national development, were taking place, the economic structure of the country continued to grow and expand.

National Economy.—A few statistics will abundantly prove this contention. During the Paraguayan War exchange had suffered, falling below par and even reaching 15 pence per milréis for a few days. But as early as 1871 the reaction set in, and quotations rose to 25 pence and for the next few years oscillated between 24 and 27. International commerce, including both exports and imports, steadily increased; even during the war it had suffered no decline. From 300,000 contos in 1866 it had risen to 356,000 in 1871-1872, and to 400,000 in 1880.[1] The curve of its development was absolutely regular, and revealed a perfectly organic process. Finances and administration were sound, and although the empire had to pass through difficult moments, the monetary situation was never really compromised.

Advance in other lines deserves notice. The first census was held in 1871. It revealed a total population of 9,930,478, of which 1,-510,806 were slaves.

Railway mileage rose from 513 kilometers in 1866 to 932 in 1872 and to 3,397 in 1880. Immigration grew apace and it was already anticipated that the advent of white labor would prove a strong factor in the solution of the slavery problem. Telegraphic lines showed the same gratifying increase; the first transatlantic cable was launched in 1874. Rio de Janeiro was illuminated by gas and was abundantly supplied with water; public sanitation was extended. Public instruction was encouraged in every possible manner.

Political Situation.—Let us now pass briefly in review the political situation during the last two decades of the empire. Unfortunately, the striking economic progress which we have just

[1] It will be recalled that the conto at par was worth approximately $500.00.—P.A.M.

noted brought no surcease to political passions. From 1871 to 1875 political interest was concentrated, as we have already noted, on the law of "free birth" and the religious question. The inextricable confusion in the two traditional parties gave the impression of disorder and eventual disintegration. No one could predict what would emerge from this confusion and clash of opinions. The republicans, though at first haltingly, were beginning to organize their forces. They successfully entered candidates in the elections, both in the municipalities and the provinces, and they narrowly missed seating one of their representatives in the parliament of 1876.

Above everything else, the political atmosphere was shot through with recriminations, and passionate criticisms of the emperor, whose "personal power" (*poder pessoal*), as it was commonly called, was looked upon as the destroyer of parties. The basis of this accusation was the fact that Dom Pedro was, so to speak, the balance wheel of the political machine by which the country was governed. It was his right and duty to impose his will on the choice and dismissal of the imperial cabinets and on the form and content of their respective platforms and programs.

We have already pointed out how this power emanated directly from the constitution and belonged exclusively to the emperor. In its application Dom Pedro remained strictly within the limits of his legal authority. Moreover, as the years passed and all things and all men changed with them, he remained the only fixed element, the axis, on which the whole machinery of state revolved. As *redresseur de torts*, he took the greatest pains to see that no political group was decisively crushed. For him, the existence of two opposing parties was a *sine qua non* of good government. In the internal struggles he was as it were a shock absorber, praised or condemned as the party leaders chanced to be in or out of power. This was because of his method of balancing opinions, holding himself aloof from them, without favorites among the contenders for office.

Such a position necessarily entailed many personal sacrifices— sacrifices which grew as the years went on. After 1843, the old system by which the emperor chose his own ministers fell into disuse. In this year Honorio Hermeto, Marquis of Paraná, the minister of justice, was entrusted by the emperor with the task of choosing his colleagues in the cabinet. This was but a transitional arrangement; in 1847 was created the presidency of the council of prime ministership, chiefly to give a greater unity to the cabinets, and greater responsibilities to the parties in power and their leaders.

This parliamentary system—for such it was in effect—could not function successfully save under certain conditions: the existence of regularly organized parties, conscious of their duties, with the necessary maturity to direct their energies on a high political and moral plane, holding themselves aloof from mere personal squabbles or struggles for spoils of office. Unhappily, as we have already seen, these conditions were largely lacking in the period under review.

During the long reign of Dom Pedro II, there were to be sure a number of really superior men, endowed with the attributes of higher statesmanship, who were admirably qualified to perform the functions of presidents of the council. Such men were Paraná, Saraiva, Rio Branco, and a few others. For men of this stamp, Dom Pedro was a model sovereign. During their incumbency, it was literally true "that the king ruled but did not govern." Each of these statesmen had his own methods of work and the emperor, recognizing the ability of each, adapted himself to his particular methods. He was, for example, quick to recognize and appreciate at their true value the unswerving and uncompromising opinions of Paraná, the magnanimity, calmness, and supreme honesty of Saraiva, the sincere devotion of Rio Branco to the empire and dynasty. With personages of lesser stature, men whose chief and ofttimes only ambition was to find a cabinet berth, the will of the emperor was supreme, not because Dom Pedro was eager to assert his authority, but because these ministers had no will of their own.

For reasons which have already been suggested, Dom Pedro was against the fusion of parties, as it left the field free for the worst kind of political intrigues. For the same reason, too, he was genuinely anxious to have the party aims and programs reflect the real opinion of the country, as revealed in honest and sincere elections. Only in this manner—and his views were shared by some of the really competent leaders of public opinion—could the parties possess unquestioned authority, based on public sentiment, independent of, though in harmony with, the personal convictions of the sovereign.

This was the point of departure for the energetic efforts he expended in the sixties to discover some practical means of destroying the highly unsatisfactory existing electoral machine, which sent to parliament only majorities belonging to the political party in power, whether it was conservative or liberal. Given this deplorable situation how could the emperor believe that the parties and the party methods reflected the real opinion of the country? This was the reason why he put into practice the system of rotation, which with all its disadvantages, was bound at one time or another to reflect the views of the nation.

Electoral Reform.—We come now to one of the really important events in the political and constitutional history of the empire—the electoral reform bill of 1881. The almost insuperable difficulties encountered by the emperor in really acclimating the parliamentary system to Brazil have already been touched upon. The serious crises to which the system was exposed in the early seventies have already been noted. Dom Pedro clearly discerned the tempest which was approaching from every section of the political horizon. He was well aware of the mounting opposition of the *fazendeiros,* the slaveowners, the clergy, and finally the military. He saw how these disgruntled elements would not scruple to employ the existing party machinery to further their own ends. And he had reached the conviction that the only effective antidote to the party venom which was poisoning parliamentary life in Brazil would be a loyal and free appeal to popular opinion. Hence the favor with which the emperor looked upon the reform bill of 1881.

Up to that time elections had been held in two degrees: the voters chose electors, who in turn chose the representatives to the chamber of deputies. Such a system gave rise to all sorts of irregularities. The only political crime that a party might commit was to lose the election; to prevent such a catastrophe every means, no matter how fraudulent, was legitimate.

There was a widespread assumption that direct election by districts for a single deputy would solve the problem. As always it was a case of the pleasing and naïve illusion that the law is capable of preventing moral lapses. Be that as it may, the idea of electoral reform was embraced by the leading politicians and above all by the emperor, desirous as he was of bringing to an end the prevailing system of fraud and chicanery.

The difficulties were many. The senate was not inclined to regard innovations favorably. The conservatives, firmly entrenched in power at the time, were opposed to changing an electoral system which guaranteed them a cohesive majority, provided the emperor did not use the moderate power to displace them by the liberals. The liberals themselves were of divided opinion as regards the proposed reform.

One formidable objection presented itself at the outset. Such an innovation would apparently require an amendment to the constitution. This gave Dom Pedro considerable anxiety as the obstacles to constitutional changes were very great. The apprehensions of the emperor were likewise shared by many senators and deputies. The reasons for their fears were obvious. Party programs of the liberals, the republicans, and other groups had favored the abolition of the life feature of the senate, and the abolition of the moderate power and the council of state. These proposed reforms, all of which would require constitutional amendments, had aroused considerable interest in the public. Once innovations were made in the constitution it was hard to tell where they might stop. Hence those in office, *beati possidentes*, hesitated to run the risk of losing what they possessed.

One group thought that a constitutional reform was necessary. Others deemed such a procedure perilous as it might open the door to dangerous reforms, which would be inacceptable to the senate, the conservatives, and even the emperor himself. Leaders of different shades of political opinion decided that the best mode of procedure would be through ordinary legislation. To this it was objected that a law might be revoked, annulled, or modified by another law, whereas a constitutional amendment could be changed only with great difficulty.

The truth of the matter was that Dom Pedro was very eager for the establishment of a system of direct election and, although he was loath to amend the constitution of 1824, he would accept this procedure if the goal could be obtained in no other manner. Accordingly, when the liberals were invited to form a government in 1878, it was understood that they would take active steps toward securing direct election by means of a reform of the constitution. Cansansão de Sinimbú, as president of the council, had the chief responsibility for this measure. The choice of Cansansão turned out to be an unhappy one. He was lacking in the necessary authority and qualities to carry such a campaign to a successful conclusion. After two years had been spent in futile skirmishes, he was forced to retire from the government.

The emperor then summoned Senator José Antonio Saraiva and asked him to organize the government. This statesman replied that his views were diametrically opposed to those of his predecessors. He was convinced that electoral reform should be brought about through ordinary legislation, without touching the constitution. The sovereign gave him full liberty of action. Saraiva showed great political acumen. In the execution of his program, he tranquilized the senate and the conservatives. Opposition gave way to coöperation. On January 9, 1881, the law for direct election was promulgated, and for the first time both Catholics and freedmen were given the same electoral rights as other voters.

The new measure received a most favorable welcome by the nation. Ruy Barbosa, then on the threshold of his glorious career, called it a guerdon of liberty, the most admirable gift within the power of the liberal party. Saraiva was recognized as the outstanding statesman of his party. The election for the next parliament was conducted with such scrupulous impartiality and such absence of official pressure that two of his own ministers were defeated. He was acclaimed as a personality far above party dissensions, and was commonly known as the "vice-emperor."

Weakness of New Law.—Unfortunately, the political life of the country could not continue long on such a high plane. Within a short time it became evident that the parties did not desire impartiality on the part of the government. In practice, they preferred the spoils system, and the smashing of one's opponents at any cost. The new law, to which they had accorded such high praise, had produced such admirable results only as long as Saraiva was president of the council and in a position to insist on an honest observance of the new electoral code. But in the hands of Cotegipe, the greatest of the conservative leaders, and president of the council in 1886, the same law permitted the almost complete exclusion of the liberal party from parliament. In other words the key to the electoral situation was so to speak the moral level of the head of the government. Did he possess the caliber of a statesman, who placed the welfare of the state above every other consideration—a man, say, of the type of Saraiva—the new law might be regarded as successful. When, however, party interests were in the ascendant, and the prime minister was subservient to them, the situation changed entirely. And yet all of the real political mentors of the nation knew perfectly well that on the honesty of elections depended the life or death of the monarchy.

Freedom of the Slaves. Joaquim Nabuco.—After the passage of the Rio Branco law of 1871, which granted freedom to all children born of slave mothers, the emancipation question went into a temporary eclipse. Such was, in fact, the intention of the sponsors of the law, who above all were anxious to avoid driving the *fazendeiros* to despair or giving them any valid pretext for revolt. But events were soon to show that such halfway measures as the law of 1871 were really futile; the avalanche had been loosened and no human force could stay its course.

Nonetheless, all of the political groups declared themselves in favor of a policy of evolution, or the settlement of the slavery question by progressive steps. They were now satisfied that the really important step had been taken; no more slaves would be born in Brazil; existing ones would gradually die off or be liberated as a result of the action of the emancipation fund. This would mean, in effect, that slavery in a progressively attenuated form would last three or four decades longer, possibly until 1910. On the other hand, the complete extinction of slavery might come as early as the turning of the century through the growth of the emancipation fund and other agencies. The slaveowners had reconciled themselves to the gradual disappearance of slavery, but unfortunately for them the tacit understanding that the whole slavery problem if left alone would solve itself, proved of short duration.

The truce in fact was broken as early as 1878. A new and portentous factor suddenly appeared to disturb the comparatively even tenor of Brazilian political life: Joaquim Nabuco, who years later died when our ambassador at Washington, was elected to the chamber of deputies. With the advent of this fiery apostle of abolition a movement which hitherto had been legal, conservative, and peaceful was suddenly diverted into new and perilous channels. Overnight, as it were, the entire slavery question was surrounded by an atmosphere in which purely economic considerations were largely displaced by motives religious, philosophical, and humanitarian.

For the proponents of the *status quo* it was a rude awakening. Their anxieties were not lessened when the cause of abolition began to strike responsive chords in the mass of the people, who were being aroused from the apathy by the vibrant eloquence of Nabuco. In his brilliant speeches both within and without parliament, the young tribune invoked principles long forgotten or ignored—the dignity of human life, the bonds of Christian brotherhood, the immortality of the souls of those unjustly condemned to a life of cruel servitude.

At first the rank and file of the Brazilians were offended by this glaring light projected into hitherto unperceived horrors and abysses. In a short time, however, the truth and fervor of Nabuco's message became clear as the light of day and he was hailed as the prophet of a new evangel. Only those who lived through those days of social and moral catharsis may adequately describe the upward surge of the abolitionist movement, the red hot lava which branded with the mark of infamy the institution of slavery, the enthusiasm of the crusade launched by Nabuco and his cohorts in favor of the new freedom.

As was to be anticipated, all of the forces of conservatism united against this daring and dangerous young innovator. He was not reëlected for the legislative session of 1881-1884. But in 1885 we find him back in parliament, and again in 1887-1889.

In 1880 he introduced a bill providing for the extinction of slavery at the end of ten years; the chamber of deputies rejected it. This defeat opened the eyes of Nabuco. He came to realize that a long and carefully formulated propaganda would be necessary. He set about to secure adherents and partisans. He published pamphlets and articles in the press. He gave frequent public lectures the burden of which was immediate abolition. Shortly afterward he founded the Brazilian Anti-Slavery Society (*Sociedade Brasileira contra a Escravidão*). These were some of the weapons he employed to force upon the attention of the parliament and the public the importance of the campaign to which he was devoting all of his efforts and resources. The supporters of slavery found it impossible to banish this burning question from the halls of parliament or to silence the protests of the human conscience.

The speeches and enthusiasm of Nabuco had an almost electric effect throughout Brazil from north to south. A veritable fire-brand, he started conflagrations throughout the empire. A regular network of abolitionist clubs was established; the Abolitionist Confederation (*Confederação Abolicionista*) was the center of the movement.

The problem began to change aspects; it was no longer simply a phase of Brazil's economic development. Shot through with popular passions it decided the fate of imperial cabinets. Saraiva, who had been president of the council since March 28, 1880, tendered his resignation and was succeeded on January 21, 1882, by Martinho Campos. His program did not mention the servile question and it was well known that he was favorable to the *status quo* in order that the abolition movement should run its course in accordance with the legislation of 1871. In June, 1882, he was overthrown by an adverse vote on a trivial question but it was public knowledge that a majority of his party in parliament did not share his views on abolition.

He was succeeded by the Viscount (later Marquis) of Paranaguá on July 3, 1882. The new president of the council felt obliged to mention the slavery question in the program of his government and to promise to give it his consideration. On May 24, 1883, LaFayette Rodrigues Pereira was called upon by the emperor to form a ministry; he declared that he would exert his efforts to hasten the extinction of slavery by enlarging the emancipation fund and prohibiting inter-provincial traffic. He had no opportunity, however, to carry out this program as he remained in power only a few weeks. The head of the new government, which came into power on June 6, 1884, was Senator Manuel Pinto de Souza Dantas. This statesman, whom we shall meet again later, held the same attitude as his predecessor.

The First Conquests.—Opinion in favor of abolition moved more rapidly throughout the empire than it did in parliament. There was an increasing and insistent demand that something definite be accomplished. The first break came in the north.

Fortaleza, the capital and chief seaport of the province of Ceará, was a wretched anchoring place and as a consequence landings were made by small and unsinkable crafts known as *jangadas*, the only kind of boat which could brave the heavy breakers outside the harbor. Their crew were known as *jangadeiros* and were an exceedingly daring and courageous type of seaman. Almost to a man they were ardent abolitionists. Aroused by the generous enthusiasm which was sweeping the country, they went on strike and declared that they would not transport slaves, irrespective of their destination. In this manner was movement of slaves along the coast effectively stopped. Ceará became a haven for fugitives and thanks to the attitude of the *jangadeiros*, who were supported by the provincial authorities, it was quite impossible for their owners to recapture them. So rapidly did the number of Negroes in servitude decrease that on March 25, 1884, the province officially declared that slavery was extinct within its confines.

On July 10 of the same year, similar action was taken by the province of Amazonas. On September 18, in memory of the Paraguayan capitulation at Uruguayana, three municipalities of Rio Grande do Sul emancipated their slaves beyond a certain age, and a month later the city of Pelotas, in the same province, freed five thousand Negroes. Within six months no less than thirty-five thousand slaves had received their freedom in this single province. In Rio de Janeiro the municipal council created a special fund for the emancipation of certain classes of Negroes unaffected by the existing legislation.

Senator Souza Dantas, who as we have seen became president of the council on June 6, 1884, was himself an abolitionist. Both from conviction and necessity, he placed himself at the head of the movement. He was virtually pledging himself to take such a step when he assumed office, since Dom Pedro had entrusted him with the formation of a cabinet owing to Dantas' well-known conviction that the operations of the emancipation fund, even if it were greatly enlarged, were quite inadequate to meet the wishes of the nation. It was his intention to free all slaves of sixty years of age, which meant in effect the granting of liberty to some one hundred and fifty thousand individuals. But parliament refused to support him and by seven votes denied the cabinet its confidence. The chamber was dissolved; the resulting election returned a chamber which again denied the government its support, this time by a scant two votes. Dantas presented his resignation, but it was evident to all that public opinion disapproved the action of the parliament.

On May 6, 1885, Saraiva assumed office with a definite program in favor of abolition. He remained in power barely long enough to secure the passage of what was to all intents and purposes the law originally sponsored by Dantas, save that its provisions were somewhat less liberal. The act of September 28, 1885, raised the age limit from sixty to sixty-five, with the result that only one hundred and twenty thousand Negroes were affected. It is a noteworthy fact, fully appreciated at the time, that his measure occasioned no disturbances and did not prejudice in any manner the harvesting of the coffee crop. The curtailment of the amount of servile labor was more than made up by the influx of immigrants from Europe.

As time went on, the desire to see the black stain removed from the national emblem grew stronger and stronger. From statistics it appeared that in the province of Rio de Janeiro, the stronghold of slavery, 15,132 manumissions had taken place between 1873 and 1885; most of these were due to the voluntary action of the slaveowners. Recourse was had to all sorts of pretexts, legal and illegal, to hasten the end of the now thoroughly discredited institution.

Organizations which were frankly outside the law sprang into being. Their purpose was to aid the slaves to escape from their fazendas, to prevent their recapture, to conceal them if need be in secure hiding places. The clergy in their prayers condemned the inhuman theory, so little consonant with the idea of divine goodness, that man could hold his fellow man as property. Magistrates took advantage of legal quibbles to grant the right of habeas corpus, sometimes collectively, to fugitive Negroes. Not infrequently these same magistrates offered asylum to the slaves. Obviously the entire fabric was crumbling.

Driven to desperation the slaveowners implored the government to use the army for the capture and return of their runaway slaves. The Military Club, in a generous and respectful message to the princess regent in 1887, begged that they be relieved from carrying out such an odious rôle. It became increasingly evident that nothing could stay the current which was sweeping away every obstacle in its path. The slaveowners were forced to cross their arms and witness a general exodus of their slaves from the plantations.

In the province of São Paulo, where the abolitionist campaign was most intense, more than ten thousand slaves were in hiding in the tropical forest in the vicinity of Santos. Their presence was known to everyone; they received protection and aid from all quarters. Many of the proprietors, reading the handwriting on the wall, hastened to free their slaves. In the province of Rio de Janeiro, for instance, two of the greatest landowners, the Counts of São Clemente and Novo Friburgo, manumitted 1,909 Negroes in 1887.

From the middle of 1887 on, the victory of the abolition cause was a foregone conclusion. The only question was to find a formula which should save from ruin thousands of *fazendeiros* who, pinning their faith on the imperial constitution and the existing legislation, had invested their fortune in lands. These men were in truth representative of the most influential and best strata of Brazilian social life. They were the genuinely conservative elements in the state; robust in their fine family life, hard-working, prudent, patriotic, full of energy. Such were the social and economic values which emancipation seemed fated to destroy.

Abolition. Isabel "A Redemptora."—The idea of indemnifying the slaveowners for the property they were about to lose was not tolerated by public opinion. The attitude of the Brazilians at large was formed by various factors. There was something shocking and repugnant in attaching a monetary value to the commerce in human flesh. Then, too, there was a resentment of the dispossessed against the wealthy, the revolt of the poor, or *popolo minuto* against the mighty, or the *popolo grasso* of the Italian republics of the Renaissance. The heirs of a situation centuries old fell a victim to a sort of divine fury bent on the destruction of an institution which at the end of the nineteenth century had become an odious anachronism. It could hardly have been otherwise. The noble propaganda of Joaquim Nabuco and his partisans, chief of whom was a Negro with a touch of genius, José do Patrocinio, rested in the final instance on the deepest feeling of Christian brotherhood. Under these circumstances, anything that smacked of compromise or sordid commercial interests was held to be unworthy of the cause to which the abolitionists had dedicated their lives and fortunes. The critical year was 1885 when Dantas and Saraiva were in power. The concessions granted to the slave-owners at that time had in reality strengthened the idealistic side of the abolitionist movement, and it rapidly became evident that nothing short of a grant of immediate freedom would satisfy the rank and file of the Brazilian people.

Thus, when Cotegipe, the prime minister, resigned on March 7, 1888, in order to avoid responsibility for administering the *coup de grâce* which was now recognized as inevitable, he was quite out of harmony with the majority of his party. Immediately, another conservative of great prestige, João Alfredo Correia de Oliveira, a member of the Rio Branco cabinet of 1870, was picked out to succeed him, with a clear mandate to bring to an end, definitely and for all time, the institution of slavery in Brazil.

On March 8, 1888, the government bill was presented to the chamber of deputies by the minister of agriculture, Rodrigo Silva. After some discussion it was agreed that the memorable act should consist of a single article abolishing slavery in Brazil. A second article, which revoked all dispositions to the contrary, was eventually added.

The bill was finally enacted into law on May 13, 1888.

Of the memorable debates and discussion which preceded the final vote only two episodes need be noted. Paulino José Soares de Souza, chief of the conservative minority opposed to slavery, consented to accept the blow with an elegant gesture, *à mourir en beauté*, striking a pose which the gladiators of ancient Rome were wont to affect with their *morituri te salutamus*. It was known that the princess regent, Dona Isabel had come down from Petropolis, where she was spending the summer, in order not to delay even for a moment the final act of emancipation. Paulino ascended the tribune of the senate and pronounced a brief but impressive discourse. "It is a matter of common knowledge, as revealed in the papers which I read this morning, that her Most Serene Highness, the Princess Regent has arrived from Petropolis and in an hour will be in the imperial palace (*Paço de Cidade*) to await the deputation of this House in order to sign and immediately to promulgate the law which has just been submitted to the Senate.

To the extent which circumstances permitted I fulfilled my duty as senator. I am now going to fulfill my duty as a gentleman (*cavalheiro*), by refusing to keep waiting a lady of such high category."

The Baron of Cotegipe had held out to the last against the measure. After the final step had been taken, the princess summoned him to the palace and pointing out the general enthusiasm provoked by the passage of the law, asked him if it would not have been wise to have voted for it. "Your Highness redeemed a race but lost a throne," was his prophetic reply.

Years afterward, the noble lady, possessed of the true spirit of Christianity, blessed by thousands of Brazilians and acclaimed Isabel the Redeemer, had the courage to declare: "Even if in those days I could have devined what was going to happen, I should have acted in the same manner." Those who had the honor of knowing the altruism and exalted virtues of this rare soul realize that such words were spoken with absolute truth and sincerity. Glorified and blessed be her memory!

The Abandonment of the Monarchical Ideal.—As has already been suggested, the one class adversely affected by emancipation were the former slaveowners who for the greater part were the *fazendeiros* or plantation owners. The economic losses and the destruction of private property were assuredly not the most lamentable consequences of the magnificent triumph of abolition. The really irremediable disaster was the sudden loss of prestige and social influence on the part of a class which, in the final instance, represented the best elements of the empire.

The really superior class of the empire, superior in experience, in prudence, in appreciation of the abiding values in national life, felt itself the victim of injustice and neglect. As a consequence of this dissatisfaction and bitterness, the bonds which for decades had united the landowning class and the empire were abruptly severed. The Braganza dynasty lost one of its most important props.

A large number of voters, though by no means a majority of the conservative party, joined the ranks of the opponents of the empire, including of course the republicans. The greater number, however, withdrew entirely from political life. There was a general feeling that the monarchy had outlived its usefulness and that a new dispensation was in order. What should it be? While no one could lift the veil of the future, speculation and conjecture were rife. The republic? Why not? But it was a tendency, rather than a definite goal.

A similar centrifugal movement took place in the army. The older chieftains, those with the rank of major and above, soldiers who had fought in the Paraguayan War, still recalled with gratitude and esteem the rôle which Dom Pedro had played in this great struggle. They could never forget that among the civilians he and he alone had unswervingly supported the military in their arduous task. But with the coming of peace the intensity of such sentiments of devotion began to decline. It was seen with increasing clearness that the chief interests of the monarch lay in the fields of letters and sciences. Though his patriotism was above all question he had no military leanings, and he possessed no real understanding of the vast sums required by the navy and army if they were to be adequately equipped for their task of defenders of the nation. He failed also to appreciate the powerful bond of unity which both branches of the national service constituted in such a vast, heterogeneous state as Brazil.

The same thing had happened in the days of independence. Parliament, as we have already seen, evinced little sympathy with the ambitious military plans of Dom Pedro I and its penuriousness was the primary cause of the loss of the Cisplatine Province. The same neglect, or shall we say ill-will, of the legislature was faced by the regency, aggravated as it was by the efforts of politicians and incompetent ministers at Rio to direct the movements of the armies in the field.

In the latter years of the reign of Dom Pedro II, there developed other causes of bitterness on the part of the army. Contrary to what happened in countries with long military traditions, the avowed pacific tendency of the imperial government, coupled with the defective method of recruiting the army, tended more and more to set the army apart from the rest of the nation. In the north and south of Brazil—somewhat less in the center—there existed a certain indifference to, if not positive antipathy toward, the officers; as was natural the latter resented this but slightly veiled malevolence and in turn made no effort to conceal their contempt for their civilian critics. The politicians they held in especial scorn.

Here a curious phenomenon occurred. The military denied these politicians any particularly competency; they were, it was alleged, mere empiricists, without any scientific basis for their actions. This charge was a consequence of the ill-assimilated teaching of the positivistic philosophy of Auguste Comte which in the eighties and nineties enjoyed a great vogue in Brazil especially in military circles.[2] As a consequence of these various factors there developed a repugnance for parliament and ministers, and the notion arose of the superiority of the military over the ignorant lawmakers, men who ignored mathematics, mere bachelors (*bachareis*) as they were scornfully called. Although in a somewhat attenuated form, such sentiments persist even to the present day.

This growing contempt for the "politicians," coupled with an increasing estrangement between the army and the rest of the population, eventually resulted in a conviction by the military that the intervention of the army in the affairs of state was quite within the bounds of possibility. To this sentiment, which in most countries would have been taxed with disloyalty, was attached an *esprit de corps*, a real feeling of solidarity. The ideas of the army underwent a further development. An ill-formulated but distinct messianic tendency began to appear. It was the soldiers who had won independence; it was the soldiers who had fought and suffered for the creation of national unity; it was the soldiers who had saved the country in the Paraguayan War. A sort of mystic belief took form and developed among the officers: they were predestined to be the saviors of Brazil from the odious machinations of party leaders and politicians. And it must be admitted in all conscience that the invectives which these same party leaders hurled against each other and even against the emperor and the imperial régime supplied the military with a certain warrant for their beliefs.

The Political Parties and the Army.—Indications of the future alignments in the conflict between the monarchy and the armed forces of the nation were beginning to appear. The politicians, inspired by what they regarded as the lesson of 1868, strove to find allies among the officers. It was the old, old story of all times:

---

[2] The most ardent votary of positivism in the last days of the empire was Benjamin Constant, whom we shall meet presently as one of the chief actors in the overthrow of the monarchy.—P.A.M.

party rivals seeking the support and protection of brute force. In the present instance, their task was comparatively easy.

Through its specialized activity, its discipline, its common aims, the army and its officials naturally formed a gregarious class, easily influenced by a few chieftains who possessed prestige and who enjoyed the confidence of their subordinates. Thus, daring and aggressive commanders, not overburdened with scruples, would have in times of crisis things pretty much their own way. Moreover, as has been pointed out by numerous acute observers, an army is a rare and notable case of survival in our own times of a caste modeled by the ideas of a close corporation with its mortality based on honor, sacrifice, and devotion to its leaders.

When these ethnic motives are placed in action, the entire machine responds. Politicians possessed of any subtlety have always known the secret of applying the maxim, *mens agitat molem*, and behind the curtain have pulled the strings to their own liking. One after another of the famous revolts of history prove this assertion; after a certain lapse of time the very officers who have most successfully resisted the political sirens and their distilled venom of pronunciamentos fall into their clutches and become their easy victims. Pretorians, Varangians, Janizaries, and many others are historic proofs of this fact.

In Brazil the liberals had made the brave and daring Osorio, later the Marquis of Herval, their military counsellor. Circumstances, rather than the conscious designs of a political party, had exalted to a pinnacle of greatness the prudent, famous, and ever victorious Caxias. Though he truly belonged to the empire as a whole, the conservatives, owing to his party affiliation, nonetheless, claimed him as their own. When both of these great soldiers died in 1887 and 1880 respectively, their succession fell to persons of less national prominence, although their military and technical abilities were rated high by those competent to judge. But, as might have been expected, the appearance of these lesser chieftains had as one of its immediate results the widening of the gulf of misunderstanding between the military and civilian camps, the more so as the very qualities which made these men efficient soldiers had little to do with their capacity to play a brilliant part in the drama of politics.

The liberals selected as their chieftain Corrêa da Camara, the

Viscount of Pelotas. Unfortunately, their new standard-bearer was little more than an impetuous cavalry leader. He represented his native state, Rio Grande do Sul, in the senate but it was soon discovered that his parliamentary abilities were slight. The conservatives chose as their leader among the military General Manoel Deodoro da Fonseca. They were wont to describe him as the heir of Caxias. While he was far from possessing the ability of Brazil's greatest soldier, he did have military qualities of a high order. His good faith as an officer was never called into question. He was loyal as steel, rash to the point of temerity, famous for his magnanimity. On the other hand, his intellectual gifts were mediocre. When crossed, he could explode like dynamite, but his intentions were always of the best, and he immediately repented of any intemperate action. If on reflection he found himself in the wrong, he readily admitted his fault and was anxious to make amends. A soldier to the core, his loyalty to his brother officers and his solidarity with the army were beyond question. In this respect, he saw eye to eye with Pelotas, despite their political differences.

In 1883 and 1884, a certain friction began to develop between the army and the civilian ministers of war. The abolition movement, as we have seen, had become a sort of crusade in which the prevailing sentiment of the officers was opposed to slavery. On the other hand, the ministry at this time, under Cotegipe, a dyed-in-the-wool conservative, was opposed to any action which went beyond the "free-birth" law of 1871. For this reason, more than once officers and cadets in the military schools had been censured and even punished for being present in public gatherings in which this question was debated. Such disciplinary steps simply added fuel to the fire. In the various institutes of learning, civilian as well as military, a critical spirit was astir which went beyond the question of abolition. It had become fashionable, for instance, to condemn the hereditary principle as the basis of government; an *esprit frondeur* was characteristic of the students, especially in the military schools. While such discussion may have raised the intellectual level of the debates, they reënforced those tendencies which were undermining the foundations of the empire.

The Military Questions.—This intellectual effervescence had reached such a point that in 1885 the minister of war felt constrained to punish a certain Lieutenant Colonel Cunha Mattos who, in a controversy in the press with a certain deputy, declared that the cause of all the discussion was a mistake committed by the minister. This censure was regarded as an insult directed against the entire army. Pelotas, in the senate, sprang to the defense of his brothers-in-arms, declaring that he would support them whether they were acting within or without the law. This was but one of a number of similar instances in which the authority of the government was flouted by the military.[3]

It was perhaps natural that this spirit of disaffection should make great headway in Rio Grande do Sul, the traditional center of revolutionary disturbances. Owing to its turbulent history and its proximity to the Platine republics, an especially large military force was stationed in this province under the command of Deodoro da Fonseca. Meetings of protest against the actions of the government of Rio were held by the officers with the full approval of Deodoro. The minister of war attempted to open the eyes of the general to the consequences of such acts of insubordination, but without success. Such a situation was frankly intolerable; the general was dismissed from his command and ordered to repair to the capital of the empire. Here, meetings of protest continued, with even greater intensity. They were presided over by Deodoro himself, who had as his secretary the insubordinate and factious Madureira who had come into conflict with the government several years earlier.

The movement continued to grow. Its ramifications spread throughout the empire. From garrison to garrison, from corps to corps, began an active correspondence for the nomination of Deodoro as representative of the military and defender of their rights. Powers were granted him to protect their interests and defend their honor.

The situation was essentially revolutionary. The republicans, as was natural, endeavored to profit from it by still further widening the breach between the army and the government. The liberals, likewise, had been following this same policy of hostility toward

[3] As early as 1883, a certain Colonel Senna Madureira came into collision with the minister of war for writing in the *Jornal do Commercio* a series of articles attacking a bill introduced into parliament by Senator Marquis of Paranaguá. Many of the students in the military schools and the higher officers in the army rallied to Senna Madureira's defense.

the conservative cabinet as a feature of their partisan opposition, until the leaders of the party in the senate finally perceived that a continuation of such tactics might result in their advent to power under the cover of a military pronunciamento. The creation of a liberal cabinet under such conditions would be awkward in the extreme. Accordingly, they tried to put on the brakes and throw a bridge over the fissure which was opening between the army and those institutions on which the very existence of the empire depended. Unfortunately, their efforts were largely futile.

As seen in retrospect, no one can doubt that this so-called military question was a preliminary of the overthrow of the imperial government. Cotegipe himself, the president of the council, confessed later that his cabinet suffered greatly from this conflict with the army and emerged from the conflict "with its dignity somewhat scratched" (*cum alguns arranhões na dignidade*), a phrase which became celebrated.

The Loss of Prestige of the Imperial Régime.—The general result of these unhappy controversies was an increasing loss of consideration suffered by the monarchy. The emperor still enjoyed the deep respect and grateful affection of the old officers who had taken part in the Paraguayan War, but the lower ranks were filled with young graduates of the military schools who did not share such sentiments, and who swallowed hook, bait, and sinker the calumnies issued by the monarchical parties themselves, who were the real, though unconscious, architects of the ruin of the empire.

The situation was aggravated by the fact that since 1887 Dom Pedro had been suffering from diabetes, a malady which was to bring him to the tomb four years later. This illness had an immediate effect upon his capacity for work and on his mental attitude. He was no longer the highly respected chief, indefatigable in his labors, *au courant* of all the *minutae* of the administration, intervening personally with all of his prestige as sovereign to exorcise a political conflict which otherwise would have had the gravest consequences. His waning health was, so to speak, a melancholy symbol of the decline of the monarchy.

Aside from an exceedingly small number of persons who utterly lacked political foresight, nobody believed in the possibility of a third reign. With the same unanimity of opinion, everyone was convinced that no change would take place during the lifetime of the emperor. An aura of affection and love accompanied Dom Pedro in his progress to the tomb, even as it had shielded the infant monarch, almost in his cradle, in the agitated days of 1831. On the other hand, any sentiment of fidelity to monarchical institutions had virtually disappeared. The clergy were still smarting under the persecution they had endured in the early seventies; the landowners, ruined in some instances by abolition, had abandoned their faith in the throne. They either remained indifferent to its fate or frankly went over to the opponents of the imperial régime. The army, as we have seen, had virtually severed relations with the empire. Its attitude was one of expectancy, but it was firmly decided to make no opposition to a democratic change.

A persistent, secret, and subtle propaganda presented the princess imperial and her consort under a false and mendacious light, distorting the mental and moral traits of this noble lady, alleging that she was a mere instrument of the clergy. Calumny had it that the Comte d'Eu was a sordid *arriviste* and had no real interest in the welfare of Brazil. The truth is that the princess showed herself one of the noblest examples of human dignity, steeped in the spirit of Christian charity, fully conscious of her duties, and firmly resolved to carry them out. And the prince was a soldier, body and soul, capable, altruistic, affectionate with his comrades, always eager to be of service, spending all that he possessed to lighten the lot or assuage the sufferings of those about him. But, unhappily, he suffered from deafness; it was maliciously said he was deaf to the Portuguese tongue. This was a libel for he knew the language as did few. On the other hand, this affliction prevented him from taking part in general conversations and tended to keep him isolated. As a consequence, he remained up to the end "the Frenchman" (*o francés*).[4]

The Disinterestedness of the Imperial Family. Affonso Celso.— From the emperor to his grandchildren none of the imperial family considered for even a moment the idea of fighting for the crown against popular will. Such were emphatically the views of Dom Pedro II and he proved his sincerity while in power, and later when in exile. Similar declarations were repeatedly made by the

---

[4] It will be recalled that the Comte d'Eu was the grandson of Louis Philippe. [See Luis da Camara Cascudo, *O Conde d'Eu* (São Paulo, 1933).—J.A.R.]

Comte d'Eu in his voyage to northern Brazil in 1888. As exponents of a certain political doctrine, the members of the Braganza dynasty were persuaded of the superiority of the formula which they defended; it was their duty, however, to maintain this doctrine in a manner which would redound to the happiness of the nation. On the other hand, they were utterly opposed to any attempt to enforce their ideas upon the country. Had events pursued their normal course, the empire would have quietly been followed by the republic when Dom Pedro came to close his eyes on this mortal life; such a peaceful and natural transition would have been applauded by the entire nation. But facts and circumstances sometimes have a way of their own quite apart from the designs of men.

The ministry of João Alfredo came to an end in the early days of June, 1889. The chief task of the new president of the council, irrespective of the choice, would be to find some means to cope with the general discontent pervading all fields of national life, including agriculture, the army, political parties, the clergy. The qualification, even more necessary than energy and competency, was tact. Saraiva was really the person to charter the course of the ship of state in such a troubled sea. Summoned by the emperor to organize a new government, he declined this arduous task on the ground of his precarious health, and advised that the mission be confided to the senator from Minas Geraes, Affonso Celso de Assis Figueiredo, Viscount of Ouro Preto.

This statesman was a model of honor, competency, and capacity for hard work. Frank, manly, and sincere, he never evaded a situation, no matter how difficult. He despised the use of tortuous means; he refused to argue or quibble with his parliamentary opponents; all his blows were delivered in the open. His was a character of adamantine rigidity, inflexible, unyielding. It is a fair question to ask if the times and circumstances were most propitious for the ultilization of such virtues and qualities. Under the delicate conditions then prevailing, would not a greater use of diplomacy and even circuitous means have produced larger results? This is a nice question on which no definitive judgment is possible.

In his noble sincerity, the president of the council accorded scant attention to the intrigues and underhanded tactics of his opponents. Rumors there were aplenty, but he gave them no heed. From the day of its assumption of power, June 7, 1889, his

ministry dedicated its entire energies to financial reorganization.
The productive forces of the nation, especially the former slaveowners, were to be the object of its special solicitude. As far as
possible, the government would endeavor through loans and other
financial concessions to tide over the crisis caused by abolition.
Such was the economic program of the Ouro Preto cabinet. The
political problem was quite a different matter. How was the government to cope with the growing menace of the military? The prime
minister never concealed his intentions. As a counterpoise to the
professional army, factious, eager to invade the sphere of politics,
largely under the control of officers long in the service, it was his
plan to create a national militia, armed and trained on the basis
of loyalty to the state. The idea was a sound one but, unfortunately, time was lacking to put it effectively into practice.

The Republicans. Benjamin Constant.—Their ranks swollen
by the influx of disgruntled ex-slaveowners, the republicans
exerted every effort, by means of intrigues and astute propaganda,
to bring the crisis to a head. They scrupled at nothing: slanders,
calumnies, downright falsehoods. They utilized any and every
weapon which might undermine the foundations of the state. They
accused the government of planning to exile the higher officials of
the army, beginning with Deodoro, to the remote, uninhabited
regions of the empire. The most sensitive part of the army, the
portion which reacted most violently to these actions imputed to
the government, was composed of young officers recently graduated
from the military schools, or students about to graduate. They
had as their idol a middle-aged professor by the name of Benjamin Constant Botelho de Magalhães. He had taken part in the
Paraguayan campaigns, he was a good mathematician, and was
held to be a profound thinker. He was a republican of many years
standing but despite this fact—which was perfectly well-known—
the emperor had selected him as tutor for his grandchildren. Between him and Dom Pedro existed a mutual esteem and even
affection based on the sincerity of their opinions. For the students
in the military school his word was that of an oracle. As a result
of his lectures and conferences with his students, his prestige
was so great that on one occasion the cadets begged him to place
himself at the head of the army and save the nation from the abyss

into which it was plunging. Many officers lent their adhesion to this subversive movement.

The chief obstacle to any military revolt was the devotion of Deodoro to the old emperor. At length, persuaded by Benjamin Constant and a number of his intimates—old comrades-in-arms for the most part—he allowed himself to be carried away by the current, although up to the last moment it was his determination that the *coup d'état* should be limited to a change of ministry. It was necessary that Benjamin point out to him, after the victory of the revolt, that if a complete change in régime did not take place, the lives of all of them would be imperiled; only then, and reluctantly, did he go over bag and baggage to the republicans.

The Proclamation of the Republic. Deodoro Da Fonseca.—The plot was hatched with the greatest secrecy. With the exception of a few civilians—in every instance republicans—the conspiracy was exclusively in the hands of the military. The uprising was set for November 20, but on the thirteenth and fourteenth, rumors began to circulate that the government was about to order the imprisonment of Deodoro. As a consequence the date was pushed forward. The powder train was ignited. Orders were hurriedly despatched. Troops began to assemble at their appointed places in the early morning of the fifteenth. The cabinet, which for the first time suspected that some plot was on foot, gathered before daylight in the large fortresslike structure occupied by the ministry of war. Here they were made prisoners by the revolting troops. The Baron of Ladario, the minister of marine, arriving late at the assignment, and seeing the armed forces in front of the building, fired at the officer who tried to take him prisoner. The baron in turn was fired upon and wounded in the leg. This was the sole casualty of the revolt.

For several hours after the deposition of Ouro Preto and his colleagues, no steps were taken to proclaim the republic. Deodoro himself declared to Ouro Preto that he would submit to the emperor a list of the new ministers. Dom Pedro had time to come down from Petropolis after the first news of the uprising. His plan was to summon a council of state and to entrust Saraiva with the organization of a new government. But when this statesman endeavored to place himself in contact with Deodoro to discuss his

mission, he was informed that an exchange of views would be futile
as the republic was already proclaimed and a new ministry organized. As has already been noted, the old soldier had yielded
against his better judgment to the arguments of his republican
associates. One of the chief reasons, perhaps the decisive one, why
Deodoro completely abandoned the emperor was the rumor relayed
to the general by Benjamin Constant that Dom Pedro had entrusted the formation of the new cabinet to Senator Silveira
Martins, a bitter personal enemy of Deodoro.

During the course of these momentous changes there was at
no time any participation on the part of the people. It was a
simple military *coup d'état* which encountered no opposition. But
in simple truth it must be said that the events of November 15
were but an anticipation of a change that was inevitable. A third
reign was held to be chimerical even by the overwhelming majority of the two imperial parties.

It was evident that the imperial family could not remain in
Brazil. Up to the last moment, however, every mark of deference
and respect was bestowed upon them. The feeling was universal
that only hard necessity was responsible for the exile of the
Braganza dynasty. The departure took place early in the morning of November 17 on the *Alagôas*. This inconvenient hour
was chosen as the government feared demonstrations and tumults
which might result in bloodshed.

There now commenced the final period in the career of the great
Brazilian, a period in which he rises perhaps to an even greater
moral stature than during his reign as emperor. Never before had
he merited as completely as he did in exile the praise of Victor
Hugo, who saluted him as the grandson of Marcus Aurelius.

Summary of the Achievements of the Empire.—Great and noble
was the task performed by the empire. At the beginning of the
reign of Dom Pedro II Brazil was obliged to face widespread
threats of disintegration, and yet it remained united. Though
they lasted two full decades local troubles eventually succumbed
to the cohesive power of the empire. Methods of governments had
passed through a striking evolution from absolutism to parliamentarism, and while the latter was not theoretically perfect, its
functioning, thanks to the emperor and his moderative power, was
at least tolerable. Elections, too, had progressed from utter dis-

order to a fairly acceptable representation of the two traditional parties. The great codes of justice and administration had been organized and had regulated social and juridical relations in a manner satisfactory to the great majority of the Brazilians. Slavery was abolished. With the insufficient training in citizenship and the existing ignorance in the use of political machinery, hardly more could have been expected. So much for the internal life of the country.

International Relations.—In foreign affairs the same forward trend was to be noticed. With the abdication of Dom Pedro I in 1831 Portuguese ideas and influence showed a marked decline. No longer was imperialism a pretext for national expansion at the expense of Brazil's neighbors. The regency and Dom Pedro II adopted as the bases of the empire's international relations the following policy: the rule of *uti possidetis* in the definition of national boundaries, a sentiment of fraternity toward all of Brazil's sister nations of the continent, and finally, arbitration as a means of settling international disputes.

Since 1828 the empire had harbored no plans of conquest. To be sure, we were forced to intervene in the basin of the Río de la Plata and adjacent territory; we even went to war at the behest of certain countries in order to free them from impossible tyranny, a fact expressly recognized by Bartolomé Mitre. But in no case was there any thought of conquest. Our conduct in the Paraguayan War reveals the same disinterestedness. We declared war on Paraguay as the direct result of the provocation of its dictator, and with the avowed purpose of restoring to this noble nation the liberty which had been filched from it by an unscrupulous tyrant.

The widespread hostility toward the empire on the part of the South-American republics, a heritage of similar sentiments in the Iberian peninsula, little by little disappeared in an atmosphere of mutual confidence. Both from Europe and from North America came additional evidence of the esteem and respect evoked by the empire. A few instances may be mentioned.

In 1871 Brazil was chosen as one of the arbiters between the United States and Great Britain in the question of the *Alabama.* Later, in 1880, the empire acted as arbiter between the United States and France in the settlement of the claims advanced by American citizens for damage suffered in the war between Mexico and Napoleon III. Still another instance occurred in 1884-1885. The war between Chile and the Peruvian-Bolivian alliance had been the occasion of great loss and damage to other nations. An agreement was signed by which an arbitral tribunal should pass upon complaints. The tribunal consisted of three members, two representing the governments immediately interested, and the third, Brazil. By this means France, England, Italy, Germany, Belgium, Austria-Hungary, and Switzerland solved their disputes with Chile. The eminent position of the empire in South America admits of no doubt; if additional proofs were needed, they were to be found in the demonstrations of esteem of which Brazil was the recipient in the Congress of Montevideo on Private International Law in 1888, and in the First Pan-American Congress held at Washington the year following.

Public Instruction.—One of the chief preoccupations of the emperor was public instruction. He was wont to attend all of the examinations, competitions, and tests to which the candidates for positions in the scientific school had to submit; often he would appear quite unexpectedly in the lecture rooms. He repeatedly declared that he considered the teaching profession the most important in society. He encouraged public lectures; he was prodigal in his aid to investigators, travelers, and scientists, foreign as well as Brazilian. It is impossible to narrate in detail all that he did for educational institutions, both primary and secondary. As for the higher institutions of learning, it may be noted that in 1889 the empire possessed two faculties of medicine and surgery, two academies of law, a school of mines, a school of fine arts, a conservatory of music, a polytechnic school, three military schools, and a naval school. Public libraries, archives, and museums were modestly but adequately endowed, and supplied mental stimulus to students without distinction. The emperor was a scholar and everything which touched education or science interested him to the highest degree.

Economic Advance.—Economic problems were, on the whole, adequately handled under the empire. Credit and exchange may be accepted as convenient yardsticks. The first may be judged by the character and success of Brazil's foreign loans. In London in 1886 was floated a 5 per cent loan at 95; the following year a 4 per cent loan was placed at 90, both with no special guarantees and with only one-half per cent sinking fund. On the Brazilian market, an internal loan of 4 per cent placed in circulation at 90 was covered twice over. In the last months of the empire currency went over par. Production rose. As measured by exports it ascended from 22,000 contos in 1879-1890 to 366,000 contos in 1886-1887.[5] Commerce in general, including both exports and imports, expanded in the same period from 400,000 contos to 676,500 contos. The blow inflicted by abolition was borne without too much loss. To be sure the immediate effect was a drop in coffee production to 40 per cent, but the three-quarters of a million bags which were sold abroad commanded an excellent price. Parallel with the emancipation of the slaves was the arrival of immigrants: 11,000 in 1881; some 28,000 per annum for the period 1882-1886; 55,000 in 1887; and 132,000 in 1888. At the end of the empire, railway mileage had risen to 9,583 kilometers, and telegraph lines to 18,-925 kilometers.

Literary Activity.—The last decades of the empire witnessed a marked literary development. Naturalism was most conspicuous in its descriptions of life and society from the psychological point of view; the outstanding representative of this school was Machado de Assis. Emotion played a larger part in the works of Julio Ribeiro and Raul Pompeia. Aluizio Azevedo was noted for his impressionism and his remarkable power of analysis. In the domain of poetry are to be found great names also. Raymundo Corrêa, whose works are pervaded by sentiments of restlessness, pessimism, and pain; Olivo Bilac, whose brilliant simplicity proved a most eloquent vehicle for the expression of national sentiments; and others. Literary critics included such names as Tobias Barreto, Sylvio Roméro, Araripe Junior, José Verissimo. In the field of history, we may cite Varnhagen (later the Viscount of Porto Seguro), Joaquim Nabuco, Oliveira Lima, and above all Capistrano de Abreu. In the case of the last two of these men it should be noted that their most notable productions came after the fall of the empire.

National Individuality.—With the aid of this group of intellectual creators, Brazil was developing a marked national individuality. Dom Pedro II was one of the most important factors

---

[5] At this time the conto was worth slightly less than $500.—P.A.M.

in keeping the civilizing evolution of Brazil within its proper historical limits. Brazil, like the majority of the South American nations, is a legitimate offspring of the ancestral Iberian stem, and as such inherited racial characteristics profoundly modified by deep-felt Catholicism, fidelity to the highest moral principles, and devotion to the stern precepts of a severe Christianity and romantic chivalry. Its aims reveal a marked leaning toward idealism. In the Brazilian soul spirituality, imponderable qualities, count for much more than material factors and in its political and social evolution duties have always taken precedence over rights. Our national history abundantly proves this contention.

It has been our constant endeavor, moreover, to maintain intact this national individuality. We do not tolerate the idea of revealing ourselves as mere imitators, more or less perfect, of foreign models, however advanced or progressive these may be, unless perchance these models are guided by the same idealistic inspiration as ourselves. Harmony, beauty, altruism, bulk much larger with us than mere wealth and comfort.

Our civilization is qualitative and is entirely beyond the comprehension of minds fixed only on quantitative superiority. Psychologically we are much closer to Europe, especially Latin Europe, than to any other part of the world. For this reason we are understood much better by these people than by any others. After Portugal and Spain, our mentality is chiefly indebted to French thought, and more recently, with the development of higher studies and immigration, to the science of Italy and Germany. The beginning of an intellectual and moral intercourse with the Anglo-Saxon soul is a more recent phenomenon. Here we are confronted with a peculiar antithesis, for the United States and England are precisely the two countries with which our greatest affinities of another kind have lasted for a century.

To Great Britain we are chiefly beholden for the invaluable assistance rendered us in Canning's days when we were struggling for independence. We also gladly acknowledged the large part Great Britain has played in fostering our material progress. As for the United States, we are indebted to that great nation for the immediate recognition of our national sovereignty, and for the Monroe Doctrine, which we have always regarded as an expression of our own ideas in regard to the relations of America and Europe, and as such have always furthered it as a common link among all the nations of our continent. In one respect, however, we disagree with the great northern republic. We regard the Doctrine, not as a unilateral instrument, a principle of self-protection for the United States, but as a rule basically continental or Pan-American in scope.

With the passage of time, such disagreements are bound to pass, and this process will be accelerated in proportion as the United States acquires a more fundamental understanding of its sisters to the south, their soul, and their feelings. The change will also be hastened by the marked progress which these same republics are making, and also in consequence of the fundamental racial developments which are taking place in the United States, developments which are giving this country a different ethnic complexion than it had, say, in 1823 when the population was overwhelmingly of English extraction.

Little by little the juxtaposition of mentalities of different ethnic backgrounds will make for the formation of a common substratum, a collective soul, as it were. This soul will be less matter-of-fact, perhaps, but as a compensation will possess a greater degree of spirituality. And, on the other hand, world competition will give to the South Americans a certain practical sense which they now lack, and which eventually will be a supplement to, though not a substitute for, the prevailing idealist inspiration.

CHAPTER XIII

THE PROCLAMATION AND CONSOLIDATION OF
THE REPUBLIC

The Republic and Dom Pedro II.—One of the first problems confronting the new régime was the attitude it should assume toward the Braganza dynasty and its loyal supporters. Thanks to the good sense of the emperor and the generous attitude of the new provisional government, few questions arose which could not be settled in a dignified and equitable manner. Little or no hostility existed between the representatives of the old and the new order. The first concern of the provisional government was to assure Dom Pedro and his family a decorous material existence while in exile. But the old monarch nobly refused any such pecuniary grant. The national treasury did, however, assume responsibility for the pensions of the old servitors of the crown and worthy families without resources who had formerly derived their support from the modest civil list of the emperor. This step, which was really a duty, met with the full approval of the Brazilians. Dom Pedro never uttered a word of complaint of the treatment which had been meted out to him; with his spirit of magnanimity, he understood everything. In the hours of his exile, he proved the sincerity with which he had repeatedly affirmed during his long reign that he was the first republican of Brazil. He even did more. Various Brazilian diplomats stationed in Europe waited upon the emperor and placed in his hands their resignations; he refused to accept them, declaring that he had no right to proceed thus as they had been appointed to serve Brazil and not its emperor. He added that as loyal Brazilians it was their duty to continue to carry on their diplomatic functions. He forbade his supporters to make any attempt to change the course of events. In this manner, he aided indirectly the recognition of the new order. More than once he declared that were he summoned by the people to return to America in order to render further service to Brazil he would be happy to do so. He represented in foreign lands the noblest qualities of the Brazilian people.

The new rulers of the nation quite naturally found their days of apprenticeship replete with difficulties, but to their credit it must be said they entered upon their task with tremendous energy and enthusiasm. As the situation was frankly revolutionary they were naturally eager to see the country restored to a legal status; on the other hand questions were pending whose decision could not be deferred until the promulgation of the new constitution. The members of the provisional government also knew that it would be easier to establish at once the reforms for which the country was prepared than to postpone them for a remote period, months or even years later, when conditions and circumstances might be far less propitious. Moreover, many of these reforms had been pledged in the republican programs issued in the latter years of the empire, and had received the approval of the republican party at that time.

The First Steps.—One of the first necessities of the new rulers was to escape from the purely *de facto* situation in which they found themselves on the proclamation of the republic on November 15. Decree Number 1, issued on November 16, met this problem: it proclaimed a federative republic until the definite adoption of a constitution. On December 3 a special commission was appointed to prepare a project for this constitution; on May 30, 1890, this project was submitted to the provisional government, which proceded to revise it, whereupon it was published as the draft to be laid before the constituent convention. Delegates to this body were elected on September 15, 1890. It held its first session on November 15, 1890, the first anniversary of the proclamation of the republic.

Until that date the government held concentrated in its hands the powers of both the executive and the legislature. Innumerable measures had been taken to meet the many problems growing out of the change of régime. The electorate was considerably enlarged; the only qualifications for voting were the enjoyment of civil and political rights and the ability to read and write. The provincial assemblies were dissolved. A general naturalization decree was issued providing that all foreigners resident in Brazil on November 15, 1889, should be regarded as Brazilian citizens unless they should make legal declarations to the contrary. A movement toward greater decentralization was initiated through the enlargement of the powers of the provinces, henceforth to be known as states.

On January 7, 1890, a decree was passed formally separating Church and State. In the formulation of this delicate and important measure, every consideration was shown the Church. The government recognized its own incompetency in spiritual matters and relinquished any attempt to regulate them; religious and civil societies were to remain each within its own limits. Official patronage, appeals to the crown, the right of approving or rejecting instruments dealing with ecclesiastical matters, were abolished. Separation under these conditions, in an atmosphere of deep respect for the Church, naturally met with the full approval of the Brazilian episcopate. From that time to the present, the law has functioned without friction and to the advantage of both parties. To such an extent is this true that in France, during the debates on the laws affecting religious congregations, our legislation was cited as a model of its kind. This inestimable boon of complete religious freedom and toleration we owe to Ruy Barbosa, the author of the law, and to the influence of positivism, a doctrine which inspired Benjamin Constant Botelho de Magalhães, one of the militant leaders of the revolution of November 15, 1889.

Certain important consequences necessarily flowed from the separation of Church and State. Civil registration of births and deaths had existed since 1888, but civil marriage and the secularization of cemeteries now came into force.

Immense and beneficent changes were introduced into civil law, both in the criminal code and the organization of justice. Never before in our history had such a display of political thought and activity occurred in an equally short time. The man who stands preëminent in this connection is the great jurist Ruy Barbosa whom we have just mentioned in connection with the separation of Church and State.

Unhappily, the financial situation under the provisional government was deplorable. We have already seen that in the last days of the empire advances had been made to the former slaveowners to tide them over the crisis caused by emancipation. Partly to prevent attacks on monarchical institutions, special facilities had been extended to various banking concerns. The inevitable result was the launching of a large number of companies having no adequate financial backing. With the coming of the republic, this situation was greatly aggravated. In order to quicken the economic forces of the nation, a number of favored banks were authorized to issue immense sums of paper money and received at the same time a long list of financial privileges. A wild orgy of speculation ensued, for which the economic resources of Brazil offered no justification. One may well ask why the members of the provisional government did not take measures to check this movement. Possibly one of the answers is the fact that the monarchists, inflamed with hopes of easily acquired wealth, spent their time and resources in the stock market instead of launching conspiracies against the newly born republic. The financial craze thus acted as a sort of lightning rod for the government.

Whatever may be the true explanation for the financial policy of the provisional government, its results were disastrous. The confidence enjoyed in the money marts of Europe disappeared as it were overnight, and it was only slowly that Brazil's credit was reëstablished. Many critics have laid the blame for Brazil's misfortunes at the door of the minister of finance of the provisional government, Ruy Barbosa. Though this brilliant but somewhat erratic personage cannot be absolved from all blame, he should not be charged with full responsibility for the debacle which followed his term of office. In many instances, he was not a free agent. Tremendous and frequently irresistible pressure was placed upon him to sanction financial measures which he frankly disapproved. It must not be forgotten that Brazil was passing through a period when political and economic conditions were frankly abnormal. And as we have already suggested, some of the minister's difficulties were inherited from his predecessor in the last cabinet of the empire.

The Recognition of the Republic.—In addition to the reforms of capital importance which we have just discussed, there remained two problems whose solution was well calculated to tax the ability and discretion of the provisional government—the admission of the republic to the comity of nations, and the maintenance of order within the country itself.

The solution of the first problem proved to be unexpectedly easy. On November 20, 1889, Argentina and Uruguay took the initiative in the recognition of the republic; on December 13 it was the turn of Chile; in the course of January, 1890, Bolivia, Venezuela, Mexico, and the United States fell into line;[1] in February, Guatemala, El Salvador, and Colombia were added to the list;[2] in March, Costa Rica, Nicaragua, and Honduras. The European governments then had to make their decisions. France was the first to recognize Brazil, on June 20, 1890. Then followed Portugal, on September 18; The Netherlands, Italy, and the Holy See, on November 23; Switzerland, on November 25; Germany, Norway, and Sweden, on November 29; Austria-Hungary and Spain, on December 6. It is to be noted that France and Portugal did not even wait for the installation of the constituent congress.

Internal Politics.—As might have been expected, the internal political situation soon caused serious difficulties. The *coup d'état* of November 15 was so sudden, the number of those initiated was so small, that the surprise was general throughout the country. But sooner or later opposition and dissension were bound to arise. The greatest danger, however, came from another quarter. One of the worst consequences of politics based on force and especially on armed force is that there is no logical goal to the process; today, generals head mutinies; tomorrow, it may be colonels, and then from rank to rank, in ever descending scale. We may even come to soviets of the common soldiers. As has happened frequently in the history of Brazil, the revolutionists refuse to admit that their own blunders might be the causes of the reaction against them; the rule has always been to accuse the defeated party of fomenting disorder. Thus from the abdication of Dom Pedro I in 1831 until his death in 1834, it was the custom to tax the absolutists and monarchists with responsibility for the commotions and revolts which caused so much difficulty to the regency. And now once more, with the monarchy overthrown, all rebellions and risings were promptly characterized as anti-republican conspiracies directed against the men in office or designed to restore the monarchical régime. But, as has already been intimated, there was no real basis for such accusations.

Not that sincere monarchists failed to support a number of these revolts but, with the exception of the partial revolt of the

---

[1] The dates were January 3, 7, 13, and 29, respectively.

[2] The dates were February 6 for Guatemala and El Salvador, and February 20 for Colombia.

fleet in 1893, their influence was virtually nil. And even in the case of the naval revolt in 1893—which we shall consider later in detail —the restoration movement did not go further than the suggestion of a plebiscite on the form of government to be adopted. Nevertheless, this tendency to descry monarchical plots even in the most unlikely quarters lasted for a long time and, as late as the opening of the twentieth century, partisan literature was full of bitter utterances against the "enemies of the republic," to whom were gratuitously attributed the responsibility for every blunder committed by the party in power.

As the months wore on the difficulties of the provisional government continued to mount. The chief problems were financial and political. The rate of foreign exchange became more and more unfavorable to Brazil. On the overthrow of the empire in 1889, it was quoted at twenty-seven pence the milréis. By 1891 it had fallen to twelve pence. The hundreds of mushroom companies, to which we have already alluded, collapsed utterly, and the discontent among the producing class increased by leaps and bounds.

Marshal Deodoro da Fonseca was a valiant soldier and warm-hearted and generous. Unfortunately, he was quite innocent of any political ability. Easily influenced by his entourage, he was usually prone to follow the advice of the last to catch his ear. He was cut out to be the leader of a successful revolution but never to be the chief magistrate of a nation. Moreover, he was a creature of impulses, swayed by sudden feelings. Though possessed of a fine sense of dignity and honor, he was rarely objective in his judgments and looked upon all criticism of his acts and policies as personal affronts. It is not surprising, therefore, that he found himself every day more entangled in the meshes of partisan conflicts in which sordid and selfish motives predominated. Helpless when confronted with these intrigues, deceived by friends, he was tortured by a real anguish to return to private life where he might die in peace. But even this course was denied him; for these same friends, intent only on feathering their own nests, persuaded the noble soldier that he was indispensable to the nation. Under these conditions the breach between Deodoro and many of the better and abler elements in Brazilian political life tended to widen. Things went so far that the normal activity of the legislature, even when it kept within strictly constitutional limits, was frequently looked upon by the chief of state as an attack on his own person. As a consequence, Deodoro tended more and more to surround himself with a small circle of advisers and devoted comrades, even the most loyal of whom were ignorant of the problems of government.

From the very beginning of the provisional government, this failure to select administrators of ability had led to the appointment as presidents of the various states young officers, many of them not much more than boys, who had just left the military schools. Under the influence of the doctrine of positivism, whose high priest at this time was Benjamin Constant, each one of these young men judged himself a prophet, a depository of the purity of faith. This naïve assurance was not surprising since these same persons, while students in the military schools, had discussed, approved, or censured the acts of their superiors.

Friction Between the Executive and Congress.—Congress had hardly assembled before sharp criticism was voiced of the prevailing methods of government. The marshal had turned over to the constituent convention the sum of the prerogatives which the republic had conferred upon him, but the convention decided that he should remain at the head of national affairs until this body had definitely elected the president and vice president. During the course of the debates two groups began to emerge, one consisting of Deodoro's supporters and the other composed of those definitely hostile to the course which had been followed by the government.

The drafting of the constitution itself gave rise to friction and recriminations. When the delegates to the constituent convention assembled, they were given a preliminary draft of the new constitution, chiefly the work of Ruy Barbosa. When, however, the convention proceeded to amend this draft, which was its elementary duty, the marshal took it ill. But this resentment on the part of Deodoro was only one of the minor causes of the growing friction between the executive and congress.

The new constitution which was finally adopted on February 24, 1891, was a remarkable achievement, both liberal and prudent in its dispositions. Exceptions may be taken to certain articles, but in all fairness it must be admitted that it is a masterpiece of political science, far superior to what might be expected of a parliament elected in a time of revolution. This happy result was due in considerable part to the presence in the constituent assembly of a number of monarchists, who were at the same time thoroughly reconciled to the change in régime. They acted as a brake on the tendencies of the extremists. It is also to be noted that a number of persons of first-rate ability were to be found among the new elements.

At this point, only a few of the more questionable dispositions may be noted. It is debatable whether it was wise to grant the states the right of formulating codes of procedure. The turning-over of the public lands to the states and of the mines to the surface owner was certainly a mistake. Some half a dozen other details of the constitution may be open to disagreement. Taken by and large the new political covenant represented liberty and progress, but it is a pity that it did not institute reforms in the territorial divisions of the country, in the sense of removing some of the inequality in the size of the states. This last topic may well engage our attention for a moment.

With the coming of independence in 1822, the provinces of the empire took as their boundaries the old colonial captaincies general. As time went on these provinces showed striking differences in their development. Some of them, vast in size and with a relatively large population, took over the direction of the country; while others, limited in area or scantily settled, possessed practically no influence. Such differences increased from year to year until in 1889 the political orientation of Brazil depended on five or six circumscriptions: Bahia, Rio de Janeiro, Minas Geraes, São Paulo, Pernambuco, Rio Grande do Sul. The influence of the remaining sixteen provinces in national affairs was all but negligible.

If the new régime had availed itself of the fact that everyone accepted the decisions of the provisional government, and had straightway divided the republic into states and territories with fairly equivalent areas and populations, a serious cause of rivalry would have been eliminated and the evils inherent in the existence of first- and second-class states could have been avoided. But tradition is one of the bases of Brazilian mentality. When the constituent congress met it was already too late, for every former province now had its representative and could oppose any curtailment of its privileges.

The Government of Lucena. Its Isolation.—The differences between the military as represented by Deodoro and the civilians who were firmly intrenched in congress have already been alluded to. So far apart were these different conceptions of the organization and function of the government that effective coöperation between the executive and congress became impossible. With ever greater frequency, the marshal turned to his personal friends both for counsel and sympathy.

The beginning of this unhappy conflict went back to the first days of the provisional government. One of Deodoro's ministers left him as early as 1890. The remaining members of the provisional government, chiefly Ruy Barbosa, Campos Salles, and Cesario Alvim, made heroic efforts to maintain a united front until the final vote on the constitution. But their labor proved unavailing and on January 21, 1891, the entire ministry resigned. On this occasion Deodoro called to his side a personal and political friend, the Baron of Lucena, to help him in his task of organizing a ministry. The friendship of these two men dated from 1885 when Lucena was appointed governor of the province of Rio Grande do Sul, of which at the time Deodoro was military commander. Both were conservatives, strongly imbued with the doctrine of order, authority, and discipline. Both were honest, worthy of confidence, and thoroughly patriotic; but both were wont to resort to force when the law might well have been invoked. Their confidence in each other was complete.

Such an appointment was natural; in fact it was expected by everyone. But it turned out to be a political error of the first magnitude. In republican circles, the baron was neither admired nor trusted; he was too much a dyed-in-the-wool conservative and too much addicted to party interests to win confidence from republicans whom he had once so uncompromisingly opposed. He, in turn, wasted no love on these same republicans whom he regarded as incompetent and untried administrators. He accordingly constituted a ministry of personal friends, respectable and competent, all save one being monarchists. Naturally, such a move played directly into the hands of Deodoro's enemies.

In many respects the baron was vastly superior to the marshal. Unlike Deodoro he possessed a real flair for politics and he realized the urgent need of peace and concord among the republicans if his government was to succeed. He bent every effort to obtain harmony, even offering to resign and retire to private life if such a move might promote conciliation and party disarmament. This laudable endeavor utterly failed owning to the intransigent opposition of Senator Prudente de Moraes of São Paulo, who was at the time president of the constituent assembly. A man of the highest character, Prudente, as we shall see later, was called upon to serve his country with heroic energy and complete self-sacrifice. But he was not without his faults and was more of a doctrinaire than an accomplished politician. At this particular juncture he saw in the policy of the marshal and in his political and administrative incapacity a standing menace to republican ideals. His distrust of Lucena was complete.

The task of framing the constitution was drawing to an end. The atmosphere of the assembly became more and more tense. Anticipating complications and a growing hostility toward the executive, Lucena seriously considered dissolving congress as soon as the final vote on the constitution was taken. But Deodoro would not hear of such a flagrantly illegal step. Once more the marshal held out the olive branch to congress only to meet another rebuff. Conditions were rapidly approaching a complete deadlock.

A new difficulty arose when it came to the election of the first constitutional president of the republic. Obviously but one logical choice was possible—Deodoro. But his adversaries, among whom were many public officials who had been elected by congress, launched a vigorous campaign in favor of a civilian. While some of Deodoro's opponents were sincere, many had no other object than the discrediting of the old soldier, who in the final analysis was responsible for the creation of the republic.

The civilian candidate was Prudente. The Paulista senator had never sought out such distinction. But when his political friends urged him to withdraw his name for the sake of harmony, he refused on the ground that his candidacy had been thrust upon him. This was a great error on his part, and an injustice toward the founder of the republic; it caused dangerous political agitation at a time when the country was in dire need of peace. The schism between supporters and enemies of Deodoro steadily widened. The disastrous consequences of this hostility were soon to appear.

The election for president was held on February 25, 1891. Of the 234 members of congress present, 129 voted for Deodoro and 97 for Prudente. As might have been anticipated, Deodoro re-

garded the actions of Prudente's supporters as a personal affront
and from now on considered them his personal enemies.

Legally, the provisional government had now come to an end
and forthwith the constituent assembly became the first constitutional congress. The new session was very active. Many bills were
presented. Demands on the executive for information on the march
of public affairs were repeatedly presented.

The president was requested, for instance, to supply information on such subjects as appointments, acts of the various
ministries, the filling of vacancies on the supreme court, or even
the law of presidential responsibility. Although the formulation
of these demands was a legitimate and proper function of the
legislature the real motive behind them was to force Deodoro from
office. The president himself was under no illusions on this score.

Dissolution of Congress.—The conflict was now clear to everyone. Both sides were at fault, although the blame was chiefly to
be laid at the door of the president. On the other hand, Prudente
cannot be absolved from the responsibility of creating an atmosphere surcharged with political passions. The majority of congress
was clearly hostile to Deodoro and made no attempt to conceal
its aversion. With the powder train thus laid, an explosion was
inevitable. The president could contain his indignation no longer
and on November 3, 1891, he dissolved both branches of the legislature.[3] On the same day, the majority of the members of congress
addressed a manifesto to the nation. This document answered with
convincing clearness and sincerity the accusations of the executive.
It pointed out that the dictatorial act of Deodoro had no constitutional warrant and that the reasons given by him were quite
without merit.

Although this document was only published after the restoration of legality, and hence had no immediate influence, it reflected
accurately the general feeling of the Brazilians. So true was this
that on November 23, scarcely twenty days after the dissolution
of congress, the entire country voiced in one way or another its

---

[3] This *coup d'etat* was defended by Deodoro in a long proclamation, in
which, after attacking the actions of congress as calculated to endanger the
safety of the republic, he asserted that the government had evidence of widespread monarchical plots and that conspirators were aiming at an armed
revolution. Rippy, Martin, and Cox, *Argentina, Brazil, and Chile*, p. 227.—
P.A.M.

disapproval. A full-fledged revolt broke out in Rio Grande do Sul; Pará was on the brink of a similar uprising; in the capital, the army and the navy, as well as congress and civilians, made clear their opposition. During the night of the twenty-second to the twenty-third of November, the president was abandoned by the better elements of his fellow-countrymen.

The shock experienced by Deodoro when he discovered his moral and political isolation can hardly be described. It was, in reality, a mortal blow from which he never recovered. In his long career as a soldier he more than once acted with real heroism. He was possessed of a great heart and a domineering soul in which kindness and patriotism were almost equally blended. In all that had to do with the army he showed himself a commanding figure. But in civil life, what a contrast! He alternated between weakness and wilfullness; he was able to command subordinates but not to direct civilians. Hating power merely for power's sake, he was now confronted with the necessity of shedding the blood of his fellow-Brazilians if he was to maintain himself as head of the state. Such a price he was quite unwilling to pay. When Lucena pointed out to him the terrible alternatives, he determined once for all to resign from the presidency.

The manifesto to the nation, in which he detailed the reasons for this step, is one of the most tragic documents in Brazilian history. In it is revealed a noble soul, wounded to the quick by the ingratitude of his so-called friends.

"Extraordinary circumstances in which, I swear before God, I had no part have led to an exceptional and unforeseen situation. I assumed that I could avoid such a dangerous crisis by the dissolution of congress, a measure which I took with great reluctance, but responsibility for which I freely assume. I thought to direct the government of the state along a path which would save it from the disastrous effects of this crisis. But the conditions in which the country now finds itself, and the ingratitude of those for whom I sacrificed myself, and the desire not to kindle war in my dear country, make clear the wisdom of resigning my authority in the hands of my successor."

In this manner did the vice president, Marshal Floriano Peixoto, assume office on November 23, 1891.

Legality. Floriano Peixoto.—Although much has been written regarding the interesting, curious, and ambiguous personality of Floriano, he still remains an historical enigma. He was a born leader, but of a temper utterly different from that of Deodoro. While the former inspired a flaming enthusiasm through his innate courage, the latter, fearless and calm, imposed his will by his coolness, foresight, and calculation. In one case we have the brilliancy of lightning; in the other the inflexibility of a theorem.

During the Paraguayan War Floriano had valiantly performed his duty, but in his own peculiar way, quietly and efficiently, without fuss or feathers. In addition to his moral qualities, which were very real, Floriano possessed a prudent distrust of his pretended friends, men whose real interest was to secure lucrative positions for themselves. He was sparing in words, kept his own opinions to himself, as far as possible avoided intimacies, was loyal to his comrades and never deserted his subordinates.

He occupied a strong position in the army, inferior to no other chieftain, not even to Deodoro. When differences arose, Deodoro could generally in the early stages of the argument rally the majority to his support; but, with the coming of reflection and more mature study, the situation was reversed, and Floriano emerged victorious, thanks to his logic, powers of persuasion, and superior intelligence.

Since we are to consider the administration of Floriano Peixoto in some detail, it will be well to cast a glance in retrospect at his activities in the latter days of the empire. In politics, he had been a pronounced liberal, with strong republican leanings. So true was this that when the so-called military question reached an acute state many suspected him of having abandoned the monarchy. Certain it is that he regarded the rule of a third Braganza as impossible of realization.

The chief of the last imperial cabinet, the Viscount of Ouro Preto, knowing that his minister of war, the Viscount of Maracajú, could not remain in office on account of his ill-health, had already invited Floriano to succeed him and the general had accepted. The fact is, however, that Floriano was aware of the coming revolution, and had held conferences with Deodoro a few days before the revolt took place. His respect for law was binding as long as it tended to reënforce his own authority; he was not the type of man to become involved in a mutiny or in the overthrow of a minister or cabinet. But when it was a question of a revolution, involving a complete change of régime, he would examine the case on its merits. In any case, he would stay with his comrades to the last.

Yet, in the events which preceded the *coup d'état* of the fifteenth of November, it is difficult to explain satisfactorily his position. The emperor and Ouro Preto simply regarded him as a traitor. This explanation of Floriano's actions is perhaps a little too easy. It seems probable that he did not realize the importance of the situation until shortly before it came to a head, that is, after his interview with Deodoro already mentioned. He then saw that the general was about to direct a rising of practically all of the forces in Rio de Janeiro, with at least the tacit support of the garrisons in the south. He knew that the civilian element was quite incapable of offering any resistance. He realized, too, that the abolition of the empire at this time merely meant anticipating by a few years an event which in any case was inevitable. To overcome one force by another would mean the division of the army into two hostile camps and the useless shedding of Brazilian blood. And to what end? Merely to postpone the advent of the new régime until the death of the reigning monarch. But though we may accept this explanation of his apparent disloyalty, it is clear that it was Floriano's duty to open the eyes of the government, even if he had decided to throw in his lot with the revolution. On this point the disloyalty of his conduct cannot be too severely censured.

The duplicity of Floriano was thoroughly understood by both parties; we have already noted the opinion of the monarchists. The attitude of the republicans is evidenced by the fact that in the provisional government he was appointed minister of war and later elected vice president of the republic in order to avoid the peril of a new betrayal. This distrust of Floriano was shared by Deodoro. He feared that if Floriano was not taken care of he might well become the center of the dissatisfied elements in the army and become their leader in any attack on the legal authorities.

Such was the man who succeeded the noble and sincere Marshal Deodoro as chief magistrate of the nation.

The Causes and Antecedents of the Naval Revolt of 1893.—The majority of the governors of the states had accepted Deodoro's *coup d'état* of November third. When the president resigned, their position became precarious. To leave them in power would be dangerous to Floriano, for like the majority of Deodoro's supporters and appointees they were hostile to the new executive. Yet, there was no legal way of removing them. On the other hand, Floriano, who already saw menacing clouds on the horizon, determined at any cost to get rid of these governors. He felt that he could not afford to allow local political situations to serve as a basis for attack on his régime. For this reason, he not only did not oppose but actually aided those state factions which rose against the former supporters of Deodoro and ousted them from power. These flagrantly illegal acts could have but one result. Floriano at once became the target for the furious imprecations of the ousted state officials and their partisans, and one and all joined the ranks of the vice president's most bitter opponents.

Difficulties growing out of the unhappy financial policy of earlier years also gave a solid basis to the growing hostility to the executive, hostility which was voiced in congress, in the press, and in the gatherings of local political groups. Opposition to Floriano on the part of both monarchists and republicans was slowly but inexorably coming to a head. Early in 1892 armed uprisings against the actions of the executive, especially the overthrow of the state governors, took place. In January two forts in Rio de Janeiro had to be silenced. In April thirteen generals wrote a joint letter to Floriano intimating that he should resign for the good of the nation; they received imprisonment and exile for their pains. In Minas Geraes, Matto Grosso, São Paulo, Rio de Janeiro, Amazonas, and Maranhão took place revolts which, however, were all suffocated. In Rio Grando do Sul, however, the disturbances assumed a very grave aspect. In this revolt the legitimacy of the republican institutions was called into question, owing to the influence of the monarchist senator, Gaspar da Silveira Martins. The headquarters of the "federal revolution," as it was called from an article of its political program, was to be found not far from the Uruguayan frontier and on frequent occasions Brazil was invaded by bands of irregulars organized on foreign soil.

Floriano's enemies, exaggerating and distorting his official acts, alleged that the vice president was aiming at the establishment of a permanent military dictatorship in order to avoid the election of a civilian at the end of the current presidential term in 1894. Such a step would assure the perpetuation in power of the military, the real authors of the proclamation of the republic in 1889.

The coördinating center of all of these plans and rumors was represented by a most heterogenous mingling of politicians of every stripe and from every quarter. Some were merely political climbers; others occupied high positions, including the minister of marine, Admiral Custodio José de Mello, who made a great parade of the resignation which he sent to Floriano in order to draw attention to himself. There were a few conscientious monarchists who hoped to abolish the republic. Still others were monarchist in sympathy but felt that the whole question of the future government of Brazil should be determined by a plebiscite. This lack of cohesion among his enemies proved the salvation of Floriano. He understood the situation perfectly and used every method at his disposal to create schisms among his opponents and to set the various factions by the ears. Events were to show that his enemies were quite incapable of sustained united action.

The Revolt of the Fleet.—There had long existed rivalries between the army and navy; intriguers and plotters against Floriano had naturally made the most of this hostility. Their task was not difficult. While the vast majority of the higher officers in the army were sincere republicans, there were many members in the navy who made no effort to conceal their monarchical sympathies. Among these officers stood out Admiral Luiz Philippe de Saldanha da Gama, a person of great prestige and remarkable achievements. He was the center of a large group of supporters. These men, principally in the younger rank, looked upon him with both affection and admiration, even though they did not all share his political views.

These disparate elements, united, as we have seen, only in their dislike and suspicion of Floriano, launched the long expected revolt on September 6, 1893, under the leadership of the ex-minister of marine, Admiral Custodio de Mello, who was, be it noted in passing, a sincere republican. Admiral Saldanha da Gama, at this time head of the naval academy, remained neutral. Later he joined the revolt with a program in which he urged that the entire nation be consulted on the form of government eventually to be adopted.

To appreciate the magnitude of the revolt one must remember that the opponents of Floriano had in their possession all of the craft anchored in the harbor of Rio de Janeiro. These included practically the entire Brazilian navy and a number of merchant ships. Admiral de Mello at once ordered the bombardment of the capital, at the same time intimating to the vice president the wisdom of resigning, even as Deodoro had resigned two years earlier. Although Floriano was taken by surprise at the outbreak of hostilities he not only refused to vacate his office, but he set about with great energy and vigor to fortify the capital.

At this critical moment he received unexpected and, as events turned out, decisive assistance from the foreign squadrons stationed in the harbor of Guanabara. Rio de Janiero was an open, unfortified city. As such, declared the commanders of the foreign fleet, it was by international law not liable to bombardment, and if it was necessary they would prevent such an act by force. Moreover, the capital had a large foreign population whose lives must not be placed in jeopardy. This decision of the foreign commanders was like a bolt from the blue. Admiral Custodio de Mello assumed, rightly enough, that the mere threat of knocking the city about the ears of its inhabitants would bring the vice president to terms. The whole success of his plans was thus predicated on immediate and decisive action. But now he suddenly found his hands tied. His most powerful weapon was wrested from him. To oppose the decision of the foreign commanders would have been the height of folly as their warships were far superior to his own both in number and effectiveness. Instead of the sudden attack and prompt issue which he had contemplated, he saw his fleet condemned to idleness. He had no foothold on the land; he had no means of raising money. To supply his crew with food, he was forced to practice virtual acts of piracy on the merchant ships which carried cargoes of provisions. The only actions in which he could engage were fruitless attempts to gain a foothold on the shores of the bay. In every instance they were beaten off by the territorial troops.

Custodio's hopes of victory began to dwindle. His initiative in launching the rebellion awakened no echo throughout the country. All of the states stuck by the legal authorities. The government of Floriano showed unexpected strength. On one occasion a number of foreign diplomats asked the vice president how he would receive small foreign contingents sent ashore to help protect the foreign residents in the capital. "With shot," answered the marshal. And he meant it. The query was never raised again.

Thanks to the tireless energy of Floriano in placing batteries in strategic localities throughout the city, the capital was finally placed in a state of defense. At great expense and effort a fleet was purchased abroad, manned, and trained. In the spring of 1894 it was finally assembled in Brazilian waters and on March 13 prepared to offer battle to the revolting squadron in the harbor itself. By this time the issue was no longer in doubt. Both the professional soldier as well as the informed civilian recognized that the game was up. Weakened by almost daily engagements with the batteries stationed along the littoral, short of crews and provisions, many of the larger of the revolting warships had abandoned the harbor of Rio de Janeiro and had made their way southward to unite their forces with the federalists of Rio Grande do Sul. The remnants of the naval forces in the harbor, under the command of Saldanha da Gama, were unfit for battle. Rather than surrender, Gama finally abandoned his ships and in company with some five hundred of his officers and men sought asylum on two Portuguese corvettes anchored in the harbor of Guanabara. The so-called legal fleet (*escuadra legal*) quietly took possession of the rebel's deserted ships. Meanwhile, Admiral Custodio de Mello had attempted in vain to seize an important harbor and establish a land basis for the revolt. After a particularly severe repulse in Rio Grande do Sul, he determined to place his vessels under the protection of Argentina. But Captain Alexandrino de Alencar, the commander of the largest ship of the fleet, the ironclad *Aquidaban*, refused to follow such a course. He advanced up the coast as far as Santa Catharina where the seat of the provisional revolutionary government was located. Here in the harbor of Desterro his ship was torpedoed by destroyers of the legal fleet on April 16, 1894. Thus ended this great naval adventure.

The Federalist Revolution.—The federalist revolt had been launched in Rio Grande do Sul as early as June, 1892. Admiral Custodio de Mello, at that time minister of marine, sympathized with the rebels from the first. Immediately after the revolt of the fleet in September, 1893, he placed himself in contact with the rebels by sending one of his ships to Santa Catharina, whose governor, he had learned, was hostile to vice president Floriano. On the arrival of this vessel a local junta was set up and a *point d'appui* on the littoral was established.

The greatest success of the federalists was in the state of Paraná. Here a concentration of troops from Rio Grande do Sul and Santa Catharina brought the entire state under subjection. The legal garrison, in the weak hands of General Pego Junior, offered no effective resistance. Some even go so far as to accuse the commander of treason. Thanks to these successes, the incursions of the federalists extended all the way from Rio Grande do Sul to Paraná and their chief, a hard fighter and capable leader named Gumercindo Saraïva, laid his plans for the invasion of São Paulo and even of Rio de Janeiro.

As long as the revolting fleet was in control of the harbor of Rio de Janeiro, it was not an easy task to organize troops to repel this invasion from the south. Little by little, however, there was accumulated in São Paulo a body of some six thousand loyal troops. Once the rebel fleet was disposed of, the government had its hands free to drive the federalists back into the southern states of the republic whence they had come. The one decisive action took place at Carovy, where Saraïva fell mortally wounded. Deprived of their leaders, the federalists began to break up into small bands and disperse.

The refugees on the Portuguese corvettes were transported on these little ships from Rio to Buenos Aires in April, 1894. Under circumstances which are still obscure, something like half of the men and officers contrived to escape and land on Argentine territory. They immediately crossed the river to Uruguay and hastened to join the federalists, who in full retreat were making every effort to reach neutral territory. On June 24, 1894, at Campo-Osorio, a bloody encounter took place between the legal troops and the remaining federalists. The major part of the sailors and officers who had escaped from Rio were slain. Among the bodies was that of Saldanha da Gama. With his death disappeared the dream of a monarchical restoration.

The revolution was crushed. To be sure, sporadic and desultory engagements took place for something like a year longer, but they were the last dying embers of a fire that was really spent. It would be hard to exaggerate the importance of the triumph of legality. The young republic had emerged triumphant though not unscathed from its first real baptism of fire. The victory of the government not only placed it on a firm foundation but also spelled the defeat of the cause of monarchy and parliamentarism. But the great service which Floriano Peixoto rendered Brazil was to consolidate and render impregnable a régime which under his predecessors was threatened with dissolution and disintegration. It was now clear to all that the republican formula alone possessed any real validity.

CHAPTER XIV

RECONSTRUCTION [1]

THE BANNER of the republic floated victoriously over a field of battle strewn with ruins, dead, and wounded. To bury the dead, to bind up the wounds of the suffering, and to reconstruct the civil and political life of Brazil was the mission of the civil government. These were tasks replete with difficulties. The new president, elected for the term 1894-1898, was Senator Prudente José de Moraes Barros, a distinguished civilian and a son of the great state of São Paulo. We have already met him as president of the constituent assembly over whose deliberations he presided with unquestioned authority. Later he filled with equal competency the post of vice president of the federal senate.

Presidential Election of Prudente de Moraes.—The tasks confronting the new executive might well be described as Herculean. In the first place it was necessary to restore peace. It was not merely a question of stopping bloodshed; the moral aspects of the problem were even more important. The civil war had barbarized the country, dividing the Brazilians into two hostile camps, and, as is only too often the case, created permanent hatred between the adversaries. It diverted into sterile and ferocious conflicts resources which were sorely needed for reconstruction.

Unhappily, the revolution had created a special kind of mental attitude which survived active hostility. The combatants, both regulars and volunteers, regarded themselves as heroes, apostles of a political credo, unique agents of the triumph of a new faith. As long as the battle was raging such psychology was comprehensible. But when the fighting was over these super patriots remained, as far as their mental outlook was concerned, still under arms, mobilized for action against the "enemies of the republic." Like the Bourbons, they had learned nothing and forgotten nothing, and refused stubbornly to let bygones be bygones.

Although Floriano does not appear to have directly intervened in the political maneuvers which preceded the election of his suc-

---

[1] The events described in this chapter are taken up from a somewhat different point of view and with greater brevity by the translator in Rippy, Martin, and Cox, *Argentina, Brazil, and Chile,* Chap. XXI—P.A.M.

cessor, a number of groups close to him, including his intimates, hoped to postpone the inauguration of the new president. They made a great parade of consulting a number of the higher officers in the army regarding the wisdom of a change in the executive while the country was still unsettled. The results in general gave no comfort to those who would prolong Floriano's rule; nevertheless, up to the very day of Prudente's inauguration, November 15, 1894, these rumors of a plot against the president-elect were so insistent that great uneasiness prevailed throughout the entire republic.

The best proof that Floriano never seriously considered such a *coup d'état* is the fact of his retirement. He possessed both the forces and resources necessary to remain in power had he so desired.

Hostility of the Army.—It is a fact, nevertheless, that Prudente was looked upon with suspicion and dislike by the army. This is no occasion for surprise. The civilian president, by virtue of his high office, was now in a position to wield the power which the military had created through great efforts and sacrifice. Did Prudente mean perhaps to deprive the armed forces of the fruits of their exertions? What were his real intentions? What would be his attitude toward them? Would he follow the same lines as his predecessor, or would he try to undo all that Floriano had accomplished? Would he prove a friend or foe of the officers and enlisted men? Had he not been Deodoro's opponent in the first presidential election when he defended the cause of the civilians against the militarists? In fine, the attitude of the army was distinctly hostile and boded no good for the new administration.

Prudente's inaugural manifesto slightly allayed this distrust. On the other hand, his program of a much-needed pacification was ill-received in Rio Grande do Sul but recently the theater for a fratricidal civil war. In addition to the regular army, there were the so-called patriotic volunteers to be reckoned with. Many of these latter were not at all anxious to have hostilities cease as they were drawing double pay for their services. Resentment against the government in Rio de Janeiro took the form of lawless agitation in the military school. This situation was due in large part to Floriano. During his administration discipline was relaxed and the higher command had lost the respect of the students, many of whom had taken part in the crushing of the naval revolt of 1893. They were so little inclined to submit to discipline that in March, 1895, the government of Prudente was forced to resort to extreme measures. As punishment for their disobedience, many of the students were reduced to the rank of privates, while the higher officers were distributed among the different states.

Restoration of Order.—It was not until August 23, 1895, that peace with the vanquished revolutionists was finally signed. Congress voted a general amnesty which it was hoped would heal the many wounds caused by the rebellion and make possible an era of reconciliation.

These hopes were slow in being realized. The navy, smarting under its defeat, was jealous of the laurels won by the army. Many elements among the military still refused to accord Prudente their full confidence. Yet, little by little, the situation improved. Rodrigues Alves, the capable minister of finance, proved successful in repairing many of the blunders of his predecessors, and brought in a much needed era of financial convalescence.

International relations also showed an improvement. Relations with Portugal which had been broken off during the naval revolt of 1893-1894 were renewed through the good offices of Great Britain. The vexed frontier question with Argentina—the so-called "Misiones" dispute—was solved by the arbitral award of President Grover Cleveland in February, 1895, with an almost complete recognition of the claims of Brazil. At this time was evidenced a real anxiety on the part of the Brazilian people to solve their various boundary controversies. The movement once launched never ceased until all of Brazil's territorial disputes with its neighbors were amicably settled. We shall have occasion to revert to this topic when we come to discuss the activities of the Baron of Rio Branco.

International difficulties of a somewhat different order arose in 1896. At two different points the national territory was invaded: by England, which seized the island of Trinidad;[2] and by France, which occupied the area in dispute between Brazil and French Guiana. When supplied with the proofs of the right of Brazil over

---

[2] This islet, lying off the coast of Brazil in south latitude 20°31′, is of course not to be confused with the British crown colony of Trinidad in the West Indies.—P.A.M.

Trinidad, Great Britain nobly withdrew all its claims to this un-inhabited islet. As for the French Government, an agreement was reached for the submission of the controversy to the arbitration of the Swiss Government. A new spirit of continental solidarity and international coöperation was inaugurated under the exceed-ingly competent direction of a great minister of foreign relations, Carlos Augusto de Carvalho.

Despite these unmistakable symptoms of convalescence, new obstacles to progress and national appeasement arose in the early months of 1897. In November, 1896, Prudente fell dangerously ill. The vice president, Manuel Victorino Pereira, took over his duties and, assuming, perhaps that he would be called upon to fill out the four-year presidential term, endeavored to follow out his own ideas and plans. In many respects these differed widely from those of the president and when Prudente, after four months' retirement, took up again the reins of power, relations between the two magis-trates became tense. It is possible that Prudente acted with un-necessary brusqueness on this occasion; in any event, Manuel Victorino, his dignity offended, became the head of the opposition to the executive.

Fanaticism in the Sertão.[3]—These differences would probably have amounted to little but for a series of strange and disquieting developments in the north which brought the administration of Prudente to the verge of disaster. In the spring of 1897 a body of federal troops, sent into the interior of the state of Bahia to disperse a body of fanatics, suffered a crushing defeat and the loss of its arms and munitions to the enemy. A wave of wrath and indignation swept the republic from north to south. The possibility of such a defeat had never even been considered. In the prevailing atmosphere of suspicions and recriminations, the most absurd and improbable rumors gained ready credence. Many Brazilians, especially the enemies of Prudente, saw or pretended to see in this disaster a conspiracy of the "enemies of the republic," intent on a monarchical restoration. Things reached such a pass that an in-surrection all but broke out in Rio de Janeiro; the lives of two of the most widely known monarchists were threatened, and a parti-san of the empire, Colonel Gentil de Castro, was assassinated.

---

[3] An excellent account of the so-called Canudos affair is given by R. B. Cunninghame-Graham in *A Brazilian Mystic.*—(New York, 1920).

In reality, the monarchical plot was pure fantasy, a figment of the imagination. The truth was utterly different. The population of the *sertão* or interior of Bahia is a mass of ignorant folk, descendants of the early Portuguese settlers crossed with Indian and Negro strains. They adhere to a Christianity *sui generis*, in which Catholic dogma is adulterated with beliefs and practices imported by the former slaves from Africa. In this curious religious amalgam, gross superstitions and downright idolatry naturally play a large part.

On various occasions since the days of independence fanatical outbreaks, the results of psychopathic conditions, have introduced this strange note into Brazilian history. Usually these outbreaks begin with the disordered activities of a penitent, who has repaired to some solitary or desert region to do penance for his sins. If, however, the religious exile is an uneducated person, he is apt to develop into an apostle of a new creed, generally repulsive both to morals and common sense. A few instances may be cited. In Ceará, during the period of the regency, one of these half-sane individuals, called Antonio Manoel de Sousa, wrought great evils. In Rio Grande do Sul in the seventies a sect known as the *Muckers*, composed of German colonists headed by a family by the name of Maurer, caused so many disturbances that they had to be put down by public force. When, in 1874, the metric system was adopted, mobs known as *quebra-kilos* started veritable riots in their endeavor to smash the new weights and measures. And finally, in recent years, from 1912 to 1915, in both Paraná and Santa Catharina very grave uprisings were caused by groups of fanatics known as *monges* (monks).

In the present instance, an old *fazendeiro* of Ceará, one Antonio Vicente Mendes Maciel, later known as Antonio Conselheiro, after suffering a great deal at the hands of local petty authorities, fled into the *sertão* of Bahia. There he wandered from fazenda to fazenda, living on alms, halting from time to time in the villages to preach and do penance for his sins. In his crude sermons he exhorted his hearers to construct chapels and oratories throughout the countryside.

It is obvious that he was not of sound mind. His doctrine was an absurd mixture of primitive Christianity, grotesque superstitions, and hatred against all authority. It was clearly a psychopathic case which at the outset should have been handled with patience and Christian charity, preferably by members of the clergy. Instead, the half-insane old man was regarded as a political menace and was hounded from pillar to post.

The ignorant crowds who little by little joined themselves to Antonio Conselheiro, as he was now called, were at first largely impelled by a gregarious instinct. Naturally inclined to fanaticism, they soon came to have unlimited faith in their leader. Multitudes arrived from the most remote *sertaões* of the state, or even from neighboring states, in order to see and hear this superman who had inspired their faith and devotion.

At length Conselheiro, apparently tired of these wanderings, settled down in an abandoned ranch known as Canudos, in a remote section of Bahia. Here, in a large town of huts, thousands of his followers carried on a lawless and promiscuous existence. Depredations and disorders, tolerated by their chief, became so numerous that the government of Bahia found itself obliged to intervene in order to put down this growing anarchy. But it proved no easy task to suppress this focus of turbulence and iniquity. Appeals by the clergy met with no response. Bodies of state police, even when reënforced by a few federal troops, were repulsed. A fundamental mistake, repeated again and again, was the failure of the authorities to recognize the seriousness of their task.

In 1896, after the defeat of a column commanded by Major Febronio de Brito, it was decided to despatch a body of troops strong enough to crush once for all Conselheiro and his followers. The expedition succeeded in overcoming the resistance of the fanatics, and managed to gain possession of their stronghold. At the close of the fight, however, a bullet struck down the military chief, Colonel Moreira Cesar. His subordinates possessed little military ability and a panic broke out followed by a riot. It was, in truth, a very serious defeat of the government forces. As a result of this fact, which in a way was quite fortuitous, the prestige of Conselheiro grew enormously and his supporters increased by thousands. Moreover arms, munitions, and military equipment of all sort had been captured in immense quantities.

The effect on public opinion of this disaster was overwhelming. The man in the street suspected that behind Conselheiro and his *sertanejos* were powerful and dangerous influences; the population at large finally came to believe that a vast conspiracy was on foot looking to the restoration of the monarchy. Though a greater mistake could hardly have been made, the opinion persisted and accounted in large part for the uneasiness in the capital.

A supreme effort was now launched by the government to bring this costly and wretched affair to an end. This time, adequate preparations were made and, after a long and bloody siege, Canudos was taken by storm on October 5, 1897. But in the interval grave events had occurred in Rio.

Once more the military school had staged a mutiny and had to be disbanded by the government. The parliamentary opposition to Prudente, which had increased as a result of the unhappy events just narrated, was composed of the most divergent elements. The representatives of the southern states, where the revolt of 1893-1894 had been most violent and where fierce political passions still smouldered, connived with the military deputies and other exalted elements to form a factious, intolerant, and aggressive group almost as large as the official majority which supported the president. In fact, the difference between the government and the opposition amounted to scarcely half a dozen votes.

In this atmosphere, surcharged with mutual recriminations, almost anything might happen. The inhabitants of Rio had the feeling that they were standing on the brink of a volcano. All feared that an explosion of some kind was imminent. The partisan press instead of trying to allay the tension added fuel to the fire. The blow fell on November 5, 1897. On this date, Prudente went to the war arsenal to meet a body of troops returning from Canudos. Here he was the object of a cowardly and murderous attacked by a common soldier who immediately committed suicide. Although the president himself escaped unscathed the minister of war, Marshal Carlos Machado Bittencourt, fell a victim to his loyalty to his chief. Another officer of high rank, Luiz Mendes de Moraes, later general and marshal, was gravely wounded. Both had nobly done their duty in protecting the person of the president.

The impression caused by this criminal attack on Prudente was tremendous. It was now clearly seen that the moral responsibility really rested with those guilty of the exaggerations and excesses of the parliamentary opposition to the president. In the reaction which followed this dastardly act the leaders and foremost members of this opposition were accused of being accomplices of the criminal. Although these charges were never really proven, they were sufficient to seal the political doom of Prudente's enemies. All those who were suspected of even countenancing such methods were avoided as if they were smitten with the plague. As a consequence, the last year of Prudente's term of office was calm. He was able to render one more service to his country, and a capital one at that, by paving the way for the financial reorganization of Brazil.

Financial Reorganization. Campos Salles President.—Prudente's minister of finance, Rodrigues Alves, had already prepared the ground for such an operation when he had courageously set forth the precarious and even desperate condition of the treasury. In March and April of 1898, he signed with the foreign holders of Brazilian securities an agreement whose chief provision was the funding of the unpaid interest for three years. By this means he hoped to find a breathing spell during which he might prepare a budget adequate to meet these new demands. Credit for this funding scheme was due the London and River Plate Bank and its emissary, Mr. Tootal, President Prudente and his then minister of finance, Bernardino de Campos, and the president-elect, Manoel Ferraz de Campos Salles. The coöperation of the future president was at this juncture all important. Campos Salles chanced to be in Europe at this time. While in London he took a personal part in the negotiations and pledged his whole-hearted support during the forthcoming administration to carry out the provisions of the funding loan.[4]

On November 15, 1898, Prudente's term as president came to an end and he left office with the affection and good will of his

---

[4] Dr. Calogeras' account of the funding loan is too brief to be entirely clear. The translator has ventured to quote a paragraph from his own account of this transaction, "Through the skillful negotiations of Campos Salles, was arranged the famous funding loan—called in Brazil *o funding*—of June 15, 1898. By the terms of this loan Brazil was able to dispose of her bonds at par for a total of £8,613,717, a financial success equalled only once before in the history of the country. These bonds were to bear interest at five per cent with one-half per cent amortization, and run for sixty-three years, the loan being secured by the collection in gold of import duties. And what was fully as important, interest payments in specie were to be suspended for three years—their place being taken by bonds—and amortization suspended for ten years." Rippy, Martin, and Cox, *Argentina, Brazil, and Chile*, p. 299.—P.A.M.

fellow-citizens. His successor was another civilian and *Paulista,* Campos Salles. As already noted, his chief concern was the financial rehabilitation of Brazil and to this task he devoted his utmost efforts. Fortunately, he was ably seconded by one of the greatest financial ministers in the history of Brazil, Dr. Joaquim Murtinho.

The new executive carried out his promises to the letter. Not only were the provisions of the funding loan scrupulously fulfilled, but a whole series of supplementary measures were taken to assure the necessary resources for meeting the deferred payments. Both the president and his able finance minister were reaping in peace what their predecessors had sown in trouble. Recovery and growing prosperity were everywhere manifest. Never before had the marvelous recuperative powers of Brazil been more in evidence. Promptly on the appointed date Brazil met its obligations in full.

The activities of the administration in other fields may be noted. During the incumbency of Campos Salles, international affairs were conducted in harmony with Brazil's traditional policy of sincerity, good faith, and continental solidarity. In 1900, the long-standing dispute with France over the boundary between Brazil and French Guiana was settled through the arbitration of the Swiss Government. In 1901, the controversy with England over the boundary with British Guiana was submitted to the arbitration of the king of Italy. To the terms of the settlement of this thorny problem we shall return later. Relations with Argentina were placed on a more friendly footing through the exchange of visits between Presidents Campos Salles and Roca. The first steps were taken toward the enactment of a federal civil code. The management of the state railroads had long been a grievous burden on the federal exchequer; arrangements were made for the leasing of most of the lines to private companies.

Presidential Election of Rodrigues Alves.—Thanks to the sacrifices of the Brazilian people and the able husbanding of national resources under Campos Salles, Brazil found itself on the eve of an era of prosperity. This happy situation was frankly recognized in the election on November 15, 1902, of the third civilian president of Brazil, Francisco de Paula Rodrigues Alves. So complete was Brazil's financial recovery that the new executive did not hesitate to declare that the country was at length in a position to face the future with complete confidence. The government, he intimated, would offer every legitimate encouragement to the development of Brazil's vast potentialities.

For the prosecution of the great program of national development the new president surrounded himself with competent aids. His ministry was an unusually strong one. For the first time the navy had at its head a minister, Julio de Noronha, who fully rose to the level of his responsibilities, both as a leader and an administrator. The portfolio of finance was turned over to the able hands of Leopoldo de Bulhões, whose achievements we shall have occasion to summarize at the end of President Rodrigues Alves' administration. The expansion of port works and railroads, and the development of the natural resources of the country were under the competent direction of Lauro Müller, the minister of industry. He shared with the municipal prefect, Pereira Passos, the responsibility of transforming Rio de Janeiro from an old colonial city into a great modern capital. Public health, one of the chief preoccupations of the president, was entrusted to Dr. Oswaldo Cruz, a brilliant young physician who was one of the first to grasp the supreme importance of sanitation.

The task of Dr. Cruz was indeed a formidable one. He was called upon to cope with those recurring scourges of Brazil: yellow fever, smallpox, and bubonic plague. He began his mission with a definite program. He was given full freedom of action and resources adequate to carry out his vast sanitary campaign. What was equally important he was assured by the president that he would be unhindered by obstacles thrown in his path by politicians. The necessity for this latter proviso was soon apparent. Hardly had Dr. Cruz's program been announced than there appeared an extremely strong opposition, recruited chiefly from a group of politicians and army officers eager to discredit the administration and to revive the old idea of a military dictatorship. The president was under no illusions as to the motives of these attacks on Dr. Cruz. He realized fully that the protests against the new measures were but pretexts to overthrow the lawful government. Calmly and unflinchingly, Rodrigues Alves carried out his duties. Despite threats and attempted intimidation, he despatched forces against the mutineers and ruthlessly quelled attempts at armed revolt. The efforts of Oswaldo Cruz, so loyally supported by the president, were crowned with complete success. At the conclusion of his term of office, the president could point with satisfaction to the extinction of yellow fever and bubonic plague, and the rapid disappearance of smallpox.

Boundary Questions.—The administration was equally successful in its handling of international relations, especially boundary controversies. Of these, the most vexatious was with the republic of Bolivia. This dispute had so many ramifications, even including a threat to the peace of the continent, that we are justified in taking it up in some detail. The boundary between the two republics had been defined by a treaty signed in 1869. The line traversed an immense, little-known area of dense equatorial forests in which rubber trees grew in great abundance. The increasing world demand for rubber eventually led to a desire to exploit this district. While access from Bolivia was difficult, no special obstacles existed on the Brazilian side. It was natural, therefore, that the area absorbed many Brazilians, chiefly from the northwestern states of the republic. Left more or less to their own ways and devices in this immense area so far from civilization, these Brazilian rubber gatherers developed a crude political and social organization of their own, in which the sovereignty of Bolivia was largely ignored. Such a situation could not last. The Acre, as this district was called, belonged to Bolivia and, as was perfectly natural, this republic determined to impose its authority. Prior to 1902 it made three different attempts, all of which were failures. In point of fact, the territory was independent. Nowhere were the lawful Bolivian authorities recognized. The population, overwhelmingly Brazilian as we have just seen, demanded annexation to Brazil. The government of Rio rejected all such overtures as it had no desire to interfere in a zone admittedly belonging to another nation.

Since Bolivia possessed no means of making its authority respected, it finally, in desperation, determined to grant the better part of the territory as a concession to a North American syndicate. The transfer of this princely domain to the virtual control of a foreign corporation caused a tremendous and painful impression throughout South America, especially in the countries adjacent to the Acre. Brazil controlled the means of access to the territory; without its consent and good will the value of the concession was nil. Not only Brazil but all of South America felt that their interests were jeopardized through the implanting in our hemisphere of the lamentable system of chartered companies, which had contributed so greatly to the growth of conflicts in Asia and Africa, as well as to the disintegration of these great continents.

Those most immediately involved were naturally the inhabitants of the territory in question. The *Acreanos* cared nothing about laws and treaty rights. But they were determined that they would not be turned over to a foreign syndicate, and forthwith began to arm themselves. The Bolivian government sent a military expedition to cope with the threatened uprising. Thereupon Brazil courteously pointed out to the government of La Paz that it could not look upon such a step, in which lives of its citizens were involved, with indifference. Brazil also raised certain questions of treaty interpretations and, to give point to these veiled remonstrances, despatched troops to protect the lives of Brazilians who had settled in the districts close to the Acre frontier.

Such was the grave problem, vital to all of South America, which our department of state had to face.

The Baron of Rio Branco.—To the post of minister of foreign affairs, Rodrigues Alves had invited the Baron of Rio Branco, the victorious defender in two thorny boundary disputes, those of the Misiones territory and the French-Guiana-Brazilian frontier, submitted respectively to the arbitration of President Cleveland and the Swiss Government. And now, at one of the most perilous junctures in the international relations of the entire continent, this great chancellor, through his skill, sense of realities, and diplomatic tact, forged an instrument of South American peace and solidarity. At the same time, he removed the threatening precedent of the establishment in the heart of the continent of a powerful and all but sovereign chartered commercial organization. The tragic example of Africa was not ignored.

The terms of the settlement were simple. Brazil acquired the rights of the syndicate which thus abandoned the concession. The treaty with Bolivia signed on November 17, 1903, provided for an exchange of territories and other compensations.[5] It was a triumph for Brazil and a service to all of South America.

---

[5] Dr. Calogeras' account of the terms of the settlement of the Acre dispute is perhaps too summary. Brazil bought out the syndicate for £100,000. By the Treaty of Petropolis, Brazil secured the major portion of the Acre, for

The settlement of the Acre difficulty inaugurated the most brilliant phase of Brazilian diplomacy, which extended through the incumbency of four presidents, from 1902 to 1912. During all of this time, the portfolio of foreign affairs was held by the Baron of Rio Branco. We have already noted the success of this able diplomat in defending the rights of Brazil in its controversy with Argentina over the Misiones District and with France over French Guiana. During the decade 1902-1910, the outstanding differences with practically all of Brazil's remaining neighbors were satisfactorily adjusted.[6] The only real disappointment suffered by Brazil was the outcome of the boundary controversy with British Guiana, submitted as we have seen to the arbitration of the king of Italy. Brazil's case was handled by Joaquim Nabuco. The decision did not grant us all we felt entitled to. No blame, however, is to be attached to the negotiator; rather was it the fault of the doctrine which in more than one case had been followed by Italy; namely, that in questions of arbitration, political as well as juridical factors are to be taken into account.

The Baron of Rio Branco died on February 11, 1912. During his term of office, Brazil's traditional policy of friendship and continental solidarity had been carried to its furthest limits. The Pan-American Conference held in Rio de Janeiro in 1906 is a case in point. Although chronologically the third of such gatherings, it was really the first to elaborate a specific and practicable program which was still further developed in the conferences of Buenos Aires (1910), Santiago (1924), and Havana (1928).

Arbitration as a means of settling difficulties between nations is for Brazil a sort of international religion whose greatest interpreter was Rio Branco. When he assumed his duties as minister of foreign affairs, the only two arbitration treaties to which Brazil was a party were with Chile and Argentina. Both had been negotiated in the early days of the republic. As a result of his initiative, twenty-nine additional treaties, designed to cover every kind of international misunderstanding, were signed. Among these

which it paid Bolivia £2,000,000 as indemnity. Brazil aso agreed to build a railroad around the falls of the Madeira, thus giving the hinterland of Bolivia access to the Atlantic. This whole subject is discussed briefly but adequately by Raul d'Eça in his article "The Boundary Settlement of Brazil," in Rippy, Martin, and Cox, *Argentina, Brazil, and Chile*, pp. 447-68.—P.A.M.

[6] The details of these settlements may be found in the article by Raul d'Eça cited above.

instruments was a treaty with Uruguay which greatly liberalized, in a sense favorable to the southern republic, the existing boundary settlement of 1851-1852.[7]

Despite the memorable achievements of the administration of Rodrigues Alves, the president was never popular among the politicians. On the other hand, he held the affection and esteem of the nation at large. He was a monarchist and as such was an object of suspicion by the more exalted adherents of the republican creed. Moreover, he did not enjoy the full confidence of the great state of São Paulo. The *Paulistas* never forgave him for his opposition to their scheme for the "valorization" of coffee and for his refusal to support one of their favorite sons, Bernardino de Campos, as his successor. In both respects the instinct of the president was sound. The candidacy of Bernardino was opposed by the majority of the states, while history has shown that attempts by the government artificially to raise the price of coffee have merely aggravated the ill they were designed to remedy.

The Election of Affonso Penna.—On November 15, 1906, Affonso Penna assumed office. An able and honest man, he was chiefly interested in the economic advance of Brazil. He was convinced that one of the chief obstacles to the increase of national production was the continual fluctuation of the exchange. In order to secure the much needed stabilization he founded the *Caixa de Conversão.* This "Conversion Bureau," as it may be translated, received gold at a fixed rate against which it issued gold certificates payable on sight in metal. Thanks to this arrangement the circulating medium henceforth had a fixed value, and as such greatly helped to foster production. Under Penna, the army was reorganized and strengthened and the efficiency of the navy was increased by the addition of a number of new units. Railway mileage showed a marked advance; by 1910, the total extension amounted to 21,467 kilometers. The exposition held at Rio de Janeiro the same year strikingly revealed the growth and extent of the nation's industries.

From the political point of view, the presidential term of Affonso Penna closed a phase in our history. Up to that time presidents had been selected on the basis of their personal qualities or their devotion to public interests. The four civilian magistrates

[7] It provided *inter alia* for the joint navigation of Lagôa Mirim and the Jaguarão River.—P.A.M.

who held office from 1894 to 1909 were citizens of outstanding ability with a long list of public achievements to their credit. Their names became symbols of honor, industry, and patriotism in the best sense of the word.

Unfortunately, during the incumbency of Penna new elements came to assert themselves. Men began to appear in public life who were more interested in feathering their own nests or advancing the interest of their party than in striving for the public weal. It must be said in all conscience that much of the responsibility for this unhappy situation rested squarely on the shoulders of the president himself. He had two grave faults—a stubbornness in pursuing his own course beyond all reason, and a certain laxity in resisting inopportune demands put forward by representatives of the army. The full effects of these attempts of the military to play once more a predominant part in politics were not to appear until the next presidential election.

Penna, who was well along in the sixties, was not a strong man physically. Kindly, affectionate, and warm-hearted, he was not cut out for the rough and tumble battle of politics. He was very sensitive by nature and looked upon all opposition as a personal affront, or at least a desertion on the part of his friends. Shortly after he assumed office, he lost his son, in whom he had placed all his hopes and affection. This blow he never survived and he died in the early summer of 1909.

Nilo Peçanha, Vice President.—On June 14, 1909, the vice president, Nilo Peçanha, took over the presidency as provided by the constitution. The new executive at once showed that he possessed real capacity and, though he remained in office but seventeen months, his influence on the march of public events was considerable. He called to his side ministers of marked ability, while keeping in office Rio Branco and Alexandrino de Alencar as ministers of foreign affairs and marine respectively. A new ministry was founded, that of agriculture; a number of ironclads built in England arrived in Brazil, and aroused great enthusiasm both in the navy and the public at large. Finances, once more under the competent guidance of Leopoldo de Bulhões, were flourishing. The ministry of public works, entrusted to Francisco de Sá, was extremely active, especially in measures designed to cope with the recurrent drouths in the northeast of Brazil. Railroad mileage showed a further increase while great impetus was given to the improvement of port facilities.

The last months of the incumbency of Peçanha were embittered by dissensions both within and without congress on the choice of the future president and vice president. Since the days of Prudente, or even earlier, the outgoing president by virtue of his position in the dominant political party had usually been able to dictate the choice of his successor. Nilo Peçanha was no exception to this rule and after some hesitancy threw the force of the administration in favor of the minister of war, Marshal Hermes Rodrigues da Fonseca, the nephew of Deodoro, the first president of the republic. On the other hand, the minister of agriculture, Antonio Candido Rodrigues, a strong *Paulista*, with a long and distinguished public career to his credit, was heart and soul opposed to any candidate who might in any wise represent the army, and in this opposition to a possible revival of militarism he had the enthusiastic backing of his native state. As was to be expected, the members of the army, with a few exceptions, rallied to the support of Hermes. The divergence of views between President Peçanha and the minister of agriculture became so marked that the latter at length tendered his resignation. His successor was a man of no consequence, a mere party hack, who, though a *Paulista*, devoted all his time and energy to furthering the cause of Hermes through the disposal of patronage and subsidies. Brazil is still paying for this practice of corrupting the electorate for the benefit of the party in power.

After interminable discussions and dissensions, in which the executive came in for a great deal of caustic criticism, the official candidates finally chosen for the succeeding quadrennium were Marshal Hermes for the presidency and Wenceslau Braz Pereira Gomes for the vice presidency.[8]

[8] For reasons which are not clear, Dr. Calogeras has chosen to pass over in silence one of the most significant and dramatic features of the presidential election of 1910, namely, the campaign of the great jurist and political figure Ruy Barbosa, the candidate of the so-called *Civilista* party. As standard bearer of this new party, Ruy Barbosa stumped the country, a procedure hitherto unknown in Brazilian political life. The chief burden of his impassioned addresses was the danger of a revival of militarism which he declared would be inevitable with the election of his opponent. Though the official candidate won by a large majority, the supporters of Ruy have always asserted he was defrauded of the election through corruption and duress at the polls. *Cf.* Rippy, Martin, and Cox, *Argentina, Brazil, and Chile*, pp. 246-47.—P.A.M.

CHAPTER XV

THE RECRUDESCENCE OF MILITARISM; TRIUMPH OF THE CIVILIAN GOVERNMENTS; THE LAST PRESIDENCIES

The Presidency of Hermes da Fonseca.—The presidency of Marshal Hermes was a disappointment from the first. As minister of war under Penna, he had shown real capacity in the reorganization of the army and had enjoyed considerable popularity. The fact, too, that he was the nephew of the glorious founder of the republic stood him for a time in good stead. But all this was to change when he became the chief magistrate of the republic. He found it impossible, it seemed, to deny anything to anybody, particularly when tearful petitioners would appeal to the emotions of the soft-hearted president. His friends, real or alleged, were quick to appreciate this weakness and exploited it to the full.

Worse was to come. Most of the president's life had been spent in army circles, and he was particularly amenable to the influence of the military. Of any knowledge of politics in the finer sense or of even the rudiments of public administration he was quite innocent. He lacked any real energy; he worked by fits and starts, and seldom chose the propitious moments to put his plans into execution. Moreover, he found himself the prisoner of an electoral platform in which he had promised much more than it was humanly possible to carry out.

One of these promises was that his government would be strictly civilian in character. But the military, who detested the *bachareis*[1] and their methods of administration, had only contempt for Hermes' efforts to carry out this pledge, with the result that the president quickly found himself on bad terms with his old brothers-in-arms.

The president was soon involved in difficulties in another quarter. In his electoral program he had promised to rid the country of its local political bosses. This meant in effect the overthrow of a number of oligarchies which had governed the smaller states for

---

[1] Literally "bachelors" (*i.e.*, graduates of the *liceu*), a term contemptuously applied by the army to legislators and long-winded speakers.—P.A.M.

many years, in some cases on their own account, in others as mere dummies of powerful local chieftains. But the chief result of Hermes' efforts to do way with these abuses was to arouse bitter local and state antagonism against the executive and the central government.

The truth of the matter was that the president did not possess either the character or will power resolutely to grapple with these problems. In a futile effort to satisfy the complaints which poured in upon him, he made promises right and left which he was powerless to keep. Naturally, he pleased no one. He was accused of following a policy of deceit, hypocrisy, and double-dealing, and his enemies did not scruple to impugn publicly his honor and sincerity.

The weakness of the administration was strikingly revealed shortly after the president's inauguration. A full-fledged mutiny suddenly flared up in the fleet as a consequence of the cruel treatment visited upon the crews of the new dreadnaughts recently arrived from England. A number of officers were murdered and the twelve-inch guns of the battleships were trained on the capital. Since the government had no means of silencing them, it made an ignominious capitulation to the rebels. When, however, a short time afterward a minor revolt occurred on other vessels and in the Naval Battalion it was crushed ruthlessly.

A feeling of uncertainty and malaise began to pervade the country. Smouldering resentment against the executive threatened to break out into open rebellion in a number of the states, notably São Paulo and Bahia. While the former state could bid defiance to the federal government with a certain degree of impunity, Hermes made short work of the opposition forces elsewhere. Partly at the behest of his ministers of war and communication, the president employed federal troops to overthrow the state governments of Bahia, Pernambuco, Ceará, and Alagoas. The resentment which this policy of violence and illegality aroused was so great that the minister of marine, Marques de Leão, resigned his office as a protest. The great Baron of Rio Branco, old and in poor health, likewise presented his resignation. He was so shocked and disillusioned by the administration of Marshal Hermes that he died soon afterward.

Pinheiro Machado.—As was to be expected, these and similar happenings brought the administration into great disrepute. Even the army and the navy voiced dissatisfaction when Hermes employed the armed forces of the country for the ousting of the governments of his political enemies. It was pointed out, however, by officers and civilians alike—and this was regarded by many as an attenuation of Hermes' offenses—that in following these illegal and arbitrary courses the president was a mere instrument in the hands of Senator Pinheiro Machado, the real chief of the party in power.

In point of fact, Pinheiro was indubitably the dominating influence in Brazilian politics at that time. He represented in the senate the state of Rio Grande do Sul. His energy and ruthlessness had won him a certain reputation and prestige which dated from the establishment of the republic. During the administration of Prudente de Moraes, he had joined the opposition, although at all times he tried to exercise a moderating influence. Campos Salles had enjoyed his unswerving support. He disapproved of the election of Rodrigues Alves, on the ground that he could not support an ex-monarchist. Yet such was his inconsistency that he later threw his support to Affonso Penna who likewise had been a monarchist. He felt no enthusiasm for Hermes, as he had already taken the measure of the nephew of the founder of the republic. But realizing the inevitability of Hermes' election, he had made a virtue of necessity and strongly supported his candidacy, hoping that after his inauguration he could exert a salutary influence on the president.

These hopes were realized only in small part, owing to the instability of the president and to his disposition to follow the advice of those who had last caught his ear, particularly if they happened to belong to the military. A growing estrangement took place between the nation and the executive. Suspension of constitutional guarantees, disregard of law and justice, unrestrained party violence became the order of the day. The financial situation aggravated by the outbreak of the European war became so parlous that in August, 1914, a new issue of paper money took place and in October of the same year a new funding loan had to be contracted in London. It is now generally recognized that the administration of Hermes da Fonseca has been the weakest in the entire history of republican Brazil.

Hermes had for Pinheiro Machado great respect and consideration and was exceedingly anxious to make him his successor. Under
normal conditions the task would have been relatively easy. But,
unfortunately, Pinheiro had become so identified in the mind of the
public with Hermes' excesses and mistakes that his prestige suffered severely. The feeling was widespread, both in military as well
as civilian circles, that Pinheiro was the real inspirer of Hermes'
political blunders.

Nonetheless, the senator from Rio Grande do Sul had certain
elements in his favor. The president, as we have seen, was devoted
to him. Rio Grande do Sul and the smaller states were under his
control. On the other hand, the great states of Minas Geraes, São
Paulo, Pernambuco, and Bahia were in frank opposition. In
general, it may be said that Pinheiro's opponents not only objected
to his domineering mood and imperious methods, but also harbored
a deep suspicion that he was responsible for the anti-liberal tendencies of Hermes' administration.

What would have been the results had Pinheiro persisted in being
a candidate for the presidency? The answer is not easy. But this
much is certain. The country would have been rent by further
dissensions at a particularly critical and delicate moment. The
European war was beginning to produce its disastrous effects,
among which were the dislocation of Brazilian finance, the virtual
suspension of our maritime commerce, the curtailment of imports,
and the catastrophic drop in the exports of our staple products.
And in addition to the concrete causes for discontent was the fact
that the government of Hermes had deeply wounded national feelings and the Brazilians' innate love of liberty. If harmony and
concord were ever necessary, it was at this critical juncture.

The situation, fraught with so many disquieting possibilities,
was saved through the discernment and good sense of one man,
Sabino Barroso, the president of the chamber of deputies and
representative of the state of Minas Geraes. He had the reputation
of being a keen psychological observer of the political and social
life of his times; in fact, his friends were wont to describe him
as a "political seismograph." To these qualities he united tact,
understanding, unselfishness, and devotion to the public weal.
Morally, he was above reproach.

Impelled solely by patriotic motives, he went to Pinheiro and opened his eyes to the realities of the situation. The senator from Rio Grande do Sul might be elected, he admitted, but at the risk of very grave dissensions at the very time when the nation was facing perils both from without and within. In this instance Pinheiro showed that he could rise to the occasion. He put his patriotism before his ambition and withdrew his candidacy, which he alleged had been put forward by his friends. The whole country breathed a sigh of relief.

Election of Wenceslau Braz.—Efforts were now made to secure the election of a statesman whose ability and experience would fit him to cope with the problems of the hour. The ex-presidents, Rodrigues Alves and Campos Salles, were seriously considered but it was soon found that neither was available. The former had barely recovered from a very severe illness and did not feel able to take up the onerous duties of the presidency. Campos Salles was opposed by a number of political groups, chiefly in his own state in São Paulo. Apparently, the only person available was the acting vice president, Wenceslau Braz Pereira Gomes.

Though not a man of exceptional ability, Wenceslau Braz possessed certain qualities which commended him both to the politicians and to the nation at large. He was a tolerant, well-meaning gentleman,[2] honest and incorruptable. As governor of the state of Minas Geraes, he had acquitted himself well. During Hermes' administration he had been, as we have seen, vice president. As such he had to share the unpopularity and odium which were heaped on the president. But to insults and abuse his sole answer at all times was a dignified silence. As the almost intolerable government of the marshal approached its end, Wenceslau Braz gained the increasing respect and confidence of his fellow-Brazilians. It was realized that as far as possible he had opposed, or at least held aloof from, the more reprehensible actions of the president.

The Difficulties of the Moment.[3]—The tasks confronting the new president were in reality formidable. As the war wore on the position of Brazil became more and more complex and difficult. Although he was a sincere believer in an absolute neutrality, Wenceslau Braz could not remain indifferent as the war began

---

[2] Dr. Calogeras uses the English word.—P.A.M.

[3] A detailed account of the relations of Brazil to the World War is given by the translator in his book *Latin America and the War* (Baltimore, 1925), Chap. I.—P.A.M.

to cast its sinister shadow across the Atlantic. Evidence continued to multiply that the imperial German Government was secretly but effectively intervening in the internal affairs of Brazil. Instances of such intervention in the affairs of a friendly country were the violations of Brazilian legislation, the utilization of Brazilian harbors as a basis of supplies for cruisers, the fomenting of strikes, and finally attempts to mobilize the German communities in the southern part of the republic. When naval operations led the warships of the empire to sink the unarmed vessels of Brazil, with the frequent loss of both crew and cargo, the president felt that the limit of patience had been reached. In harmony with the wishes of the executive, congress proclaimed on October 26, 1917, that the nation accepted the state of war imposed on Brazil by Germany because of the disloyal conduct of the latter and the constant attack on our merchant marine.

To appreciate in full the significance of this act, we must pass in brief review a number of diplomatic events which had occurred earlier in the year. As a consequence of the sinking of the steamer *Paraná*, we were obliged to suspend political and commercial relations with the German Empire on April 11, 1917, a few days after the declaration of war against Germany by the United States. Somewhat paradoxically, however, we still remained a neutral in the conflict between these two powers. In a dispatch to Washington, President Wenceslau Braz explained that

"The [Brazilian] government could go no further than this;[4] but the Brazilian nation, through its legislative organ can . . . adopt the attitude that one of the belligerents (*i.e.*, the United States) forms an integral part of the American continent; and that to this belligerent we are bound by a traditional friendship and a similarity of political opinion in the defense of the vital interests of America and the principles accepted by international law.

"Such has always been the conduct of Brazil; the Republic remains faithful to the uninterrupted tradition of Brazil's foreign policy; it could not today repudiate the ideas which inspired the note of protest of the Brazilian empire of May 15, 1886, when a European squadron bombarded a South American city.[5]

---

[4] *I.e.*, the severance of relations with Germany.

[5] The allusion is to the bombardment of the Chilean harbor of Valparaiso by the Spanish Admiral Méndez Núñez on March 31, 1866.—P.A.M.

"In submitting this matter to the judgment of the national congress we must emphasize that this policy of continental solidarity is not merely the policy of this administration and that of the present republican régime, but the traditional one of the Brazilian nation. We are convinced that any resolution adopted by congress will stress the fortunate understanding which must exist between Brazil and the United States."

The ensuing legislative measures naturally reflected the views thus set forth by the executive. Of these measures the most important was the revocation of neutrality between Brazil and the United States on June 1. To clear away any possible doubt as to the attitude of the government on this occasion, an explanatory circular letter was dispatched on June 2 to all friendly powers. This communication declared *inter alia:*

"If hitherto the relative lack of reciprocity on the part of the American republics has withdrawn from the Monroe Doctrine its true character, permitting a scarcely well-formed interpretation of the prerogatives of their sovereignty, the present events, by placing Brazil, even now, at the side of the United States, in the critical moment of the world's history, continued to give our foreign policy a practical form of continental solidarity—a policy indeed which was that of the old *régime* on every occasion on which any of the other friendly sister nations of the American continent were in jeopardy."

The aggressions of the German marine against our ships continued. On October 26, 1917, as we have already seen, congress in full agreement with the executive formally recognized the state of war forced upon Brazil by the imperial government. From that time on, there was complete collaboration between Brazil and the Allies, and appropriate measures were voted by congress and carried out by the president.

The Financial Policy of the Administration of Wenceslau Braz. —To understand the financial aspects of the government of Wenceslau Braz, one must compare the state of the national treasury as it was inherited from Marshal Hermes with the results obtained after three years of operation of the funding scheme of 1914.

At the outset, however, it is necessary to point out the large difference between the first funding operation, that of 1898, and the second, consummated in 1914-1917. When the first of these transactions was negotiated, the international money marts were bursting with gold and rates of interest were low. Brazilian trade and commerce, in a state of frank convalescence, were on the point of acquiring the solidarity of earlier days. Imposts and taxes were relatively low, and the tributary field was almost untouched.

What a contrast with the second funding loan! To begin with, liabilities dating from the preceding presidential term amounted to the equivalent of some twenty million dollars in foreign countries and eighty million in the domestic market. The situation was enormously aggravated by the outbreak of the war. Custom dues, the chief source of national income, suffered a rapid decline. Export duties, from which the states derived much of their revenue, were similarly affected. As a consequence of the ship famine, foreign commerce all but collapsed. An intolerable economic crisis afflicted almost every phase of national activity. New taxes, though urgently needed, were difficult to create and still harder to collect. While the war was in progress, there was naturally no possibility of raising money in Europe.

The amount of the liabilities of the two periods was in the ratio of 33 to 166, or one to five. Moreover, the second funding loan had to face the overwhelming difficulty of immediately raising the sum of one hundred million dollars or its equivalent. Only those who had to grapple with these terrible problems can appreciate the magnitude of the task which made a veritable agony of each day's labor.[6] But when Wenceslau Braz left the presidency, he might affirm without boasting that the financial crisis was a thing of the past.

Other evidences of the careful husbanding of national resources may be noted. Public expenses were sharply reduced. Onerous contracts and liabilities, which had been blithely assumed by previous administrations, were drastically revised, with a resultant saving to the treasury of 500,000 contos or $100,000,000 at the average rate of exchange of the period. Payments on Brazil's foreign obligations were made promptly and in gold. All of the floating debt was refunded. Both in the foreign and domestic markets the quotations on Brazilian bonds rose steadily.

[6] Dr. Calogeras may write feelingly on this subject, as he held the portfolio of finance for the years 1915-1917.—P.A.M.

In the field of politics, the firm but just policy of the executive brought an end to party conflicts. As a result of his prestige and personal exertions, the president was able to settle a very delicate and vexatious boundary conflicts between the states of Paraná and Santa Catharina. He put an end to a bitter armed clash between rival political factions in the distant state of Matto Grosso. Local uprisings in various other parts of the republic were suppressed. The civil code, on which some of the ablest jurists in Brazil had labored for many years, was at length completed.

Had Wenceslau Braz followed the example of his predecessors, he would have bent every effort to secure the election for the next quadrennium of one of his personal friends or adherents. Instead, he frankly coöperated with the most responsible elements in the country in their endeavors to find a candidate who could fully measure up to the duties of his office.

Rodrigues Alves and Delfim Moreira.—Rodrigues Alves, whose model administration we have already discussed, was chosen for the second time, and should have been inaugurated on November 15, 1918. But he was advanced in years and, as a result of his unflagging devotion to the public service, his health was gravely impaired. The new responsibilities thrust upon him resulted in a crisis from which he never recovered. His death occurred on January 16, 1919, before he took possession of his office.

From November 15, 1918, to July 28, 1919, the vice president, Delfim Moreira da Costa Ribeiro, acted as chief magistrate. He had no liking for the office, but he was willing to sacrifice himself to his duty. His health was precarious, and he was worn out by his arduous labors as president for four years of the state of Minas Geraes. Moreover, he felt that his freedom of movement was seriously restricted because of the fact that he was merely a stopgap executive. His position was in fact slightly awkward; he felt as if he were something of a guest in the presidential palace. Yet, despite this somewhat anomalous position, his solid good sense, high moral qualities, and experience in government enabled him to tide over these difficult months with a fair degree of success.

Election of Epitacio Pessôa, 1922.—The choice of the new president turned out to be a surprising and happy one. Epitacio had, to be sure, given ample proof of his exceptional abilities, both as minister of state and member of the supreme tribunal of justice. At the moment of his election, he was senator from the northern state of Parahyba and was absent from Brazil as head of the Brazilian delegation to the Versailles Peace Conference. The surprise consisted in this: He represented one of the smallest states of the federation; hitherto it had been an unwritten law that the executives should be chosen from the two great states of São Paulo and Minas Geraes.

The disproportionate prominence of these two states has already been alluded to. It was a consequence of a great political error which went back to the days of independence in 1822. Colonial Brazil, as we have already seen, was divided into captaincies, differing widely in size, wealth, and population. When the empire was established, the imperial provinces were made coextensive with these same captaincies, and the provinces in turn were made the basis for the states of the republic. The practical consequence of this inequitable division of the country was deplorable. With no political or moral justification was set up a sort of hierarchy of states by which Brazil was divided into states of the "first" and the "second" class. It was inevitable that the states in the first category, of which São Paulo and Minas Geraes were the most important, should strive to exert a predominating influence in national affairs, with all the evils which this policy brought in its train. Neither the empire nor the republic had possessed the courage to remedy this essentially vicious situation.[7]

In practice, this system resulted in the presidential candidates being chosen almost exclusively from the out-going executives of São Paulo and Minas Geraes. This is not at all surprising when we recall these men had in their control the electoral machinery of their respective states. When the candidate chanced to be a real statesman of the caliber, say, of Rodrigues Alves, no harm resulted. But frequently the candidate belonged to a lower intellectual and moral level, and his competency at the best extended only to local or regional matters; by no stretch of the imagination could they be regarded as first-class presidential timber. The nation at large naturally suffered the consequences of this faulty political system.

We have here a glaring proof of the unfitness, in a political sense, of the party leaders. It is clear that those who inspire and

[7] See above, p. 283.

guide public opinion in Brazil have often failed to attain a mental
or moral majority in their political thinking. They are apt to be
much more concerned with success at the polls, irrespective of
means they employ, than with an adequate solution of national
problems. In other words, issues are only too often subordinated
to personalities. And in all of these respects it must be conceded
that the present situation shows few signs of improvement.

When Rodrigues Alves died, the traditional custom was invoked.
As the most likely candidates for the ensuing presidential term
were put forward the names of the executives of São Paulo and
Minas Geraes, although the head of the last-named state promptly
declined the honor. The field was thus apparently left clear for the
president of São Paulo, Altino Arantes. But a strong body of
opinion was in favor of the election of the eminent jurisconsult,
Ruy Barbosa, and a period of great political agitation was seemingly at hand. Despite the widespread sympathies which Ruy, as
standard bearer of the civilian elements, enjoyed both in São Paulo
and other parts of Brazil, the majority of the *Paulista* politicians
were clearly in favor of Altino Arantes. Minas Geraes was lukewarm in regard to Ruy Barbosa and sought a "candidate of conciliation" in order to avoid tumults and perhaps military revolts.
As a matter of fact, Ruy was supported by very respectable sections of public opinion throughout the entire country. In military
circles, however, he encountered a deep hostility, which was in part
a survival of the dissensions which had taken place during the administration of Marshal Hermes. The great majority of the officers never forgave him for his campaign of 1910 in which he had
inveighed against militarism and all its works.[8] This resentment
on the part of the military, though unjust, was very real and was
perfectly understood in those political circles where elections were
made or unmade.

A way out of this impasse was found by Senator Sabino Barroso who once more, as in the days of Hermes, acted as a sort
of political *deux ex machina*. He suggested the name of Epitacio
Pessôa, senator from the little state of Parahyba, hitherto quite
divorced from national politics. The idea made rapid headway,
particularly as the politicians were very anxious to avoid a campaign which might degenerate into violence and bloodshed. Ruy

[8] *Cf.* footnote to p. 311.

Barbosa and Altino Arantes were both dropped as candidates and Epitacio became the official choice of the dominant political party.

The senator from Parahyba knew nothing of the maneuvers which were being carried on in Rio in furtherance of his candidacy. The cablegrams bearing the news of his selection—in this case tantamount to election—took him by surprise in Paris where he was busy as president of the Brazilian delegation to the Peace Conference. He had not lifted a finger to further his own cause.

Achievements of the Administration of Epitacio Pessôa.—With the election of Epitacio began one of the most notable presidential terms in our entire history. Space permits a reference to only a few of the accomplishments of the next four years. Especial emphasis was placed on the development of our foreign relations, resulting in the tightening of the bonds of friendship between the governments of both hemispheres. Our presence in the League of Nations, which we had helped to establish, afforded us an opportunity to collaborate in the labors of this body. The difficulties with Germany and France[9] arising from the Great War were adjusted to the satisfaction of all concerned. For the first time two heads of European governments crossed the Atlantic to visit Brazil: King Albert of Belgium in 1920 and the President of Portugal in 1922. Numerous statesmen from the different American republics came to our shores. As practically all frontier questions with our neighbors had been settled, this perennial source of international discord had disappeared.

The most important landmarks in Epitacio's administration, if we leave aside the bitter dissensions which preceded the presidential succession of 1922, were the celebration of the first centenary of independence, beginning with September 7, 1922; and the revocation on September 3, 1920, of the banishment of the imperial family. The first of these events furnished a material proof, in the shape of the International Exposition of Rio de Janeiro, of the extent of Brazil's progress. The extensive and surprising advance in the fields of industry, agriculture, and stockraising, as evidenced in this exhibit, aroused very real enthusiasm, and revealed to foreign-

---

[9] The reference is to the disposal of the German ships which were interned in Brazilian harbors, and which the government took over in 1917. *Cf.* Martin, *Latin America and the War*, p. 99.—P.A.M.

ers as well as to the Brazilians themselves the country's unsuspected capacity for production.

The second event made clear that the bitterness engendered by the overthrow of the empire had entirely disappeared and that the acceptance of the new régime was complete. For almost thirty years the mortal remains of Emperor Dom Pedro II and Empress Dona Tereza Christina had been deposited in the memorial church of São Vicente de Fóra of Lisbon, the pantheon of the Braganza dynasty. As a token of respect to the memory of this august pair, their ashes were now transported to Brazil on the *São Paulo*, one of the most powerful dreadnaughts of our fleet. They were accompanied by the Comte d'Eu, husband of the Princess Imperial Dona Isabel, *A Redemptora*,[10] and by his eldest son, Dom Pedro, known as the Prince of Grão-Pará. As marshal of the Brazilian army during the last phases of the Paraguayan War, the Comte was received with full military honors by the descendants of the officers whom he had commanded in this international conflict.

The efforts of President Epitacio were successfully employed in the settlement of a number of thorny boundary controversies between the states. So successful were his endeavors that the twenty disputes which existed as he entered office were reduced to two: Santa Catharina with Rio Grande do Sul, and Bahia with Pernambuco.

The navy was the object of his special care. It was Epitacio's desire that the portfolios of both the navy and army be entrusted to civilians. This policy was carried out with great success. The entire organization was infused with a new spirit. New ships were built and old ones modernized. Auxiliary services were raised to a high pitch of efficiency. Large-scale maneuvers, accompanied by intensive target practice, became the order of the day. No pains were spared to build up effective reserves both in men and *matériel*.

A similar progress is to be noted in the army, as a result partly of the influx of a group of younger officers. They were filled with patriotic enthusiasm and had a full appreciation of their double duty: to raise their professional level and to avoid all partisan

---

[10] Literally "The Redeemer," a name given to the princess after she had signed the act of 1888 freeing the remaining slaves in Brazil.—P.A.M.

and political entanglements. The new minister of war,[11] himself a civilian, had lent this movement his full support and shared the new mental outlook of corps of officers. In 1919 a special mission of instruction, under the command of General Gamelin, was contracted for in France. The responsibility for this important initiative, which marked an epoch in the military history of the country, belonged to acting President Delfim Moreira and to his minister of war, General Cardoso de Aguiar.

Under President Pessôa, as just intimated, progress in the reorganization of the army was noteworthy. The system of recruiting by lots was improved; military justice was strengthened. Particular attention was devoted to armaments, campaign equipment, modernization of ordnance, military aviation, instruction and drill, barracks, field training and the like. The grand parade of 1922, on the celebration of the centenary of independence, was composed of thirty thousand men, with the most modern type of equipment. Yet this body of troops constituted but one of the five divisions of which the Brazilian army was composed.

The department of agriculture, through its schools, experimental stations, and other agencies, vastly increased its efficiency and usefulness. Public works, railways, telegraph lines followed the same curve of progress. In 1922 the railway system amounted to 29,389 kilometers; the number of telegrams rose to 47,055,667 transmitted over lines measuring 83,778 kilometers. For the first time the reclamation service (*obras contra secas*) was supplied with adequate funds, and the terrible problem of droughts in northeastern Brazil, which had baffled the efforts of successive administrations since 1909, was in a fair way toward solution. A new spirit was kindled throughout the nation.

Activity, progress, and patriotic enthusiasm for the development of the country were everywhere in evidence. The only discordant note was sounded by the professional politicians and their supporters who found their leadership challenged and their advice unheeded.

Artistic Expansion.—*Pari pasu* with this material advance

---

[11] The new minister was Dr. Calogeras himself who held the portfolio of war from September 19, 1919, to November 15, 1922. The reforms noted above were largely owing to his initiative.—P.A.M.

came a renaissance in the domain of letters. Literature, criticism, historical investigation—all were quickened by this new spirit. Many of the authors mentioned in earlier pages continued their labors and to this period belong some of their most notable productions. New names began to appear, including a legion of poets concerned in their writings with the eternal problems of life, suffering, and death. Their chief trait in common was a deep-seated spiritualism.

Though romanticism seemed dead and buried, a few belated representatives survived. They served to throw into greater relief the works of the newer writers whose great preoccupation was the writing of fiction based on careful study and observation. Remarkable studies and novels were written by Euclydes da Cunha, Affonso Arinos, Coelho Netto, Graça Aranha, Afranio Peixoto, Gastão Cruls, and Alberto Rangel. They derived their inspiration from such disparate subjects as colonial Brazil, immigration and its resultant problems, the population of the *sertão*,[12] life in the great basin of the Amazon, the new racial fusions which were emerging from the South American melting pot. But above and beyond all of this, we find a growing concern with a sounder and truer nationalism, based, as we have just seen, on a careful study of the Brazilian milieu both past and present.

Literary criticism became more exact and scholarly. The men preëminent in this field were Tristão de Athayde, Agrippino Grieco, Humberto Campos, and Madeiros de Albuquerque. The activity of our Brazilian Academy of Letters increased both in quantity and quality in every domain of literary and esthetic production.

A deeper religious note began to pervade the current literature in the form of a healthy reaction against paganism, which had been largely an outgrowth of a deceptive kind of naturalism. Writers concerned themselves more and more with moral problems, the soul, future life, and human destiny. These men ran the gamut from mere religiosity to the most profound and sincere Catholicism. The names of Jackson de Figueiredo, Tasso de Silveira, Perillo Gomes, Hamilton Nogueira, the Jesuit fathers, Leonel da Franca and Madureira, are to be remembered in this connection.

---

[12] The most famous of this type of novels is *Os Sertões* of Euclides da Cunha. —P.A.M.

Social thought was represented by essayists such as Vicente Licinio Cardoso, Oliveira Vianna and a few others. History, much of it erudite, was cultivated by the members of the *Instituto Historico e Geographico do Rio de Janeiro*, and by members of other assocations with similar aims both in the capital and in the various states. Even the daily press was caught up by the new spirit. Both in scope and content it had risen to a higher intellectual level than had ever before been reached in Brazil.

Political Crisis at End of Epitacio's Administration.—As the time approached for the choice of Epitacio's successor, there arose grave dissensions which for a moment threatened to plunge Brazil into civil war. The origin of this crisis was to be found in the determination of certain elements in the army once more to play an important if not decisive rôle in the political life of the country. It will be recalled that Epitacio had entrusted to civilians the portfolios of war and navy. In certain sections of the army this action was violently resented. Ex-president Hermes, of unhappy memory, at the time president of the powerful Military Club, was in full sympathy with these malcontents. At the conclusion of his disastrous presidency he had declared his intention of holding aloof from politics. To prove the sincerity of his statement, he refused a senatorship from Rio Grande do Sul and retired to Europe for some six years. But the temptations of the old life were too strong, and in 1920 we find him back in Rio intriguing with his old friends and supporters.

We have already seen that during Epitacio's administration the majority of the army, largely under the influence of younger officers, had ceased to interest itself in politics. Nonetheless, Hermes could find a considerable number of pseudo friends among both soldiers and civilians who pretended to be devoted to him but who, in reality, wished to use him for their own purposes when it came time to select the new president.

In the preliminary caucuses held by the leaders of the party in power it became evident that Minas Geraes desired the election of its own state executive, Arthur da Silva Bernardes. When asked what were his own wishes President Epitacio Pessôa declared that in the approaching electoral campaign he would remain absolutely neutral and consequently would favor no particular candidate.

At this juncture, the situation was greatly complicated by the return from Europe of ex-President Nilo Peçanha. While abroad Nilo had made it clear that he was a strong supporter of Bernardes, for whom he professed great admiration and friendship. But on his arrival at Rio he fell into the hands of a group of designing army officers and deserting his own candidate and personal friend he made a complete *volte-face*. As leader of the disaffected if not rebellious military and civilian elements, he determined to make a bold bid for the presidency himself.

The campaign now resolved itself into a bitter struggle between Bernardes and Nilo Peçanha with Hermes and his supporters lurking in the background. The contest was conducted with a complete lack of moral scruples. One episode became famous. A number of Nilo's followers, probably without the knowledge of their chief, resorted to a despicable forgery in the shape of a letter purporting to have been written by Bernardes, in which both the army and navy came in for gross calumnies and slanders. Instead of exposing this contemptible subterfuge, Nilo kept silent. Hermes, who also knew it was a forgery, likewise kept his own counsel and bided his time.

As may readily be imagined, when the incriminating letter was made public, the agitation in the military circles soon rose to a dangerous height. Such was, in fact, the aim of the plotters. It was their hope to introduce such confusion and turmoil into the election that they could secure by hook or crook the election of Nilo or Hermes. The former was the choice of the majority of the plotters, the latter of the officers who were most deeply involved in the conspiracy.

It is unnecessary to rehearse the different stages by which this conspiracy approached its climax. The situation was enormously complicated by the decision of Senator Raul Soares, the manager of Bernardes' candidacy, to submit the whole matter of the forged letter to a tribunal of honor. Bernardes opposed this procedure, but allowed himself to be overruled. When it came to the selection of a tribunal Raul Soares was so naïve as to accept the Military Club, one of the strongholds of opposition to Bernardes. In fact, the president of this club was, as we have seen, none other than Hermes himself! It is no occasion for surprise, therefore, that the decision of this "tribunal of honor" was to the effect that the insulting letter was indubitably genuine and that Bernardes had grossly libeled the armed forces of the nation.

But the triumph of the military and the opponents of Bernardes was short-lived. Doubts regarding the handwriting experts employed by the club became more and more insistent, until finally the forger himself, who was of course a tool of higher-ups, made a full confession. The result was naturally disastrous to the candidacy of Nilo Peçanha. His supporters were quick to see that, in the existing state of public opinion, the election would go against him. The more daring of the conspirators then determined that what they could not accomplish legally they would secure by force. They, therefore, set about systematically to stir up disloyalty and dissension in the garrisons throughout the nation, particularly in the states in the north. The motley crew of civilians and disloyal officers who now made up the opposition to Bernardes came to be known as the "Republican Reaction" (*Reacção republicana*). In general the civilians supported Nilo and the military, Hermes. From its very nature this hybrid association would have quarrelled over the spoils had their plot been successful; it would have been a veritable *journée de dupes*. But events fell out somewhat differently. It was Hermes himself who brought the crisis to an issue. On June 28, 1922, the marshal, in his capacity of the president of the Military Club, violated all military discipline by sending an insulting telegram to the military commander of Pernambuco. Confronted by this overt act of insubordination, the government placed Hermes under arrest.

Exactly a week later the revolt broke out. But it was suffocated almost before it got started, as a result of the forehanded and decisive action of the government. The great conspiracy of the "Republican Reaction" collapsed utterly and its two leaders, Hermes and Nilo, were entirely discredited.

A great political lesson is to be drawn from this conspiracy. The prompt and easy suppression of this plot showed that only a handful of disloyal troops was implicated and that the heart of the army was perfectly sound. The overwhelming majority of the officers, irrespective of their personal feelings, remained true to the code of their profession and to the principles of military discipline. It was now clear to everyone that, both in spirit and morale, the army had made an immense step forward. No longer could it supply a fertile field for the intrigues and machinations of unscrupulous politicians. No longer could it be led astray into the path of revolutions and armed uprising to further the ambitions of a particular party or clique. A chapter in the military history of Brazil had been definitely closed.

Arthur Bernardes, President.—The inauguration of the new president took place without incident on November 15, 1922. A fair and unbiased judgment of his administration is most difficult. It may be asserted without fear of contradiction that few presidencies in Brazilian history have been more disturbed by bitter partisan strife. It was a case of four long years of latent civil war. Save for rare intervals, constitutional guarantees were suspended. Dissatisfaction with the administration was all but universal.

While the historian is too close to the event to treat these critical four years with the necessary objectivity, certain points stand out with considerable clearness. The simple truth is that Bernardes did not attempt to govern in the accepted sense of the term. Rather did he stick to his post as he might have defended a beleaguered fortress and to this task he devoted all his energies. That he committed errors admits of no doubt, but it must be said in partial extenuation that his opponents were equally ruthless. He was willing to make every sacrifice to what he conceived was his duty.

Bernardes was ill-equipped to grapple with the difficult and trying problems which confronted him when he assumed office. He had no familiarity with the problems of the federal government or with the handling of the vast federal civil service. Practically his entire life had been spent within the limits of his native state of Minas Geraes. During the election campaign, his innermost sentiments of pride and honor had been wounded to the quick by odious maneuvers of his opponents who were responsible for the forged letter. He was not apt to forget or pardon offenses of this nature, although he stated in his inaugural manifesto that "the president would never remember the attack on the candidate." Bernardes never learned that the prerequisites of mental and moral superiority have always been understanding, tolerance, patience, and above all the power to forgive.

He considered any dissent from his opinion as an evidence of personal enmity. He possessed a sort of mystic conviction that he was called upon to carry out a superhuman mission. His personal enemies, therefore, were foes of the nation and of the public weal. It was particularly unfortunate that the president should hold such views at this time. The embers of the revolt of 1922 still smoldered. The army was frankly distrustful. The president in turn looked upon all officers—insubordinate as well as law-abiding—with suspicious and hostile eyes. Here he was guilty of a grave injustice. The most convincing proof of his error lies in the unquestioned fact that whatever their personal opinions, the bulk of the officers did their duty and crushed the insurrection of 1924-1926.[13] Of the five thousand officers in the regular army, less than two hundred were guilty of acts of insubordination.

Election of Washington Luis.—It was with a great sense of relief that the Brazilians saw the term of Bernardes approach its close. But the restoration of anything like normal conditions could be assured only through the election of a president who could inspire confidence in the nation at large. As successor of Bernardes was elected without opposition Washington Luis Pereira de Souza, minister of justice in two previous administrations and governor of São Paulo from 1920 to 1924. In these various posts he had acquitted himself with unusual competency. Such, in fact, was the confidence which he inspired that his election was hailed as the dawn of a new and better era for Brazil.

These generous hopes were, in part at least, realized. To be sure the tasks facing the new president were not easy, particularly when it came to the liquidation of the tremendous liabilities he had inherited from his predecessor. Yet it was soon evident that a new hand was at the helm of state. Order was at once restored. After four long years, the nation enjoyed the blessings of peace and tranquillity. The government made every effort to bring about a renewal of public confidence. Two of its policies may be singled out for special mention: the scrupulous care with which vacancies were filled in the supreme court and the insistance of the executive that all of its acts be clothed with perfect legality. Washington Luis endeavored also to stabilize exchange, the fluctuations of which had had such a demoralizing effect on Brazilian finance. There is a wide

---

[13] Dr. Calogeras here alludes to a revolt which broke out in São Paulo in the summer of 1924 and was suppressed by federal troops. *Cf*. Rippy, Martin, and Cox, *Argentina, Brazil, and Chile*, p. 260.—P.A.M.

difference of opinion regarding the success of his efforts; certain it is that his stabilization scheme could not weather the economic crisis of 1929.

In its relations with foreign powers, Brazil neglected no opportunity to set forth its belief in the principles of international solidarity, especially as regards the nations of the western hemisphere.[14] In this connection may be noted its active participation in the Sixth Pan-American Conference held in Havana in 1928, the reception of President Hoover in Rio de Janeiro, and the visit of President Guggiari of Paraguay to our capital. Brazil thus furnished eloquent proofs of a return to its traditional policy of friendship and coöperation with its sister republics of the three Americas.

Conclusions.—On the basis of this summary exposition of four centuries of Brazilian history, we may venture to point out a few permanent tendencies in our historical evolution.

The first is an ever-growing sense of national unity. That the immense, amorphous, thinly populated territory of Brazil, with its diversity of regional interests, has been welded into a national whole is owing in the last analysis to the empire. We must note at once that the ideal of the empire was in sharpest contrast to that of Portugal when Brazil was still a colony. At all times the mother country strove to keep as tight as possible the bonds between colony and metropolis and, on the Roman theory of divide and rule, tried to thwart all efforts of the captaincies to draw closer one to the other. Any attempts at closer union were discouraged.

During the first two decades of independence, the nation was distraught by survivals of these old colonial methods, but after 1845 there was no further serious menace to imperial unity. It was early recognized, however, that local and regional differences would have to be taken into account and to a certain extent encouraged if all parts of the vast empire were to develop and progress. Hence we find the grant of a certain amount of provincial autonomy under the empire and the organization of the republic on a federal basis. History has shown, however, that concessions by the central

---

[14] During the last months of the Bernardes administration Brazil withdrew from the League of Nations under circumstances which even now are not entirely clear. *Cf.* Rippy, Martin, and Cox, *Argentina, Brazil, and Chile,* pp. 260-62.— P.A.M.

government to the local units are apt to be more or less belated. As a consequence, the cry of independence has been occasionally raised and a few exalted minds insist that the only proper solution is secession of the dissatisfied states from the union.

In point of fact, however, at no time after the consummation of independence did there exist a desire to dismember Brazil. Our history clearly shows it. The proof to the contrary would seem to be furnished by the long and bitter rebellion in Rio Grande do Sul in 1835-1845, but even in this instance the aim of the leaders of the revolt was autonomy rather than independence. This is abundantly proven by the collapse of the rebellion once Brazil was threatened by the Argentine dictator Rosas.

Another significant tendency in our historical evolution has been the gradual but profound change which has taken place in our attitude toward, and relations with, our Spanish American neighbors. During colonial days, there existed a rivalry, at times amounting to hatred, between the American possessions of Spain and Portugal. It was inevitable that something of this suspicion and dislike should be bequeathed to the scions of the two Iberic nations once independence was achieved. In fact, it still exists in an attenuated form in certain of the more ignorant elements of the population.

In political circles, this feeling of mutual distrust between Brazil and Spanish America declined sharply after the fifties, although there remained in the higher levels of society a few individuals who clung with an almost atavistic instinct to old rivalries based on differences of racial stock. But it must be said at once that our diplomats never shared this sentiment. One of the great moral victories of our twentieth century has been to foster openly and sincerely a greater intimacy between Spanish and Portuguese Americans. It is no exaggeration to say that we are rapidly approaching an era of unrestricted and heartfelt solidarity throughout the whole of South America.

As regards the United States it would be idle to deny that differences do exist. Yet, of all the nations south of the Rio Grande, Brazil is perhaps the closest to the great North American republic. Our deep friendship and community of ideas date from the first days of our independence. The Monroe Doctrine contributed to the growth of this atmosphere of cordiality and mutual esteem. From the first we considered ourselves as sharing in the responsibility of its enforcement since it is a rule common to both countries and not merely a unilateral North American instrument.[15]

It should be made clear that while Brazil will bend every effort to draw ever closer the bonds of fellowship with its sister republics both in North and South America, it is firm in its determination never to lose its individuality, either spiritual or social, as a great Catholic people. Brazilians of all shades of political opinion are as one on this point. We shall never cease to be what we are.

As a people, we have many obligations and duties, of which perhaps the gravest and most pressing is the attainment and maintenance of our political majority in the art of government or the science of statesmanship. Many of our leaders have been men of whom any country might legitimately be proud. On the other hand, as has been repeatedly pointed out in the course of our study, our political guides and mentors have all too often failed to rise to a full appreciation of their responsibilities. Intent on furthering their personal ambitions, they have frequently fallen short of possessing what we may call a collective national and international point of view. As in all countries, there have been violent oscillations in the curve of our efficiency in that most difficult art of self-government.

Our ideas on some of these important matters were authoritatively set forth by the great Baron of Rio Branco at the Latin-American Scientific Congress held in Rio de Janeiro in 1905.

"Even when Brazil, under a régime different from the present one, was described by the famous General Mitre as a 'crowned democracy,' and the difference in governmental forms might suggest a difference of political ideals; even then our sentiments of friendship with our neighboring republics suffered no abatement and we never succumbed to a spirit of aggression, expansion, or conquest as has been very unjustly charged against us. Today, as yesterday, the sole ambition of the Brazilian nation is to grow through the fruitful labors of peace. It wishes to expand by its own exertions and within the frontiers in which is spoken the language of its ancestors. It wishes to be strong among neighbors

---

[15] This view was clearly enunciated by the Brazilian government during the course of the World War. See above, p. 318.—P.A.M.

equally strong and great, for the honor of all and for the security of our continent which others, perchance, may feel is inadequately occupied."

In 1906, in the closing session of the Pan-American Conference of Rio de Janeiro, he once more made clear the norms of Brazil's foreign policy.

"Popular opinion frequently goes astray. Even the most peaceful and cultivated of peoples are sometimes swept by gusts of insanity which arouse the most barbarous instincts. It is the duty of a statesman and of every man possessing true political sense to combat unflinchingly all propaganda designed to stir up hatred and international rivalries.

"There have been occasions when states, overpopulated and condemned by an ungenerous nature to a hard material existence, have aroused fears and suspicions in their neighbors. Brazil happily could never fall into this category. To all of the republics whose boundaries coincide with our own, in fact, to all American nations, we wish peace, intelligent initiative, and productive labor, in order that through their development and prosperity they may act as examples and stimuli not only to our own exertions in these fields of endeavor, but also to those of our great sister nation in the North which has promoted these useful conferences. And to the countries of Europe, to which we have been bound and always will be bound by so many moral ties and economic interests, we shall continue to offer, as we have in the past, our firmest guarantees of order and progress.

"We beg of you, gentlemen, delegates of all of these friendly powers, to present to your governments and your people these declarations which sincerely express the sentiment of the government and people of Brazil. May these sentiments serve to destroy such remnants of unfounded distrust and suspicion—if any still exist—and bring us in return the ever growing friendship of all the peoples of America, a friendship which we shall do everything in our power to foster."

A noble and high-minded ideal and one that can be carried out only by men of good will and intelligence. All countries throughout the world need men of this caliber. It is not to the United States alone that are applicable the words which Ambassador James Watson Gerard wrote in his interesting book, *Four*

Years in Germany: "There are too many thinkers, writers and speakers in the United States; from now on we need the doers, the organizers, and the realists who alone can win this contest for us, for democracy, and for permanent peace."

This, succinctly stated, is the task and ideal of Brazil. We have come to a full realization of the difficulties on the road before us; let us strive to overcome these difficulties with all the faith and enthusiasm of which we are capable. Behind our efforts lies the conviction that just as the nineteenth century has been described as the "Century of the United States," so may the twentieth, in which we are living and working, deserve to be known as the "Century of South America."

Neglected:
1 education
2 land reform
3. health improvement
4 broadening of political representation
5. class

CHAPTER XVI

THE LAST DECADE OF BRAZILIAN HISTORY[1]

IN HIS *Formação Historica do Brasil* Dr. Calogeras has carried
the narrative history of his country up to the election of Washington Luis in 1926. When the work was planned in 1929 this seemed
a logical place to stop. Along with millions of others Dr. Calogeras
honestly supposed that the major political and social problems of
Brazil were approaching something like a definite solution. We now
realize that such hopes were too optimistic. As events have turned
out, the last decade of Brazilian history has been fraught with far-
reaching changes in almost every domain of public life. It has
therefore seemed desirable, both to the editor of the Inter-American
Series and to the translator of the present work, to bring the story
up through 1937. It is obvious that such a survey of contemporary
Brazil must from the very nature of things be tentative. For many
of the changes anything like complete and authoritative data are
lacking. A satisfactory perspective is next to impossible. Yet the
translator has embarked on this ungrateful task in the conviction
that the momentous events of the last few years are destined to have
such profound and far-reaching effects that they cannot be passed
over in silence.

Dr. Calogeras conveys the impression that the election of Washington Luis in 1926 ushered in an era of appeasement and progress,
this despite the many grave responsibilities which the president
inherited from his predecessors. Such in fact were the views of the
nation at large but it soon developed that such expectations had a
very slender foundation. To be sure the first three years of the new
administration were reasonably prosperous. The executive took
energetic measures to cope with Brazil's perennial financial difficulties. For a time such measures enjoyed a fair degree of success
but they eventually proved ineffectual to exorcise the economic
and political crisis which overwhelmed Brazil at the end of the
presidential term. It will be recalled that 1930 was a fatal year for

---

[1] In preparing this chapter the translator was kindly granted permission by
the George Washington University Press to utilize some of the material which
he had already published in *Argentina, Brazil, and Chile since Independence*
(Washington, 1935).

South America. The greater part of the continent was visited by an epidemic of revolutions from which Brazil could not escape. We may consider briefly the cause and development of this movement in so far as it affected Brazil.

Prior to the promulgation of the constitution of 1937 the larger states of the Brazilian republic enjoyed a degree of influence in national affairs of which we in the United States have little conception. The state executives were often known as presidents and were assisted by a cabinet modelled somewhat on that of the federal government. The states themselves enjoyed wide powers, including the right to levy export taxes and to contract foreign loans. A number of the states in practice were almost *imperia in imperio*. They might even have their own military forces; the militia of São Paulo, for instance constituted a veritable state army. It was natural that between the larger and more popular states jealousies and rivalries should appear, particularly as regards their influence in the affairs of the national government. An unwritten law had grown up to the effect that no state might furnish a president for two consecutive terms. Between 1889 and 1926, the presidency had with few exceptions alternated between the states of São Paulo and Minas Geraes. But as time went on other states began to assert their claims, particularly Rio Grande do Sul, whose wealth, influence and population have greatly increased since the advent of the republic. The president of the nation usually plays no passive rôle in these assertions of "state rights." As head of his political party—usually the only one in the country—he has naturally great influence on the choice of his successor. As a matter of fact such is generally the case throughout Hispanic America.

Washington Luis was, as we have seen, a Paulista. His successor, according to the traditional method of state rotation, should have been a Mineiro.[2] But the campaign of 1930 was hardly under way when the governor of Minas Geraes, looked upon by many as the logical candidate for the presidency, threw his support to Dr. Getulio Vargas, the able and energetic governor of the state of Rio Grande do Sul. Under these circumstances, Dr. Vargas looked to the outgoing president for support, or at least acquiescence in his candidacy, but on July 25, 1929, Washington Luis announced

---

[2] A native of the state of Minas Geraes.

that he would favor the election of Dr. Julio Prestes, the governor of São Paulo.

In thus defying the unwritten law that two successive presidents should not come from the same state Dr. Washington Luis was doubtless perfectly sincere. He was probably convinced that the election of another Paulista was necessary, in the words of the party platform, as a "guarantee of the continuation of policies which during the present four-year administration have contributed to the greatness and glory of our institutions." Unfortunately for Dr. Washington Luis, the candidacy of Prestes was coolly received throughout the country. The opponents of Dr. Prestes proceeded to sink their various rivalries and under the designation of "Liberal Alliance" lined up behind Dr. Vargas. Though the election, which took place on March 1, 1930, resulted in a victory for Dr. Prestes, hostility against Washington Luis and his protegé rapidly increased. Against the outgoing president were charged his refusal to grant amnesty to the revolutionists of 1922 and 1924, his responsibility for the economic situation, and above all his attempt to foist as his successor another Paulista upon the nation. He was likewise accused of favoring the coffee and other interests of São Paulo while neglecting industries in other states.

Such, in brief, was the political background of the revolution. There were, of course, economic bases for the revolt. It may be recalled that the post-war years had witnessed a vast increase in Brazil's foreign indebtedness, encouraged, it must be said in all conscience, by our own bankers. According to *Moody's Investment Service*,[3] the total foreign indebtedness of Brazil, including federal, state, and municipal loans, amounted at that time to the enormous sum of $1,181,000,000, of which some three-fourths was owed by the federal government. Service on this foreign debt, together with the return on foreign capital investments, was placed somewhere between $175,000,000, and $200,000,000. These large remittances could, of course, be met only by a favorable balance in Brazil's international trade or by further borrowing. The export balance for 1929, however, amounted to barely $40,000,000 and for 1930, a trifle over $50,000,000. The situation was aggravated by the large internal debt amounting to at least a quarter of a billion

---

[3] July 17, 1930.

dollars. President Washington Luis, though he had effected some economies, was forced to continue the pernicious practice of additional foreign loans. With the coming of the world depression in 1930, such sources were automatically closed.

The most important single factor in Brazil's economic crisis was coffee. As is well known, Brazil furnishes from one-third to one-half of the world's production of this article. Thanks to this happy situation, the country enjoyed for a time a quasi-monopoly of this commodity, and within certain limits could dictate prices. It could do this, however, only with government assistance, and at various times the federal and state authorities have been called upon for the "valorization" or "defense" of coffee. The ultimate result has been a vast amount of overproduction. By November, 1930, for example, the amount available in São Paulo for export was estimated at 26,600,000 bags of 132 pounds each. This was 1,000,000 bags more than the entire world consumption in 1929 and twice the amount of Brazil's normal export of this commodity. An organization known as the Coffee Institute was created in 1928. By means of foreign loans it endeavored to hold the surplus coffee out of the market and keep the price at a high level, but in 1930 the situation got beyond its control. No more foreign loans were possible. Prices dropped catastrophically, and many of the planters were ruined. So great was the economic importance of coffee that almost every phase of Brazil's life was adversely affected. The responsibility for this situation was naturally laid at the door of the government.

In September, 1930, the long threatening revolution broke out. The details of the struggle we may omit. A long-drawn-out civil war was in prospect. Fortune seemed to favor the government forces when on October 4, 1930, a number of generals in Rio de Janeiro rose against President Washington Luis and gave him but half an hour to resign. He refused and was held prisoner until November 20 when he was allowed to embark for Europe. Exactly one month after the outbreak of the revolt a provisional military junta turned over the office of chief executive to Dr. Getulio Vargas. The *gauchos* of Rio Grande do Sul kept their promise to tether their horses at the foot of the obelisk fronting the Monroe Palace. One episode of the revolution deserves mention. Just before the collapse of the government forces, the United States Secretary of State, Stimson, placed an embargo on the arms intended for the revolutionists. This act was naturally ill-received in Brazil and for a time caused some coolness between the new government and the administration at Washington. The fact that the United States was the first of the great powers to recognize the Vargas régime was looked upon by many as a recognition that Mr. Stimson's action was to say the least precipitate. It may be noted in passing that this was the first time that the United States had declared an arms embargo in the case of a revolution in South America.

It was at once evident that a strong hand was at the helm of the ship of state. On November 11, an executive decree dissolved congress; by the same decree Dr. Vargas assumed absolute powers for himself and his government. Constitutional guarantees were suspended; a special tribunal to try political crimes was established. The place of the governors of the states was taken by men known as *"interventors"* appointed by Dr. Vargas himself. As the personal representatives of the executive, these officials were granted wide discretionary power. Unfortunately, many of them were young military officers without political experience and their rule occasioned much dissatisfaction. Their power soon waxed so great that they became known as *O partido dos tenentes* (the party of the lieutenants). Especially was their rule resented in São Paulo which, as we shall see, revolted against the central government in 1932.

Dr. Vargas was on the whole happy in his choice of members of his cabinet. As minister of justice was appointed Dr. Oswaldo Aranha. Many regarded him as the strong man of the cabinet. Later he became, in succession, minister of finance, ambassador to the United States, and minister of foreign affairs. Dr. Afranio de Mello Franco, former head of the Brazilian delegation at Geneva, and one of the greatest jurists in South America, received the portfolio of foreign affairs. In this position he showed marked capacity, particularly in his successful efforts to settle the Leticia controversy between Colombia and Perú. He was regarded by many Brazilians and others as the logical candidate for the Nobel peace prize in 1936. The other cabinet members though less well known were all men of ability.

Before taking up the accomplishments of the government of

Dr. Getulio Vargas, we must in a parenthesis refer to an event which for a time threatened to jeopardize the success of the revolution. The reference is, of course, to the revolt which broke out in the state of São Paulo in the summer of 1932. The great coffee state had particular occasion to complain of the course of the revolution of 1930. The *interventors* and other officials sent by the government at Rio apparently failed to rise to the level of their responsibility and their actions aroused intense opposition. It is alleged that a number of these men were intent only on furthering their own interests. The Paulistas objected to the mounting expenses of both the state and federal governments to which they were naturally heavy contributors. Since the state contributed something like thirty-three per cent of the funds in the national treasury, it felt that it should receive a more equitable treatment. Even in normal times, however, only four and one-half per cent of its contribution is expended in the state. So bitterly did the Paulistas resent the attitude of the government at Rio that the local political parties as well as every class of the population formed the so-called "united front" (*frente unica*) against the national government. In order to regain their own autonomy and also, as one writer put it, to "reconstitutionalize" the country, they determined to take up arms. At the outset of the revolt they were led to believe that they could count on the support of Rio Grande do Sul and Minas Geraes. The uprising took place on June 9, 1932. At the last moment, Senhor Flores da Cunha, the *interventor* in Rio Grande, abandoned São Paulo and went over with all his forces to the national government. Minas Geraes also left its former ally in the lurch and directed its troops against the state of São Paulo. None the less, São Paulo continued the struggle. In point of troops engaged, it was one of the most serious revolts in the entire history of Brazil. At the outset, the federal forces consisted of more than 70,000 men against 28,000 of the revolutionaries. In the face of this menace, the city and state rose, as it were, en masse. Volunteers to the number of 200,000 offered themselves, of which it was possible to equip barely a fifth. The capital of the state was transformed into a veritable arsenal for the manufacture of arms and ammunition. Even women and children feverishly labored for the success of the movement. The belligerents possessed the largest and best equipped armies that have ever taken the field in South America. The revolution lasted eighty-three days. Early in August the federal forces surrounded and cut off the Paulistas, and forced them to yield to overwhelming odds. It is the opinion of the Paulistas that had it not been for the defection of Colonel Herculano de Carvalho, commander of the state army, São Paulo would have been victorious. Yet the Paulistas believed that their enormous sacrifices had not been in vain. They allege that their heroic resistance to the dictatorship resulted in a different orientation in the government with the consequent adoption of a number of important reforms, including the convocation of a national constituent assembly. It is their conviction, too, that the representatives of São Paulo in this body were responsible for many of its most salutary measures.

The provisional government extended from the autumn of 1930 to the summer of 1934. During this period, Dr. Vargas, who exercised dictatorial power, issued a multitude of decrees, some of immense importance. Perhaps the most noteworthy were those abolishing interstate taxes, eliminating a number of useless holidays, appointing a committee to study the reform of the judiciary, and a variety of decrees designed to cope with the ever-present problem of coffee. This latter topic we shall consider in another connection. Among the other accomplishments of the Vargas administration were those dealing with labor legislation, child welfare, and recurrent droughts in northern Brazil. Decrees were even passed looking toward the eradication of leprosy, which is a scourge in certain of the more backward portions of the country. Not the least important of the decrees issued by the new government were those which provided for the partial resumption of interest payment on dollar loans of the Brazilian federal government, states, and municipalities, beginning with 1934. The terms of these decrees were rather complicated but in general they included a resumption of payment from one hundred per cent on certain types of federal loans to seventeen and one-half per cent on certain state and municipal loans. This latter percentage, however, steadily rose until the year 1937, when the whole subject was reopened. In general it may be said that in this respect the provisional government made heroic efforts to meet its international obligations within the limits of its capacity. So many and wide-sweeping were the changes introduced into the fabric of national life that the term *Republica nova* (New Republic) was used to designate the régime in contradistinction to the "Old Republic" inaugurated in 1889.

Brazilians of all shades of political opinion were eager for the reëstablishment of a constitutional régime. Yielding to overwhelming pressure, Dr. Vargas on May 3, 1933, signed a decree calling for the election of a constituent assembly. Elaborate preparations were made for the election of members to this body. Nearly a million and a quarter voters out of a total population of forty-two million were registered. The proportion would undoubtedly have been larger had not the electoral code required that the voters be fingerprinted, photographed and otherwise identified. There was also the qualification of literacy. Though barely a million persons actually cast their ballots for delegates to the assembly this number was remarkable when compared with past elections which seldom exceeded two hundred thousand voters.

As the constitution adopted by the constituent assembly remained in power for less than four years it will not be profitable to make more than a brief summary of its provisions. The executive power was vested in a president elected for four years by the direct suffrage of all male and female citizens over eighteen. The president was ineligible for reëlection. The legislative power was in the hands of a chamber of deputies of three hundred members, including two hundred and fifty chosen by popular vote and fifty by trade and professional groups. A senate of forty-two members (two from each state and from the federal district) was designed to preserve administrative continuity, to act as a coördinator of federal powers and to watch over the constitution. It also acted as arbiter of interstate disputes.

In some respects the constitution of 1934 was extremely conservative; in others, astonishingly liberal. The influence of the Catholic hierarchy was seen in the prohibition of divorce and the fact that Church weddings were to have the status of civil marriages. On the other hand, women were made eligible for all political offices including the presidency. The constitution forbade discrimination in wages on the basis of age, sex, nationality, or marital status; it fixed a maximum working day of eight hours, and a working week of six days; it set minimum wage scales, prohibited child labor, stipulated annual vacations with pay, and recognized the rights of collective bargaining. A number of these and similar pro-

visions merely reaffirmed the decrees issued by Dr. Vargas during
the provisional government. The document was infused with a
strong spirit of nationalism. The government was empowered to
control traffic in war material, regulate banking and insurance,
and progressively nationalize resources and their exploitation. One
important article dealt with immigration. It provided that henceforth the entry of immigrants into Brazil was to be subject to the
restrictions necessary to guarantee the "ethnic integration" of
the immigrants, who in no year should exceed in number two per
cent of their total nationals resident in Brazil during the preceding
half century. During the course of the debates of the assembly the
charge was freely made and vehemently denied that this provision
was directed against the Japanese, of whom there are now some
two hundred thousand in Brazil. In many respects the Constitution
of 1934 embodied the hopes and aspirations of some of the best
political minds in Brazil. An immense amount of time and thought
had gone into its preparation. A conscientious effort was made to
correct the shortcomings of the constitution of 1891 and to provide Brazil with a fundamental charter adequate to cope with the
pressing economic, social, and political conditions of our own day.
It is unfortunate that it has never been given a really fair trial
under anything like normal conditions.

The return to a constitutional government, though it was
coupled with a certain amount of economic recovery, brought
little abatement of the social unrest throughout the country. The
two most pressing internal problems with which President Vargas
and his government had to cope were the rapid growth of fascism
and ultraradical political agitation. In many respects the soil
was favorable for the growth of subversive movements. During
the previous three years the provisional government had been so
absorbed with its struggle against internal strife and the prevailing economic depression that it was forced to postpone or
neglect the promised fundamental reforms in the social, economic,
and political fields. The great bulk of the agricultural laborers,
especially in the more remote areas, were the victims of an in-
tolerably low standard of living, while the growing mass of the
industrial workers complained that the *Republica nova* had brought
them little improvement in their lot. The class consciousness of the
workers had been stimulated by the presence in Brazil of radical

elements from Europe and the United States, many of which were frankly communistic. The result was an increasing number of industrial strikes for which the illegal Brazilian communistic party had a large responsibility.

As might have been anticipated the spread of these radical doctrines was matched by the rapid development of fascist organizations of which the most important was a group known as the *Integralistas*. Headed by an astute fanatic named Plinio Salgado, the *Integralistas* developed a program of extreme nationalism and anti-communism. At the same time they were anti-Semetic and pro-Catholic. They had as their uniform the green shirt and as their symbol the Greek letter sigma. Estimates of the size of this movement have run as high as three quarters of a million, though this figure is probably exaggerated.

With the ground thus prepared for some kind of a subversive movement an outbreak was almost inevitable. The explosion came on November 25, 1935. The focus of the disorder was in Natal, the capital of the state of Rio Grande do Norte, though sporadic uprisings took place elsewhere, notably in Pernambuco and Rio de Janeiro. The immediate instigators were apparently an outlawed radical organization known as the Alliança Nacional Libertadora and an agitator named Luis Carlos Prestes, a former captain in the Brazilian army. The government took energetic measures to crush the movement. The whole of Brazil was placed under martial law and in three days the revolt was put down. This abortive revolution had a long aftermath. With but brief interruption, Brazil remained under martial law through the rest of 1935 and through 1936. First and last nearly 10,000 arrests were made, including some 6,000 in Rio alone. Among the prisoners were a number of university professors, the prefect of the Federal District (an eminent physician by the name of Pedro Ernesto Batista), Senator Chermont, several deputies, and other persons of prominence and distinction. Though the spokesmen of the government insisted that communism was the sole cause of the insurrection, the opinion was general that the government feared hostile opinion and that the causes of the unrest lay far deeper than the grievances of certain extremists in the rank and file of the army.[4]

---

[4] The prisoners were judged by special tribunals which sat during the closing months of 1936 and all of 1937. Many cases were dismissed for lack of evi-

The year 1937 was a momentous one in the history of Brazil. During the spring and summer the attention of the country was centered on the presidential election for the period 1938-1942. The government early announced that it would remain aloof from the campaign. The various parties were therefore free to utilize all electoral methods commonly employed in such democracies as the United States and Great Britain, such as, for instance, mass meetings, processions, newspaper articles, and above all radio addresses. It is safe to say that since the establishment of the republic in 1889 no election had been carried on with equal fervor or had aroused greater public interest. Eventually three candidates entered the lists. Of these the best-known was Armando Salles de Oliveira, former governor of the state of São Paulo. He had enlisted the support of many of the powerful political elements opposed to the continuance of the régime of President Vargas. He was generally regarded as the spokesman of the big business interests in São Paulo and Rio Grande do Sul. His numerous lucid and able political speeches dealt largely with economic and educational problems. He denounced alike fascism, communism, and what he declared were the dictatorial tendencies of the president. He demanded the restoration of constitutional guarantees and the release of the political prisoners held in large numbers since the abortive revolt in 1935. In brief, Armando Salles was a sound, middle-of-the-road candidate who endeavored to carry on the fine political traditions of the great Paulista executives.

The other important candidate was José Americo de Almeida, a native of the northern state of Parahyba. Though he had gained some reputation as minister of communication he was chiefly notable as a regional novelist. He was strongly nationalistic and in some respects more liberal than Armando Salles. His appeal throughout the campaign was to the emotions rather than to the reason of his listeners. He had a wide following among the younger elements of the electorate. Rumor had it that his allegedly "demagogic" speeches alarmed certain military circles which did not

dence. No death sentences were imposed but the ringleaders received prison sentences up to twenty-seven years. A number of the defendants appealed to the supreme court; in the majority of cases their sentences were confirmed but in the instance of the most celebrated defendant, Dr. Pedro Ernesto Batista, ex-prefect of the federal district, the court ordered his release on September 13, 1937. He received an immense ovation from the people of the capital.

have too much difficulty in persuading Dr. Vargas that internal peace could only be assured through the president's continuance in power.

Fascism made its first appearance in a presidential campaign when the chief of the Integralistas, Plinio Salgado, announced his candidacy. Not even his most ardent partizans expected him to be elected. On the other hand, the Integralistas were a power to be reckoned with. It is conceivable that were the contest between the major parties at all close they might hold the balance of power. They also constituted a proof of the extent and vitality of fascism in Brazil.

To many observers, both Brazilian and foreign, the conflict between two such able candidates as Armando Salles and José Americo was a heartening demonstration that popular suffrage was a reality in Brazil and that the election scheduled for January, 1938, would be a triumph of democratic principles. But as the campaign wore on optimism began to wane. There were evidences that powerful revolutionary forces were waiting only for an opportunity to assert themselves. Deep-seated personal and sectional rivalries began to emerge. There were not lacking Brazilians who subsequently asserted that the election of either of the major candidates would have been the signal of a civil conflict between the north and the south. In wide circles, especially among the military, it was believed that radicalism and communism still constituted subversive elements which only a strong hand could hold in check. A general feeling of malaise and apprehension continued to spread throughout the country.

The entire world was startled when on November 10, 1937, President Vargas staged a *coup d'état* by the assumption of dictatorial power. Congress was dissolved, the state governors (with few exceptions) were deposed, and a new constitution written by Dr. Francisco Campos, the minister of justice, was promulgated. Not since the overthrow of the empire in 1889 has so momentous a change taken place in the whole political and constitutional fabric of the nation. Over night, as it were, Brazil became the closest approach to an authoritarian state yet established in the western hemisphere.

It is obviously too early to attempt anything like a final appraisal of the new constitution. Some of the articles are obscure.

Others are doubtless provisional in character and will be modified as occasion dictates. But this much is certain: the constitutional framework of Brazil based on the constitutions of 1891 and 1934 has suffered sweeping modifications. The underlying purpose of the new instrument is apparently to bring about a fusion of an authoritarian régime with democratic principles. In practice, this has meant a vast increase in the power of the president, the strengthening of the federal government at the expense of the states, the curtailment of the powers of congress, and the adoption of extensive measures for the maintenance of domestic peace. A few examples of the way these principles are translated into practice may be noted.

The position of the executive, though already great, is immensely increased. Subject to a plebiscite the presidential mandate will be extended for six years. At the expiration of this period an ingeniously constituted electoral college will choose a candidate for the presidency of the republic. If the outgoing president, however, should nominate a candidate, the election will be by direct and universal suffrage between the candidate chosen by the president and the one selected by the electoral college. There is nothing in the constitution to prevent the president from indefinitely succeeding himself. It is unnecessary to analyze in detail the faculties of the president. Paragraph 73 states the matter succinctly: "The president of the republic, the *supreme authority of the state,* coordinates the activity of the representative organs of higher grade, directs internal and foreign policies, furthers legislative policies of national interest, and superintends and administers the country."

Although the constitution explicitly declares that Brazil is a federation a study of the document itself will show that in practice the country has moved a long direction toward a unitary state. The faculties of the individual states are greatly abridged. The president's right of intervention suffers an enormous extension. The states may not contract external loans without the previous authorization of the federal council (which takes the place of the senate); they may not levy export taxes higher than ten per cent ad valorem. The control of primary and secondary education, hitherto within their incumbency, is apparently to be taken away from them. By appropriate action of the national government the smaller states may be merged into larger units, or even be converted into territories. The constitution says nothing about the method of choosing their governors; at present these officials are supplanted by *interventors* appointed by the president of the republic.

As already suggested, the executive has assumed many of the most important powers hitherto enjoyed by the national congress. He shares the legislative functions of this body through the right of issuing so-called "decree-laws" (*decretos-leis*). The president is authorized to prorogue or postpone a session of congress and call it in extraordinary session. Coincidently with the president's assumption of these augmented powers, congress is deprived of much of its representative character and former authority. Congress is to consist of a chamber of deputies elected indirectly and a federal council composed of representatives of the states, chosen by the state legislatures, plus ten members appointed by the president. The chamber of deputies is authorized to initiate tax measures involving increase in expenditure, but the initiative can only be taken by a third of the deputies. The federal council—which offers the nearest approach to the former senate—is not much more than an appanage of the executive. Its competency is almost exclusively confined to matters relating to the federal district, the territories, and Brazil's foreign relations.

The powers of the central government extend to fields unrecognized by the constitution of 1891 and only adumbrated in the constitution of 1934. The most striking innovation in the new charter is the provision for a "national economic council" composed of representatives of the various branches of national production. Many of its activities still remain to be determined by legislation, but it seems reasonably clear that it is designed to further a system of planned economy and rationalization of industry, as well as to banish all labor conflicts through the creation of syndicates. At first sight it would seem that this body is to have purely consultive powers. But article 63 of the constitution permits the assumption of legislative powers covering all matters under its jurisdiction through a plebiscite held at the instance of the president. Thus is laid the legal basis for the gradual transformation of Brazil into a corporative state in fact as well as in name.

The *coup d'état* of November 10 plus the promulgation of the new constitution have been interpreted by many as signalizing the entry of Brazil into the group of fascist or near fascist states, and the charge is freely made that the recently formed anti-communist combination of Germany, Italy, and Japan has acquired an important ally in the shape of the largest of the South American nations. At first sight there might seem some warrant for this view. Those conversant with the situation have long been aware of the unremitting propaganda—by radio, press, lecture platform, and other means—which the fascist powers have been carrying on in South America. Nazi activities among the large population of German birth or descent in Southern Brazil have steadily grown during recent years. The German National Socialist Party has had its agents everywhere. It is not without significance that the Nazi leader, Herr von Sossel, was appointed cultural attaché to the German embassy in Rio. While definite proof is apparently lacking, there is excellent reason to believe that a connection existed between the now outlawed Integralista party and representatives of German fascism in Brazil. It may be further noted that German propaganda in Brazil was reënforced by the close economic relations developed between Brazil and Germany through the medium of Germany's trade policy and especially the employment of the famous "compensated mark." In fact, so successful was this maneuver from the German point of view that, in 1936, Germany became the chief source of imports to Brazil, a primacy which had been held by the United States since the outbreak of the World War.

In any appraisal of the character of the new régime in Brazil one thing is abundantly clear. However one may describe the present government, certainly Brazil has not become a satellite of Germany, ideologically or any other way. One of the first acts of President Vargas after the adoption of the constitution was the suppression of the Integralista party; and its leader is now a fugitive from justice. The German ambassador, at the request of the Brazilian Foreign Office, has been recalled from Rio de Janeiro, owing to his improper activities in Brazil. As early as September, 1937, the Brazilian authorities in the states of Santa Catharina, Paraná, and Rio Grande do Sul declared that Portuguese must be the principal language used in private schools. The prohibition of the use of German was a severe blow to the spread of Nazi propaganda. A number of the schools immediately closed. Economically,

Germany is losing its grip on Brazil, thanks in considerable part to the negotiation of the reciprocal trade treaty between Brazil and the United States, which went into effect on January 1, 1936, and also to the gold purchase agreement of July 16, 1937.

President Vargas himself emphatically denied that the new state was fascist and repudiated any intention of contracting an alliance with the fascist states of Europe or with Japan.

His actions since the *coup d'état* are in harmony with such a pronouncement. Brazil has made it abundantly clear that it will not accept foreign dictation of any kind. An authoritarian régime has indeed been set up, but in many respects it is *sui generis*. One looks in vain for some of the most characteristic features of present-day Germany and Italy. The Brazilians are a tolerant, kindly, and peace-loving people. Brazil cherishes no hostile designs on its neighbors, or on any nation for that matter. No pseudoscientific theory of racial purity has been advanced. Anti-Semitism has not raised its ugly head. The only important ideological feature borrowed from any of the fascist powers is the national economic council, set up for the coördination of the economic forces of the country; here we see a certain parallel to the Italian corporative state. On closer scrutiny, it will be seen that, through the increase of his faculties and prerogatives, Dr. Vargas has merely been invested with powers, most of which have long been characteristic of Hispanic American dictators. As for the perpetuation of his mandate, it does not differ so greatly from the system of *continuismo* long in vogue in certain portions of Spanish America.

There is another and very powerful reason why Brazil is extremely unlikely to join the anti-democratic fascist camp, and that is its close relations with the United States. With no other Hispanic American country has the friendship of the North American republic been so profound and enduring. The history of the past century furnishes a wealth of historic examples. It may be recalled, for instance, that less than two months after the reading of President Monroe's famous message the Brazilian government issued instructions to its representative at Washington to propose to the United States an offensive and defensive alliance on the basis of the newly enunciated Monroe Doctrine, acting on the belief that sacrifices such as those which the United States undertook to make for the other American nations should not be accepted gratuitously. Though this proposal bore no fruit, the United States was the first foreign power to recognize the empire, this event taking place on May 26, 1824. In the latter days of the Civil War, President Lincoln, on refusing all offers of mediation from the European powers, is reported to have declared that if mediation should ever be acceptable it would only be that of the Emperor Dom Pedro II of Brazil. When the United States and Great Britain agreed to submit the *Alabama* claims to arbitration, Dom Pedro was requested to name one of the arbitrators. The visit of Dom Pedro to the United States in 1876 on the occasion of the Centennial Celebration and the keen interest he took in our educational institutions are still remembered. On the overthrow of the monarchy and establishment of the republic in 1889, the United States was the first power to recognize the new régime. Still more recently, when in 1914 the attitude of the Mexican dictator Huerta caused the United States to withdraw its ambassador from the City of Mexico, the United States interests in Mexico were entrusted to the Brazilian minister, Sr. Cardoso de Oliveira. And when the World War projected its shadow across the Atlantic, Brazil was the only South American country which entered the conflict as a full belligerent. Among the compelling motives for this step, as was stated by the Rio de Janeiro government at the time, were the traditional friendship with the United States and Brazil's adherence to the cause of continental solidarity. And when we come to the present juncture, we find the most responsible elements among the Brazilians voicing these century-old sentiments. At the very time the new régime was launched in Brazil, President Vargas and Dr. Francisco Campos (the author of the new constitution) went out of their way to declare that Brazil adheres to the principle of Pan-Americanism and regards friendship with the United States as a fundamental factor in its foreign policy. It is significant that Dr. Oswaldo Aranha, whose admiration for the North American Republic during his ambassadorship at Washington was patent to all, was called upon by Dr. Vargas to assume the all-important portfolio of foreign affairs.

Before concluding this rapid survey of contemporary Brazilian history, one important topic remains to be considered. The question naturally arises—why did Dr. Vargas, to the surprise of the world at large and of the great majority of the Brazilians, carry

out the *coup d'état* of November 10? At the present moment no
fully satisfactory answer is possible. Pressure from various
quarters, including the army, must certainly have been a factor.
The president may have honestly felt that the safety of the state
was threatened by subversive elements, headed by the communists,
and that the powers of the executive needed a strong reënforce-
ment.[5] In the non-political sphere there was apparently equal
need for drastic action. Dr. Vargas seemingly was convinced that
Brazil's many and pressing internal problems could only be solved
by the maintenance of a strong government, fully conscious of its
responsibilities and determined to carry out a long-range program
of economic rehabilitation. Unlike Argentina, Brazil is still within
the shadow of the great depression. It has not yet been able to
resume full payment on its foreign obligations.[6] The country's
rail systems—especially the government owned lines—are quite
inadequate for the transportation of products from the interior
to the seaboard, and demand rehabilitation and in part reconstruction. The country needs additional immigrants, but the process of selection is admittedly a difficult one. Increased capital
investment is necessary for the adequate exploitation of Brazil's
vast national resources. A case in point is the iron deposits of
Minas Geraes, which are among the largest in the world. The
encouragement of agricultural products other than coffee is of
supreme importance.[7] The country can never look forward to a
healthy economic life until "polyculture" has displaced mono-
culture.[8] These are only a few of the most immediate problems

[5] Dr. Vargas is explicit on this point. In the preamble of the new constitution
he justified the need of this instrument on the grounds of "the growing aggre-
gation of dissatisfied partizans . . . which threatened to develop into a class
struggle . . . placing the nation under the imminence of civil war; the apprehension created in the country by communist infiltration; the fact that under the
former institutions the state did not have the normal means of maintenance
of the peace and safety of the people."

[6] At the time of the *coup d'état* of November 10, Brazil suspended even the
partial payments of interest which had been in effect since 1934.

[7] It is unfortunate that space will not permit a discussion of the marvelous
progress which Brazil has made during recent years in its cotton industry. In
1924, the value of the exports of cotton amounted to less than $12,000,000; in
1936 it had risen to $60,818,000, and is now second only to coffee in importance.
Such commodities as citrus fruit, cacao, etc., figure more and more prominently
on Brazil's export list.

[8] The perennial problem of coffee is perhaps the most striking case in point.
Allusion has already been made to the attempts to "valorize" coffee through the

which are crying for solution. Of equal and possibly greater importance are the problems related to illiteracy and the raising of the standard of living of the mass of the population.

The writer of this chapter believes, after a careful study of the evidence available, that the majority of the Brazilians are in favor of the new order. The conviction would seem to be general that the continuance of the mandate of President Vargas is necessary if Brazil is successfully to cope with the many difficulties—political, economic, and social—with which it is beset. The widespread acquiescence in the present authoritarian régime is due, in other words, to the confidence which the Brazilians have in their president. Without such confidence the duration of the present government would probably be only a matter of months.

Since the days of the establishment of national independence Brazil has had to face crises more serious and ominous than that of the past few years and has come forth in every case strengthened and rejuvenated. Its history shows that the country possesses a marvelous capacity for recuperation. There is no valid reason for believing that the present emergency is an exception to the rule. Nothing in Brazil's past history warrants the belief that it has permanently abandoned the principles of democracy or departed in the slightest measure from its policy of enduring friendship with the United States.

---

medium of such organizations as the Coffee Institute. The chief result was over-production. In 1931, a disastrous policy of burning the inferior grades was inaugurated. During the next seven years something over fifty million bags were destroyed but in the summer of 1937 coffee stocks were higher in Brazil than they had been in 1931, and the government had meanwhile spent millions of dollars to maintain an artificial price level. The Brazilians at length came to realize that successive attempts at valorization were failures and—which was equally disconcerting—that Brazil was playing the game of its rivals, especially Colombia. When the Havana coffee conference failed in the summer of 1937 to agree on any policy of world stabilization, the government of Dr. Vargas determined to abandon, in large part, the scheme of coffee control. A few days before the *coup d'état* of November, it was officially announced that the export tax on coffee would be reduced by seventy-five percent and that a program of open competition with coffee growers of other countries would be adopted. The result was a tremendous, but, happily, temporary, dislocation of the whole industry. But virtually all authorities now agree that had Brazil adopted this sensible policy years ago some of its greatest economic difficulties might have been avoided.

The great majority of books and other printed material on Brazil is naturally written in the idiom of the country, which is Portuguese. The eminent Lusitanian novelist, Camilo Castelo Branco, once declared that Portuguese is the sepulcher of literature, and in truth this interesting language is little known outside of Portugal and its former colony, Brazil. It is this widespread ignorance of the language of Camões which has led the translator to restrict these bibliographical notes largely to works in English, French, and German. In recent years, however, an increasing number of advanced students and specialists are recognizing the importance of Portuguese as an indispensable tool for the serious study of Ibero-American history; for the guidance of these has been added a number of the more important and accessible works in Portuguese.

BIBLIOGRAPHIES

Among the bibilographical aids in English are the following: P. Lee Phillips, *A list of Books relating to Brazil in the Library of Congress,* Washington, 1901; C. K. Jones, *Hispanic American Bibliographies,* Baltimore, 1922; R. H. Keniston, *List of works for the Study of Hispanic American History,* New York, 1920; E. M. Borchard, *Guide to the Laws and Legal Literature of Argentina, Brazil, and Chile,* Washington, 1917; W. W. Pierson, Jr., *Hispanic American History, a Syllabus,* Chapel Hill, N. C., 1926; A. Curtis Wilgus, *Histories and Historians of Hispanic America,* Washington, 1936; *Bibliographical and historical Description of the rarest Books in the Oliveira Lima Collection at the Catholic University of America,* compiled by Ruth E. V. Holmes, Washington, 1927 (the vast majority of the items deal with Brazil); J. D. M. Ford, A. C. Whittem, and M. I. Raphael, *A Tentative Bibliography of Brazilian Belles-Lettres,* Cambridge, Mass., 1931. The more important current publications are listed in the *Hispanic American Historical Review,* 17 volumes to date, Baltimore, 1918-1922, Durham, N. C., 1926—. A useful survey of books and articles which appeared in 1935 is to be found in the *Handbook of Latin American Studies* prepared by a number of specialists and edited by Lewis Hanke, Cambridge, Mass., 1936. Works on Brazilian history are noted on pp. 136-48; it is hoped to publish this volume annually. Also to be noted is the voluminous catalogue of Maggs Bros., *Bibliotheca Brasiliensis ou Manuscriptos, Livros Antigos e Gravuras sobre o Brasil,* London, 1930. Descriptions of the four hundred items are in English.

Of the various bibilographical aids in foreign languages other than Portuguese should be noted: Chadenat, *Biblioteca Braziliensis* in number 38 of his catalogue entitled *Le Bibiliophile américain*, Paris, *ca.* 1910; A. L. Garraux, *Bibliographie brésilienne: Catalogue des ouvrages français et latins relatifs au Brésil, 1500-1898;* Oskar Canstatt, *Kritisches Repertorium der Deutsch-brasilianischen Literatur,* Berlin, 1902, Nachtrag, 1906. Finally, much material may be found scattered through the *Ibero-Amerikanisches Archiv,* the official organ of the *Ibero-Amerikanisches Institut,* 10 vols. to date, Berlin, 1926—.

Of the bibliographies in Portuguese, in every way the most important is the comprehensive work of J. C. Rodrigues, *Biblioteca Brasiliense: Catalogo annotado dos livros sobre o Brasil.* Parte I. *Descobrimento da America: Brasil Colonial, 1492-1822,* Rio de Janeiro, 1907. More than 2,600 items are listed, many with extended comments. The second volume was never published. A comprehensive work, concerned with literature rather than history, is that of A. V. A. Sacramento Blake, *Diccionario bibliographico brazileiro,* 7 vols., Rio de Janeiro, 1883. The firm of J. Leite e Cia, which has the largest stock of new and second-hand books in Brazil, issues from time to time extensive bibliographical bulletins. The address is Rua São José 80, Rio de Janeiro.

GENERAL

Apart from works in Portuguese there is no adequate survey of Brazilian history as a whole. Brief but comprehensive accounts of Latin-American history, with chapters on Brazil, have been written by W. S. Robertson, *History of the Latin-American Nations,* New York, 1932; Mary W. Williams, *The People and Politics of Latin America,* New York, 1930; H. G. James and P. A. Martin, *The Republics of Latin America,* New York, 1925. The nearest approach to a satisfactory account in English of the Portuguese background is H. Morse Stephens, *Portugal* (in "The Story of the Nations Series"), New York, 1891. There is one comprehensive history of Brazil in German: Heinrich Handelmann, *Geschichte von Brasilien,* Berlin, 1860. The eminent Brazilian historian, Oliveira Lima, delivered in 1912 a series of twelve brilliant lectures on Brazil at the Sorbonne in Paris. They have been published under the title of *Formation historique de la nationalité brésilienne,* Paris, 1912.

Of the works in Portuguese on Brazilian history which carry the story from the beginnings up to modern times may be mentioned: José Francisco do Rocha Pombo, *Historia do Brasil,* 10 vols., Rio de Janeiro, 1905; Rafael Galanti, S. J., *Compendio de Historia do Brasil,* 5 vols., São Paulo, 1896-1910; and João Ribero, *Historia do Brasil,* 5th ed., Rio de Janeiro, 1914. This latter excellent work is widely used in secondary schools in Brazil. In 1900 was published in Rio de Janeiro the three-volume *Livro do Centenario* in which a number of specialists discussed various phases of Brazil's evolution during the preceding four centuries. Max Fleiuss, the erudite perpetual secretary of the *Instituto Historico* has written and edited an immense amount of historical material, of which may be noted *Paginas de Historia*, 2nd ed., Rio de Janeiro, 1930, and·*Apostilas de Historia do Brazil*, Porto Alegre, 1934. Of the various collections of material on Brazilian history, that put out by the *Instituto Historico e Geographico Brasileiro* (established 1838) is by all odds the most important. In addition to its *Revista trimensal*, it has published a large number of special volumes, among the more noteworthy of which is the *Diccionario historico, geographico e ethnographico do Brazil*. The first two volumes of the *Diccionario* were issued in 1922 and none has appeared since. A scholarly and comprehensive Lusco-Brazilian encyclopaedia—a long felt want—is at length being published. The *Grande Enciclopedia Portuguesa e Brasileira*, Lisboa, 1935, is slowly issuing *fasciculos*. The second, still unpublished, par of this work is to be devoted exclusively to Brazil. Announcement has been made in the Rio de Janeiro press (1936) that under the auspices of the Ministry of Education plans are being formulated for an *Enciclopedia Brasileira*.

The Discovery of Brazil. Portuguese Colonial Policy and Administration
(Chaps. I-II)

Of the works in English on the colonial period the most important is that of the English poet Robert Southey, *History of Brazil*, 2nd ed., 3 vols., London, 1817-1819. R. G. Watson offers a survey of the whole period in his *Spanish and Portuguese South American during the Colonial Period*, 2 vols., London, 1884. Edgar Prestage, *The Portuguese Pioneers*, London, 1933, has chapters on the first voyages to Brazil. *The Histories of Brazil* by Pedro de Magalhães, translated by J. B. Stetson, Jr., 2 vols., New York, 1928, is an interesting work originally published in 1576. A. G. Keller, *Colonization*, New York, 1908, has a valuable chapter entitled "The Portuguese in Brazil." A fascinating description of life in the capital toward the end of the colonial period is to be found in the work of Luiz Edmundo, *Rio de Janeiro in the Time of the Viceroys*, translated by Dorothea H. Momsen, Rio de Janeiro, 1936. The following articles published in the *Hispanic American Historical Review* may be noted: Fidelino de Figueiredo, "The Geographical Discoveries and Conquests of the Portuguese," VI (February-August, 1926), 47-70; Charles E. Nowell, "The Discovery of Brazil—Accidental or Intentional?" XVI (August, 1936), 311-38; Alan K. Manchester, "The Rise of the Brazilian Aristocracy," XI (May, 1931), 145-68; P. A. Martin, "Portugal in America," XVII (May, 1937), 182-210.

Of works in foreign languages other than Portuguese may be noted: Gonzalo de Reparaz (Hijo), *La Época de los grandes descubrimientos españoles y portugueses,* Barcelona, 1931; Charles de Lannoy and Herman Vander Linden, *Histoire de l'expansion colonial des peuples européens,* Bruxelles, 1907; P. Leroy-Beaulieu, *De la colonisation chez les peuples modernes,* 2 vols., Paris, 1902; A. Zimmermann, *Die Kolonialpolitik Portugals und Spaniens,* Berlin, 1896; H. Wätjen, *Das Hollandische Reich in Brasilien,* Berlin, 1921 (best account of conflict with the Dutch).

Literature in Portuguese on the colonial period is very voluminous. Only a few of the more significant works will be noted. The most important work covering the period as a whole is that of Francisco Adolpho de Varnhagen (Viscount of Porto Seguro), *Historia Geral do Brasil,* third edition annotated by Rodolpho Garcia, Rio de Janeiro, no date, but *ca.* 1926. By many, Varnhagen (died, 1878) is regarded as Brazil's greatest historian. A recent and comprehensive work on the discovery and early settlement of Brazil is *Historia da Colonização portugueza do Brasil,* 3 vols. in 2, Porto, 1921. In vol. I of his *A Politica Exterior do Imperio: As Origens,* João Pandiá Calogeras treats of the period 1500-1821. Capistrano de Abreu, one of the most brilliant of recent historians, has illumined various phases of the colonial epoch through his *Capitulos da Historia Colonial* (1500-1800), Rio de Janeiro, 1928. The most important work which has yet appeared on the social evolution of Brazil during this period is that of Gilberto Freyre, *Casa Grande & Senzala,* Rio de Janeiro, 1933. The works of Pedro Calmon, notably *Historia da civilização brasileria,* São Paulo, 1933, and *Espirito da Sociedade Colonial,* São Paulo, 1935, also deserve notice. The well-known book by Oliveira Martins, *Brasil e as Colonias Portuguezas,* Porto, 1904, though a bit antiquated is very useful. Probably the best study of colonial types is that of F. J. Oliveira Vianna, *Populações Meridionaes do Brazil; Paulistas, Fluminenses, Mineiros,* São Paulo, 1920. Of collections of documents, perhaps the most noteworthy is *Alguns documentos do Archivo Nacional da Torre do Tombo, acerca das navagações e conquistas portuguezas,* Lisboa, 1892 (published on the occasion of the fourth centenary of the discovery of America).

RIO DE JANEIRO, CAPITAL OF THE PORTUGUESE MONARCHY (1808-1821)
(Chap. III)

The one work in English which covers this period with some adequacy is John Armitage, *History of Brazil*, 2 vols., London, 1836. The book is designed as a continuation of Southey and embraces the years 1808-1831. Much information on this important period is to be found in the accounts of foreigners, some of whom visited Brazil at the invitation of Dom João VI. Among them may be mentioned: John Mawe, *Travels in the Interior of Brazil*, London, 1815; Henry Coster, *Travels in Brazil*, London, 1816; John Luccock, *Notes on Rio de Janeiro and the southern parts of Brazil*, London, 1820; Alexander Caldcleugh, *Travels in South America*, London, 1825; Maria Graham, *Journal of a Voyage to Brazil, and Residence there, during part of the Years 1821, 1822 and 1823*, London, 1824; James Henderson, *A History of the Brazils*, London, 1821 (largely descriptive); A. de St. Hilaire, *Voyage dans les Provinces de Rio de Janeiro et Minas Geraes*, 2 vols., Paris, 1830; Maximilian, Prince of Wied-Neuwied, *Travels in Brazil 1815, 1816, 1817*, London, 1920; Spix and Martins, *Travels in Brazil in the years 1817-1820*, 2 vols., London, 1824 (translations of the works of eminent German scientists who visited Brazil at this time). An increasingly important phase of Brazil's foreign policy is adequately treated by Lawrence F. Hill in his *Diplomatic Relations between the United States and Brazil*, Durham, N. C., 1932. An excellent account of the commercial and economic conditions in Brazil in this and subsequent periods is given by Alan K. Manchester, *British Preëminence in Brazil, its Rise and Decline*, Chapel Hill, N. C., 1933. A magisterial survey in Portuguese of these crucial years is that of Oliveira Lima, *Dom João Sesto no Brasil (1808-1821)*, Rio de Janeiro, 1908.

THE INDEPENDENCE OF BRAZIL; ITS RECOGNITION BY THE
"COMITAS GENTIUM"
(Chap. IV)

No work in English is devoted solely to this period, though it is discussed in some of the works listed in the previous section, notably Armitage, *History of Brazil*. Thomas Cochrane (Earl of Dundonald) describes his share in the stirring events of the period in his *Narrative of Services in the Liberation of Chile, Peru and Brazil*, London, 1858. The rôle of the "Patriarch of Independence" is set forth by Paul Vanorden Shaw in "José Bonifacio and Brazilian History," *Hispanic*

American Historical Review, VIII (November, 1928), 527-50. F. Renaut has discussed the matter especially from the diplomatic side in a series of articles in the *Revue d'Histoire Diplomatique:* "L 'Emancipation du Brésil," année 33, pp. 540-99 (1918); "L'Organisation Constitutionelle du Brésil," année 33, pp. 39-89 (1919), année 35, pp. 164-86 (1921); "Le Brésil et l'Europe," année 36, pp. 50-95 (1922). The two most scholarly works in Portuguese are by Oliveira Lima: *O Movimento da Independencia, 1821-1822,* São Paulo, 1822, and *O Reconhecimento do Imperio,* Rio de Janeiro and Paris, 1902. The older, classic treatise on the period is by Manoel Pereira da Silva, *Historia da Fundação do Imperio Brasileiro,* 7 vols., Rio de Janeiro, 1864-1868. In 1922, on the occasion of the centenary of independence, the Brazilian government published most of the relevant documents in a collection of six volumes entitled *Archivo diplomatico da Independencia.*

THE REIGN OF DOM PEDRO I AND THE REGENCY
(Chaps. V-VII)

The majority of the works mentioned in the previous section cover this period at least in part. Especially is this true of Armitage for the reign of Dom Pedro I. An excellent appreciation of the rôle of the first emperor is given by Alan K. Manchester, "The Paradoxical Pedro, First Emperor of Brazil," *Hispanic American Historical Review,* XII (May, 1932), 176-97. Only three new works in Portuguese need be noted: F. A. Varnhagen, *Historia da Independencia do Brasil,* Rio de Janeiro, 1917; Tobias Monteiro, *Historia do Imperio, a Elaboração da Independencia,* Rio de Janeiro, 1927; J. P. Calogeras, *A Politica Exterior do Imperio: O Primeiro Reinado,* Rio de Janeiro, 1928. This last work is especially valuable for the relations of Brazil with the Platine republics. No really adequate history for the regency alone exists.

THE REIGN OF DOM PEDRO II
(Chaps. VIII-XII)

There is abundant literature on this, the most interesting period in Brazilian history. A fascinating and authoritative biography of Dom Pedro II has been written by Mary W. Williams *Dom Pedro the Magnanimous, Second Emperor of Brazil,* Chapel Hill, N. C., 1937. A good French biography is that of B. Mossé, *Dom Pedro II, Empereur du Brésil,* Paris, 1889. The material was supplied Mossé by the eminent diplomat, Baron of Rio Branco. A historical sketch of the period is supplied by P. A. Martin in Chaps. 13-23 of *Argentina, Brazil and Chile since Independence,* A. C. Wilgus, ed., Washington, 1935. A fascinating account of political and social conditions during the earlier years of this period are given by two missionaries, D. P. Kidder and J. C. Fletcher, *Brazil and the Brazilians,* Philadelphia, 1857. Relations between Brazil and the United States are adequately discussed in the work by L. F. Hill already mentioned. Of the many works by travellers may be noted: Thomas Ewbank, *Life in Brazil,* New York, 1856; Professor and Mrs. Louis Agassiz, *A Journey to Brazil,* Boston, 1868; F. Biard, *Deux Années au Brésil,* Paris, 1862; Adophe d'Assier, *Le Brésil contemporain,* Paris, 1867; Charles Expilly, *Le Brésil tel qu'il est,* Paris, 1862 (unflattering though in the main truthful). The following articles published in the *Hispanic American Historical Review* may be noted: Harold F. Peterson, "Efforts of the United States to Mediate in the Paraguayan War," XII (February, 1932), 2-17; Lawrence F. Hill, "The Abolition of the African Slave Trade to Brazil," XI (May, 1931), 169-97; Gilberto Freyre, "Social Life in Brazil in the Middle of the Nineteenth Century," V (November, 1922), 597-628; P. A. Martin, "Slavery and Abolition in Brazil," XIII (May, 1933), 151-96, and "Causes of the Collapse of the Brazilian Empire," IV (February, 1921), 4-48. Two articles published by the eminent French geographer, Elisée Reclus, in the *Revue des Deux Mondes* deserve mention: "Le Brésil et la colonisation: le bassin des Amazones et les Indiens," June 15, 1862; "Les provinces du littoral, les noirs et les colonies allemandes," July 15, 1862.

Of the enormous literature in Portuguese only a few works will be singled out. Joaquim Nabuco, *Um Estadista do Imperio: Nabuco de Araujo, sua Vida, suas Opiniões, sua Epoca,* 2nd ed., 3 vols., Rio de Janeiro, 1936, is by all odds the best treatise on the period. An admirable synthesis of every phase of the empire is Dr. Oliveira Lima's *O Imperio Brasileiro, 1822-1889,* São Paulo, 1927. The third volume of Calogeras, *A Politica Exterior do Imperio* is entitled *Da Regencia á Queda de Rozas,* São Paulo, 1933. It covers the years 1831-1852. Carolina Nabuco has written a charming and scholarly biography of her father, the great abolitionist and diplomat: *A Vida de Joaquim Nabuco,* 2nd ed., São Paulo, 1929. This work is being translated into English by Professor F. W. Ganzert. Possibly the most important single volume of documentary material on the reign of Dom Pedro II is that assembled by Max Fleiuss with the title of *Contribuições para a Biographia de D. Pedro II* (Tomo Especial of the *Revista do Instituto Historico e Geographico Brasileiro,* Vol. IX, Rio de Janeiro, 1925).

THE REPUBLIC
(Chaps. XIII-XV)

Material on the history of Brazil since 1889 is inadequate. Brief surveys of the period are given by C. E. Akers, *A History of South America,* 3rd ed., New York, 1930, Chaps. XIII-XVII; and P. A. Martin, *Argentina, Brazil and Chile since Independence* (ed., A. C. Wilgus), Chaps. XX-XXIII. Of the many books dealing with contemporary Brazil may be mentioned H. G. James, *Brazil after a Century of Independence,* New York, 1925; Pierre Denis, *Brazil,* London, 1911 (translation of a work of an able French scholar); L. E. Elliott, *Brazil Today and Tomorrow,* New York, 1917; C. S. Cooper, *The Brazilians and Their Country;* Roy Nash, *The Conquest of Brazil,* New York, 1926. Pierre Walle, *Au Brésil,* 4 vols., Paris, n.d. Brazil's relations to the World War are discussed by P. A. Martin in *Latin America and the War,* Baltimore, 1925. H. G. James, *Constitutional System of Brazil,* Washington, 1923, though rendered partly obsolete by the adoption of the constitution of 1934, is still valuable. Two articles dealing with the activities of Brazil's great minister of foreign affairs, Rio Branco, have been published in the *Hispanic American Historical Review* by F. W. Ganzert: "The Boundary Controversy in the Upper Amazon between Brazil, Bolivia, and Peru, 1903, 1909," XIV (November, 1934), 427-49, and "The Statesmanship of Rio Branco," August, 1937. Conditions since 1930 are discussed in two *Foreign Policy Reports* by the Foreign Policy Association, New York: "The Revolution in Brazil" (Vol. VI, No. 26, November, 1931), and "Brazil's Political and Economic Problems" (Vol. XI, No. 1, March 13, 1935). The nearest approach to an economic history of Brazil is the work of J. F. Normano, *Brazil, A Study of Economic Types,* Chapel Hill, N. C., 1935. Brief biographical sketches of many of the most notable living Brazilians are to be found in *Who's Who in Latin America,* edited by P. A. Martin, Stanford University, 1935. From the immense mass of material in Portuguese (much of it ephermeral) may be noted *A Decada da Republica,* Rio de Janeiro, 1901-1902 (an extremely critical appraisal of the various activities of the first ten years of the republic); and José Maria dos Santos, *A Politica Geral do Brasil,* São Paulo, 1930 (a critical account of the political evolution of Brazil from 1889 to 1930). Finally, one of the most eminent of contemporary jurists and writers, Rodrigo Octavio, is the author of a delightful study of the most notable figures of the republic, *Minhas Memorias dos Outros,* ser. Rio de Janeiro, 1934-1936.

INDEX